Air Conditioning Applications and Design

Air Conditioning Applications and Design

W. P. Jones

M.Sc.,C.Eng., F.Inst.E., F.C.I.B.S., M.A.S.H.R.A.E.

Edward Arnold
A division of Hodder & Stoughton
LONDON NEW YORK MELBOURNE AUCKLAND

© 1980 W. P. Jones

First published in Great Britain 1980
Reprinted 1988, 1990

British Library Cataloguing in Publication Data

Jones, William Peter
  Air conditioning applications and design.
  1. Air conditioning
  I. Title
  697.9′3   TH7687

  ISBN 0-7131-3423-2

Printed and bound in Great Britain for Edward Arnold, a division of Hodder and Stoughton Limited, Mill Road, Dunton Green, Sevenoaks, Kent TN13 2YA by Athenaeum Press Ltd, Newcastle upon Tyne.

Preface

This book is essentially a text on system design and application, primarily intended for the use of the more advanced student of building services at a university or technical college but with its content also offered for the practising engineer. A knowledge of the basic principles of air conditioning is therefore presupposed, notably in the topics of climate, comfort, psychrometry, fluid flow in ducts, fans, refrigeration, automatic controls, heat gains, the determination of supply air quantity and simple system design. In this respect it is, therefore, a sequel and complement to *Air Conditioning Engineering* and is the outcome of my experience over many years, not only in lecturing but also in the practical design and installation of air conditioning systems. Despite this presupposition and the fact that reference to the psychrometric data published by the Chartered Institution of Building Services may be necessary, the book is, nonetheless, self-contained. Upon this foundation a more advanced study of air conditioning is established, theoretical considerations being used wherever possible to justify the choice and design of particular systems for their correct applications. The practical consequences of design are dealt with in so far as they affect performance, system space requirements, commissioning, the diagnosis and solution of the problems that inevitably arise, energy conservation, and comparative capital and running costs.

The evolution of the Institution of Heating and Ventilating Engineers into the Chartered Institution of Building Services, upon the acquisition of a royal charter, has been accompanied by a raising to degree standard of the level of technical qualification acceptable for admission to corporate membership—a move in line with other chartered institutions and professional bodies. Further, many academic centres now offer courses of study leading to the award of higher degrees in environmental engineering and building services. This elevation of standards has meant that a knowledge of design applications and system characteristics, extending beyond an appreciation of first principles, is increasingly necessary for aspirants to corporate membership. Although simplicity is a desirable feature of all systems there has been a growing trend to complication and the designer may now have more options available for an application than hitherto. This, coupled with advances in technique and the proliferation of packaged plant, makes mid-career training an increasing necessity among professional engineers in building services. Furthermore, because of the widening recognition in the United Kingdom of the need for successful air conditioning design and installation overseas, guidance on system performance at altitudes significantly above sea level has been included and, where apt, the consequences of system operation in hot climates mentioned in the text.

A chapter on economics has been provided, in the face of continuing inflation, aiming to allow the capital costs of various systems to be established at a budget level for an historical date, the contemporary costs then being evaluated by the application of an appropriate inflation index, obtainable from official sources. As a guide, inflation indices for the building services industry in the United Kingdom are given up to 1978.

I am grateful to Haden Young Ltd for kind permission to reproduce some of the data in the Appendix and elsewhere in the text, as indicated.

W.P.J.

1979

Contents

x   Contents

1
Practical load assessment

1.1 The aims of load assessment

Most air conditioning systems operate at their design loads for only a small part of their life and it follows, therefore, that the designer should be concerned not only with the maximum heat gains and cooling loads but also with the way these change throughout the day and over the year. Establishing the pattern of such variations will be of help in choosing the correct system and in selecting the best form of automatic control. Applications lie in the commercial, industrial, institutional and domestic sectors for the climates of the United Kingdom, Europe and the rest of the world. It must therefore be expected that the size of the contribution made by each of the principal elements in the heat gain will not be constant but, nonetheless, the approach to the calculation will be essentially the same in all instances, although the same importance will not be attached to each element. Consequently, as a starting point, we shall examine the practical assessment of loads for one particular application—an office block in London. This will provide a theme for later development.

1.2 A hypothetical office block

Figure 1.1 illustrates a notional office block of simple design, with details of a typical module for an intermediate floor. The areas to accommodate lifts, escape staircases, builders' voids for ducts and pipes, lavatories, etc., are assumed to be in a pair of relatively small service blocks, one at each end of the building, adjoining the two short walls where there are no windows. For simplicity in the calculations, and probably without introducing significant error, it is further assumed that the presence of these two blocks does not influence the U-value of the two end walls or the heat flow through them. The other basic assumptions for the building are:

Area of glass (A_g): 50% of the outer facade on the two long walls only
Type of glass: single, able to be opened, clear, float or plate, 6 mm in thickness
Natural infiltration in summer: $\frac{1}{2}$ air change per hour
Natural infiltration in winter: 1 air change per hour
Shading on windows: internal, white, Venetian blinds, drawn by the occupants to exclude the entry of the direct rays of the sun
Surface density of the floor slabs: 300 kg m^{-2}

1

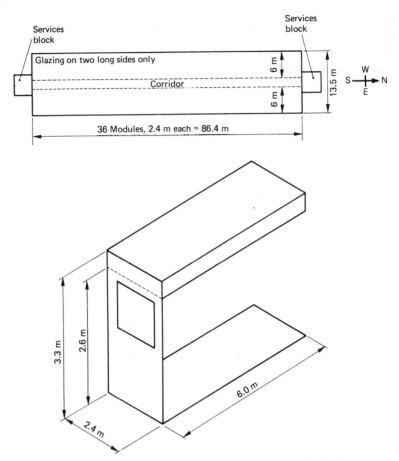

Figure 1.1 Plan and typical module of a hypothetical office block 12 storeys high

Surface density of the roof slab: 300 $\mathrm{kg\,m^{-2}}$
Surface density of the walls: 300 $\mathrm{kg\,m^{-2}}$
Thermal transmittance of the glass (U_g): 5.6 $\mathrm{Wm^{-2}{}^{\circ}C}$
Thermal transmittance of the wall (U_w): 0.91 $\mathrm{Wm^{-2}{}^{\circ}C}$
Thermal transmittance of the roof (U_r): 1.1 $\mathrm{Wm^{-2}{}^{\circ}C}$.
  It is customary to suppose that the occupied area, and hence the area for which the loads are calculated, is the pair of peripheral strips, each 6 m wide. The central corridor is not subjected to the same loads because its population is transient, it is shielded from climatic effects and its lighting may well be at a lower level than elsewhere. The treated floor area, on the other hand, is often taken to include both the corridor and the peripheries.
  In order to determine the air conditioning loads for the model building, the additional design assumptions listed below must be made:

Outside states: 28°C dry-bulb, 19.5°C wet bulb (sling), regarded as occurring at 15.00 hours sun time in July, and −2°C saturated as the design winter condition

Room states: 22°C dry-bulb, 50% saturation in summer with 20°C dry-bulb, 36% saturation in winter

Fresh air allowance: $1.3 \, \mathrm{l \, s^{-1} m^{-2}}$ of lettable floor area

Population density: 9 m² per person in general, but 2 persons per module in cases where an office is only one module in width

Metabolic rate: for sedentary workers, 90 W sensible and 50 W latent, per person

Power dissipated by electric lights: 25 Wm⁻², including control gear

Power dissipated by business machines: 5 Wm⁻².

There is general agreement on the practical assessment of sensible heat gains, except in the estimation of solar gains through glass and the determination of the heat flow through walls and roofs; the first issue being of far greater importance than the second. Opinion on the better approach to both calculations is divided between methods advocated by American authorities and those proposed in the United Kingdom. Each will be considered here.

1.3 Solar heat gain through glass

Solar heat gains through glass may be calculated from first principles using data published by two authorities[1,2], but it is much more convenient to use tabulated results for a particular window, defined by its orientation, the time of the day, the month of the year, the latitude of the place, etc. In the CIBS guide[1] the cooling load arising from solar gain through vertical glass, i.e. the sensible heat gain from this source with due allowance for the storage effect of the building, is tabulated for lightweight and heavyweight structures, with and without internal shading on the windows, for latitude 51.7°N (approximately that of north London), assuming that the air conditioning system runs for 12 hours a day to maintain either a constant environmental or a constant air temperature inside. Current engineering practice does not attempt to use environmental temperature in practical air conditioning and so only air temperature (dry-bulb) is relevant for determining heat gains. Further, maintaining a constant environmental temperature in a room imposes a bigger cooling load than does keeping the air temperature constant. Tables A.1 and A.3, in the Appendix, provide tabulated solar loads based on an American method[3] for latitude 51.5°N (approximately that of central London) and for typical building construction.

Although the influence of the storage effect of a building upon the solar gain through glass is principally exercised by the floor slab, the other room surfaces also play a part and are often taken into account when estimating the average surface density of a room, per unit area of floor, prior to determining the solar load. The procedure is best illustrated by an example.

Example 1.1 Estimate the mean surface density of a typical module in the hypothetical office block (Figure 1.1), using the following additional information.

Floor slab: hollow pots in concrete plus 50 mm cement screed and a carpet; overall thickness 200 mm; approximate surface density 300 $kg\,m^{-2}$

Walls: 112 mm brickwork with a 50 mm airgap, 100 mm lightweight concrete block and 13 mm of lightweight plaster; overall thickness 275 mm; approximate surface density 258 $kg\,m^{-2}$

Partitions: 2 × 12 mm perlite plasterboard sheets on timber studs, continued up to the soffit of the slab; approximate surface density 22 $kg\,m^{-2}$

Door: 50 mm deal, 800 mm wide × 2000 mm high; approximate surface density 3 $kg\,m^{-2}$

Suspended ceiling: Proprietary acoustic panels; approximate surface density 7 $kg\,m^{-2}$.

Note it is customary to halve the density of a floor slab if it is covered with a carpet and to ignore the mass of the window glass as irrelevant. The two side partitions are only half effective because they share their mass with the adjoining air conditioned offices. On the other hand, the corridor and the door are fully effective because the corridor is not necessarily air consitioned.

Answer

Floor: 0.5 × (2.4 × 6.0) × 300	=	2160 kg
Door: (0.8 × 2.0) × 3	=	5 kg
Side partitions: 0.5 × (3.1 × 12) × 22	=	409 kg
Corridor partition: (3.1 × 2.4 − 0.8 × 2.0) × 22	=	128 kg
Wall: 0.5 × (3.1 × 2.4) × 258	=	960 kg
Suspended ceiling: (2.4 × 6.0) × 7	=	101 kg
Total relevant mass	=	3763 kg

The average surface density per unit of floor area = 3763/(2.4 × 6.0) = 261 $kg\,m^{-2}$. This falls in between the densities of 500 and 150 $kg\,m^{-2}$ for which Tables A.1 and A.3, giving direct values for solar loads through windows, are compiled. Note that if the floor had not been carpeted the figure would have been 5923/14.4 = 411 $kg\,m^{-2}$. The designer must exercise his engineering judgement at this point but it is suggested that the tables for 150 $kg\,m^{-2}$ be used with the carpeted floor and those for 500 $kg\,m^{-2}$ with the bare floor slab, in this case.

Example 1.2 Using the appropriate tables, compare the solar heat gain through the windows of a typical module (Figure 1.1) by the CIBS[1] and Carrier[3] methods, for the month of July. Assume the floor is fitted with a

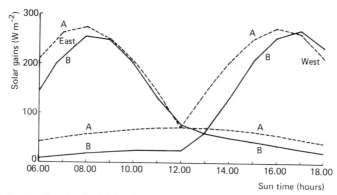

Figure 1.2 Cooling loads arising from solar gain through single clear glass which is west-facing and shaded internally by white venetian blinds. A, CIBS data for a lightweight building; B, data from Tables A.1 and A.2 for a room surface density of 150 kg m^{-2}, based on the Carrier method

carpet and that the steel-framed windows are virtually flush with the outer facade, i.e. ignore the shadow cast by any reveal.

Answer Reference to Example 1.1 shows that the appropriate, modular, surface density is 150 kg m^{-2} and so, for glass internally shaded by Venetian blinds, Tables A.1 and A.2 (in the Appendix) yield the answers directly by the Carrier method. These are plotted as full lines in Figure 1.2 and, assuming office hours of 08.00 to 16.00, sun time (09.00 to 17.00, clock time in the UK), we see that the peak loads are 253 Wm^{-2} at 08.00 h on the east face and 256 Wm^{-2} at 16.00 h on the west.

Interpreting the building as light-weight, as recommended in the CIBS guide[1] for the case of offices having light-weight demountable partitions, suspended ceilings and carpeted floors, tabulated data in the CIBS guide for latitude 51.7°N, windows protected internally by Venetian blinds and a constant air temperature maintained by a plant operating for 12 hours a day may be referred to. It must be noted, however, that these assume a sky clarity of 0.95 whereas the information in Table A.1 uses a haze factor of 0.9. The CIBS figures should therefore be multiplied by the ratio 0.90/0.95 to yield a comparison. Having done this, the results are plotted as broken lines in Figure 1.2.

The results using Table A.1 are generally a little less than those from the CIBS guide, particularly the peak values. It is not easy to say which are the more correct but it must be pointed out that the American-based answers (Table A.1) are proved in use over a longer period than are the CIBS values and are related to a continental-type (American) climate with longer stretches of continuous sunshine than are experienced in the UK. For these reasons, the Carrier[3] figures are commonly in use throughout the world.

A difficulty arises when dealing with windows of heat-reflecting or heat-absorbing glass. Table A.2 lists factors for various glass types, to be applied to the loads given in Table A.1. Note that the factors in Table A.2 are not applied to the loads for bare, clear glass, quoted in Table A.3. This is because windows or window and shade combinations that absorb a lot of solar heat transmit this to the interior, and exterior, virtually instantaneously by convection and long-wave radiation and this form of heat transfer is not influenced by the thermal inertia of the building. Only the directly transmitted shortwave solar radiation is so affected. Therefore, the storage factors for windows shaded internally with Venetian blinds are larger than those for bare, clear glass. A proprietary type of bare glass that is strongly heat-absorbing therefore corresponds more closely to clear glass with internal blinds than it does to bare, clear glass. So the factors in Table A.2 are applied to the gains through shaded windows, in Table A.1, yielding answers that are approximately correct.

It should be noted that heat-absorbing glass invariably requires internal shades as well, if people within the room are not to feel uncomfortable when subjected to the direct solar radiation that is still transmitted through the glass. Blinds may be omitted with certain types of proprietary glass that are strongly heat-reflective, provided that the shading coefficient of such glass is low enough. There is no absolute yardstick for this but a tentative suggestion is that the shading coefficient should not exceed 0.27.

Example 1.3 Calculate the shading coefficient for a proprietary brand of single, heat-absorbing glass, denoted as 49/66 bronze, with the following properties in comparison with 4 mm, single, clear glass.

1	2	3	4	5	6
		Fraction of the absorbed heat convected			
			Direct	Total	
	Absorbed	and reradiated	trans-	trans-	Shading
Glass type	heat	to the room	mittance	mittance	coefficient
4 mm clear	0.08	0.03	0.84	0.87	1.00
49/66 bronze	0.34	0.10	0.56	0.66	0.76

The figures in column 3 are obtained by assuming that approximately 30% of the absorbed heat (column 2) enters the room, 70% being lost to the outside. Adding the value in column 3 to that in column 4 yields the total transmittance in column 5.

Answer The shading coefficient is defined as the ratio of the total thermal transmittance of a particular glass, or glass and shade combination, to that of single, clear, 4 mm sheet. For 49/66 bronze it is thus $0.66/0.87 = 0.76$ and internal Venetian blinds will certainly be needed if people in the room are to feel comfortable when the sun shines on them through the windows. Although adding blinds will not reduce the shading coefficient to as low as 0.27, the short-wave direct solar radiation that causes the discomfort can be excluded.

Example 1.4 Calculate the solar load at 15.00 h sun time in July through a west-facing, proprietary brand of single, heat-absorbing glass, with the characteristics listed in Example 1.3. Assume a surface density of 150 kg m^{-2}. *Answer* From Table A.1 the load through single, clear glass fitted with internal Venetian blinds is 205 Wm^{-2} and from Table A.2 the factor for the glass is 1.43. The load is, therefore, 205 × 1.43 = 293 Wm^{-2}. Answers obtained by this method are reasonably correct for peak values but for lesser loads, at other times, the accuracy of the method is in some doubt.

1.4 Variations in outside air temperature

It is seldom obvious initially at which time of the day a maximum heat gain will occur, so it is useful to have a means of estimating outside air temperature, t_o, at various times. A reasonable assumption is that temperature varies sinusoidally against time, θ; the peak, t_{15}, occurring at 15.00 h sun time. The difference between this and the minimum value equals the diurnal range, D. Then

$$t_o = t_{15} - \frac{D}{2}\left[1 - \sin\frac{(\theta\pi - 9\pi)}{12}\right] \tag{1.1}$$

Meteorological records[4] quote mean monthly maximum dry-bulb temperatures, corresponding to t_{15}, and mean daily maximum and minimum values whose difference yields D. Table 1.1 shows the monthly variation in t_{15} and D obtained from records at Kew.

Table 1.1 Monthly variation in t_{15} and D obtained from records at Kew

	March	April	May	June	July	August	September
t_{15}	15.5°C	18.7°C	23.3°C	25.9°C	26.9°C	26.2°C	23.4°C
D	6.8°C	7.8°C	8.4°C	8.8°C	8.4°C	8.2°C	7.2°C

The use of Equation (1.1) is relevant to the calculation of air-to-air transmission gains through glass, the determination of heat gain by infiltration and the estimation of sol-air temperatures. Two problems sometimes arise in the choice of a value for t_{15}. First, although it is customary to take the summer design value of the outside air temperature as that prevailing at 15.00 h sun time, this does not always equal the value of t_{15} given in tabulated meteorological data. For example, the design brief in Section 1.2 for the hypothetical office block quotes 28°C, which can be interpreted as t_{15} but Table 1.1 gives a value of 26.9°C for July. In such a case, 28°C is adopted for t_{15} in July but the tabulated value of 8.4°C for D is associated with it. This is because the diurnal range is typical of the month and is not tied to a particular maximum value. Secondly, we may wish to determine heat gains for a month other than that having the peak value of t_{15}, taken usually as July in the northern hemisphere. If so, although the choice is open to the designer, it is suggested that if the design value chosen for t_{15} in July is not the same as that in the meteorological tables, the values of t_{15} for adjacent months be altered by the amount of the difference. Thus, if 28 °C were the design value for t_{15} in July, at Kew, 1.1 °C would be added to the tabulated values for June and August to give 27 °C and 27.3 °C for t_{15} in those months.

1.5 Heat gain through walls and roofs

Although sol-air temperatures offer the only practical way of dealing with unusual structures, the heat gain through walls and roofs is most conveniently calculated by using equivalent temperature differences[5] that take account of the diurnal variations in air temperature and solar radiation plus the time lag and decrement factor of the wall or roof. Equivalent temperature differences are given for some typical walls and roofs at a latitude of 51.5 °N in the United Kingdom in Table A.7. The table is based on an air-to-air temperature difference of 6 °C at 15.00 h sun time; if the difference is otherwise at 15.00 h, for a particular case, then the difference from 6 °C must be applied as a correction to the tabulated values. No allowance should be made for any hourly variation of air temperature each side of 15.00 h since this has already been taken into consideration in the table.

Example 1.5 Determine the equivalent temperature difference for an east wall of 300 kgm^{-2} surface density at 09.00 h sun time in June at latitude 51.5 °N, given that the outside air temperature is 27 °C at 15.00 h sun time and the room is held at a constant value of 22 °C.

Answer Table A.7 quotes a value of 9.5 °C. Since the room temperature is 22 °C and that outside at 15.00 h is 27 °C, the air-to-air difference is only 5 °C and a correction of − 1 °C must be applied, yielding 8.5 °C as the required answer. The fact that the outside air temperature at 09.00 h is less than 27 °C plays no part in the use of the table, having already been allowed for. The equivalent temperature difference is then multiplied by the U-value of the wall and its area, to give the heat gain to the room at 09.00 h.

Using sol-air temperature, t_e, is a more tedious process because of the way it is defined which is, in approximate terms,

$$t_e = t_o + \alpha(I_\delta + I_s)/h_{so} \tag{1.2}$$

where longwave radiant exchanges between the wall or roof and its surroundings are ignored, α is the absorption coefficient for solar radiation, I_δ is the intensity of direct radiation normally incident on the surface, tilted at an angle δ to the horizontal, I_s is the intensity of scattered solar radiation (sky plus ground) normally incident on the surface and h_{so} is its outside surface film coefficient of heat transfer. The heat gain, Q, through the wall or roof is then expressed by

$$Q = AU(t_{em} - t_r) + AUf(t_e - t_{em}) \tag{1.3}$$

where A is the area of the wall or roof, f is its decrement factor, t_{em} is the 24-hour mean sol-air temperature and t_r is the room temperature.

Sol-air temperatures may be calculated by means of Equation (1.2) or obtained directly from tables for a particular place. Table A.8 quotes values of t_e and t_{em} for Kew, and Tables A.5 and A.6 give approximate figures for time lags and decrement factors. Values of I_δ and I_s may be obtained from several sources[1,2,3,6].

Example 1.6 Calculate the heat gains through the east and west walls of a typical module in the hypothetical office block (Figure 1.1) at 08.00 h and 16.00 h sun time, respectively, in July (a) using equivalent temperature differences and (b) using sol-air temperatures. Assume the wall is 200 mm thick with insulation on the inside.

Answer
(a) Since the design brief for the hypothetical building has 6°C for the inside to outside air temperature difference, Table A.7 can be used directly to give values of -2.2°C for the east wall and 12.2°C for the west. Then

$$Q_{east} = 0.5 \times 3.3) \times 0.91 \times (-2.2) = -8 \text{ W at } 08.00 \text{ h in July}$$

$$W_{west} = 0.5 \times (2.4 \times 3.3) \times 0.91 \times 12.2 = 44 \text{ W at } 16.00 \text{ h in July.}$$

(b) A 200 mm thick wall with a surface density of 300 kgm^{-2} has an actual density of 1500 kgm^{-3}, to be used in Table A.5. Also, because the design brief is for $t_{15} = 28$°C, whereas Table A.8 is for $t_{15} = 26.9$°C, hourly values in the table must be corrected by $+1.1$°C and the 24-hour mean values by $+0.6$°C ($\simeq 0.55$°C). Table A.5 gives a time lag of 6.4 h and so we are interested in sol-air temperatures at 01.36 h for the east face and at 09.36 h for the west. Interpolation of Table A.8 gives respective values of 19.1°C and 26.6°C for the east and west walls which are corrected to 20.2°C and 27.7°C. The 24-hour mean values are 29.9°C and 30.2°C, corrected to 30.5°C for the east and to 30.8°C for the west. Table A.6 quotes a decrement factor of 0.33 and so the heat gains by this method are

$$Q_{east} = 0.5 \times (2.4 \times 3.3) \times 0.91[(30.5 - 22) + 0.33 \times (20.2 - 30.5)]$$
$$= 18 \text{ W at } 08.00 \text{ h in July}$$

$$Q_{west} = 0.5 \times (2.4 \times 3.3) \times 0.91[(30.8 - 22) + 0.33 \times (27.7 - 30.8)]$$
$$= 28 \text{ W at } 16.00 \text{ h in July}$$

The discrepancy between the answers obtained by the use of equivalent temperature differences and those obtained by using sol-air temperatures is of no great concern; in most instances the heat gain through the wall is only about 5% of the total sensible heat gain.

The advantage of sol-air temperatures in dealing with complicated structures can be seen in the following example.

Example 1.7 Determine the sensible heat gain at 15.00 h sun time in July at latitude 51.5°N through a flat roof consisting of felt-bitumen layers on 25 mm of expanded polystyrene fixed to metal decking and provided with a vapour seal. There is a substantial air space and a suspended ceiling constructed from 10 mm thick gypsum plasterboard. Recessed light fittings liberate a total of 10 Wm^{-2} into the ceiling void. Use 28°C and 22°C for t_o and t_r, respectively.

Answer The U-value for the flat roof is 1.1 Wm^{-2}°C, according to the CIBS guide. From the same source, the inside surface film resistance of a roof is 0.15 m^2°CW^{-1} for heat flow downwards and the thermal conductivity of gypsum plasterboard is 0.16 Wm^{-1}°C. Because of the light structure, it is wise to assume a zero time lag and a decrement factor of one. Denoting the air temperature in the void by t_v, a heat balance may be struck:

Heat flow through the roof into the void + heat flow into the void from the lights = heat flow from the void into the room below through the ceiling.

Using U_r and U_c for the thermal transmittance coefficients of the roof and ceiling, respectively, the following equation can be formed:

$$U_r[(t_{em}-t_v)+f(t_e-t_{em})]+10 = U_c(t_v-t_r)$$

From Table A.8, t_e has a value of 55.9°C at 15.00 h sun time, to which a correction of 28°C − 26.9°C, namely 1.1°C must be added, giving a value of 57°C. Also from Table A.8, t_{em} equals 37.3°C, to which a correction of 0.5 × 1.1°C, namely 0.6°C, is added, giving 37.9°C.

Therefore

$$U_c = 1/[0.15+(0.01/0.16)+0.15] = 2.76 \, Wm^{-2}°C$$

and

$$1.1[(37.9-t_v)+(57-37.9)]+10 = 2.76 \, (t_v-22).$$

Therefore

$$t_v = 34.6°C$$

and the heat gain to the room is

$$2.76 \times (34.6-22) = 34.8 \, Wm^{-2}.$$

1.6 Heat gain from electric lights

Most air conditioning systems in commercial premises such as office blocks rely on the use of extract ventilated light fittings to remove a significantly large part of the heat liberated by the luminaires and their control gear. This extracted heat then largely becomes a load on the cooler coil in the central air-handling plant, instead of on the conditioned rooms. As a result, the air quantity that must be supplied is reduced and the capital and running costs of the installation made cheaper. Figure 1.3 illustrates the possibilities, and it can be seen that with an unducted extract light fitting, about 40% to 50% of the heat is transferred to the central plant. It is not worthwhile, technically or economically, to make duct connexions directly to the light fittings. The most effective method is to permit free airflow through the fitting into the ceiling void, from where it ultimately enters a rudimentary system of horizontal extract ducting connected at one or two places to vertical extract ducts, which may be in builder's work, leading to the plant. Fire dampers are located in the duct system, as required by the local authority. Such a system of horizontal ducting is as simple as possible and limited in its extent by the position of the dampered spigots in its walls. These spigots allow the air to flow from the ceiling void into the duct system and no extract luminaire should be further

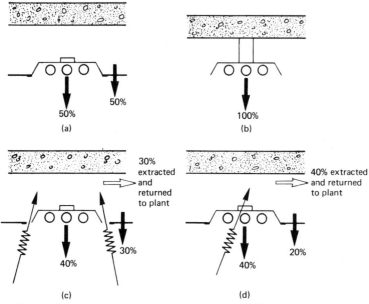

Figure 1.3a, Unventilated flush-mounted luminaire. All the heat enters the treated spaces, mostly to the room below although some goes to the room above;
b, Unventilated surface-mounted luminaire. As (a); c, Air extracted into the ceiling void. Heat goes to the room directly as well as indirectly through the ceiling and through the slab to the room above. Total gain to both rooms is 70%; d, As (c) except that the luminaire is directly extract-ventilated and the total gain to both rooms is 60%

than 20 m from an extract spigot. The reason for this restriction is that otherwise air will prefer to leave the rooms through ill-fitting ceiling panels rather than through the lights and those luminaires remote from the spigots will liberate more heat into the conditioned space than was intended. There may also be some variation in the colour rendering. The IES code[7] recommends that between 15 and 30 l s^{-1} be extracted through a ventilated luminaire for best results. More than 30 l s^{-1} is not recommended as there is a fall in light output when the lamps are overcooled. It is generally thought that there is no problem with dust deposits on extract-ventilated light fittings.

Figure 1.4[8] shows an approximate relationship between the illumination from fluorescent luminaires and the total heat liberated in Wm^{-2} of treated floor area. This figure can be used for provisional design estimates when precise details of the heat output from the lamps are not known.

1.7 Practical heat gains

The designer is interested in two sets of heat gain calculations: the maximum for individual modules or rooms, so that supply air quantities can be determined or air conditioning units selected, and the maximum for the whole building so that the minimum necessary refrigeration duty may be established. For the first type of heat gain the solar load through the glass is usually the dominant factor whereas, for the second, the time of maximum outside wet-bulb temperature is of prime importance because this significantly influences the size of the fresh air load which is a large part of the total refrigeration duty.

Example 1.8 Calculate the maximum sensible heat gains to (a) west-facing and (b) east-facing modules on an intermediate floor of the hypothetical building (Figure 1.1).

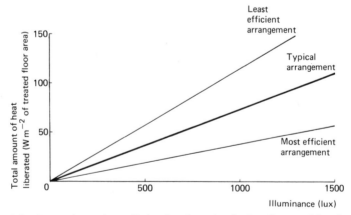

Figure 1.4   Approximate heat dissipation from luminaires for provisional estimating purposes

Answer Reference to Table A.1, for a surface density of 150 $\mathrm{kg\,m^{-2}}$, as suggested in Example 1.1, shows that, during the assumed hours of office occupancy (08.00 h to 16.00 h sun time) the peak solar gains through glass are 256 $\mathrm{Wm^{-2}}$ and 253 $\mathrm{Wm^{-2}}$ for the west and east faces, respectively, both in July. This virtually fixes the times for which the calculations should be done. From the design brief (Section 1.2) $t_o = 28°C$, which may be taken to be t_{15} in July, and $t_r = 22°C$. From Equation 1.1 it can be calculated that, with $t_{15} = 28°C$ and $D = 8.4°C$ (Table 1.1), $t_{08} = 22.7°C$ and $t_{16} = 27.9°C$. From Table A.7 the equivalent temperature differences for the west and east walls at 16.00 h and 08.00 h are, respectively, 12.2°C and $-2.2°C$ for walls of 300 $\mathrm{kg\,m^{-2}}$ surface density (Section 1.2).

It is convenient, when working out sensible heat gains arising from the infiltration of warm air from outside, to use a factor by which the air changes per hour of infiltrating air, the room volume and the temperature rise, outside to inside, may be multiplied to yield an answer directly in watts. The CIBS guide refers to this as a ventilation allowance and quotes a value of 0.33. A similar factor, equal to 0.79, may be determined from first principles for latent heat gain by infiltration; then the product of this factor, the infiltrating air change rate per hour, the room volume in $\mathrm{m^3}$ and the moisture content difference in $\mathrm{g\,kg^{-1}}$, outside to inside, gives the latent heat gain in watts.

Using the other relevant data from the design brief the total gain can now be calculated as follows:

(a) West-facing module

Item	Calculation		Gain
Glass:	$(0.5 \times 2.4 \times 3.3) \times 5.6 \times (27.9 - 22.0)$	=	131
Wall:	$(0.5 \times 2.4 \times 3.3) \times 0.91 \times 12.2$	=	44
Infiltration:	$(0.5 \times 2.4 \times 2.6 \times 6.0) \times 0.33 \times (27.9 - 22.0)$	=	36
Solar gain through glass:	$(0.5 \times 2.4 \times 3.3) \times 256$	=	1014
Lights:	$(2.4 \times 6.0) \times 25$	=	360
People:	2×90	=	180
Business machines:	$(2.4 \times 6.0) \times 5$	=	72
Total gain at 16.00 h sun time:		=	1837 W

(b) East-facing module

Item	Calculation		Gain
Glass:	$3.96 \times 5.6 \times (22.7 - 22.0)$	=	15
Wall:	$3.96 \times 0.91 \times (-2.2)$	=	-8
Infiltration:	$0.5 \times 37.44 \times 0.33 \times (22.7 - 22.0)$	=	4
Solar gain through glass:	3.96×253	=	1002
Lights:	14.4×25	=	360
People:	2×90	=	180
Business machines:	14.4×5	=	72
Total gain at 08.00 h sun time:		=	1625 W

The latent heat gains are the same for the west as for the east, in this case, because both are for the month of July, when the outside moisture content is virtually constant throughout the day at 10.65 g kg^{-1}, for 28°C dry-bulb and 19.5°C wet-bulb. Similarly, the room moisture content is fixed at 8.366 g kg^{-1}, for 22°C and 50% saturation.

Example 1.9 Calculate the latent heat gains to a module in the hypothetical · building, coincident with maximum sensible gains.
Answer

Infiltration: $0.5 \times 37.44 \times 0.79 \times (10.65 - 8.366)$	=	34
People: 2×50	=	100
Total:	=	134 W

Determining the maximum heat gain with sol-air temperature takes somewhat longer because of the more involved calculations that their use entails.

Example 1.10 Calculate the maximum sensible heat gains to (a) west-facing and (b) east-facing modules in the hypothetical building, using sol-air temperatures from Table A.8 and CIBS data for the solar load through glass. Assume a wall thickness of 200 mm and a density of 1500 kg m^{-3} with insulation on the inner face.
Answer From the CIBS guide, the solar loads through glass with internal blinds in a light-weight building maintained at a constant air temperature by a plant running for 12 hours a day are 294 Wm^{-2} for the east at 08.00 h and also for the west at 16.00 h, both in June. Example 1.6 established the gains through the walls in July when, according to Table 1.1, t_{15} is 1°C more than in June. Hence the sol-air temperatures at 08.00 h and 16.00 h in Example 1.6 must be modified to 19.2°C and 26.7°C for the east and west walls, respectively, the means being correspondingly changed to 30°C and 30.3°C. The revised wall gains are then

$$Q_{east} = 0.5 \times (2.4 \times 3.3) \times 0.91[(30.0 - 22.0) + 0.33 \times (19.2 - 30.0)]$$
$$= 16 \text{ W at 08.00 h in June.}$$
$$Q_{west} = 0.5 \times (2.4 \times 3.3) \times 0.91[(30.3 - 22.0) + 0.33 \times (26.7 - 30.3)]$$
$$= 26 \text{ W at 16.00 h in June.}$$

Equation (1.1) and Table 1.1 show that for $t_{15} = 27$°C in June, with $D = 8.8$°C, $t_{08} = 21.5$°C and $t_{16} = 26.9$°C. The heat gains can now be summarised as follows:
(a) West-facing module

Item	Calculation		Gain
Glass: $3.96 \times 5.6 \times (26.9 - 22.0)$		=	109
Wall:		=	26
Infiltration: $0.5 \times 37.44 \times 0.33 \times (26.9 - 22.0)$		=	30

Solar gain through glass: 3.96 × 294   = 1164
Lights: as in Example 1.8   = 360
People: as in Example 1.8   = 180
Business machines: as in Example 1.8   =   72

Total gain at 16.00 h sun time: = 1941 W
(b) East-facing module

Item	Calculation		Gain
Glass:	3.96 × 5.6 × (21.5 − 22.0)	=	− 11
Wall:		=	16
Infiltration:	0.5 × 37.44 × 0.33 × (21.5 − 22.0)	=	− 3
Solar gains through glass:	3.96 × 294	=	1164
Lights:	as in Example 1.8	=	360
People:	as in Example 1.8	=	180
Business machines:	as in Example 1.8	=	72

Total gain at 08.00 h sun time: = 1778 W

These results are 106% and 110% of the answers obtained for the west and east faces, by the method used in Example 1.8. Furthermore, by either method, the gains through the wall are of the order of 1 or 2% of the total sensible heat gains. It does not make sense to spend a great deal of time in attempting to calculate wall gains, to a doubtful degree of accuracy, when they constitute such an insignificant proportion of the whole. The exception to this is the case of gains through roofs, particularly if they are of flimsy construction and over a large plan area.

1.8 Heat gains and refrigeration load

Refrigeration load is the sum of sensible and latent heat gains, fresh air load, fan power, duct heat gain and, in the case of water chillers, a small allowance for pump power and heat gains to pipes. In the case of poorly designed systems there may also be an additional item for wasteful reheat that cancels part of the refrigeration capacity. Because the fresh air load is a significantly large proportion of the total, the refrigeration load is often calculated for the time when this will be greatest, e.g. 15.00 h in July or August (in the UK). However, this does not always follow, as Table A.9 (Appendix) shows. At such a time, the simultaneous sum of the sensible heat gains in the various treated areas in a building will be less than the sum of their maximum individual gains, because diversity factors may be applied to the gains from lights, people and machines and also because the solar load through the glass varies with time. However, it is not always the case that the maximum refrigeration load will occur at the times mentioned and the designer must use his common sense. For example, the peak load for a dining room may occur at 13.00 h sun time (14.00 h clock time) when the occupancy is most dense. With office blocks it is reasonable to suppose that some of the people will be on holiday or absent because of illness and that a proportion of the lights will be switched off or need replacing. Business machines may have the same diversity factors as people, if they are manually operated. On the other hand, no such diversity factors can be applied to places like concert halls, for example, where the occupancy and the lighting is obviously predictable. Table 1.2 gives diversity factors for application to sensible and latent heat gains; they are only approximate and must be used at the designer's discretion.

Table 1.2 Diversity factors for application to sensible and latent heat gains

	Diversity factor	
Application	Lights	People
Peripheral areas of offices to a maximum depth of 6 m, 20%–50% glazed	0.7–0.85	0.7–0.8
Core areas of offices and peripheral areas with less than 20% glazing	0.9–1.0	0.7–0.8
Apartments and hotel bedrooms	0.3–0.5	0.4–0.6
Public rooms in hotels	0.9–1.0	0.4–0.6
Department stores and supermarkets	0.9–1.0	0.8–1.0

Where machines or appliances are used in an industrial application the only sure way to establish the maximum combination at any one time, and also the combination at 15.00 h sun time in July, is to question the operating staff. Assessing the maximum combination is also usually necessary to calculate the required supply air quantity, since this may be the largest item in the heat gains.

Where appliances are used in a random fashion the only approach may sometimes be to determine the mathematical probability that the appliances can be simultaneously in use, as one does with the case of flow from a number of HWS draw-off points. When adopting this technique the disparity in the size of the machines must be considered: one large heat-producing item will dominate the heat gain calculations.

Table A.9 in the Appendix provides an indication of the times of the day and months of the year that the maximum refrigeration load is likely to occur for an office block like the hypothetical one considered earlier. Climatic loads in Wm^{-2} of treated floor area, including the corridor, are suggested and these include transmission and solar gains through the building envelope plus a fresh air allowance of $1.3 \, l s^{-1} m^{-2}$. There is a spread of times from 11.0 h sun time in August to 18.00 h sun time in July. No maxima occur earlier or later than this and none other than in the months of July and August. If an allowance is made for people, lights and business machines, with proper attention to diversity, plus latent gain, fan power and duct gain, the building cooling load can be assessed.

Example 1.11 Determine the refrigeration load for the hypothetical office block, assuming that a perimeter-induction system is to be used for air conditioning with a low velocity extract system.

Answer Reference to Table A.9 shows that the peak load will occur at 17.00 h sun time in July and will have an approximate value of about 70 Wm^{-2} for its climatic component. Table 1.1 quotes $t_{15} = 26.9°C$ in July but it must be corrected to 28°C to conform with the design brief (Section 1.2), whilst retaining the tabulated diurnal range of 8.4°C. Equation (1.1) is then used to give $t_{17} = 27.4°C$. From Table A.1 the solar gains at 17.00 h sun time in July for a building surface density of 150 $kg\,m^{-2}$ (see Example 1.1) are 28 and 268 Wm^{-2}, respectively, for the east and west windows. Table A.7 quotes respective equivalent temperature differences of 3.9°C, 14.4°C, 5.0°C, 16.7°C and 17.2°C, for the north, south, east and west walls and the roof. There is no need to correct these since they are based on $t_{15} = 28°C$. Diversity factors of 0.775 for lights and 0.75 for people and business machines are chosen from Table 1.2. The sensible gains for the building as a whole at 17.00 h sun time in July can now be calculated.

Item	Calculation		Gain
East glass:	$(0.5 \times 86.4 \times 3.3 \times 12.0) \times 5.6 \times (27.4 - 22.0)$	=	51 732
West glass:	$(0.5 \times 86.4 \times 3.3 \times 12.0) \times 5.6 \times (27.4 - 22.0)$	=	51 732
North wall:	$(13.5 \times 3.3 \times 12.0) \times 0.91 \times 3.9$	=	1897
South wall:	$(13.5 \times 3.3 \times 12.0) \times 0.91 \times 14.4$	=	7005
East wall:	$(0.5 \times 86.4 \times 3.3 \times 12.0) \times 0.91 \times 5.0$	=	7784
West wall:	$(0.5 \times 86.4 \times 3.3 \times 12.0) \times 0.91 \times 16.7$	=	25 998
Roof:	$(86.4 \times 13.5) \times 1.1 \times 17.2$	=	22 068
Infiltration:	$0.5 \times (86.4 \times 13.5 \times 2.6 \times 12.0)$		
	$\times (27.4 - 22.0) \times 0.33$	=	32 425
East glass solar gain:	$(0.5 \times 86.4 \times 3.3 \times 12.0) \times 28.0$	=	47 900
West glass solar gain:	$(0.5 \times 86.4 \times 3.3 \times 12.0) \times 268.0$	=	458 473

Total sensible gain through the envelope:	=	707 014 W
Lights: $(86.4 \times 13.5 \times 12.0) \times 25.0 \times 0.775$	=	271 188
People: $[(86.4 \times 13.5 \times 12.0)/9.0] \times 90.0 \times 0.75$	=	104 976
Business machines: $(86.4 \times 13.5 \times 12.0) \times 5.0 \times 0.75$	=	52 488

Total sensible heat gain:	=	1 135 666 W

At the outside design state the moisture content is 10.65 $g\,kg^{-1}$ and the enthalpy is 55.36 $kJ\,kg^{-1}$ when the time is 15.00 h. When the sun time is 17.00 h the temperature is only 27.4°C although the moisture content is still the same.

It can, therefore, be deduced from psychrometric tables that the enthalpy is 54.74 kJ kg⁻¹, which enables the latent gains and the fresh air load to be determined.

People: $(86.4 \times 13.5 \times 12.0/9.0) \times 50 \times 0.75$ =   58320
Infiltration: $0.5 \times (86.4 \times 13.5 \times 2.6 \times 12) \times (10.65 - 8.366) \times 0.79$ =   32832

Total latent gains: =   91152 W

It is likely that the fresh air will ultimately be expressed as a percentage of the supply air quantity. It is, therefore, reasonable to assume a specific volume of $0.822 \, m^3 \, kg^{-1}$ for the fresh air, at a supply state of, say, 14°C dry-bulb and about 7 g kg⁻¹. Reading the enthalpy at the design room state from psychrometric tables as 43.39 kJ kg⁻¹, the fresh air load may now be assessed as

$$(0.0013 \times 86.4 \times 13.5 \times 12.0) \times (54.74 - 43.39) \times 1000/0.822 = 251\,244 \text{ W}.$$

With an induction system, primary air is distributed at high velocity and so a practical assumption for the fan total pressure is 2kPa. It has been shown[9] that the temperature rise across a fan is about 1°C per kPa of fan total pressure and hence the rise through the supply fan will be 2°C, to which must be added a further 2°C, say, to cover duct heat gain. It is probable that the primary air will be a mixture of recirculated and fresh air and something, therefore, ought to be included to cover the fan power and duct gain in the extract system. The extract air distribution will certainly be at low velocity and estimates of 0.25°C for fan power and another 0.25°C for duct gain are appropriate, the air returned to the plant for recycling being 0.5°C warmer than the room air. To induce enough secondary air over the cooler coils in the terminal units an induction system usually handles about 2.5 to 3.5 l s⁻¹m⁻² of treated floor area. If the primary air supply rate is 3.25 l s⁻¹m⁻² then the fresh air rate of 1.3 l s⁻¹m⁻² is 40% of the total handled.

The heat input to the airstream flowing through a fan by virtue of the work done upon it in adiabatic compression equals the product of the air mass flow rate, the specific heat and temperature rise. This is most conveniently expressed (see p. 316 in the Appendix) in terms of the volumetric flow rate, the temperature rise and a Charles' Law density correction by the equation

$$\text{Volumetric flow rate at a temperature, } t, \text{ in m}^3\text{s}^{-1} = \frac{\text{Heat input in kW}}{\text{Temperature rise in °C}} \times \frac{(273 + t)}{358} \qquad (1.4)$$

The contribution of the fan powers and duct gains to the total cooling load of the building can now be determined:

Supply fan power $[0.00325 \times (86.4 \times 13.5 \times 12.0) \times 4$
and duct gain: $\times 358]/(273 + 14)$ = 226.972

Extract fan power $[0.6 \times 0.00325 \times (86.4 \times 13.5 \times 12.0)$
and duct gain: $\times 0.5 \times 358]/(273 + 14)$ $= 17.023$

Total: 243.995 kW

The total refrigeration load for the entire building may now be summarised:

Sensible heat gain:	= 1 135 666
Latent heat gain:	= 91 152
Fan power and duct gain:	= 243 995
Fresh air load:	= 251 244
Subtotal:	= 1 722 057 W
Pump power and pipe heat gain, say 1%:	= -17 251
Total refrigeration load:	= 1 742 308 W

The specific cooling load is 124 Wm^{-2} of treated area.

Referring back to the sensible heat gain and the fresh air load it can be seen that the climatic cooling load is 707 014 W for the building envelope plus 251 244 W for the fresh air, representing 68.5 Wm^{-2}, a value that is can be compared with the value of about 70 Wm^{-2} in Table A.9. If we made an allowance for the poorer U-values of the wall and the absence of an infiltration load in the tabulated values, the correspondence might be closer.

Because of the large contribution of the fresh air load (14%) the result at 17.00 h sun time should be checked with that at 15.00 h sun time, in July, when the fresh air load would be greatest. Taking the appropriate values from the tables in the Appendix, the sensible gain at 15.00 h sun time in July is as follows:

Item	Calculation		Gain
East glass:	$(0.5 \times 86.4 \times 3.3 \times 12.0) \times 5.6 \times (28.0 - 22.0)$	=	57 480
West glass:	$(0.5 \times 86.4 \times 3.3 \times 12.0) \times 5.6 \times (28.0 - 22.0)$	=	57 480
North wall:	$(13.5 \times 3.3 \times 12.0) \times 0.91 \times 2.2$	=	1070
South wall:	$(13.5 \times 3.3 \times 12.0) \times 0.91 \times 16.7$	=	8124
East wall:	$(0.5 \times 86.4 \times 3.3 \times 12.0) \times 0.91 \times 5.0$	=	7784
West wall:	$(0.5 \times 86.4 \times 3.3 \times 12.0) \times 0.91 \times 8.4$	=	13 077
Roof:	$(86.4 \times 13.5) \times 1.1 \times 13.9$	=	17 834
East glass solar gain:	$(0.5 \times 86.4 \times 3.3 \times 12.0) \times 44$	=	75 272
West glass solar gain:	$(0.5 \times 86.4 \times 3.3 \times 12.0) \times 205$	=	350 698
Infiltration:	$0.5 \times (86.4 \times 13.5 \times 2.6 \times 12.0)$		
	$\times (28.0 - 22.0) \times 0.33$	=	36 028
Total sensible gain through the envelope:		=	624 847 W
Lights, people, business machines: as before		=	428 652

Total sensible gain to the building: $= 1\,053\,499$ W
Latent gain: as before $=\quad 91\,152$
Fan power and duct gain: as before $=\quad 243\,995$
Fresh air load: $[(0.0013 \times 86.4 \times 13.5 \times 12.0)$
$\times (55.36 - 43.39) \times 1000]/0.822$ $=\quad 264\,969$

Subtotal: $= 1\,653\,615$ W
Pump power and pipe gain, say 1%: $=\quad 16\,536$
Total refrigeration load: $= 1\,670\,151$ W

It is a sound principle to check any refrigeration load against that obtained at the time of maximum outside enthalpy because of the importance of the fresh air load. This is particularly true where the outside air proportion is high. In this case, however, the time and month suggested in Table A.9 has been shown to yield the maximum cooling load.

Exercises

1 Determine the mean surface density per unit of floor area for a double module (4.8 m wide $\times$ 6.0 m deep) in the hypothetical office block, making the same assumptions as in Example 1.1.   (*Answer* 248 kg m^{-2})

2 Using the design brief (Section 1.2), calculate the maximum sensible heat gain to a south-facing, single-width module on an intermediate floor of the hypothetical office block, assuming that its major axis points east-west. Take the sky clarity as 0.9 and assume that the windows are steel-framed and flush with the outer facade.   (*Answer* 1732 W)

3 Repeat Example 1.11 to show that with $2.61\,\mathrm{s}^{-1}\mathrm{m}^{-2}$ of floor area as the fresh air supply rate, the maximum total refrigeration load occurs at 15.00 h sun time in July and is 128 Wm^{-2}.

Symbols

A	Area of a wall or roof	m^2
A_g	Area of glass	m^2
D	Diurnal range	°C
I_s	Intensity of scattered radiation (sky plus ground) normally incident on a surface.	Wm^{-2}
I_δ	Intensity of direct radiation normally incident on a surface tilted at an angle δ to the horizontal	Wm^{-2}
Q	Heat gain through a wall or roof	W
U	Thermal transmittance coefficient of a wall or roof.	Wm^{-2} °C
U_c	Thermal transmittance coefficient of a ceiling	Wm^{-2} °C

U_g	Thermal transmittance coefficient of glass	Wm^{-2} °C
U_r	Thermal transmittance coefficient of a roof	Wm^{-2} °C
U_w	Thermal transmittance coefficient of a wall	Wm^{-2} °C
f	Decrement factor	—
h_{so}	Outside surface film coefficient	Wm^{-2} °C
t_{15}	Outside air temperature at 15.00 h sun time	°C
t_{17}	Outside air temperature at 17.00 h sun time	°C
t_e	Sol-air temperature	°C
t_{em}	24-hour mean sol-air temperature	°C
t_o	Outside air temperature	°C
t_r	Room temperature	°C
t_v	Temperature in a ceiling void	°C
α	Absorption coefficient for solar radiation	—
δ	Angle	degrees
θ	Sun time from 0.00 to 24.00 hours	h

References

(1) *CIBS Guide*, Volume A, 1970
(2) ASHRAE, *Handbook of Fundamentals*, 1972
(3) Carrier Air Conditioning Company, *Air Conditioning System Design Manual*, McGraw-Hill Book Company, 1965
(4) Meteorological Office, *Tables of Temperature, Relative Humidity, Precipitation and Sunshine for the World*, Part III, Europe and the Azores, 1972
(5) Stewart, J. P., Solar heat gain through walls and roofs for cooling load calculations, *Trans ASHVE*, 1948, **54**, 361–388
(6) Jones, W. P., *Air Conditioning Engineering*, 2nd edition, Edward Arnold Publishers, 1973
(7) The IES Code, *Interior Lighting*, The Illuminating Engineering Society, January 1973
(8) Järnkonst A. B., *Integrated Environmental Design*, Landskrona, Sweden, April 1972
(9) Jones, W. P., *Designing Air Conditioned Buildings to Minimise Energy Use*, Integrated Environment in Building Design, Applied Science Publishers, London, 1974

2
System characteristics

2.1 System type and usage

Although much of the progress in the development of system types and designs stems from the growth of air conditioning for office blocks, many of the methods adopted are appropriate for other commercial applications and even for some of the less exacting aspects of industrial work. Consequently, much but not all of the following is directly applicable to office blocks, having been conceived with this use primarily in mind but, where apt, can also be considered for other uses.

Because of the very substantial amount of air conditioning done outside the United Kingdom, particularly for places situated at considerable heights above sea level, the first step to be considered is the influence of altitude upon system performance, from a general viewpoint.

2.2 Altitude effects

For any specific place an increase in altitude is accompanied by a drop in both pressure and temperature. However, it is not possible to establish a simple equation that will accurately predict the influences of both height and temperature on barometric pressure and, since the air temperature in the atmosphere near the surface of the earth is much affected by seasonal changes and the local topography, it is unwise to attempt to forecast barometric pressure for an unfamiliar place. Reference should always be made to local meteorological data, where this is available. When such information is not to hand, useful reference can be made to the CIBS guide[1], which tabulates approximate barometric pressures against altitudes. There can be discrepancies but in some instances the agreement is good. For example, the altitude of Tehran is 1220 m above sea level and the mean barometric pressure is about 875 mbar. Interpolation in the table yields 873 mbar, which is well within the probable variation of atmospheric pressure ($\pm 5\%$) arising from changes in the weather.

A fall in barometric pressure has a principal influence on the following: psychrometric properties; air mass flow rate; heat transfer coefficients for air;

22

evaporation rates; air pressure loss in ducts and plant; pressure gauge indications; available net positive suction head (NPSH); electric motor cooling.

Psychrometric properties

For atmospheric pressures of 950 mbar or less, psychrometric charts and tabulated data for the accepted standard pressure of 1013.25 mbar should not be used if progressively serious error is to be avoided. Psychrometric charts are published[2] at intervals of 25 mbar down to 725 mbar and these are very convenient to use. Alternative approaches are to use the corrections for changing barometric pressures published in the CIBS guide, or to employ the ideal gas laws[3] to calculate the desired properties, or even, if the situation demands, to construct a special psychrometric chart.

Example 2.1 Air enters a cooler coil at 39°C dry-bulb, 24°C wet-bulb (sling) and 875 mbar. If 2 m^3s^{-1} of air at 16°C dry-bulb, 15°C wet-bulb (sling) leaves the coil, calculate the cooling load and compare the answer with that obtained when the barometric pressure is 1013.25 mbar.

Answer The CIBS guide quotes tabulated additive corrections to be applied to enthalpy values read for standard barometric pressure. The corrections are expressed in terms of adiabatic saturation temperatures but can be interpreted as the same as sling wet-bulb values without significant loss of accuracy. Thus at an atmospheric pressure pressure (p_{at}) of 875 mbar and a wet-bulb of 24°C sling, the correction is 7.90 kJ kg^{-1} and at 15°C wet-bulb it is 4.34 kJ kg^{-1}. Taking the enthalpies at 39°C dry-bulb, 24°C wet-bulb and 16°C dry-bulb, 15°C wet-bulb from the guide as 71.03 kJ kg^{-1} and 42.08 kJ kg^{-1}, respectively, we can deduce that the enthalpies at 875 mbar are

$$h_{on\,coil} = 71.03 + 7.90 = 78.93 \text{ kJ kg}^{-1}$$

$$h_{off\,coil} = 42.08 + 4.34 = 46.42 \text{ kJ kg}^{-1}$$

To establish the specific volume, v, of the air leaving the coil we can use an approximate formula quoted in the guide as

$$v = (T/p_{at})(2.87 + 4.61 \, g) \text{ m}^3 \text{ kg}^{-1} \tag{2.1}$$

where T is the absolute dry-bulb temperature and g is the moisture content, also given in the guide as

$$g = [(\mu/100)(0.624 \, p_{ss})]/(p_{at} - 1.004 \, p_{ss}) \text{ kg kg}^{-1} \tag{2.2}$$

in which μ is the percentage saturation and p_{ss} the saturation vapour pressure at the dry-bulb temperature, all pressures being in mbar.

The value of μ is not necessarily known, since conditions on and off the coil are usually quoted as dry- and wet-bulb temperatures. However, for a given pair of such values the percentage saturation is approximately independent of atmospheric pressure, so μ can be read from psychrometric tables at 1013.25 mbar, without much error.

At 16°C dry-bulb, 15°C wet-bulb (sling) and 1013.25 mbar, μ is 90% and we can use this value also for 875 mbar. The value of p_{ss} depends solely on termperature and has nothing to do with barometric pressure. Therefore, this can be read directly from psychrometric tables for 1013.25·mbar at 100% saturation and any desired temperature. Thus at the off-coil state, $p_{ss} = 18.17$ mbar (read from CIBS tables at 16°C saturated) and by Equation (2.2) the moisture content of the air leaving the cooler coil at 875 mbar is

$$g_{\text{off coil}} = [(90/100)(0.624 \times 18.17)]/(875 - 1.004 \times 18.17)$$
$$= 0.01191 \text{ kg kg}^{-1}$$

Hence, by Equation (2.1) the specific volume off the coil at 875 mbar is

$$v_{\text{off coil}} = [(273 + 16)/875][2.87 + 4.61 \times 0.01191]$$
$$= 0.9661 \text{ m}^3 \text{ kg}^{-1}$$

The cooling load can now be calculated as

$$(2/0.9661)(78.93 - 46.42) = 67.30 \text{ kW}$$

Referring to psychrometric tables at 1013.25 mbar, for comparison, it is seen that the cooling load would be

$$(2/0.8322)(71.03 - 42.08) = 69.57 \text{ kW}$$

As a matter of interest, if the published psychrometric charts[2], which are based on the ideal gas laws, had been referred to values of enthalpy and specific volume yielding a cooling load of $(2/0.965)(79 - 46.5) = 67.36$ kW would have been obtained, the discrepancy being largely attributable to error in reading values from the chart. If the values had actually been calculated by means of the ideal gas laws[3] a load of $(2/0.9661)(78.76 - 46.27) = 67.26$ kW would have been obtained.

The superficial deduction from this example is that the cooling load is not much influenced by altitude, which may be true. However, the performance of the cooling coil is considerably influenced, and the cooling capacity of the air supplied to the conditioned room is reduced, by altitude effects. Plotting the on and off coil states on a psychrometric chart for 875 mbar shows that the sensible/total heat removal ratio across the coil is about 0.72 whereas the same states on a chart for 1013.25 mbar give a ratio of 0.81. This will affect the air-side film resistance and the overall U-value for the cooler coil. It can also be seen that the mean coil surface temperatures (apparatus dew points) are 14.2°C at 875 mbar and 14.1°C at 1013 mbar. This is not of much significance in this example but might acquire greater importance for other entering and leaving psychrometric states for the cooler coil. Therefore, reliance should not be placed on calculated coil duties without plotting the performance on a psychrometric chart for the correct atmospheric pressure.

Air mass flow rate

Air mass flow rate is probably the most important effect of barometric pressure changes upon system performance. It is the air mass flow rate that transfers heat between cooler coils or condensers and airstreams and removes the sensible and latent heat gains from the conditioned space. Therefore, it is of vital imprtance that the correct air density or specific volume be used in calculations.

Example 2.2 If the air leaving the cooler coil in Example 2.1 suffers a rise in temperature of 2°C because of fan power and duct heat gain on the way to the conditioned space, calculate the room temperature and humidity maintained in the face of sensible and latent heat gains of 19.82 kW and 2.67 kW, respectively, (a) when the barometric pressure is 875 mbar and (b) when it is 1013.25 mbar.

Answer (a) The specific heats of dry air and water vapour change very little with a fall in pressure and so, using the off-coil moisture content of 0.01191 kg kg^{-1} previously calculated, the specific heat of the supply air is $1.012 + 1.89 \times 0.01191 = 1.035$ kJ kg^{-1} °C^{-1}. The temperature maintained in the room, t_r, is then obtained from

$$19.82 = (2/0.9661)(1.035)(t_r - 18) \text{ from which } t_r = 27.3°C$$

Taking the latent heat of evaporation of water as 2454 kJ kg^{-1} the moisture content in the room, g_r, is obtained from

$$2.67 = (2/0.9661)(g_r - 0.0119) \times 2454 \text{ from which } g_r = 0.01244 \text{ kg kg}^{-1}$$

giving a humidity of about 46%.
(b) The answer can be obtained by similar calculations to (a) or by using the following two formulas (derived in the Appendix, p. 316):

Supply air quantity (m^3 s^{-1}) at temperature t

$$= \frac{\text{Sensible heat gain (kW)}}{(t_r - t_s)} \times \frac{(273 + t)}{358} \quad (2.3)$$

Supply air quantity (m^3 s^{-1}) at temperature t

$$= \frac{\text{Latent heat gain (kW)}}{(g_r - g_s)} \times \frac{(273 + t)}{856} \quad (2.4)$$

where t_s is the supply air temperature in °C, g_r and g_s the room and supply air moisture contents in g kg^{-1} and t is the temperature in °C at which the airflow is expressed. These will yield answers of 26°C dry-bulb and 50%, at

1013.25 mbar. Equations (2.3) and (2.4) are only valid at the standard, sea level barometric pressure of 1013.25 mbar.

Heat transfer coefficients for air

In order to express both the latent and sensible heat transfer to a cooler coil in terms of a U-value and a logarithmic mean temperature difference (LMTD), air-to-air, it is customary to enhance the value of the air film coefficient, h_a, by dividing it by the value of the sensible total ratio, S, for the cooling process. If r_w and r_m are the water film resistance and metal resistance, respectively, both referred to the external surface area of the coil, then

$$U = 1(r_w + r_m + S/h_a) \tag{2.5}$$

Thus the value of 0.72, obtained for S in Example 2.1 at 875 mbar, will give a slightly larger U-value for the coil than at sea level when $S = 0.81$, in the same example.

Heat transfer by forced convection is expressed in terms of the Nusselt number, (Nu), equal to $h_a d/k\theta$, the Reynolds number, (Re), equal to $ud\rho/\mu$, and the Prandtl number, (Pr), equal to $c_p\mu/k$, in which d is a relevant linear dimension, θ is a temperature difference, k is the thermal conductivity of air, u is its velocity, ρ its density, μ its absolute viscosity and c_p its specific heat capacity. It transpires that for forced convection over parallel plates, corresponding to the fins on a cooler coil,

$$(\text{Nu}) = 0.36 \, (\text{Re})^{0.8} \, (\text{Pr})^{0.33} \tag{2.6}$$

Little work has been done to establish the values of c_p, μ and k, at sub-atmospheric pressures but it is generally thought that they do not alter very much from their values at sea level. Therefore, it can be concluded that the influence of (Pr) is negligible and that heat transfer depends principally on (Re). It appears that for air, the dependence of heat transfer is upon $(\text{Re})^{0.8}$, and this implies that it is, in turn, proportional to the mass velocity, $u\rho$, to the 0.8 power. The change in the value of S alone, or the mass velocity alone, can influence the U-value of a coil significantly, but their combined effects can sometimes almost cancel each other.

Example 2.3 Given that, for the cooler coil in Example 2.1, working at sea level, $r_w = 0.00425 \, \text{m}^2 \, °\text{C} \, \text{W}^{-1}$, $r_m = 0.0035 \, \text{m}^2 \, °\text{C} \, \text{W}^{-1}$ and h_a (dry) $= 64 \, \text{Wm}^{-2} \, °\text{C}^{-1}$, all referred to the external surface area, calculate its U-value at (a) sea level and (b) a barometric pressure of 875 mbar.

Answer (a) From Example 2.1, $S = 0.81$ at sea level and so h_a (wet) $= 64/0.81$ $= 79 \, \text{W m}^{-2} \, °\text{C}^{-1}$, and r_a (wet) $= 0.01266 \, \text{m}^2 \, °\text{C} \, \text{W}^{-1}$.

$$U = 1/[0.01266 + 0.0035 + 0.00425] = 49.0 \, \text{W m}^{-2} \, °\text{C}^{-1}.$$

(b) From Example 2.1, $S = 0.72$ at 875 mbar and whereas $v = 0.9661$ m^3 kg^{-1} at the same pressure, it equals 0.8322 m^3 kg^{-1} at sea level. Thus the factors affecting the value of h_a are: $0.81/0.72 = 1.125$ for the change in senseible heat ratio and $(0.8322/0.9661)^{0.8} = 0.887$ for the mass flow effect. Therefore, h_a (wet) at 875 mbar $= 79 \times 1.125 \times 0.887 = 78.8$ Wm^{-2} °C^{-1} and r_a (wet) $= 0.01269$ m^2 °C W^{-1}.

$$U = 1/[0.01269 + 0.0035 + 0.00425] = 48.9 \text{ W m}^{-2} \text{ °C}^{-1}.$$

Evaporation rate
The water cooling effect in a cooling tower or an evaporative condenser depends on the evaporation rate of the water circulated. At a given dry-bulb temperature saturated air has a larger moisture content at a smaller barometric pressure. An airstream passing through a cooling tower can therefore take up more moisture, as it approaches saturation, at a higher altitude. The effect is fairly small, amounting to only about 3% at a height of 3000 m above sea level.

Air pressure loss in ducts and plant
For all practical purposes, the pressure loss through both ducting and plant is proportional to the density of the airstream. Thus the loss calculated at sea level conditions should be multiplied by the ratio of the barometric pressures and by the inverse ratio of the absolute temperatures, to determine the loss at altitude.

Example 2.4 A system of plant and ducting has a total pressure loss of 2 kPa, calculated for sea level conditions of 20°C and 1013.25 mbar. Calculate the total loss at a barometric pressure of 875 mbar and a temperature of 39°C.
Answer

$$\text{Total pressure loss} = 2 \times \frac{875}{1013.25} \times \frac{(273 + 20)}{(273 + 39)} = 1.62 \text{ kPa.}$$

Pressure gauge indications
Since a pressure gauge compares the measured pressure with the ambient atmospheric pressure, higher pressure indications will be given at higher latitudes. The correction is simple.

Available net positive suction head (NPSH)
This decreases with altitude, as Equation (4.16) shows, giving an increased risk of cavitation within a pump and a subsequent loss of performance. It is countered by reducing the resistance on the suction side of the pump and by increasing the position head, that is, the distance between the surface of the

water in the open tank, e.g. feed and expansion tank or cooling tower pond, and the centre-line of the pump suction branch.

Electric motor cooling

The mass flow rate of air for cooling a motor is proportional to the air density and so decreases with altitude according to reductions in pressure and changes in absolute temperature. These effects may be dealt with by using insulation able to withstand higher operating temperatures, or by using an oversized motor or one of special design.

2.3 Unitary systems

The distinction drawn between air handling units and air conditioning units is that the latter contain a refrigeration compressor, with or without its condenser, and the former do not. This section is primarily concerned with room air conditioning units, sometimes termed window units, and with the larger, air conditioning packages, free-standing in the conditioned space or suspended at high level in it or just outside it, that are used to treat large rooms, small commercial premises, or even whole individual floors of office blocks.

Self-contained, air-cooled, room air conditioners

Room air conditioners have had a very wide usage all over the world for many years, their chief advantages being relatively low capital cost for a small cooling load and the possibility of installing them room-by-room, as required, without the need to air condition the rest of the building and without taking up a lot of space for ducts and central plant. These advantages disappear as the cooling load increases and the scope of the air conditioning gets larger. Their chief defects are relatively short life of 3 to 10 years; noise, which increases with age as bearings wear, fixings are loosened by vibration and corrosion sets in; comparatively poor air distribution; poorer automatic control and poorer air filtration than is provided by central systems; low rate of fresh air ventilation; and, in the case of air-cooled units, a sometimes unsightly interference with the building facade caused by the need to cut openings in it to accommodate the condensers. Heating is commonly electrical, proving costly to run, but better quality units frequently offer an LTHW option. Heat pump units that reverse the roles of the evaporator and condenser in cold weather are also available. Units of this type are very popular, and one reason at least is their relatively easy installation, provided a hole can be cut in an outside wall or the unit allowed to sit on the sill, the window being raised sufficiently and any gaps around the unit being blocked.

Room air conditioners are available in the range from 1.75 kW of refrigeration to 8.5 kW. The standard of test adopted in the United States to establish unit ratings is often 26.7°C dry-bulb, 19.4°C wet-bulb (sling) in the room and 35°C dry-bulb, 23.9°C wet-bulb (sling) outside, but not every manufacturer states the basis upon which the outputs offered have been established. The cooling capacities listed in manufacturers' published leaflets and catalogues are seldom sufficient for a designer to assess the conditions of temperature and humidity likely to prevail in the conditioned space. At best, little more than an estimate of temperature is possible and that only with doubtful accuracy.

Example 2.5 An air-cooled room conditioner has the following published characteristic performance when the outside air temperature is 28°C and a volumetric flow rate of $150 \, \text{l s}^{-1}$, expressed at the room condition, is handled.

Room temperature (°C)	18	21	24
Sensible cooling capacity (W)	1947	1992	2028
Total cooling capacity (W)	2767	2943	3118
Absorbed compressor power (W)	1385	1432	1475

If one of these units is installed in a west-facing module on an intermediate floor of the hypothetical office block, described in Section 1.2, investigate the variation in room temperature, t_r, if the controlling thermostat is set at 22° ± 2°C and exercises a two-position control over the compressor.

Answer From Example 1.8 the maximum sensible heat gain is 1837 W which may be expressed as

$$1.66 + 0.03(27.9 - t_r) \, \text{kW} \tag{2.7}$$

The first element can be regarded as a constant and the second, representing the infiltration gain and the transmission through glass, as virtually instantaneous and unaffected by the thermal inertia of the building. The cooling capacity of the unit may be determined from the characteristic data by making linear interpolations, and may be expressed approximately as

$$1.667 + 0.015 t_r \, \text{kW in the range } t_r = 18°C \text{ to } 21°C \tag{2.8}$$

$$1.740 + 0.012 t_r \, \text{kW in the range } t_r = 21°C \text{ to } 24°C \tag{2.9}$$

When the inside temperature reaches 24°C and the unit switches on, starting to cool the room, the way that the temperature decays can be determined approximately by using the following equation,[3, 4] that assumes Newtonian cooling and ignores the influence of thermal capacity.

$$H = H_0 e^{-n} + M(h_s + H(\theta))(1 - e^{-n}) \tag{2.10}$$

in which

H = sensible heat content of the air in the room at any time θ (kJ)
H_0 = initial sensible heat content of the air in the room at time $\theta = 0$ (kJ)
n = number of air changes in time θ
M = mass of air in the room (kg)

h_s = specific sensible heat content of the air supplied to the room (kJ kg^{-1})
$H(\theta)$ = sensible heat gain to the room expressed in kJ s^{-1} for each kg s^{-1} of air
     supplied (kJ kg^{-1}).

It is argued that with the relatively rapid cycling of the room unit the influence of the admittance of the room surfaces is reduced to an unimportant level.

Assuming 0.847 m^3 kg^{-1} as an average specific volume of the air in the room and 1.026 kJ kg^{-1} °C as a mean specific heat capacity, then

$\quad$ M = (2.6 × 2.4 × 6.0)/0.847 = 44.2 kg
$\quad$ Mass flow rate of air supplied to the room = 0.15/0.847 = 0.177 kg s^{-1}

and

$$h_s = 1.026 \, t_s \text{ kJ kg}^{-1} \tag{2.11}$$

where t_s is the supply air temperature.
Then, from Equation (2.7)

$$H(\theta) = [1.66 + 0.03(27.9 - t_r)]/0.177$$
$$= 14.1 - 0.17 t_r \text{ kJ kg}^{-1}. \tag{2.12}$$

Using numerical subscripts to denote room temperatures at a particular time and starting from $\theta = 0$ when $t_r = 24$°C, the following is obtained for the cooling down process after the unit starts:

$\quad$ H_{24} = 44.2 × 1.026 × 24 = 1088 kJ = room heat content
$\quad$ Unit capacity = 1.74 + 0.012 × 24 = 2.028 kW.

From Equation (2.3)

$$t_s = 24 - (2.028/0.15)(273 + 24)/358 = 12.8°C$$

and from Equation (2.11)

$$h_s = 1.026 × 12.8 = 13.1 \text{ kJ kg}^{-1}$$

and from Equation (2.12)

$$H(\theta) = 14.1 - 0.17 × 24 = 10.0 \text{ kJ kg}^{-1}$$

After one air change, from Equation (2.10),

$$H = 1088 \, e^{-1} + [44.2(13.1 + 10.0)](1 - e^{-1}) = 1046 \text{ kJ}$$

which is the sensible heat content of the room air at a temperature t_r, and so

$$t_r = 1046/(44.2 × 1.026) = 23.1°C$$

Starting afresh, with $t_r = 23.1°$ at $\theta = 0$

$$H_{23.1} = 1046 \text{ kJ} = \text{room heat content}$$

Unit capacity $= 1.74 + 0.012 \times 23.1 = 2.017 \text{ kW}$
$t_s = 23.1 - (2.017/0.15)(273 + 23.1)/358 = 12.0°C$
$h_s = 1.026 \times 12 = 12.3 \text{ kJ kg}^{-1}$
$H(\theta) = 14.1 - 0.17 \times 23.1 = 10.2 \text{ kJ kg}^{-1}$, from Equation (2.12),

and, after a further air change, i.e. two in total,

$H = 1046 \, e^{-1} + [44.2(12.3 + 10.2)](1 - e^{-1}) = 1013 \text{ kJ}$
$t_r = 1013/(44.2 \times 1.026) = 22.3°C.$

Proceeding in this way it is found (see also Figure 2.1) that when $t_r = 20°C$, the unit switches off after a total of 7.33 air changes and after 30 min 30 s. If the unit did not stop but continued to run for an infinite time, the internal heat gains, the solar gain and the outside air temperature remaining constant, the room temperature would approach a lower potential value of 18.4°C. Letting the unit try and do this is not wise because it implies a continually falling evaporating temperature and a possible frosting condition with the attendant risks of complete failure by compressor motor burn-out.

When the unit is off, under thermostatic control, room temperature will climb towards a new, upper potential value, with the same stipulations about heat gains as before. Ignoring thermal capacity, as before, this can be calculated from Equation (2.7) by putting -1.660 kW equal to $0.030(27.9 - t_r)$, yielding $t_r = t_{lim} = 83.2°C$ at $\theta = \infty$. Then assuming Newtonian heating the heating-up law may be expressed as

$$t_r = 20 + (t_{lim} - 20)(1 - e^{-n}) \qquad (2.13)$$

and with $t_{lim} = 83.2°C$ the heating-up curve shown in Figure 2.1 is obtained, which indicates that the rise to 24°C is rapid, occurring after only about 15 s.

To complete the picture of the behaviour of the unit, a similar approach for reduced heat gains is used, when $t_o = 27.9°C$ but the solar gain through glass is by sky radiation only, the lights are off, there are no business machines working but there is one person present. Equation (2.12) then becomes $H(\theta) = 5.9 - 0.17 \, t_r$, which may be verified, and it can be calculated that, starting with $t_r = 24°C$ at $\theta = 0$, $t_r = 20°C$ after 0.46 air changes, and 1 min 57 s. The new upper potential value is found from the revised form of Equation (2.7) by solving $0.213 = 0.030(t_r - 27.9)$, for the revised heat gains, to yield $t_{lim} = 35°C$. Using Equation (2.13) it can then be calculated that $t_r = 24°C$ after 1.62 air changes or 6 min 44 s. The broken line in Figure 2.1 illustrates this reduced load performance. It can be seen that the room cools more rapidly but takes longer to warm up, which is characteristic of two-position control. The time between successive starts at light load is 8 min 41 s but 30 min 45 s at design duty, corresponding to about 7 and 2 starts per hour respectively, which is tolerable. As the load reduces further, towards zero, the number of starts per hour becomes fewer again.

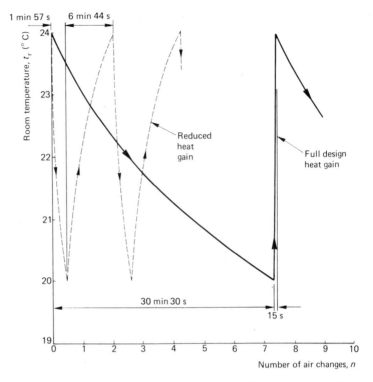

Figure 2.1   Performance of an air-cooled room-conditioning unit at full and partial load (see Example 2.5). A similar performance is to be expected from any air-conditioning unit under two-position control when the unit capacity exceeds the load

If these sort of units are run in cold weather, condensing pressures will fall with a consequent drop in evaporating pressures that is likely to be lowered even more because the dry- and wet-bulb temperatures entering the evaporator will be less, by design, in winter than in summer. The windings of the motor driving the hermetic compressor are cooled by the suction gas and the mass flow of this, and the cooling capacity, reduces in proportion to the fall in evaporating pressure. This reduction in cooling effect far outweighs any possible improvement resulting from the drop in refrigerant suction temperature. If frost forms on the evaporator fins the effect is exacerbated since an extra resistance to airflow is provided, inducing another drop in the load and so in the evaporating pressure. Operating a unit with a very dirty air filter produces a similar effect.

The outcome of inadequate motor cooling is burnt-out windings, and the presence of a safety cut-out thermostat, buried in the windings, is not always sufficient protection. Repeated motor starts at short intervals, or continued running at low evaporating temperatures, tends to bake the winding insulation without necessarily reaching the set point of the cut-out at its location. Eventually the insulation fails and the motor burns out. The chemical products of a burn-out poison the refrigeration system and it follows that it must be very carefully cleaned out before a new hermetic compressor is fitted and the system recharged[5]. Failure to clean the system properly will result in further, early burn-outs.

One method of guarding against the risk of motor burn-out is to use a hot-gas valve to maintain the evaporating pressure in the face of a falling duty accompanied by cold ambient air temperatures, by imposing a false load on the evaporator. The best way of doing this is to inject the hot gas into a hot-gas header, specially made on the side of the evaporator receiving the liquid refrigerant. However, packaged units seldom have this facility. The best alternative is to inject the gas between the expansion valve and the distributor, although even this is not always possible with small commercial units as there is no room between the two. On larger sizes of unit, self-acting hot-gas valves to inject in this manner are sometimes available.

Before selecting a packaged air-conditioning unit, other than the small room conditioner discussed earlier, with a direct-expansion cooler coil, it is generally advisable to calculate the minimum expected conditions onto the cooler coil and the corresponding cooling load, as well as the design maximum duty. If this information is supplied to the manufacturer he should be able to assess the risk of frost formation and the need for a hot-gas valve.

A cheaper alternative to hot-gas valves is cylinder unloading, actuated by changes in suction pressure. However, this method is not always as effective and is not available for the small sizes of unit considered so far.

Split systems
Room air conditioners and the larger, direct-expansion units are also available either with separate, air-cooled condensers or with remote, air-cooled, condensing units. Such installations are often a convenient alternative to single, self-contained packages. Hermetic condensing sets are made in a range of sizes able to deal with as much as 60 kW of refrigeration. Air-cooled condensers, however, have a much wider application for duties that can exceed 500 kW of refrigeration.

Packaged units generally are designed to supply about $50 \, l \, s^{-1}$ of air to a conditioned room for each kW of refrigeration. This is a restriction that limits the choice of the designer and tends to reverse the usual order of the design process, i.e. a packaged unit is selected and the designer estimates what it can do, rather than the selection being aimed at achieving a particular performance. There is often some difficulty in doing this since catalogue data is seldom adequate for a full technical exploration and sometimes the best that can be hoped for is merely to get an idea of the room temperature that will be

Table 2.1   Typical performance of a direct-expansion air-handling unit

Unit size	Entry wet-bulb (°C)	−1 T	−1 S	+1 T	+1 S	+3 T	+3 S	+5 T	+5 S	+7 T	+7 S	+9 T	+9 S
		Cooling capacities (kW)											
1	22.0					22.6	11.4	20.7	10.53	18.8	9.77	16.9	9.02
	19.5			20.0	12.86	18.5	12.2	16.5	11.28	14.5	10.4	12.5	9.61
	17.0	18.5	14.8	16.5	13.78	14.6	12.8						
2	22.0							24.3	12.47	21.8	11.6	19.4	10.7
	19.5					21.8	14.6	19.4	13.49	16.9	12.5	14.6	11.6
	17.0	21.9	17.9	19.5	16.55	17.1	15.4	14.7	14.4				

The column group heading above −1 … +9 is: Evaporating temperature (°C). T = total cooling duty, S = sensible cooling duty.

T = total cooling duty; S = sensible cooling duty
No. 1: fan power = 600 W; by-pass factor = 0.18; air quantity = 700 l s^{-1}
No. 2: fan power = 900 W; by-pass factor = 0.25; air quantity = 950 l s^{-1}

maintained. Conditions of humidity can rarely be forecast with assurance but fortunately this is of secondary importance in comfort conditioning as long as the temperature is satisfactory.

Table 2.1 shows the typical performance of two similar commercial air-handling units, of different sizes, which would be piped up to air-cooled condensing sets having the sort of performances listed in Table 2.2. The duty of the direct-expansion cooler coil in an air-handling unit is given in terms of evaporating temperature, and that of a condensing set in terms of saturated

Table 2.2   Typical performance of an air-cooled condensing set

Unit size	Saturated suction temperature (°C)	Cooling capacity (kW)	Saturated condensing temperature (°C)	Compressor motorpower (kW)	Cooling capacity (kW)	Saturated condensing temperature (°C)	Compressor motorpower (kW)
			Air temperature entering the condenser (°C) 29.4			Air temperature entering the condenser (°C) 35.0	
1	−1.1	10.1	50.0	4.0	9.5	53.3	4.1
	+1.7	11.2	51.7	4.3	10.5	55.0	4.4
	+4.4	12.2	53.3	4.6	11.5	56.7	4.7
	+7.2	13.4	55.0	4.9	12.5	58.3	5.0
	+10.0	14.5	57.2	5.2	13.6	60.6	5.3
2	−1.1	13.8	45.6	5.1	12.7	50.0	5.3
	+1.7	15.3	47.8	5.5	14.1	52.2	5.7
	+4.4	16.9	50.0	5.9	15.4	54.4	6.1
	+7.2	18.4	52.2	6.2	16.9	57.2	6.6
	+10.0	20.2	53.9	6.6	18.4	58.9	7.0

Note. Actual performances can differ considerably from the above figures

suction temperature. If the actual pressure prevailing at the compressor suction connexion were saturated, which it is not, the corresponding temperature would be called the saturated suction temperature. In fact, it is several degrees warmer because it is superheated by the action of the thermostatic expansion valve. It is customary to size the suction line for a pressure drop relating to a fall of 1°C in saturated temperature and it can, therefore, be inferred that the saturated temperature in the evaporator is 1°C higher than the saturated suction temperature.

In Table 2.1 it is assumed that the entering air dry-bulb temperature in all cases is 27°C. Interpolation is allowable but extrapolation is not. Actual performances can differ considerably from these figures.

If the performance of a condensing set is plotted in terms of kW of refrigeration against saturated suction temperature plus one degree, its intersection with the evaporator curve plotted for kW of cooling against evaporating temperature gives the duty achieved when the pair of units is piped together.

For a given evaporating temperature the mean coil surface temperature (apparatus dew-point) of the cooler coil in an air-handling unit is constant as long as the cooling load is also constant, regardless of variations in the entering dry-bulb. If a constant entering wet-bulb is regarded as synonymous with a constant entering enthalpy, an approximate assessment can be made of coil performance at various entering dry-bulbs, other than that on which the tabulated data is based.

Although the intersection of the characteristic performance curves for the evaporator and the condensing set will give the total cooling load for a particular entering wet-bulb temperature, it will not yield the sensible and latent proportions, the slope of the process line on the psychrometric chart and hence the state of the air leaving the cooler coil. However, this can be calculated if the tabulated data includes the by-pass factor or the sensible component (see Table 2.1).

Example 2.6 950 l s^{-1} of air at 27°C dry-bulb, 17°C wet-bulb (sling) enters the cooler coil of a size 2 air-handling unit having a performance as given in Table 2.1. If the unit is piped up to a size 2 condensing set (see Table 2.2) and the air temperature onto the condenser is 29.4°C, determine the following, assuming that the thermostatic expansion valve is large enough to pass the correct flow rate of refrigerant:

(a) The state of the air supplied to the room by the air handling unit
(b) The state of the air supplied if the entering air state is 23°C dry-bulb, 17°C wet-bulb.

Answer

(a) Adding 1°C to the saturated suction temperatures given in Table 2.2 enables the cooling capacity of the condensing set to be plotted against

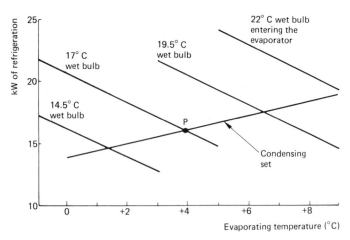

Figure 2.2   Typical performance characteristics for an air-cooled condensing set, with air onto the condenser at 29.4°C dry-bulb, and an air-cooler coil, at various entering wet bulbs (see Tables 2.1 and 2.2)

evaporating temperature and, using the data from Table 2.1, the characteristic curve of the cooler coil in the air-handling unit can be plotted on the same coordinates (Figure 2.2). At the point of intersection, P, the duty is 16 kW and the evaporating temperature is 3.9°C.

At the entering air state of 27°C dry-bulb, 17°C wet-bulb, the specific volume is 0.8607 m³ kg⁻¹ and the enthalpy is 47.21 kJ kg⁻¹. The air mass flow rate is thus 0.95/0.8607 = 1.1038 kg s⁻¹ and the enthalpy drop across the cooler coil is 16/1.1038 = 14.5 kJ kg⁻¹. From Table 2.1, the by-pass factor is 0.25 hence the enthalpy at the apparatus dew-point, A, is 47.21 − 14.5/0.75 = 27.88 kJ kg⁻¹. Figure 2.3 shows the psychrometry of this. The apparatus dew-point is 9.4°C and since the by-pass factor is 0.25, the temperature at state W, leaving the coil, can also be calculated as 27 − 0.75(27 − 9.4) = 13.8°C. The fan power, from Table 2.1, is 900 W and so the temperature of the air supplied to the room is 13.8 + (0.9/0.95) × (273 + 27)/358 = 14.6°C at state S, from Equation (2.3).

The sensible component of the cooling load is [0.95 × (27 − 13.8) × 358]/(273 + 27) = 14.96 kW and the latent component is 16 − 14.96 = 1.04 kW. Since the moisture content at state R, onto the coil, is 7.86 g kg⁻¹ the moisture content off the coil is 7.86 − (1.04/0.95) × (273 + 27)/856 = 7.48 g kg⁻¹. The state of the air supplied to the room is thus defined as 14.6°C dry-bulb and 7.48 g kg⁻¹.

(b) If the state of the air entering the cooler coil, M, is 23°C dry-bulb, 17°C wet-bulb (sling), 47.6 kJ kg⁻¹, 0.8515 m³ kg⁻¹ and the total cooling load is unchanged at 16 kW, then by the earlier reasoning the mean coil surface temperature stays at 9.4°C and the evaporating temperature remains at 3.9°C.

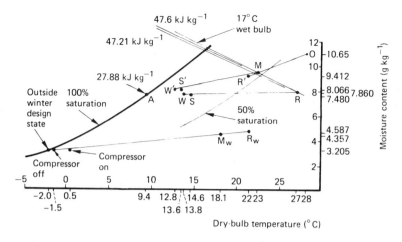

Figure 2.3   Psychrometry for Examples 2.6, 2.7 and 2.8

Figure 2.3 shows this. The coil leaving state, W', can then either be established geometrically on the psychrometric chart because WW' is parallel to RM or can be calculated as $12.8°C$ dry-bulb and 8.066 g kg^{-1} by the methods used in answering part (a). The supply temperature is then $12.8 + 0.8 = 13.6°C$.

Most air-handling units deal with a mixture of fresh and recirculated air. This poses a problem in determining the performance of the sort of unit that has just been considered. Although a match between the sensible cooling capacity of the air supplied to the conditioned room and the sensible heat gains suffered in it can be achieved thermostatically, by proportional reheating or cycling under two-position control, it is possible that the latent capacity will exceed the latent gains in many cases. As a result the room wet-bulb temperature will fall. Figure 2.2 shows that this will reduce both the total cooling capacity and the evaporating temperature, with a risk of frosting and its disastrous consequences.

Example 2.7 For the plant used in Example 2.6, determine the sensible and latent cooling capacities of the air supplied to a room conditioned at $22°C$ dry-bulb, assuming that the outside state is $28°C$ dry-bulb, $19.5°C$ wet-bulb and ignoring any effect that the reduction in outside dry-bulb has on the capacity of the condensing set. Of the air supplied, five-sixths is recirculated and one-sixth is fresh.

Answer Plotting O and R' on Figure 2.3, the line OR' passing through M, the moisture content in the room can be determined as follows:

$$[10.65 - (10.65 - 9.618) \times 6.0]/5.0 = 9.412 \text{ g kg}^{-1}.$$

The sensible gains to the room that can be dealt with are

$$[0.95 \times (22.0 - 13.6) \times 358]/(273 + 23) = 9.65 \text{ kW}$$

and the latent gains that may be offset are

$$[0.95 \times (9.412 - 8.060) \times 856]/(273 + 23) = 3.714 \text{ kW}.$$

These are substantial latent gains and the slope of the room ratio line would be 0.72, whereas, in Examples 1.8 and 1.9, the sensible and latent heat gains to a single, west-facing module in the hypothetical office block were 1.837 and 0.134 kW, respectively, yielding a slope of 0.93 for the room ratio line. The result of using the split system will be to cause the moisture content of the room state to fall, reducing the mixture wet-bulb onto the cooler coil, until some sort of balance is ultimately achieved, with the room temperature controlled at 22°C but its humidity a good deal lower than the customary 50%. When the wet-bulb onto the cooler coil falls, the latent component in its total cooling capacity reduces, as we may verified by Table 2.1, but it is difficult to predict the exact performance without access to full technical information, seldom, if ever, provided in a catalogue. The risks of low entering wet-bulbs can also arise, quite apart from the mismatch of latent capacity and load, because of the presence of the fresh air itself in the mixture and the advent of colder, non-design weather. It is desirable that an attempt should always be made to establish the minimum likely entering air state for the cooler coil.

Example 2.8 Five west-facing modules on an intermediate floor of the hypothetical office block (see Section 1.2) are to be grouped to form a dining room for thirteen people. If the split system considered in Examples 2.6 and 2.7 is to be used for air-conditioning the dining room, determine the minimum on-coil state for the cooler coil.

Answer First we must establish the revised heat gains, assuming an internal temperature of 22°C with a humidity of about 50%:

	Sensible gains (W)	Latent gains (W)
Previously calculated gains for one module:	1837	134
Less gains from 2 people:	180	100
	1657	34
Gains for five modules without occupants:	8285	170
Gains for 13 people (see CIBS guide):	1170	650
Totals:	9455 W	820 W

The minimum condition will occur when the cooling capacity of the unrefrigerated supply air, allowing for the temperature rise from fan power, equals the sensible heat gain. Anticipating that the heat balance will occur in

January or February the lower outside air temperature and the reduced solar load through glass must be taken into account. Assuming the balance occurs in February at 16.00 h sun time, Table A.1 gives 164 W m^{-2} as the solar load through glass, as against 256 W m^{-2} in July. In Example 1.8 the total sensible gain of 1.837 kW can be separated into a transmission gain of 0.03 $(t_o - t_r)$ and a gain from other sources of 1.66 kW. If the solar gain through glass is reduced from 256 W m^{-2} to 164 W m^{-2} the second part of the sensible gain diminishes by 3.96 m$^2 \times 92$ W m^{-2}, or 0.36 kW and an expression for the revised gain to the five modules, in terms of the outside air temperature t_o and the room temperature t_r, is, therefore,

$$\text{Sensible gain} = 5[(1.66 - 0.36) + 0.03 \ (t_o - t_r)]$$

If $t_r = 22°C$ this becomes

$$\text{Sensible gain} = 5[(1.66 - 0.36) + 0.03 \ (t_o - 22)]$$
$$= 3.2 + 0.15 \ t_o \ \text{kW}.$$

Since the temperature rise across the fan is 0.8°C the temperature of the air supplied by the unit when the refrigeration plant is off is $t_s = t_m + 0.8$ and its sensible cooling capacity is expressed by $0.95 \times (22 - t_m - 0.8) \times 358]/(273 + t_s)$, according to Equation (2.3). Since the value of t_s in the Charles' Law correction term for air density does not significantly affect the answer but complicates the arithmetic, a value of 17°C can be assumed for it. The natural cooling capacity of the unit with the refrigeration plant off can therefore be expressed by

$$[0.95 \times (22 - 5t_r/6 - t_o/6 - 0.8) \times 358]/(273 + 17)$$
$$= [0.95 \times (22 - 5 \times 22/6 - t_o/6 - 0.8) \times 358]/(273 + 17)$$
$$= 3.36 - 0.2 \ t_o$$

A heat balance can now be struck between sensible gain and natural cooling capacity:

$$3.2 + 0.15 \ t_o = 3.36 - 0.2 \ t_o, \text{ and } t_o \simeq 0.5°C.$$

If the proportion of fresh air had been greater this balance temperature would have been higher.

The outside air thermostat that would be used to switch the refrigeration plant on and off must have a differential, and $\pm 1°C$ might be suitable; the cooling plant would run until $-1.5°C$ was reached and not be switched on again until $+0.5°C$ was attained. The value of 0.5°C calculated above assumes the coincidence of solar gain through glass and a low outside air temperature; this may not be the rule and a decision could have been made to adopt a smaller value of solar load than that chosen, say the gain in December. The dry-bulb temperature onto the cooler coil is, thus,

$$[-1.5 + (22.0 \times 5.0)]/6.0 = 18.1°C.$$

The value of $-1.5°C$ must now be coupled with a moisture content in order to determine the natural latent cooling capacity of the air-handling unit with refrigeration off. The approach to be followed is a matter of opinion but here it will be assumed that temperatures between -1.5 and $+0.5°C$ occur during a stable, cold spell when the winter design state of $-2°C$ saturated, with a moisture content of 3.205 g kg^{-1}, has prevailed for some time. Then 3.205 g kg^{-1} can be associated with $-1.5°C$.

In winter, the infiltration latent load is usually either zero or negative and, since it is not possible to estimate infiltration accurately, it will be ignored here. The only latent load in the room is, therefore, that for thirteen people, i.e. 650 W. The moisture content of the uncooled supply air is $[5.0\ g_r+\ 3.205]/$ $6.0 = 0.833 g_r + 0.534$ g kg^{-1} and, from Equation (2.4), natural latent cooling capacity can be balanced with latent gain:

$$[0.95 \times (g_r - 0.833 g_r - 0.534) \times 856]/(273 + 17) = 0.65$$

and $g_r = 4.587$ g kg^{-1}. With a temperature of $22°C$ in the room, the corresponding humidity is 27%.

The moisture content of the air onto the cooler coil, just before the refrigeration plant is switched off by the outside air thermostat is, thus, $[(5.0 \times 4.587) + 3.205]/6.0 = 4.357$ g kg^{-1}. Since we know the dry-bulb as well, it can be stated that the minimum state onto the cooler coil is about $18.1°C$ dry-bulb, $10.1°C$ wet-bulb (sling). Figure 2.3 shows the psychrometry involved.

The $14.5°C$ wet-bulb line in Figure 2.2 gives an indication of the theoretical evaporator performance for an entering wet-bulb temperature of $10.1°C$. It implies that the evaporating temperature is less than $-1°C$ and that there will, therefore, be a distinct risk of frosting and its consequences. It is strongly recommended that evaporator pressure control be provided and the best way of doing this is by hot-gas injection into the evaporator.

A plant of this type and size would probably cycle under two-position control from a thermostat in the recirculated airstream, the single compressor in the condensing set being switched on and off, with a behaviour similar to that of the small, room air conditioner examined in Example 2.5. Larger units might have several compressors, offering step control over room temperature, but eventually the last compressor running will face the low load problems discussed.

The balance between an evaporator and a condensing unit will not be achieved at the steady-state level desired unless the thermostatic expansion valve passes the correct mass flow rate of refrigerant. The flow rate through the valve is a function of the pressure drop across it and, when calculating this, allowances must also be made for pipe friction loss, the change of position head in the liquid line before the valve, and the substantial pressure loss through the distributor and the tubes from it that feed the evaporator circuits. Since expansion valves are made in commercial size increments, an exact balance at the desired duty will not, in general, be obtained. If the valve is slightly oversized it will partly close, reducing the flow rate of refrigerant and raising the liquid level in the condenser. Since only the part of the condenser surface above the liquid line is effective in the condensation process, the condensing pressure will rise until it reaches a value that is consistent with the flow rate through the valve, the load on the evaporator and the capacity of the compressor. If the valve is undersized, stability would be reached at a higher condensing pressure than anticipated and less than the design duty would be achieved.

The fluid that is thermodynamically desirable in the system is the refrigerant but oil must also be present for the proper mechanical working of the compressor. The need to minimise the compression ratio, and the power absorbed, plus the necessity of ensuring oil return to the compressor, are the two restraints that limit the lengths of refrigerant pipe runs and the vertical distances between the items of plant. It follows that the location of the condensing set in relation to the air-handling unit is critical, and condensers, evaporators and compressors should be as close to each other as possible for the proper running of the system.

When a dry expansion refrigeration plant under thermostatic control is switched off, the thermostatic expansion valve is left open and the evaporator is filled with liquid, some of which may flow along the suction line. Slugs of liquid can then enter the compressor and damage it when it next starts. To prevent this happening, a pump-down control system must be adopted. Under this mode of operation a solenoid valve, located in the liquid line immediately before the expansion valve, is closed when the controlling thermostat is satisfied but the compressor is not switched off. Instead, it continues to run, pumping refrigerant vapour from the evaporator and so boiling off all the liquid within it, until the suction pressure has fallen to a pre-set, low value at which a pressure sensor switches off the compressor. During the period that follows, leakage past the expansion valve and back-leakage through the compressor can cause the suction pressure to rise. If the compressor were started again when the upper end of the differential of the low pressure cut-out was reached, there would be a risk of short-cycling, which means the compressor pumping-down repeatedly at intervals of time dependent on the leakage rate. A non-cycling relay is therefore included in the control circuit to prevent this. As a consequence, the compressor cannot restart after pumping-down unless both the low pressure cut-out and the controlling thermostat require it and, of course, the necessary high pressure cut-out and oil pressure safety switch permit it.

The refrigerant pumped out of the evaporator is delivered to the condenser or the liquid receiver and stored as a liquid until needed. Although a shell-and-tube, water-cooled condenser usually has enough space in its shell to store the quantity of liquid involved, many others, e.g. air-cooled, have not. A liquid receiver is then essential and it must be big enough to contain all the refrigerant from the rest of the system. It is strongly recommended that direct-expansion air-conditioning systems include pump-down control, particularly if the compressor is likely not to be running for any length of time. These considerations apply equally to air-conditioning units of size larger than exemplified here. Pump down must never be used with water chillers.

With many compressors the crankcase contains a mixture of oil and refrigerant. In such instances, since the crankcase is under suction pressure, foaming may occur when first starting up after a shut-down or when a large fall in the refrigeration load causes a drop in suction pressure. Refrigerant in solution in the oil during the shut-down period suddenly reverts to the gaseous phase in the form of myriads of small bubbles throughout the body of the oil, forming a substantial quantity of foam that lacks the lubricating properties of oil and may cause damage to the bearings and cylinders. This is highly undesirable and is to be prevented by including an electrical crankcase heater, wired to be energised whenever the compressor is off. The oil in the crankcase is then generally free of dissolved refrigerant, since it has been evaporated away during the shut-down period. Crankcase heaters may be fitted within the crankcases of open or semihermetic machines but in the case of hermetic compressors they are wrapped around the outside of the crankcase.

Condenser pressure should be controlled to stabilise the performance of the system under conditions of low ambient air temperature. The two preferred methods are liquid level back-up in the condenser and, as a second best, variable condenser fan speed under solid-state control.

Water-cooled air-conditioning units

When water-cooled units are fed from a cooling tower their capacities are related to outside wet-bulb rather than dry-bulb temperature, so condensing pressures are lower than with air-cooled units. The consequent reduction in compression ratio reduces their power requirements and, since they are working against a lower head pressure, they are likely to be quieter. Water-cooled units are available as single air-conditioning packages up to about 230 kW of refrigeration. Their catalogue ratings take into account the balance between evaporators and condensing sets and capacities are expressed in terms of condensing temperature, cooling water flow rate and entering temperature. Published ratings are sometimes in error and it is not always wise to adopt the lowest cooling water flow rate listed, even if the associated, necessary, low water temperature is available. A major advantage of such units over their air-cooled counterparts is a freedom in the choice of location, since a cooling tower can be on the roof and water pumped from it to units throughout the whole of the building. The condensers in the units are generally coiled-tube-in-shell, rather than shell-in-tube as used in the larger and better quality units, necessitating chemical cleaning when they become fouled with use. It is much better to

Table 2.3   Typical performance of a commercial, single-package, water-cooled air-conditioning unit, for an airflow rate of 950 1 s⁻¹ entering the unit and a by-pass factor of 0.22

| Entering state | | 41°C condensing | | | 43°C condensing | | |
Dry-bulb (°C)	Wet-bulb (°C)	Total cooling (kW)	Sensible cooling (kW)	Compressor motor power (kW)	Total cooling (kW)	Sensible cooling (kW)	Compressor motor power (kW)
28	20	18.0	13.6	5.40	17.7	13.4	5.70
	19	17.4	14.5	5.33	17.0	14.2	5.63
	18	16.8	15.4	5.27	16.3	15.0	5.57
	17	16.2	16.2	5.20	15.7	15.7	5.50
22	18	16.8	8.4	5.27	16.3	9.7	5.57
	17	16.2	9.3	5.20	15.7	10.7	5.50
	16	15.5	11.8	5.13	15.2	11.6	5.43

ensure clean water for the condensers by interposing a plate heat exchanger in the cooling water circuit between the tower and the condensers, if it can be afforded, even at the cost of raising the condensing temperature by a few degrees.

A further significant advantage is that the onset of warmer weather has less impact on the capacity of a water-cooled unit than on an air-cooled one because the wet-bulb temperature changes more slowly than the dry-bulb. For example, an increase of one degree in the dry-bulb at the design state to 29°C, at constant moisture content, causes a rise of only 0.4°C in the sling wet-bulb.

Table 2.3 shows abbreviated details of performance for a commercial, water-cooled, air-conditioning unit, which must be interpreted in conjunction with the requirements for cooling water listed in Table 2.4. Most catalogues also quote performances for air quantities that are roughly 25% above and below the nominal air quantity in Table 2.3.

Unfortunately, as with published data for air-cooled units, tabulated errors and inconsistencies are not uncommon. Interpolation within tables is generally permissible but extrapolation is decidedly risky and this is particularly so with low entering wet-bulbs when most of the cooling is

Table 2.4   Condenser cooling water requirements

| Condensing temperature (°C) | Water flow rates in 1 s⁻¹ for various entering water temperatures in °C | | | | | | |
	15.0	17.5	20.0	22.5	25.0	27.5	30.0
41	0.27	0.30	0.35	0.41	0.49	0.61	0.84
43	0.24	0.26	0.29	0.33	0.39	0.48	0.76

sensible. When a cooler coil does only sensible cooling, because the mean coil surface temperature must be above the dew-point of the air flowing over the coil, the apparatus dew-point does not lie on the saturation curve and the usual geometrical method of determining the by-pass factor cannot be used. There is often also doubt as to whether the air quantities quoted are referred to the state entering or leaving the unit. Since there is something like 5% difference in the air densities at these two states a corresponding, minimum inaccuracy is immediately set for the tabulated data.

Selecting a unit depends upon the choice of a temperature for the cooling water fed to the condenser in the unit and the source of this water is usually a cooling tower.

Example 2.9 Determine the total and sensible cooling duties and the necessary cooling water flow rates of a water-cooled, air-conditioning unit with a performance as listed in Tables 2.3 and 2.4. Assume an ambient wet-bulb of 19.5°C sling outside and a state of 23°C dry-bulb, 17°C wet-bulb sling entering the unit. Take a condensing temperature of 41°C.

Answer By interpolation, Table 2.3 shows that when condensing at 41°C the total cooling duty is 16.2 kW for the entry condition given and the sensible duty is 10.4 kW. The compressor motor power is 5.2 kW and so the heat rejected at the condenser will be 21.4 kW. A practical cooling tower can cool water to within 5° to 8°C of the ambient wet-bulb and it can, therefore, be assumed that a water temperature of 27.5°C is attainable. To condense at 41°C and give the listed duties a water flow rate of 0.61 l s^{-1} is needed (Table 2.4) and it can be calculated that this will rise to $27.5 + [21.4/(0.61 \times 4.187)] = 35.9$°C. This cooling range of 8.4°C is also a practical proposition for a cooling tower.

It is generally unwise, because of lack of confidence in the accuracy of all tabulated data, to adopt the extreme values of performances. It is much better to choose plant items to operate in the middle of their listed duties. This is also true of cooling water flow rates where it is sometimes risky to select the lowest quoted flow rate, even if the associated low temperature is available. It is generally a good policy to try and verify the psychrometric performance of the equipment chosen because in doing so any inconsistences in the tabulated information will become apparent.

Example 2.10 Examine the psychrometric performance of the water-cooled unit considered in Example 2.9 and determine the sensible and latent heat gains that could be dealt with if the conditioned space were maintained at 22°C dry-bulb and 50% saturation.

Answer The state of the air entering the unit is 23°C dry-bulb, 17°C wet-bulb,

9.618 g kg^{-1}, 0.8515 m^{3}kg^{-1}, but if it is accepted that the unit handles a constant quantity of 0.95 m^3 s^{-1} of air at this state then the fan blows through the cooler coil. The mass flow rate of air is thus 0.95/0.8515 = 1.116 kg s^{-1}. The catalogue will quote fan power, probably with the assumptions of a clean filter and a wet coil. If it is assumed here that the fan power is 600 W, the temperature rise across the fan can now be calculated as $[(0.6/0.95) \times (273 + 23)]/358 = 0.5°C$. Thus, the state entering the cooler coil is 23.5°C dry-bulb, 9.618 g kg^{-1} and 48.11 kJ kg^{-1}. The enthalpy leaving the coil is, therefore, 48.11 − (16.2/1.116) = 33.59 kJ kg^{-1} and, as the by-pass factor is 0.22, the enthalpy at the apparatus dew-point is 48.11 − [16.2/(1.116 × 0.78)] = 29.50 kJ kg^{-1} and, as the by-pass factor is 0.22, the enthalpy at the apparatus dew-point is 48.11 − [16.2/(1.116 × 0.78)] = 29.50 kJ kg^{-1} These states can be identified on a psychrometric chart and it can be seen that the state leaving the coil is 13°C dry-bulb, 8.116 g kg^{-1}. In the absence of supply air ducting outside the conditioned space, this is also the supply state. Consequently:

Sensible gain absorbed in the room
$$= [0.95 \times (22 - 13) \times 358]/(273 + 23) = 10.34 \text{ kW}$$

Latent gain absorbed in the room
$$= [0.95 \times (8.366 - 8.116) \times 856]/(273 + 23) = 0.687 \text{ kW}.$$

This unit would be able to cope with the sensible heat gains of 9.45 kW calculated and used in Example 2.8 for an air-cooled unit but, because the latent cooling capacity is less than the figure of 0.82 kW calculated in the same example, the humidity in the room would be higher than the value of 50% assumed. A precise solution is not readily obtained but the indications are that the unit capacity would balance the room load at a comfortable condition of 22°C dry-bulb and less than 60% saturation, in the process of which the state of the air entering the cooler coil would be a little different from that used in Example 2.9.

2.4 Terminal heat recovery units

Terminal heat recovery units are basically water-cooled, room air-conditioning units with a manually selected heat pump facility. Water is circulated in a one-pipe or two-pipe system and units either reject heat into it from their condensers when they are cooling or absorb heat from it when heating. Since units in different parts of a building may, in a temperate climate, be both heating and cooling simultaneously, energy is conserved by transference through the water loop. Most of the time there will be a net imbalance of energy, and surpluses and deficits of heat in the water system must be corrected by a cooling tower and a boiler. Because such units are sensitive to variations in water flow, it is absolutely essential that plate heat exchangers be incorporated to separate the dirty water circuits through the cooling tower, particularly, and the boiler, from the necessary clean water circuit through the units. A closed cooling tower could be used directly, instead of an open tower and a plate heat exchanger, but closed towers are invariably bulky, heavy and expansive. Further, their water circuit usually needs a glycol additive for winter frost protection and this imposes penalties on heat transfer.

There are two major variations of unit: a conventional one where heating in the winter is done solely by heat pumping, a third or a quarter of the heating being electrical by virtue of the compressor; and a heat pump/LTHW version in which the compressors do not run at all in the winter and the heating is by means of LTHW (low temperature hot water). The latter has two subclasses.

Conventional heat recovery terminals
Nominal total cooling capacities of conventional heat recovery terminals are in the range 1.5 to 3.8 kW of refrigeration with sensible heat ratios between 0.83 and 0.74. Heating capacities are from 2.2 to 5.3 kW, implying coefficients of performance of 2.1 to 2.5. Hence, the proportion of electrical heating mentioned above. Supply airflow rates are about 90 to 250 l s^{-1} and the units are therefore quite suitable for dealing with the heat gains encountered in the peripheral areas of buildings to depth of 6 m from the glazing. Fresh air may be provided by an auxiliary, central ventilation system handling filtered, tempered air but, since one advantage of using terminal units of this type is that plant space is cut to a minimum, fresh air is commonly admitted through a hole in the wall behind the unit. Although having a central ventilation system is better because air distribution and filtration are superior, as much as 22% of the supply air quantity can be introduced through the unit locally, either directly or through an adjoining cabinet fitted with its own centrifugal fan, air filter and silencer. In this latter case the direction of airflow can be reversed, in the event of a fire, to evacuate smoke from the room.

Most units are available as floor or wall-mounted options or for installation at high-level above suspended ceilings, Some terminals are designed for use with auxiliary, local duct systems, fitted with acoustic linings or attenuators. Selection procedures are likely to be similar to those for water-cooled air-conditioning units for summer operation. In winter, on the other hand, allowance must be made for the work done by the refrigeration compressor when assessing the boiler power. The critical feature of their performance is the water flow rate: for some units this can be as low as 0.08 ls^{-1} at 27°C but for others twice this quantity is needed. During commissioning it is essential that the correct water flow rate be achieved and demonstrating this may be difficult; it is of little use to measure the water temperature rise because this is dependent on the cooling load which in turn depends on many things and may be even more difficult to determine. It is better to use reliable water regulation devices, possibly to aim at having about 10% more than the nominal water quantity at each unit, regulation downward then being practical. Flushing through the piping system, with the terminals out of the circuit, is vital before they are connected.

It is feasible, sometimes, to use much of the distribution piping in a two-pipe LTHW heating system, after checking that its condition and size is adequate in all respects, if the building served is to be upgraded from heated to air-conditioned, by replacement of the radiators with heat recovery terminal units and by the addition of a cooling tower, plate heat exchangers, a condensate drainage system in plastic or copper from the units, pumps, automatic controls, switchgear and, possibly, an auxiliary ventilation system. It is good practice to introduce random start relays so that large numbers of units cannot come on together. Controls should include a minimum flow water temperature cut-out, with a probable set-point of about 15°C. Units themselves are generally controlled by cycling the compressor on-off from a return air or room thermostat, the supply fan running continuously.

Heat pump/LTHW versions
Figures 2.4 and 2.5 show two less usual varieties of heat recovery terminal unit. A one-pipe instead of a two-pipe system of water distribution may be used but the water flow rate is highly critical, and a special tee-piece is used with the one-pipe system to ensure that one-eighth of the flow in the main is diverted into the unit. This seems to set a limit of eight units for each one-pipe main and, since units appear to require 0.14 ls^{-1}, the main handles 1.12 ls^{-1} and is often 32 mm nominal bore medium grade steel.

The unit has three modes of operation. For summer cooling nothing unusual happens and water at about 27°C enters the condenser. As the outside air temperature falls, with the onset of autumn, the flow water temperature is compensated upwards towards a maximum of about 52°C. When winter arrives (say less than about 6°C outside) the compressors are switched off and the water temperature is further elevated to perhaps 85°C for design outside conditions. The units are working as fan coil heaters during this season of the year. Refrigerant 22 is used and it is evident that operation in marginal outside weather (see Figure 2.4) with the high condensing pressures involved will have thermodynamic and mechanical consequences, reducing the coefficient of performance, possibly raising the noise produced and perhaps reducing the life. However, many such units have been used, principally in the United States, with the advantage over the conventional type that all the winter heating is by the boilers, rather than there being a significant proportion of electrical energy used.

The alternative form of heat pump/LTHW unit is illustrated in Figure 2.5, where water always flows through the condenser, instead of by-passing it in winter. This has the minor advantage that a unit can cool and dehumidify and reheat. Again the water flow rate is critical.

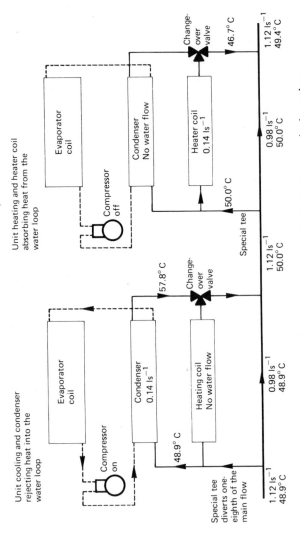

Figure 2.4   Operation of a heat recovery terminal unit during marginal weather. Expansion valve or capillary tube not shown in the refrigerant liquid line

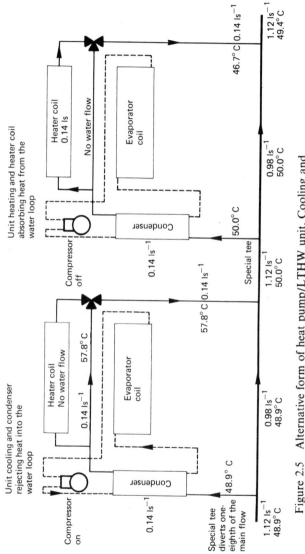

Figure 2.5 Alternative form of heat pump/LTHW unit. Cooling and dehumidification can be combined with reheat, if desired, when the compressor runs, since the evaporator coil precedes the heater coil and the condenser is in series with the heater (not shown)

2.5 Constant volume re-heat systems

These are essentially simple systems, comprising a cooler coil that reduces the dew-point of the supply air in order to match the latent gain in the conditioned room, with a reheater to elevate the supply air temperature to a value which will match the sensible heat gain or loss. If a sprayed cooler coil, or sometimes a washer, is used, the system offers the possibility of tight control over both humidity and temperature in the treated space, for an industrial application. In commercial uses it is a wasteful system in both capital and running costs, for other than the smallest duties. No advantage can be taken of diversity in heat gains, if several reheat zones are involved, because a reduction in heat gain is promptly cancelled by reheat and it follows that the installed refrigeration capacity will exceed that which would be needed for a more economical system (e.g. perimeter induction). The only fall in the refrigeration duty throughout the year is that resulting from variations in the weather that influence the fresh air load and hence these systems run at nearly full refrigeration load for long periods and are wasteful of energy, heating fuel being used to cancel unnecessary refrigeration.

Constant volume reheat systems are best used for industrial applications, for cases where the variations in the sensible gain are very small, as in some tropical places, or for very small commercial loads where the waste may be insignificant compared with the advantage of system simplicity.

Example 2.11 Determine the refrigeration load for the hypothetical office block (Figure 1.1), assuming it is conditioned by a constant volume reheat system. Make use of the appropriate information from Examples 1.8, 1.9 and 1.11 and from Table A.7. Assume occupancy finishes at 17.00 h sun time.
Answer Table A.7 suggests that the maximum gains will occur at 17.00 h sun time for the north wall and roof but at 16.00 h for the south wall. The greatest infiltration gain and the biggest fresh air load will be at 15.00 h. The maximum latent gain will also occur at 15.00 h and, being unaffected by reheat cancellation, a diversity factor of 0.75 can still be applied to the latent gain from people. The fan power will be much larger than it was with the induction system (Example 1.11) because a lot more air must be supplied and extracted. In this instance, to avoid irrelevant calculation, although accepting some possible error, let us assume three and a half times as much air is handled. It is reasonable to suppose a high velocity distribution for supply but low velocity for extract. The refrigeration load can then be assessed.

West face: 1.837 (kW) × 36 (modules) × 12 (storeys)   =   793.6
East face: 1.625 (kW) × 36 (modules) × 12 storeys)   =   702.0
North wall: [(13.5 × 3.3 × 12) × 0.91 × 3.9]/1000   =   1.9
South wall: [(13.5 × 3.3 × 12) × 0.91 × 17.2]/1000   =   8.4
Roof: [(86.4 × 13.5) × 1.1 × 18.3]/1000   =   23.5

Infiltration: $[0.5 \times (86.4 \times 13.5 \times 2.6 \times 12) \times (28 - 22)$
$\times 0.33]/1000$ = $\underline{36.0}$
Total sensible gain: = 1565.4 kW
Total latent gain: = 91.2
Fresh air load: $[(0.0013 \times 86.4 \times 13.5 \times 12) \times (55.36$
$-43.39)]/0.822$ = 265.0
Supply fan power: $[(3.5 \times 0.0035) \times (86.4 \times 13.5 \times 12) \times 4$
$\times 358]/(273 + 14)$ = 855.5
Extract fan power: $[(3.5 \times 0.00325 - 0.0013) \times (86.4 \times 13.5$
$\times 12) \times 0.5 \times 358]/(273 + 14)$ = $\underline{88.0}$
Subtotal: 2865.1 kW
Pipes and pumps, say 1%: $\underline{28.7}$
Refrigeration load: $\overline{2893.8}$ kW

This represents 207 Wm^{-2} for the treated floor area and 60% more than that calculated for the induction system in Example 1.11. There are, of course, some inaccuracies in the above, not just because of the supply air quantity assumption but also because it does not follow that the maximum gain to end modules and to modules on the top floor will be exactly as assumed. A computer analysis would clear this, but the error is very small compared with the total load.

2.6 Roof-top units

Although almost any weatherproofed, air-handling or air-conditioning unit can be located on a roof, the term 'roof-top unit' tends, by common usage, to have a special meaning. It is generally understood to denote a self-contained, air-conditioning unit that comprises mixing box, filter, direct-expansion cooler coil, air-cooled condensing unit, direct-fired air heater batter (gas or oil) and supply fan with motor, drive and switchgear. The unit is weatherproofed, prewired and factory tested. It only requires electrical connexions and a gas or oil feed, after errection on the roof, to operate. Condensate from the cooler coil runs to waste on the roof, preferably in a gully.

Such units are available in a range of capacities from 5 to 75 kW of refrigeration and from 17 to 120 kW of heating. The filters provided as standard are generally washable polyurethane foam or oil-impregnated glass fibre, but electrical filters can also be obtained. Although end connexions for ductwork are possible the standard and most convenient arrangement is to have supply and extract spigots on the underside of the unit to connect with ductwork running beneath the roof.

Anti-vibration mountings for the moving parts are generally built into the unit, as is also thermal/acoustic lining, but before locating a unit it is always wise to establish that the mass, span and stiffness of the roof is adequate for the prevention of a noise and vibration problem in the occupied space below (see Sections 7.12 and 7.26).

The advantages of roof-top units are that they are simple and cheap, no boiler plant is needed, duct distribution systems can be reduced to a minimum, multiple units can be used to provide multiple zone control and they are ideal for single-storey commercial buildings in a highly competitive application, such as a shopping centre development. One of their limitations is that the degree of control offered is simple, just on/off cooling, in sequence with one or two-step heating, but this is not necessarily a disadvantage for the correct application. Two-speed fans are sometimes available, permitting operational economy in winter when the refrigeration plant is off. It is also possible to include an assembly of variable position, automatic, motorised dampers that offer varying proportions of fresh and recirculated air and allow the refrigeration plant to be switched off when the outside air is cool enough. Some manufacturers will not let their units be operated with 100% fresh air in winter because, in cold weather, flue gases condense on the primary surfaces of the direct-fired heater battery, with a consequent risk of corrosion. Other units, designed specifically for the American market, have burners that are not easily set up to meet the UK need to establish a flame within three seconds of ignition.

2.7 All-air ceiling systems

Sometimes, office blocks are conditioned by one, or more, air-conditioning units or air-handling units, located on each floor and treated air is ducted to the plenum chamber formed by the soffit of the slab and the suspended ceiling, for distribution through circular, square, or linear slot diffusers or through perforated ceiling tiles, to the conditioned office space. Vitiated air is extracted through sidewall grilles and returned to the plants for recycling along the builders' work duct formed by the soffit of the slab and the suspended ceiling in the central corridor (Figure 2.6).

To be successful, this form of air distribution relies upon the ceiling plenum being air and vapour tight, i.e. an initial sealing of the plenum chamber followed by proper thermal insulation with a vapour barrier on its air side. Failure to do this properly may result in air leakage from the plenum, moisture migration through the building materials and insulation, and a subsequent departure from design conditions in the treated space. Since the air distribution system also deals with heat losses, downdraughts and infiltration are not countered at the windows and, if these are single-glazed, some local discomfort in witner may ensue.

The advantages of the system are that water and electrical services are confined to the plant rooms, no terminal units are used and no lettable floor area is occupied, other than in the plant rooms; maintenance work is limited to

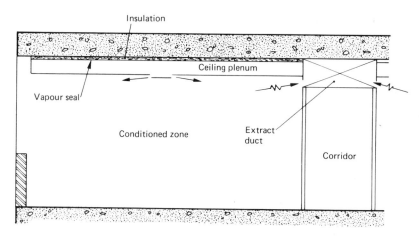

Figure 2.6   Supply and extract air distribution for an all-air ceiling system

plant areas and only those floors actually occupied need to be treated, so the installation may be progressive if desired, as successive floors are let. On the other hand, such a system is best used for open plan offices or for large, clearly defined zones having uniform variation in sensible heat gain or loss, as it is essentially a constant volume reheat system with only two reheaters, one for each side of the office floor, although there may be occasional exceptions. Clearly, individual thermostatic control in multiple private offices is out of the question if the simplicity of this approach is to be preserved and its competitiveness maintained. Because the plant rooms are actually on the occupied floors, particular attention must be paid to the acoustic qualities of their building construction if the break-out of noise and vibration is to be prevented (see Sections 7.12 and 7.26). Further, fresh air inlets and discharge air outlets must be provided in the outer face of the building at each plant room. Fixed proportions of fresh and recirculated air are the rule and the refrigeration plant may thus have to run throughout much of the winter which, in conjunction with the reheat principle, tends to make the system expensive in running costs.

Units may be air-handling, comprising mixing box, filter, cooler coil, heater batteries, supply fan and silencers, or air-conditioning with a self-contained condensing unit or, more often, a remote air-cooled condenser. Whichever condensing arrangement is adopted the cooling air must enter the plant room and leave it in a way that avoids short-circuiting, unless, as with low-rise buildings, the remote condensers can be installed on the roof.

The selection of plant must depend on the judgement of the individual engineer but, as a guide, direct-expansion cooling might be apt for refrigeration duties of less than about 150 kW but chilled water cooler coils fed from a central chilling plant better for larger duties. Overall capital cost dictates the choice. Since typical refrigeration loads (see Examples 1.11 and 2.10) are of the order of 100 to 250 Wm^{-2} of treated floor area it follows that office blocks of more than about 1000 m^2 floor area are likely to have central water chillers distributing chilled water to multiple air-handling units, if this type of system is chosen. Although electric reheat is a proposition for very small applications most installations include central boiler plant feeding LTHW to multiple plant reheaters.

Systems of this type should really only be considered for relatively small duties, in competitive situations, where the attendant disadvantages of control, running cost and possible downdraughts at windows, are clearly understood.

2.8 Variable air volume systems

Application

Conventional methods of air distribution, e.g. side-wall grilles and circular, square or linear diffusers, set a limiting range of air supply rates from about 1.7 to 15 $1s^{-1} m^{-2}$, within which variable air volume (VAV) systems may be used whenever the application favours an all-air system with thermostatic control in multiple rooms or zones.

Although lacking intrinsic heating ability, VAV may be modified in three ways that allow its extension to the peripheral areas and top floors of buildings where heat losses occur:

(1) The cheapest and simplest method is to provide auxiliary, perimeter heating using compensated LTHW in finned tube, convectors or radiators. As little as 100 mm of floor space inwards from the wall is used, representing only about 2% of lettable floor area for a module 6 m deep.

(2) The addition of a reheater at each VAV terminal unit is the second possibility and this is not wasteful of energy because reheat is only used after the air quantity has been turned down to about 40% of its summer design volume, in response to reductions in sensible heat gain. Thereafter, the volume handled stays constant but is progressively warmed as the heat losses increase. The use of terminal reheaters sometimes imposes restrictions on the layout of the VAV units and the ducts feeding them, tending to make this approach less adaptable to changes in the arrangement of partitions. Further, the delivery of low volumes of hot air at high level may introduce stratification problems, with uncomfortably low air temperatures in the occupied part of the room.

(3) A double duct VAV system may be used, which operates in a similar way, the cold air being throttled to a constant minimum of about 40% and then mixed with air from the hot duct to offset heat loss. This system can also suffer from the stratification problems mentioned previously and, in addition, the presence of the second duct poses accommodation difficulties.

With deep-plan offices it may be argued that VAV should be used for the interior zones whilst the periphery is treated with a constant volume system having a heating capacity, such as an induction scheme. The contrary view, of considerable merit, is that it is simpler and cheaper to have a single VAV system to cover the entire area and to offset heat losses at the perimeter with finned tube, or the like. Hence, one finds VAV applied to both shallow and deep buildings. Where the top floor of a building is treated by VAV the heat loss through the roof of the core area, beyond the reach of the perimeter heating, should be countered by LTHW coils fitted above the suspended ceiling. As an alternative, and also to deal with core areas on intermediate floors, before the lights are switched on in the early morning, it is possible to deliver warmed air from a heater battery in the central air-handling plant, through the VAV system, the controlling thermostats at the terminals being instructed to hold open the VAV units to full airflow. When this method is used and all terminals kept temporarily fully open, more air will be delivered to those areas nearest to the central plant, which will thus tend to be warmer than more remote areas. Once normal operation and control is resumed, prior to occupancy commencing, room temperature variations should even out.

VAV can be successfully applied to buildings other than offices, notably, hospitals, libraries, museums, department stores and schools. The system generally is not suitable for areas such as computer suites where high heat gains are usual and air supply rates exceeding $15 \text{ s}^{-1} \text{ m}^{-2}$ are needed.

Air distribution
The success of a VAV system depends very much on the choice of a terminal unit that can give satisfactory air movement, and comfortable conditions, over the full range of variation in the supply air quantity. VAV terminal units may be mounted beneath sills and blow air up the window face, or, more commonly, above the suspended ceiling and blow air across it. The latter is generally favoured because no lettable floor area is used while the possible objection that floor-to-floor building heights, and costs, are increased is seldom strong enough to out-weigh the commercial advantage of the saving in floor area. Occasionally, units are mounted above the dropped ceiling in the corridor and air delivered to the rooms through side-wall grilles, this being possible because floor-to-ceiling heights in corridors are invariably less than in rooms. Arrangements like this offer more space to accommodate terminal reheaters.

When an airstream flows from a supply opening across a ceiling, or any other flat surface, frictional losses occur and the static pressure on the ceiling side of the airstream becomes less than that on the room side. The airstream tends to cling to the ceiling and this phenomenon is termed the 'Coanda effect'. Air entrained from the room by the supply airstream increases its mass and, because momentum is conserved, its velocity falls. Since frictional loss at the ceiling is a function of air velocity, the static pressure difference that presses the airstream to the ceiling diminishes with increasing distance from the supply opening and the airstream eventually leaves the ceiling. If enough entrainment has occurred the air velocity is not very great when this separation takes place and the temperature of the airstream is virtually that of the room. If the initial velocity of the airstream is not very large, separation occurs earlier and if the airstream is initially much colder than the ambient air its temperature at separation will be noticeably less than that of the room and negative buoyancy will assist the earlier separation. This is called 'dumping' and is associated with local discomfort. Research work[6] and experience suggests that dumping does not occur very often if VAV units are chosen properly and it is evident that the selection of terminals to give good air distribution over the range of expected duties is vital.

There are two forms of VAV terminal: fixed area and variable area. With the former, the air velocity through the supply opening varies with the volume and so dumping is more likely. With the latter, the area available for delivery through the slot decreases under thermostatic control as the volume falls and so, with a constant static pressure upstream, the air velocity through the supply slot is virtually constant, regardless of volume changes, and dumping is less likely. With the fixed area type, supply air rates can be turned down to about 40% of design flow whereas the other form allows a reduction to about 20%. Whichever kind is adopted it is always possible that natural convection air currents, caused by sources of heat gain within the room or downdraughts or updraughts at the window, can upset the expected pattern of air distribution. The presence of ceiling obstructions such as down-stand beams or light fittings can also introduce problems.

Catalogue data for VAV units should always quote maximum and minimum throws. It is essential that units are not selected to have throws less than the minimum listed, otherwise draughts are inevitable. Where a problem like this arises during the layout planning stage of a design, it is often possible to solve it by rearranging the positions of the air distribution units. For example, if a linear slot VAV diffuser with a minimum listed throw of 1.95 m when handling $80 \, l \, s^{-1}$ is arranged with its axis along the major centre-line of the 6 m × 2.4 m module in the hypothetical office block, draughts will occur because the distance to the walls of the module, or to the opposing airstream from the VAV unit in the adjoining module if there is no partition separating them, is only 1.2 m. On the other hand, if the linear diffuser is turned through 90°, the distance to the window or the corridor wall is 3 m, which exceeds the minimum listed throw and no draughts will occur (see Figure 2.7).

Reducing the supply air quantity also reduces the ventilation rate at times when a fixed proportion of fresh air is handled but even at peak load a difficulty arises. Using the data in Example 1.8 and in the Appendix it can be calculated that, at 16.00 h sun time, an east-facing module suffers sensible gains of 934 W (only 57% of the design gain at 08.00 h sun time) and will therefore receive only $75 \, l \, s^{-1}$. It is calculated in Example 2.12 that the total supply air quantity for the whole building, including central corridors, is $90.7 \, m^3 \, s^{-1}$, of which 0.0013

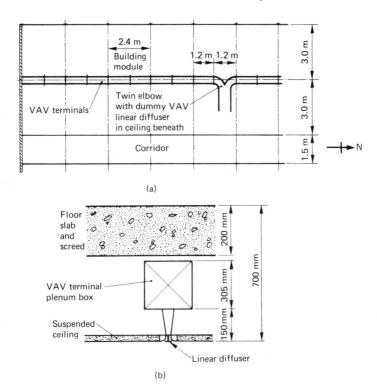

Figure 2.7a, VAV terminal and duct layout; b, Cross-section of a VAV terminal in a ceiling void

× 14000 = 18.2 m³ s⁻¹ must be fresh, 20% of the total in an afternoon in July. An eastern module will then receive $(0.57 \times 0.2 \times 130)/14.4 = 1.04 \, \text{ls}^{-1} \, \text{m}^{-2}$, whereas a western module will get $(0.2 \times 146)/14.4 = 2.03 \, \text{ls}^{-1} \, \text{m}^{-2}$. At 08.00 h sun time the positions will be approximately reversed. It can be argued that this is satisfactory since the building, on average, is getting the correct rate of $1.3 \, \text{ls}^{-1} \, \text{m}^{-2}$ and the system operates with the fresh air damper in the minimum position for only a small proportion of the year. Alternatively, increasing the minimum design amount of fresh air in a July afternoon to $(18.2 \times 1.3)/1.04 = 22.75 \, \text{m}^3 \, \text{s}^{-1}$, ensures that eastern modules always receive enough, western modules getting rather more than enough, without incurring a very severe penalty in extra refrigeration load. Referring to Example 1.11 and assuming that the refrigeration load calculated for an induction system is roughly the same for a VAV system, it can be estimated that the fresh air component of 251 kW will be increased by $[(22.75 - 18.2) \times 251]/18.2 = 63 \, \text{kW}$, which is only about 3.5% of the total of 1742 kW of refrigeration. Under partial load for the whole system the fresh air dampers are opened progressively as the total supply quantity is diminished.

System type
There are many different forms of VAV terminal unit available on the market, but the following two typify a basic difference of approach:
(1) A self-contained unit, often actually forming part of the air distribution ducting, in which air is handled directly at medium velocity and high pressure in the process of being thermostatically controlled
(2) A split system that uses two devices, the first a pressure reducing valve and the second a thermostatically controlled, motorised, variable volume diffuser.

An example of the first type comprises a linear diffuser, 75 mm in width, flush-mounted in the suspended ceiling and fed from an acoustically lined plenum box above, several such boxes usually being connected in series to form part of the distribution ducting (see Figure 2.7) Proportional thermostatic control is self-acting, the static pressure of the air in the duct itself being used as a power source, providing it is above a minimum value of about 100 Pa and less than a maximum of about 1250 Pa. There are thus no electrical or pneumatic connexions required and the thermostatic element, a bimetallic strip, and its set point adjustment are unobtrusively located in the end part of the unit, where entrained room air permits a representative assessment of room temperature. Constant volume as well as variable volume units are available and it is also possible to have as many as five slave units linked with one master control unit, where the thermostat is fitted, to provide automatic control of larger rooms at a reduced cost.

There are two bellows in such units and each may be thermostatically controlled from its own side of the diffuser slot, independently of the other. The resulting important advantage of this type of unit is that there is complete freedom for partition rearrangement, even after the system has been commissioned and the building occupied. Also, all the control modifications may be done from below and ceiling panels need not be removed, it being unnecessary to change duct connexions to the units since they will have been chosen to provide controlled, flexible air conditioning on a modular basis; partitions can be erected along the centre line of the linear diffuser and independent control achieved in the offices on each side.

The other principal form of VAV system is available in many versions, including motorised, circular, square or rectangular ceiling diffusers and pneumatically-actuated side-wall grilles. There are electric reheat options and slots or grilles that permit distribution upwards at the window sills. The pressure reducing valves can cope with upstream pressures as high as 1 kPa when they are of the inflatable, neoprene bellows type that are operated by compressed air at a pressure of 100 kPa. The diffusers are able to deal with upstream duct pressures from about 12 to 60 Pa and the side-wall grilles can manage with 25 to 125 Pa. A modification to units of this type (2) introduces an induction principle to the diffusers with single and dual duct possibilities. The single duct unit comprises a plenum chamber fitted with high velocity nozzles

Table 2.5 Typical performance of a self-contained VAV unit

	Air quantity (l s^{-1})										
	20	30	40	50	60	70	80	90	100	110	120
Minimum throw (m)	0.6	0.6	1.0	1.3	1.6	2.0	2.3	2.6	2.9	3.2	3.6
Maximum throw (m)	1.5	2.4	3.2	4.0	4.8	5.6	6.5	7.3	8.1	8.9	9.7
Minimum pressure (Pa)	370	330	290	255	225	190	165	135	150	100	100

inducing air from the ceiling void, which is warmed by the recessed light fittings, at a rate that is varied under thermostatic control. Obviously, no heating is possible until the lights are switched on. The dual duct version has a ducted, primary, fresh air supply at constant volume and compensated temperature fed to its plenum chamber to offset heat loss. A separate, variable volume, secondary supply of cold air at constant temperature is also delivered to the chamber. Under conditions of minimum secondary airflow, maximum induction of warm air from the ceiling void occurs but there is no induction at all when maximum secondary air is flowing under summer design heat gains.

VAV units of type (1) have a typical performance as shown in Table 2.5. The minimum pressures quoted are the static pressures in the duct immediately upstream of the unit. The maximum allowable static pressure in the duct is about 1250 Pa. Each unit has a nominal length of 1200 or 1500 mm and a width of 290 mm, but the depth of the plenum box varies according to the air quantity handled (Table 2.6). To obtain the overall height of the unit, the height of the approach to the linear diffuser, i.e. 150 mm, must be added to the plenum depth (see Figure 2.7).

Example 2.12 Referring to Example 1.8 and the design brief in Section 1.1, as necessary, determine the maximum supply air quantities needed for the modules on intermediate floors of the hypothetical office block. Assume that the dry-bulb temperature leaving the cooler coil is 10°C and allow 2°C rise for duct heat gain. Assume also that a blowthrough cooler coil is used and, therefore, that the temperature rise for the fan power occurs before the cooler coil. A VAV system is used.

Table 2.6 Variation in plenum box depth in a self-contained VAV unit

	Unit size			
	1	2	3	4
Maximum inlet air quantity (l s^{-1})	330	470	710	940
Plenum box depth (mm)	168	216	305	400

Answer From Equation 2.3, the maximum required supply air quantities are:

West-facing modules: $\dfrac{1.837}{(22-12)} \times \dfrac{(273+12)}{358} \times 1000 = 146 \ \mathrm{l\,s}^{-1}$

East-facing modules: $\dfrac{1.625}{(22-12)} \times \dfrac{(273+12)}{358} \times 1000 = 130 \ \mathrm{l\,s}^{-1}$

Table 2.5 shows that two units will be needed, each handling 73 and 65 $\mathrm{l\,s}^{-1}$ with minimum throws of 2.1 and 1.8 m for the west and east modules respectively. A satisfactory arrangement is for the units to be positioned on the smaller centre-line of each module with their own centre-lines parallel to the windows. The minimum throws are then less than the distance to the corridor wall or the window and no draughts will be felt (see Figure 2.7). Each unit has a nominal length of 1.2 m and so a pair connected in series can be accommodated in the 2.4 modular width.

The maximum air quantity required for the whole building, i.e. the supply fan duty, will not be the sum of the maximum individual values. Instead, it is necessary to evaluate the maximum simultaneous sensible gain to all the modules, taking proper account of diversification for the loads from lights, people and business machines. Example 1.11 showed that the maximum sensible gain for the whole building, including corridors, was 1136 kW. In fact, it can be shown that the biggest gain is 1142 kW and occurs at 16.00 h sun time in July, but the slight error is insignificant in comparison with the doubt that exists in the diversity factors chosen.

The supply fan should therefore deliver a maximum quantity of

$$\dfrac{1136}{(22-12)} \times \dfrac{(273+12)}{358} = 90.4 \ \mathrm{m^3 s}^{-1} \text{ at } 12°C.$$

It is most important to appreciate that the benefits of diversity in the solar heat gain through windows can only be achieved if the air-handling plant and main duct system serve opposing faces of a building, for example, east and west.

The difference between floor-to-floor and floor-to-ceiling heights is 700 mm, which must include the structural slab and screed, a void for ducts and extract-ventilated light fittings, the suspended ceiling and its supports. A surface density of 300 $\mathrm{kg\,m}^{-2}$, previously accepted for the floor, implies a slab thickness of 143 mm, assuming an actual density of 2100 $\mathrm{kg\,m}^{-3}$ for concrete. Allowing 200 mm for the slab and screed, plus 75 mm for the ceiling structure, leaves a clear space of 425 mm beneath the soffit of the slab, although it must be remembered that, in places, downstand beams may encroach upon this and due provision must be made when planning the duct layout. Table 2.6 shows that a size 3 plenum box is the largest that will fit

(Figure 2.7b). Such a unit can handle a maximum of $710\,\mathrm{ls^{-1}}$ at its inlet and this sets a limit on the number of VAV terminals that may be fed in series, i.e. 9 units for the west face and 10 for the east. Ducts can be arranged to feed the end of a series group of 9 units, for the west face, or to feed the middle of a series group of 18 units at a twin-elbow. Figure 2.7a shows this and also that the half-module containing the twin-elbow will receive no air, which is unavoidable. If the minimum size of an office is two modules wide, say, then where a twin-elbow was present the three live linear diffusers would deliver a total of $4 \times 73 = 292\,\mathrm{ls^{-1}}$, or $97\,\mathrm{ls^{-1}}$ each, when under thermostatic control during periods of peak heat gain for the west face.

It is possible to use low velocity, as opposed to medium velocity, VAV terminal units which feed air through linear ceiling diffusers. One make on the market is not a true VAV system in that the supply fan handles a constant quantity of air, although the supply to the room is variable as unwanted air is delivered to the ceiling void in the cold state for mixing with used air relieved from the room through extract light fittings prior to return to the plant for recycling. This air may sometimes leak back to the room through the ceiling. A motorised damper regulates the amount of air supplied to the room or diverted to the ceiling void according to the signal received from a wall-mounted thermostat. Floating rather than proportional control is the mode exercised, although this may not be always satisfactory since it should only be applied to a system with a quick response, and with something like ten air changes per hour typical for a core area the air diffusion lag will be six minutes, probably too long for good floating control, which will then degenerate to two-position control. In some instances, of course, this form of control may be adequate.

A roof-top packaged air-conditioning unit is also available for VAV. It usually comprises an air-cooled condensing set, direct-expansion cooler coil and gas or oil, direct-fired, heater battery. Variable position, motorised, inlet guide vanes are fitted to the centrifugal supply and extract fans. Any make of VAV air-distribution terminals can be ducted at low or medium velocity from the packaged unit. The unit is appropriate for low-rise developments requiring all-air systems with multiple, individual, thermostatic control and covers a range from 5000 to $12500\,\mathrm{ls^{-1}}$. It is most important to stabilise the evaporating pressure, preferably by a hot gas valve, to ensure that the coil will not frost at light load with the consequence of burnt out windings in the motor of the semihermetic compressor and a poisoned refrigeration system.

Duct system design
Generally, to avoid noise and to minimise energy consumption by fan power, it is best to design VAV systems as medium velocity, in the range 10 to 12.5 m s^{-1}, rather than as high velocity, in the range 15 to 20 m s^{-1}. Exceeding a velocity of 15 m s^{-1} should be avoided and 20 m s^{-1} should never be exceeded. Run-outs feeding VAV terminals, of whatever type, should be sized for 10 m s^{-1}, or less.

To assist in balanced air distribution, main ducts should be sized by static regain where building space permits. It is wise to keep a distance of at least six duct diameters between successive fittings and to adopt conical tees. An air-tight supply system is essential and this means ducting must be pressure-tested after installation. It is possible that, with the conservative approach to sizing suggested above, the fan total pressure may not be high enough to bring the system within the range of pressures that codes of practice regard as necessary for pressure tests. Pressure tests should be carried out nevertheless. Well-designed systems are likely to have fan total pressures of the order of 1.0 to 1.25 kPa, rather than 1.5 kPa upwards. Duct layouts should be simple and circular, spirally-wound duct is preferable to rectangular ducting, the cost of the latter, if air-tight, being some four times that of the former. Spirally-wound oval duct is acceptable, to a limited extent, and is better than rectangular. Extract systems are generally much less extensive than supply duct schemes, since the location of the supply terminals dictates the quality of the air distribution. Wherever possible, air should be extracted through ventilated light fittings (see section 1.6) but extract duct systems should never be sized by high velocity methods. Steel ducts under large suction pressures are structurally unstable and, in any event, suction pressure reducing valves, where used, will tend to get fouled with dirt and become increasingly unreliable in performance. Supply air terminals will not give good air distribution and will perform badly if erected above egg-crate ceilings and, even when located flush with the lower surface of the egg-crate, air distribution is likely to be poor. When such a form of installation is being considered it is wise to test the proposed arrangement in a full-scale mock-up.

Another ceiling effect can be experienced with the by-pass type of VAV unit. At low loads, large amounts of cold air are returned to the ceiling void and the ceiling surface itself may then act as a thermal sink, the room overcooling by radiant loss to the ceiling, with a further reduction in the air flow to the room as a consequence, giving less air movement and, possibly, a poorer ventilation rate. A remedy sometimes adopted is to raise the temperature of the supply air, at the central plant.

VAV in tropical climates
It does not follow that VAV is an acceptable solution for all climates. For example in the hot, humid weather of part of the West African coast, with imperfect building construction, natural infiltration can impose a very large latent load which can stay constant throughout twenty-four hours, while sensible heat gains vary. Thus at start-up in the early morning a VAV system can be delivering only a small amount of air to meet the much reduced sensible heat gain but can be facing a very high latent load, simultaneously. Humidity will rise as a result. For instance, outside design conditions in Lagos in March could be taken as 33.5°C dry-bulb, 28°C wet-bulb (sling), 21.74 g kg^{-1}. An

inside condition might be $25 \pm 1°C$ dry-bulb, with a maximum of 60% saturation. Under design conditions inside (26°C, 60%) the moisture content is 12.86 g kg^{-1} and, for a module of our hypothetical office block, one air change of infiltration causes a latent heat gain of 263 W (see Section 1.7). At 26°C each person will liberate 70 W of latent heat and so the total latent heat gain becomes 403 W.

Example 2.13 A variable air volume system delivers 251 l s^{-1} of air at 20°C dry-bulb, 12.37 g kg^{-1} to an office module, maintaining it at 26°C dry-bulb, 60% saturation in the presence of sensible gains of 1837 W and latent gains of 403 W, when the outside state is 33.5°C dry-bulb, 28°C wet-bulb (sling). Determine the humidity in the room if the sensible gains reduce by 80% to 367 W, the latent gains and the supply air state remaining constant.
Answer For a proportional band of 2°C quoted, the room temperature will be 24.4°C when the sensible gains are only 20% of their design maximum.

$$\text{Reduced supply air quantity} = \frac{0.367}{(24.4 - 20)} \times \frac{(273 + 20)}{358} = 0.068 \text{ m}^3\text{s}^{-1}$$

$$\text{Room moisture content} = 12.37 + \frac{0.403}{0.068} \times \frac{(273 + 20)}{856} = 14.4 \text{ g kg}^{-1}$$

At this moisture content and 24.4°C the humidity is about 75%.

Automatic control
The many different types of VAV terminals available offer a wide variety of control methods. Most, however, share the facility for operating several slave units in unison from a master controller or control unit. This is worth doing because of the saving in control costs when dealing with large rooms containing more than one VAV terminal. The majority of units require electrical or pneumatic power to actuate their thermostatic throttling mechanism but a few types use duct pressure directly, with a saving in control costs. A second aspect of automatic control concerns the need to maintain the ventilation rate as the total system flow is diminished. In principle it is possible to measure velocity at the outside air dampers and to open these as it tends to fall. The difficulty is that quite small velocities are involved, i.e. 2.5 to 4.0 m s^{-1}. This means the corresponding velocity pressures are only 3.75 to 9.6 Pa, which are not easy to measure. A possible alternative is to divide the variable fresh air dampers into several sections, each with its own actuator, and to link their openings in sequence with the control of the inlet guide vanes on the supply fan so that more sections of the dampers open as the vanes move from fully open to fully closed. Site calibration is necessary, using a velocity traverse of the main supply duct.
    The third feature of the control system that requires attention is the need to

reduce the capacity of the supply and extract fans as the VAV terminals throttle. Figure 2.8 shows what happens in a simple system. The index VAV terminal needs a minimum pressure drop across it for proper functioning, namely, $p_b - p_a$, at its full design flow, $V_b = V_a$, when the point of operation on the fan curve is B. As the room thermostat needs a reduced duty, V_c, the bellows or dampers in the terminal throttle the flow to this value and the system curve shifts counter-clockwise from OB to OC. The new point of rating on the fan characteristic is C. If there is no fan capacity control, the pressure drop across the terminal unit increases to $p_c - p_e$, the rest of the system loss at the reduced duty being p_e. When a pressure sensor is located at fan discharge and is used to adjust blade pitch angles or inlet guide vanes it must sense a rise in pressure, its proportional band, in order to modify the blade or vane positions. If it does this to achieve the reduced duty, $V_c = V_d$, the fan total pressure will rise from p_b to p_d and the new point of operation will be at D. Since the system loss without the terminal is p_e, the new pressure drop across the VAV terminal will be $p_d - P_e$. For intermediate duties we would expect the point of operation to follow the control curve shown by the broken line from B to D in the figure. If we shift the position of the sensor from the fan discharge to immediately behind the terminal unit, then as the unit throttles to reduce the duty from $V_b = V_a$ to $V_c = V_f$, and the rise in pressure from $p_b - p_a$ to $p_f - p_e$, which is the proportional band of the sensor, the inlet guide vanes close partially. The operating point is at F on the new fan curve. The control is represented by the broken line from B to F in Figure 2.8.

The main purpose of controlling fan capacity is to ease the job that the terminal VAV units have to do. As the pressure drop across the terminals increases, the noise they produce also increases, for a given air flow rate, so minimising the rise in pressure behind the terminals as they throttle is highly desirable. It is best achieved by locating the pressure sensor at a position remote from the fan, which also keeps the fan total pressure at a minimum and so helps to economise in energy consumption. Because systems contain many terminals arranged in a complicated array of branch ducts, locating the sensor at the index terminal will prejudice the performance of units nearer to the fan, since their duties are unlikely to vary in parallel with that of the terminal unit. It is often suggested that the pressure sensor should be located in the main duct at a position where the flow rate is between 50 and 75% of the total design quantity, which is usually interpreted as being at a position between two-thirds and three-quarters of the way along the index run from the fan discharge. More complicated and expensive control arrangements are also sometimes advocated, involving the use of multiple static pressure sensors in the many branch ducts, the lowest signal being used through a selector relay to regulate the guide vanes. A high limit sensor at fan discharge is usually also recommended.

A fourth feature of control that must be attended to is the regulation of the

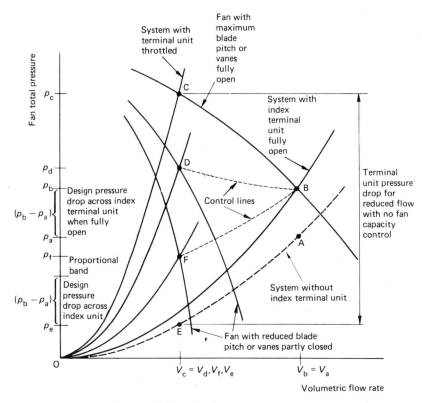

Figure 2.8   Automatic control in a simple VAV system by reduction of the capacity of the supply and extract fans as the VAV terminals throttle.

The total pressure drop across a terminal unit, for a given flow rate, is the static pressure measured on its upstream side plus the velocity pressure of the airstream leaving the diffuser slots. When the sensor is near the fan discharge position, the static pressure sensed is not p_b or p_d, but it is the fan total pressure, p_b or p_d, minus the total pressure loss on the upstream side of the measuring point minus the velocity pressure at the point. The static pressure sensed at the reduced duty, V_d, when the fan total pressure is p_d, will exceed that sensed when the fan total pressure is p_b by the amount allowed for the proportional band of the sensor. However, p_d will not necessarily exceed p_b, as shown, because the velocity pressure will be less at the reduced duty. The exact relationship of p_d to p_b can only be established by calculation for a particular case. It is to be noted that the duct velocity pressures near index terminal units is often insignificantly small, e.g. at 5 ms^{-1} the velocity pressure is only 15 Pa whereas the minimum required unit static pressure is likely to be about 150 Pa (see Example 8.4)

capacity of the supply fan in step with the extract fan. The latter will be a forward-curved centrifugal, or axial flow, chosen to operate at a low fan total pressure of the order of 400 Pa. The supply fan, on the other hand, will be an aerofoil blade, backward-curved centrifugal, or axial flow, selected for a high fan total pressure, of the order of 1.5 kPa. The pressure-volume characteristics will thus be quite different. The simplest approach is to use the signal from the pressure sensor in the supply duct to regulate both sets of guide vanes in unison. The vanes are set up during commissioning to give the correct supply and·extract flow rates, at the maximum and minimum duties. However, in between there will not be a match and static pressures within the building will vary as a result. The simplicity and stability of this approach has much to recommend its, particularly if the reduction in flow rate is only down to 50%. An improvement is made by locating a velocity pressure sensor near the inlet of the extract fan and using this to control its guide vanes. Another velocity pressure sensor is positioned in the main duct after the supply fan and used to reset the velocity pressure sensor in the extract system. The quantity of air supplied can then always be maintained at a required amount above the extract quantity and a small positive pressure in the building assured. When using velocity pressure sensors it should be remembered that the relation between velocity pressure and velocity is not linear. One solution is to use a linear approximation over the relevant part of the pressure-velocity curve; another and more expensive is to use a square root signal extractor. Variable inlet guide vanes are not liked by some engineers. First, they are well-known for overshooting the control point and to minimise this the proportional band must be widened with the result that there is an increased amount of offset between the actual and desired flows as the duty alters, although adding integral action to correct the offset is a solution. Secondly, the design of the linkage between the actuating arm and the vanes must be sound and the linkage itself must be well-made. Thirdly, most of the flow control is when the vanes lie between fully closed and half open. It is worthwhile using positioners on inlet guide vanes and it is also possible to obtain an actuating mechanism that opens the vanes slowly at first and then more quickly over the end of the movement. It should always be arranged that the vanes move to the fully closed position upon fan shut-down or failure.

Axial flow fans with variable pitch blades offer better control than do guide vanes on centrifugal fans. The principles outlined for control and illustrated in Figure 2.8 hold equally well for variable pitch blades. The only possible points of difficulty in using axial flow fans are that more attention must be paid to silencing and, plant room layout is sometimes more difficult because of the need to have gradual expanders and reducers in the duct connexions on each side of axial flow fans.

Noise

The noise produced by a VAV terminal is a function of the air quantity and the upstream duct static pressure. If either rises, the other staying constant, the sound power level (see Section 7.5) also increases. Table 2.7 gives some typical values of sound power level for units tested under ideal conditions of airflow in

Table 2.7 Typical values of sound power levels of VAV terminals

		Sound power level (dB: re 10^{-12}W)						
Air quantity (ls^{-1})	Duct pressure (Pa)	Mid-octave band frequencies (Hz)						
		125	250	500	1000	2000	4000	8000
20	250	35	28	24	20	16	14	14
	375	36	20	26	22	20	18	19
	500	36	32	28	25	24	24	21
	750	37	36	32	28	27	27	27
	1000	38	38	34	33	32	33	35
	1250	39	39	36	35	34	35	39
40	250	41	34	32	28	26	23	18
	375	41	36	36	30	28	26	23
	500	42	39	37	31	30	28	27
	750	43	42	38	32	32	30	32
	1000	44	43	40	34	34	33	36
	1250	45	44	41	35	35	35	40
60	250	44	43	41	35	33	26	21
	375	45	44	42	36	34	29	26
	500	45	45	43	37	35	31	31
	750	46	48	44	38	36	33	35
	1000	47	49	45	39	37	35	39
	1250	48	50	46	40	39	37	41
80	250	46	46	46	40	37	29	22
	375	47	48	47	41	38	33	26
	500	48	50	47	42	40	36	30
	750	49	53	48	43	41	37	35
	1000	50	54	49	44	42	39	41
	1250	51	55	50	45	43	40	43
100	250	46	49	49	44	41	34	24
	375	49	51	50	45	42	37	31
	500	50	53	51	46	43	39	36
	750	51	55	52	47	44	40	42
	1000	52	56	53	48	45	42	46
	1250	54	57	53	48	46	43	46

a laboratory. The units are of the variable area type, feeding air through linear diffusers and provided with self-acting bellows for throttling the airflow through the use of duct static pressure as the power source. No account is taken of residual noise in the ducted air supply to the unit. Inadequate plant silencing and regenerated noise arising from air turbulence in the duct system will give greater values than those tabulated. Poorly made units will also generate more sound power.

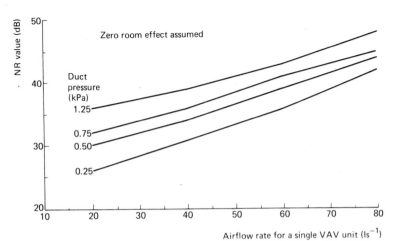

Figure 2.9   Typical NR values produced by a single VAV unit with a performance as given in Table 2.5 and a sound power level as in Table 2.8 (reproduced by kind permission of Haden Young Ltd)

Making use of the data in Table 2.7, it is possible to estimate the noise rating (NR value) (see Section 7.9) likely in a typical module of the hypothetical office block (see Section 1.1), assuming that the room effect (see Section 7.8) is zero. Figure 2.9 shows this.

Example 2.14 If two VAV terminals installed in a west-facing module of the hypothetical office block each deliver $73 \, \mathrm{l \, s^{-1}}$ with a duct pressure of 500 Pa, estimate the NR value likely (a) under design conditions, (b) when the units throttle to $36 \, \mathrm{l \, s^{-1}}$ to meet a reduced heat gain but the duct pressure rises to 1250 Pa and (c) when each unit handles $36 \, \mathrm{l \, s^{-1}}$ but the duct pressure has been controlled at 250 Pa. In all cases assume a room effect of $-5 \mathrm{dB}$.
Answer
(a) From Figure 2.9 one unit handling $73 \, \mathrm{l \, s^{-1}}$ at 500 Pa gives about NR 42. For two units in our softer room the noise level will be $42 + 3 - 5 =$ NR 40.
(b) Two units each handling $36 \, \mathrm{l \, s^{-1}}$ at 1250 Pa will give $38 + 3 - 5 =$ NR 36.
(c) Two units each handling $36 \, \mathrm{l \, s^{-1}}$ at 250 Pa will give $30 + 3 - 5 =$ NR 28. Unattenuated residual plant noise, regenerated air noise in the supply duct feeding the units and the fact that the actual installation departs from the ideal test conditions used to establish the table, mean that higher NR values are to be expected.

It is characteristic of VAV systems that they operate at less than their design flow rates for most of the time. Solar gains through glass often represent over 50% of the maximum total gains, e.g. in Example 1.8 it was 55% for a west module, and vary greatly on both an hourly and a seasonal basis. The peak solar gains can be regarded as prevailing for only about an hour in a day and this can be as little as 5% of the total working hours of the system. It follows that most VAV terminals will be operating at less than their maximum noise rating for the majority of the time. It can be inferred that NR values of 40 to 45 can be specified with safety for west-facing modules with 50% of their external facades glazed, because the units will give noise levels much less than this throughout most of their life.

Practical aspects

Since about two-thirds of the capital cost of an all-air system may be in the handling and distribution of air, efforts to minimise design supply air quantities are worthwhile and have the side advantage of assisting in the choice of quiet VAV terminals. When seeking to reduce air quantities it must be remembered that less than about $3 \, \text{ls}^{-1} \text{m}^{-2}$ supplied to an occupied room sometimes gives rise to complaints of inadequate air movement, although as little as $1.3 \, \text{ls}^{-1} \, \text{m}^{-2}$ is more than enough to keep an unoccupied room fresh. Design supply air quantities may be minimised by selecting 8-row cooler coils with chilled water flow temperatures of 5.5°C to give a leaving air temperature of 9°C. If there is sufficient room to ensure a smooth expansion onto the upstream face of the cooler coil and a uniform velocity across it then the coil can be installed on the discharge side of the fan and the penalty of temperature rise across it avoided. Thus, assuming a 2°C rise for duct heat gain, air can be delivered to the VAV terminals at 11°C. If a design room temperature of $22\frac{1}{2}$°C or 23°C is selected each $1 \, \text{s}^{-1}$ of air supplied at 11°C can then deal with 14.5 to 15 W of heat gain and systems handling $12.5 \, \text{ls}^{-1} \, \text{m}^{-2}$, near the limit for VAV, can cope with as much as $187 \, \text{W} \, \text{m}^{-2}$. It must be emphasised, however, that sprayed blow-through cooler coils should never be used as it is virtually impossible to prevent water leakage from them. The only way of doing this is to ensure that the static air pressure outside the sprayed coil equals or exceeds that within.

Having reduced the supply air quantity to a practical minimum, the secret of an installation low in capital cost is to arrange an economical duct layout to feed the VAV terminals. Furthermore, as few VAV terminals as possible should be used, consistent with avoiding noise problems, providing satisfactory air distribution and offering the facilities for individual, modular, thermostatic control and easy partition re arrangement that characterises certain types of VAV system. Air zoning is generally unnecessary.

VAV systems probably only run at their design duties for 10% of the time and for the rest of the year they handle much less (see Section 8.3). Fans should therefore, be selected to have their peak efficiencies at about 75% of their design flow rates, in order to conserve energy. It is claimed by some manufacturers that their VAV terminals, operating from duct static pressures, control room temperature within a proportional band of as little as 1°C and it is certainly true that properly slaved units, operating in unison from a single control terminal, give better air distribution and control than do multiple ceiling diffusers fed with low velocity air from a single control VAV terminal, e.g. octopus box. Figure 2.10 shows the difference in layout. With the second arrangement, individual diffusers are not themselves VAV terminals–they receive variable quantities of air at low velocity from the central control box–and will not necessarily always be in volumetric balance.

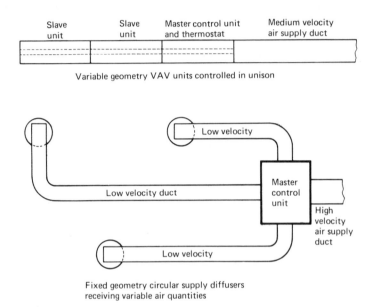

Figure 2.10   Different layouts of VAV systems

Shut-off leakage at VAV units can be as little as 15% of the design duty but this may still be enough to overcool an unoccupied space, although room temperatures should soon reach a comfortable level with the return of the occupants and the switching on of lights. In exceptional circumstances auxiliary heating may be needed. Since VAV systems can inherently deal with reductions in volumetric flow rates, it follows that ducts feeding untenanted floors in an office development can be dampered off, provided this is not carried to excess, and the fan capacity still controlled in a satisfactory way at the reduced duty. It appears that properly designed, variable linear diffusers can give better air distribution for VAV systems than can circular or square diffusers, or side-wall grilles. Also, with properly designed VAV installations the time spent in air balancing during commissioning may be minimised, but not entirely dispensed with. A well thought out balancing procedure must be followed. The use of electrostatic filters is not recommended because, with reduced air velocites through them, the amount of ozone produced is unacceptably high.

2.9 Dual duct systems

The chief advantage of the double duct system is that full cooling and full heating capacity are simultaneously available at all times, under thermostatic control. Further, it has, in common with other all-air systems, the facility of free cooling when the outside air temperature is low enough, which is about 10°C in the UK, the refrigeration plant being off. It is suitable for any application needing an all-air system with thermostatic control in a multiplicity of rooms and it has been used succesfully for offices, hotels, hospitals and ships. One advantage over induction or fan coil systems is that since no air is induced or recirculated from the room over a local cooler coil, there is no local contamination at the unit, hence its suitability for hospitals. However, the system is expensive in capital and running cost and needs a large amount of building space to accommodate ducts. These are formidable objections which have restricted its use in comparison with other systems, notably perimeter-induction and, more recently, variable air volume.

The supply air quantity for a dual duct system will always exceed that for a variable volume scheme and because it takes no account of load diversification more plant space is required. Furthermore, since two supply ducts must be accommodated, the designer of a dual duct system will always tend to use higher air velocities than for a single duct system. It follows that noise will often be a problem and, since fan total pressures will be high, the component of the cooling load attributable to fan power will be large, increasing both the size of the installed refrigeration plant and its energy consumption.

Terminal mixing boxes may be used in two forms: either installed beneath window sills, when rather more floor space is used than with an induction or fan coil system; or located above suspended ceilings. Mixing box terminals require minimum operating duct static pressures from about 70 Pa to 400 Pa and have listed sound power levels for working pressures up to 1500 Pa, when handling between 25 and 1900 ls^{-1}.

The only stable dual duct system is one having constant volume regulators on all mixing terminals so that each can deliver a fixed quantity of air, regardless of upstream duct pressure variations caused by changes in the ducted volumes of hot and cold air consequent upon load fluctuations at the other terminals. It should be noted that so-called constant volume regulators are factory-set to deliver a nominally constant amount of air with a tolerance of about $\pm 5\%$, corresponding to their proportional band. However, it is not uncommon for such factory setpoints to be highly inaccurate, and a check on site is essential. The design volume at each terminal is the cold air quantity required to meet the local design sensible heat gains and this is the nominal setting of the constant volume regulator. The sum of the terminal cold volumes is the duty of the supply fan. The hot duct quantity is less than the cold duct amount because a bigger temperature difference, supply-to-room, can be adopted to deal with the heat losses, and the room that has the smallest ratio of supply air quantity to design heat loss will need the warmest air. This index room fixes the design hot duct temperature and its design hot quantity will be the same as its design cold quantity. Elsewhere, terminals will require less hot air to satisfy their design heat losses and so, progressing back to the fan, the hot duct will become smaller than the cold duct. It is claimed[5] that the maximum airflow in the hot duct will seldom occur when meeting the design winter heat loss but will do so during light summer loads or marginal weather, when the hot duct temperature is compensated down from its winter design value. Because the dual duct system, for the building as a whole, takes account of diversity in heat gain, e.g. that maximum solar gains through east and west modules do not coincide, the maximum cold duct quantity is less than the fan duty, some small amount of warm air being mixed with cold air to provide a higher supply temperature to those rooms not suffering peak gains. It has been suggested[7] that the ratio of the design cold duct quantity to the fan duty is a basis for deciding on the maximum hot duct quantity (Table 2.8). Exact relationships between hot and cold duct sizes probably depend very much on particular system designs and computer-aided techniques should be able to resolve individual cases.

If excessively high hot duct temperatures are chosen the adverse consequences are stratification in the room, stratification in the hot duct, which often reasserts itself even after a deliberate attempt to remove it by turbulent mixing, excessive duct heat loss and a tendency to underheat some rooms. It is suggested that air temperatures above about 40°C, with conventional ceiling heights of about 2.7 m, are best avoided. High hot duct temperatures will also aggravate the effects of hot air leakage, as much as 10%, past the nominally closed valve in the mixing box.

Table 2.8   Suggested relationship between hot and cold duct sizes

Design cold duct quantity	Hot duct area
Fan duty	Cold duct area
1.0 –0.9	0.8
0.9 –0.85	0.8
0.85–0.80	0.85
0.80–0.75	0.85
<0.75	0.9

Many dual duct installations have a pair of ducts running above the suspended ceiling in the corridor with connexions to terminal units mounted above the ceilings in the rooms on either side. Making connexions that have to cross over the main ducts to feed the terminals poses a problem of accomodation, space being at a premium. Flexible ducts from the mains to the terminals, therefore, tend to be used, very often conveying air at high velocities. Such flexible ducts frequently generate a good deal of noise, particularly if they are sharply bent. In addition, noise break-out through the relatively light-weight material of the flexible ducts is common. The mixing boxes themselves generate noise in the process of reducing the air pressure from the high velocity inlet side to the low velocity, single duct outlet side to the air diffusers. Although the boxes are lined with sound-absorbing material this is often inadequate and additional acoustic lining is recommended for the downstream, low velocity ducting. A further problem is that boxes radiate sound outwards from their casings and this passes unhindered through the light-weight suspended ceiling tiles into the room. The temptation to use high velocities should be resisted and it is recommended that velocities be kept as low as possible, preferably to below 15 m s^{-1} and never over 20 m s^{-1}. High velocity ducts with rectangular sections should be avoided as they regenerate more noise than do spirally wound ducts at the same velocity. Branch dampers are of little value in a dual duct system where air volumes are constantly changing. Duct layouts should be designed to give smooth airflow around bends and through branch take-offs, where conical fittings are preferred. Square mitred bends are undesirable but, if they must be used, they should be fitted with small section turning vanes. Large section turning vanes should not be used as there is a tendency for vortices to form and act as sound generators.

2.10 Multizone units

A system using a multizone air-handling unit is essentially the same in principle as a dual duct scheme, the difference being that thermostatic mixing of hot and cold air occurs at the plant and not at a terminal unit in the room. Single ducts conveying air at low velocity feed each room or zone, i.e. two or more rooms with similar change patterns for their sensible heat gains. Multizone units are applied to small buildings or parts of buildings where running several low velocity ducts, one to each zone, does not use up too much building space. Multizone systems have been used for treating groups of public rooms in hotels that need an all-air design approach and share similar usage routines. Blow-through air handling units are commonly available with up to twelve zones but best results are achieved with fewer zones that each require approximately equal amounts of supply air. The poorest control performances are obtained when there is a large disparity in zone duties. Damper characteristics of position versus flow rate are by no means linear and it is highly probable that the air quantities delivered to zones will alter as damper positions change under thermostatic control. It is absolutely essential that the flow temperature of the LTHW feeding the heater battery in the hot deck be compensated against outside air temperature. If this is not done control will become difficult when the hot deck dampers are nearly closed and small amounts of very hot air mix with air from the cold deck. It is also desirable to compensate the chilled water flow temperature to the cooler coil in the cold deck. If direct-expansion cooler coils are used (on small jobs) it is vitally important that their evaporating temperatures be stabilised by means of hot gas valves.

The quality of dampers provided with commercial multizone units is usually not good enough to give the best proportional control and the control mode may often degenerate to two-position. Leakage past the dampers in their closed positions is of the order of 15% and introduces additional operating and control problems. Even specially made, tight shut-off dampers can still have 5% leakage. For installations of any size, particularly where better quality of control is needed, the double duct system is worth considering as an alternative, althrough the capital cost is greater.

2.11 Air curtains

Air curtains and air doors include a variety of types: complete air curtains (Figure 2.11), industrial warm air curtains (Figure 2.12a), industrial cold air curtains (Figure 2.12b) and simple door heaters (Figure 2.12c). There are other

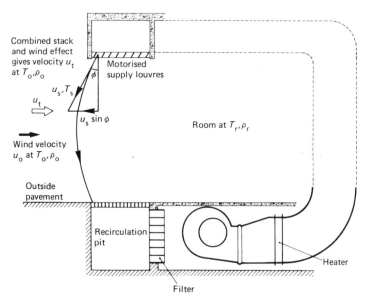

Figure 2.11   Complete air curtain

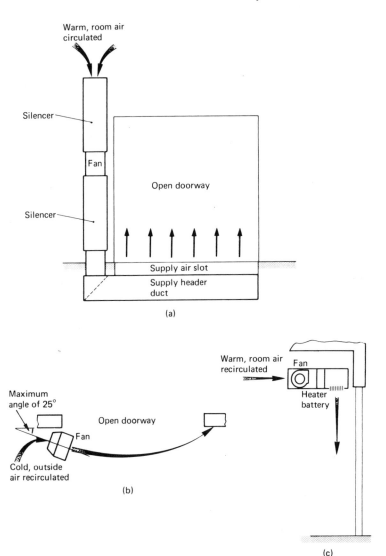

Figure 2.12a, Front elevation of an industrial warm air curtain; b, Plan of an industrial cold air curtain—several fans are stacked on top of each other, the number depending on the door height; c, Section of a fan coil door heater

subtypes such as that used above the door of a cold store, blowing air downward and inward to retain the large mass of cold, dense air within the store when its door is opened.

A simplified analysis developing the basic principles of complete air curtains is as follows. Two columns of air, one of density ρ_0 and absolute temperature T_0

outside the building and the other of density ρ_r and temperature T_r within, share a common stack, height H. The pressure difference across the open door at the base of the column is $\rho_o gH(1 - T_o/T_r)$ and is the stack effect. At the same time the wind speed, u_o, exerts a velocity pressure of $0.5\,\rho_o u_o^2$ and the combined stack and wind effect on the open doorway is a pressure difference of $0.5\rho_o u_o^2 + \rho_o gH(1 - T_o/T_r)$ which will produce a velocity of airflow, u_t, trying to enter the doorway and which must be countered by the horizontal, outward component of the airflow supplied by the air curtain. Over the upper half of the doorway the combined effect is held at bay by the outward-curving supply airstream of the curtain but, over the lower half of the doorway, the supply airstream is defeated and is curved inward by the combined effect to be extracted through a floor grille (Figure 2.11). Therefore,

$$0.5\rho_o u_t^2 = 0.5\rho_o u_o^2 + \rho_o gH(1 - T_o/T_r)$$

and so

$$u_t = \sqrt{u_o^2 + 2gH(1 - T_o/T_r)} \tag{2.14}$$

Since force is the rate of change of momentum, a balance exists between the momentum of the airstream trying to enter the doorway and that opposing it. Introducing a coefficient of discharge, c_d, for the quantity of air, Q_t, trying to enter the upper half of the doorway, gives

$$c_d Q_t \rho_o u_t = Q_s \rho_s u_s \sin \phi$$

$$(c_d hw\rho_o u_t^2)/2 = Q_s \rho_s u_s \sin \phi$$

$$Q_s = (c_d hw\rho_o u_t^2)/(2\rho_s u_s \sin \phi)$$

$$= (c_d hw T_s u_t^2)/(2T_o u_s \sin \phi) \tag{2.15}$$

where Q_s, ρ_s, T_s and u_s are the quantity, density, absolute temperature and velocity, through the actual open area of the grille, respectively, of the supply airstream at an angle ϕ to the vertical. The height of the doorway is h and w its width.

A choice of supply grille is dictated by the equation

$$Q_s = f c_s u_s wd \tag{2.16}$$

in which f is the free area ratio of the grille, c_s its coefficient of discharge and d its depth. A certain amount, depending on the wind velocity and stack effect, of cold outside air is entrained by the air curtain and a corresponding quantity of air from within the building is lost to the outside, some entrainment of inside air also occurring. The net effect is to reduce the supply air temperature from its initial value and so the recirculated air must be warmed. Deciding on a value to which the air temperature should be raised is difficult but, in the UK, 32°C has been found practical for an outside temperature of -1°C and an inside one of 20°C. Selecting a supply air velocity is also empirical. It must not be so high that serious draughts are felt by people passing through the air curtain in a commercial application, although transient, perceptable warm air movement at head level is generally acceptable. For a door height of 2.5 m a value for u_s of 10 ms^{-1} is often found practicable, but operating experience could dictate other values, hence the desirability of control over the air volume handled by the fan.

Example 2.15 A complete air curtain is to be fitted in a doorway of dimensions 2.5 m high × 4.0 m wide to combat a wind speed of 4 m s^{-1} (14.4 km h^{-1} or 8.9 mph) when the outside air temperature is -1°C and the room temperature is 20°C. The stack height is 10 m. Determine the duties of the fan and heater battery and establish the dimensions of the supply grille. Assume the vanes of the supply grille are turned at an angle of 45° to the vertical.
Answer From Equation (2.14)

$$u_t = \sqrt{16 + 2 \times 9.81 \times 10(1 - 272/293)} = 5.48 \text{ m s}^{-1}$$

Taking a coefficient of discharge for the doorway of 0.65

$$Q_s = (0.65 \times 2.5 \times 4.0 \times 305 \times 5.48^2)/(2 \times 272 \times 10 \times \sin 45°)$$
$$= 15.48 \text{ m}^3\text{s}^{-1}, \text{ from Equation (2.15).}$$

The heater battery duty is to warm this quantity of air from an assumed value of 293 K to 305 K and, from Equation (2.3), this equals $[15.48 \times (305 - 293) \times 358]/305 = 218$ kW.

Assuming a free area of 60% for the supply grille and a coefficient of discharge of 0.7 Equation (2.16) gives

$$15.48 = 0.6 \times 0.7 \times 10 \times 4.0 \times d, \text{ so } d = 0.921 \text{ m.}$$

The floor grille should be the full width of the doorway, w, as should the supply grille, and not less than the depth of the supply grille, d. The floor grille must be specially designed to withstand heavy traffic and must have spacings between its bars that will not catch pedestrians' heels or umbrella tips. The louvres on the supply grille ought to be motorised for easy adjustment to suit the wind velocity and the fan should be variable speed to economise on running costs and to permit the empirical modification to supply velocity, mentioned previously. The pit beneath the floor grille must be accessible for cleaning out and, preferably, should have an arrangement for washing down. Fans may be required to run at fan total pressures of the order of 500 Pa and the noise they produce must not be overlooked.

It is evident from the example that complete air curtains use a lot of air and will be expensive to run. Further, a large amount of space is occupied by plant and ducting. It is also clear that only a modest wind speed can be dealt with. An air curtain must, therefore, be regarded as a device that allows doors to be kept open only when the outside wind velocity and air temperature are within stated design limits. It is not really practicable to consider coping with a wind speed greater than about 14.5 $km h^{-1}$ (9 mph) in a commercial application and it follows that an air curtain must never be used without a door that can be properly shut during weather conditions outside the design scope.

Industrial air curtains of two types, warm and cold, are also in use. Their purpose is to minimise heat loss and draught through doorways with a high traffic frequency. It is arranged that the air curtain only runs when the door is open, a microswitch turning off the fans when it is closed. Industrial air curtains are claimed to be effective in dealing with wind speeds of up to 32 km h^{-1} (20 mph) but with noise levels in the vicinity of 85 dB(A), in spite of silencing.

Air curtains, or air doors, are also used to keep flying insects out of food processing plants. The average flying speed of an insect is about 1 ms^{-1} and research by the US Department of Agriculture has shown that insects can be effectively screened if the moving airstream of the curtain is at least 125 mm thick; the velocity at a level 1 m from the floor exceeds 6.6 $m s^{-1}$; and the air curtain covers the full width of the doorway. A typical arrangement is to use recirculated air at high level and to blow it downwards with an outward direction of about 10° to the vertical. The air screen, or curtain, is switched on only when the door is opened and it is, therefore, important that the full airflow is attained as quickly as possible if insects are to be excluded. It is thought that axial flow or propeller type fans are better than centrifugals, because they come up to full duty within 2 or 3 s of being switched on, whereas centrifugals take as much as 20 s.

Fan heaters installed over the doors in some shops are intended to diminish the worst effects of cold draughts when the doors are temporarily opened to admit customers. They are not installed to permit the doors to remain open for any lengthy period in the winter. Air curtains, air doors and door heaters must never be regarded as allowing the conventional door to be discarded.

2.12 Perimeter-induction systems

Changeover systems

There is no doubt that the perimeter-induction system, in its various and improved forms since 1935, has been a satisfactory one for air conditioning in commercial office blocks. However, in its original, two-pipe changeover version it has not proved an outstanding success in temperate climates, except in limited instances where the winter mode of operation, with hot secondary water flowing to the terminal units, has been adopted for early morning pre-heat, the system reverting to the summer mode prior to occupancy and the thermostats at the units changing their action. The reasons why the changeover system has not succeeded are:

(1) During winter, the limited cooling capacity offered by the primary air is seldom enough to match the maximum sensible gains experienced at some time of the day

(2) Typical changes in the sensible gains throughout the day, in winter, caused by the variations in outside air temperature and solar radiation, impose changeover demands on the system that it cannot respond to because of its thermal inertia.

The two-pipe, non-changeover system was innovated to meet these objections, the winter mode being abandoned and the system operating in its summer style throughout the year.

Primary air quantity

Because the amount of primary air handled influences capital cost, running cost and the space occupied by ducts, the designer is concerned with its minimisation, provided that the four functions it serves—heating, inducing the necessary sensible cooling capacity from the secondary coil, dehumidification and ventilation—can be fulfilled. The restraint imposed by the need to offset heat loss depends on the primary air temperature chosen for design winter operation. With conventional flow and return values of 85°C and 65°C, respectively, for LTHW, an upper limit of primary air temperature might be 50°C, if stratification within ducts and excessive heat loss from them, with consequent uneven distribution of heating capacity at the induction units, is to be avoided. It is wise to use less than such a limiting value but the limit of 40°C, previously suggested for all-air systems (Section 2.9) can be exceeded, because the primary air at the terminal unit mixes with about four volumes of induced secondary air before delivery to the room.

Example 2.16 Estimate the heat losses from typical modules on an intermediate floor and a top floor of the hypothetical office block and calculate the primary air quantity at 50°C needed to offset them. Assume the primary air is handled at a temperature of 14°C, corresponding to the probable summer design performance.

Answer Using data from the design brief (Section 1.2) gives

Glass: $(0.5 \times 2.4 \times 3.3) \times 5.6 \times 22$ = 488
Wall: $(0.5 \times 2.4 \times 3.3) \times 0.91 \times 22$ = 79
Infiltration: $(1.0 \times 2.4 \times 2.6 \times 6.0) \times 0.33 \times 22$ = 272
Subtotal for intermediate floors: = 839 W
Roof: $(2.4 \times 6.0) \times 1.1 \times 22$ = 348
Total for top floor: = 1187 W

From Equation (2.3)

$$q_p = \frac{839}{(50-20)} \times \frac{(273+14)}{358} = 22.42 \ \mathrm{l\,s^{-1}} \text{ for intermediate floors}$$

$$q_p = \frac{1187}{(50-20)} \times \frac{(273+14)}{358} = 31.72 \ \mathrm{l\,s^{-1}} \text{ for the top floor.}$$

It is technically correct to choose a primary air temperature, with the use of reheat if necessary, that allows summer design transmission heat gain, by virtue of air-to-air temperature difference, to be offset by the primary air alone, leaving the secondary coil to cope with the random gains from people, lights and sunshine under local thermostatic controi. This permits one primary air reheat zone and schedule to be used for the entire building and allows the problems associated with the movement of shadows cast by adjacent buildings over the sunlit facades to be disregarded. Achieving this invariably means reheating the primary air in summer design weather slightly above the lowest available temperature, with a consequent loss in its capacity to deal with part of the maximum sensible heat gain. This imposes a bigger load on the secondary cooler coil and tends to increase the size of the induction unit needed. The disadvantages of a single primary air zone treatment are, therefore, increased capital cost and increased running cost by wasteful reheat. For these reasons it is common to use the lowest practical temperature at the induction units, after allowing for the rise accruing from fan power, about 1 °C per kPa of fan total pressure, and duct heat gains.

A practical state for the air leaving the cooler coil in the primary air-handling plant is 10°C dry-bulb, 9.7°C wet-bulb (sling) and 7.4 g kg^{-1}. From Equation (2.4) it can be calculated that, to deal with 134 W of latent gain, when maintaining 22°C dry-bulb and 50% saturation in the room, 30.65 l s^{-1} of primary air is needed. For ventilation, on the other hand, there is no problem. The CIBS recommends a minimum of 1.3 l s^{-1} m^{-2} over the treated floor area, i.e. 18.7 l s^{-1} over 14.4 m^2.

It remains to consider the amount of primary air needed to induce the necessary cooling capacity from the unit. Example 1.8 gave the sensible heat gains for modules on intermediate floors of the hypothetical building but to complete the picture so as to assess more completely its total needs the heat gains for modules on the top floor should be estimated.

Example 2.17 Calculate the sensible heat gains for the modules on the top floor of the hypothetical office block.
Answer Table A.7 gives the equivalent temperature differences for a roof of surface density 300 kg m^{-2} at 16.00 h and 08.00 h sun time and the relevant gains for the top floor are, therefore:

	West	East
As previously calculated for an intermediate floor:	= 1837	1625
Roof (west module): $(2.4 \times 6.0) \times 1.1 \times 15.5°$	= 246	—
Roof (east module): $(2.4 \times 6.0) \times 1.1 \times 0.6°$	= —	10
Gains for modules on the top floor:	= 2083 W	1635 W

Induction unit cooling capacity
The sensible capacity of the unit depends on the finning, the number of rows (usually one), and the amount of air induced, for a specified chilled water flow rate. Table 2.9 shows the approximate variation in capacity for different flow rates.

Table 2.9 The variation in capacity of a secondary cooler coil for various flow rates

Flow rate (%)	10	20	30	40	50	60	70	80	90	100	115	130	145
Capacity (%)	24	48	64	86	88	92	94	96	98	100	102	104	106

The induction ratio is a function of the air velocity issuing from the nozzles and their diameter. More air is induced by many small nozzles than by few large ones, at a given velocity. The cooling capacity of the secondary coil is usually regarded as proportional to the room air temperature (t_r) onto the coil and the entering secondary chilled water temperature (t_w), without appreciable error. Primary air cooling capacity is defined by Equation (2.3) in terms of the primary air temperature (t_p) and t_r. Unit capacities and noise levels are, therefore, expressed in terms of unit size, nozzle arrangement and pressure, for nominal water flow rates and stated values of t_r, t_p and t_w. Tables 2.10 and 2.11 show typical performances and noise levels for a commercial range of induction units. It must be noted that catalogue ratings are always published for a specified standard form of unit installation and any deviation from this results in a loss of performance.

Example 2.18 Select an induction unit from Tables 2.10 and 2.11 for a non-changeover system suitable for a west module on the top floor of the hypothetical building. Assume $t_w = 11°C$ and allow 4.4°C rise for fan power and duct gain.
Answer It is often convenient to adopt a relatively high water velocity through the primary air cooler coil, so that the water temperature rise through it is about 5°C. The reason for this is to try and get a primary water flow rate that exceeds, or is not much less than, the secondary water flow rate. Table 2.12 shows that a six-row cooler coil with a water velocity of $1.83 \, \mathrm{m \, s^{-1}}$ will give a primary air leaving state of 9.6°C dry-bulb, 9.0°C wet-bulb (sling) when the entering state is about 24°C dry-bulb and 17°C wet-bulb (sling). Using this and an assumed rise of 4.4°C for fan power and duct heat gain gives a primary air temperatue of 14°C at the induction units in summer. To make the best unit

Table 2.10   Typical performance of a commercial range of induction units

Unit size and nozzle type	Primary air quantity ($l\ s^{-1}$)							
	47.5	50.0	52.5	55.0	57.5	60.0	62.5	65.0
	Primary air cooling capacity (W)							
	474	499	524	549	574	599	624	649
Secondary coil cooling capacity (W) d3	1480	1520	1560	1590	1620	1640		
Nozzle pressure (Pa)	575	640	695	755	810	865		
Secondary coil cooling capacity (W) c4	1270	1305	1340	1380	1405			
Nozzle pressure (Pa)	580	645	705	760	840			
Secondary coil cooling capacity (W) d4	1375	1420	1450	1500	1540	1575	1605	1640
Nozzle pressure (Pa)	345	380	420	460	505	545	595	640
Secondary coil cooling capacity (W) b5	1075	1105	1130	1150				
Nozzle pressure (Pa)	575	640	695	755				
Secondary coil cooling capacity (W) c5	1190	1225	1260	1295	1325	1350	1380	1400
Nozzle pressure (Pa)	380	425	465	510	555	605	655	705
Secondary coil cooling capacity (W) d5	1305	1340	1375	1410	1445	1480	1515	1550
Nozzle pressure (Pa)	220	245	270	295	325	355	385	415

Note. The coil cooling capacity is based on a room temperature of 22°C and a chilled water temperature of 11°C onto the coil. For other values of these temperatures, assume coil capacity is directly proportional to their difference. The primary air cooling capacity is based on t_p equal to 14°C and the use of Equation (2.3)

Table 2.11   Typical noise levels for a commercial range of induction units

Unit size and nozzle type	NR values for various nozzle pressures (Pa)			
	125	375	625	825
b3	25	26	34	41
c3	26	27	35	42
d3	27	28	36	43
b4	28	27	35	41
c4	28	29	36	43
d4	28	29	37	44
b5	29	29	37	43
c5	29	30	38	44
d5	31	31	39	45

Note. The noise ratings are for a single unit in an office with zero room effect. Many catalogues assume a room effect of 8 or 12 dB, yielding correspondingly lower NR values, and it is important to take this into account when interpreting unit performance

choice we must investigate performances with primary air quantities greater than the minimum of $30.65 \, \mathrm{ls}^{-1}$ needed for dehumidification. To offset the heat gains of 2083 W (Example 2.17) data can be abstracted from Tables 2.10 and 2.11, as follows:

Primary air quantity (ls^{-1})	Primary air cooling capacity (W)	Cooling load on secondary coil (W)	Unit size and nozzle type	Nozzle pressure (Pa)	NR (dB)	Secondary coil cooling capacity (W)
52.5	524	1559	d3	695	38	1560
55.0	549	1534	d3	755	41	1590
57.5	574	1509	d4	505	33	1540
60.0	599	1484	d5	355	31	1480

The cooling loads on the secondary coil are obtained by subtracting the primary air cooling capacity from the sensible gain of 2083 W.

The costs of distributing and lagging primary airflow are very roughly the same as the costs of the associated induction units, in many cases. So choosing a larger unit, requiring less primary air, could cost about the same as selecting a smaller unit with more primary air. There is some merit in adopting a larger unit, provided it will fit in the building space available, as its cooling capacity can always be increased by feeding more primary air to it, with what may be an acceptable rise in the NR value. Nozzle pressures exceeding about 500 Pa are sometimes regarded as being on the high side because the fan total pressure becomes rather large, with increased fan motor power and running costs. Bearing all this in mind the selection made for a west module on the top floor is d4, handling $57.5 \, \mathrm{ls}^{-1}$ with a nozzle pressure of 505 Pa and giving NR 33 in an office with zero effect. Catalogue acoustic claims are frequently optimistic and it is generally wise to expect a room effect to be less than the catalogue anticipation.

For a west-facing module on an intermediate floor, having a heat gain of 1837 W, the reader can verify that a suitable selection is a d5 unit, handling $52.5 \, \mathrm{ls}^{-1}$ with a nozzle pressure of 270 Pa and giving NR 31 in an office with zero room effect. The east-facing modules pose a special problem, their selection being influenced by the fact that with a non-changeover system the primary air temperature is only 14°C when it is 28°C outside. Example 1.8 showed that maximum heat gains in the east occur at 08.00 h sun time, when the outside air temperature is 22.7°C. If a primary air supply rate of $47.5 \, \mathrm{ls}^{-1}$ is assumed it can be calculated, from Equation (2.3) that the primary air temperatures to deal with losses in winter of 839 W and 1187 W on the intermediate and top floors, are 34°C and 40°C, respectively. Assuming a primary air reheat schedule that gives these temperatures at the units when it is $-2°C$ outside, and 14°C when it is 28°C, it can be established that the primary air temperatures at the induction terminals must be 17.5°C and 18.6°C, on intermediate and top floors, when it is 22.7°C outside. These values, not 14°C, must then be used in estimating the primary air cooling capacities which, from Equation (2.3), are:

Primary air quantity (ls^{-1}):   47.5 50.0 52.5 55.0 57.5 60.0 62.5 65.0
Cooling capacity, intermediate
  floors (W):   266 281 295 309 323 337 351 365
Cooling capacity, top floor (W): 201 212 223 233 244 254 265 276

From this information, the possible unit selections can be abstracted from Tables 2.10 and 2.11, as follows:

Primary air quantity (ls^{-1})	Primary air cooling capacity (W)	Cooling load on secondary coil (W)	Unit size and nozzle type	Nozzle pressure (Pa)	NR (dB)	Secondary coil cooling capacity (W)
East face, intermediate floors (heat gain 1625 W)						
47.5	266	1359	d4	345	29	1375
East face, top floor (heat gain 1635 W)						
47.5	201	1434	d3	575	34	1480
50.0	212	1423	d4	380	29	1420
52.5	223	1412	d4	420	30	1450

The cooling loads on the secondary coil equal the sensible heat gain minus the cooling capacity of the primary air.

The selection for the intermediate floors is clearly a d4 unit handling $47.5 ls^{-1}$ and for the top floor a d4 unit at $50 ls^{-1}$ is apt. The total primary air quantity for the building can now be estimated and the performance of the primary air cooler coil considered.

Example 2.19 Calculate the total primary air quantity for the hypothetical building, using the induction unit selections already made.
Answer
West face, top floor: 36×57.5 = 2070
West face, intermediate floor: $11 \times 36 \times 52.5$ = 20790
East face, top floor: 36×50.0 = 1800
East face, intermediate floor: $11 \times 36 \times 47.5$ = 18810
Total: $\overline{43470\ ls^{-1}}$
As a specific supply rate over the treated floor area this is $3.11\ ls^{-1}\ m^{-2}$. For preliminary planning purposes, a useful figure to use is $3.25\ ls^{-1}\ m^{-2}$, when estimating the probable duct and plant sizes.

Primary air cooler coil
Wet-bulb temperature onto a cooler coil is much more significant than dry-

Table 2.12   Typical performance of a six-row cooler coil

Wet-bulb on (°C)	19.5	19.0	18.5	18.0	17.5	17.0
Dry-bulb off (°C)	10.7	10.4	10.2	10.0	9.8	9.6
Moisture content off (kJ kg^{-1})	7.6	7.5	7.4	7.3	7.1	6.9
Enthalpy off (kJ kg^{-1})	30.0	29.4	28.9	28.5	27.8	27.0

bulb for the range of values commonly encountered in the UK and most areas abroad. The CIBS recommendation for the amount of fresh air handled is 1.3 l s^{-1} m^{-2}, which is 42% of the total primary air quantity of 3.11 l s^{-1} m^{-2}, from Example 2.20. Therefore, typical fresh air proportions are between 35% and 45%. Using a figure of 40%, the mixture state onto the primary air cooler coil can be established as 24.4°C dry-bulb, 17.1°C wet-bulb (sling), 9.28 g kg^{-1} and 48.18 kJ kg^{-1}. Accepting 5.6°C as a practical chilled water flow temperature for a centrifugal or screw machine a cooler coil performance may be deduced from a manufacturer's catalogue. Table 2.12 gives a typical performance for a six-row coil with a face velocity of 2.5 m s^{-1}, a water velocity of 1.83 m s^{-1} and an entering water temperature of 5.6°C when the entering air dry-bulb is about 24°C or 25°C.

A six-row coil of the type in Table 2.12 is a reasonable choice that fits in with the earlier assumptions, but it has a slightly lower leaving moisture content that will give a room humidity of about 48%, as can be verified by Equation (2.4). This is, however, acceptable.

Example 2.20 Determine the cooling load on the primary air cooler coil discussed above.
Answer The primary air state at the induction units of 14°C dry-bulb and 6.9 g kg^{-1} has a specific volume of 0.822 m^3 kg^{-1}. The primary cooling load is, therefore,

$$\frac{43.47}{0.822} \times (48.18 - 27.0) = 1120 \text{ kW}.$$

It is generally not a practical proposition to use one air-handling plant to deal with more than about 35 m^3 s^{-1}. If packaged plants are adopted the limit is roughly half this. It is likely that four packaged plants would be selected in Example 2.20 and reference to a catalogue would show that the chilled water flow rate for one of the four primary coils is 13.9 kg s^{-1}, for which the pressure drop is 24 kPa. The water temperature rise is, therefore, 280/(4.18 × 13.9) = 4.8°C, giving a leaving water temperature of 5.6° + 4.8° = 10.4°C, available for the secondary circuit.

Primary/secondary water flow relationships
If three-port, mixing valves or air dampers are used to control the induction

units, the secondary chilled water flow rate will be virtually constant. The catalogue from which the induction units were selected shows that their nominal flow rate is 0.1 kg s^{-1} each. With 864 units (one per module) needed in the hypothetical building the secondary chilled water flow rate will be 86.4 kg s^{-1}, which exceeds the primary flow rate of $4 \times 13.9 = 55.6$ kg s^{-1}. This difficulty can be resolved by increasing the primary rate to 86.4 kg s^{-1}, of which 30.8 kg s^{-1} permanently by-passes the primary coil. If two-port throttling valves are adopted the maximum secondary flow rate will be less than the sum of the nominal rates and must be calculated to establish the primary/secondary water flow relationship.

Example 2.21 Determine the maximum secondary chilled water flow rate for the hypothetical building, assuming two-port throttling valves are used at the units.

Answer Example 1.11 gives the sensible heat gains at the time of peak cooling load as being 353 438 W for the eastern half of the building and 782 225 W for the western half. Further, Example 2.19 shows that induction units in the eastern modules handle a total of 20 610 1s^{-1} of primary air and those in the west, 22 860 1s^{-1}. With a room temperature of 22°C and a primary air temperature of virtually 14°C (not quite 14°C because t_o at 17.00 h sun time is not quite 28°C), the primary air sensible cooling capacities can be calculated as 205 669 W in the east and 228 122 W in the west. Therefore, the cooling duties of the secondary coils are $353 438 - 205 669 = 147 769$ W in the east and $728 225 - 228 122 = 554 103$ W in the west. Example 2.18 shows that the units have been selected for maximum secondary coil duties of

		West	East
West, top floor:	1509×36	= 54 324	—
West, intermediate floors:	$1313 \times 36 \times 11$	= 519 948	—
East, top floor:	1359×36	= —	48 924
East, intermediate floors:	$1423 \times 36 \times 11$	= —	563 508
		574 272 W	612 432 W

Hence the proportional duties on the unit coils at 17.00 h sun time in July are $(147\ 769 \times 100)/612\ 432 = 24\%$ for the east and $(554\ 103 \times 100)/574\ 272 = 97\%$ for the west. It can be inferred that the corresponding secondary flow rates are 24% of 43.2 kg s^{-1}, or 10.37 kg s^{-1}, for the east and 97% of 43.2 kg s^{-1}, or 41.90 kg s^{-1}, for the west. The total maximum secondary flow rate is thus 52.17 kg s^{-1}, which should be compared with the primary rate of $4 \times 13.9 = 55.6$ kg s^{-1}. More than enough water at 10.4°C is thus available in the primary circuit to give the secondary flow rate necessary at 11°C.

Night-time heating
With a heavy-weight building of slow thermal response there is no case for

energy conservation by intermittent operation and so the system should run continuously. However, it is clearly wasteful to run the primary fan all night as there is no need for fresh air. Circulating hot water, with its flow temperature compensated against outside air temperature, through the secondary circuit in winter is worth consideration. Since supply and extract fans are off, heat transfer from the secondary coils is by natural convection, 'gravity heating', but there are several practical problems that must be dealt with if the method is to be successfully adopted:

(1) Automatic control action at the induction units must be reversed, or by-passed, if heating is to be possible at night

(2) The secondary circuit should include a heat exchanger to warm the water when necessary

(3) Tight shut-off valves must be used to prevent warm water entering the primary circuit at night

(4) The heat in the secondary system must be dissipated in the morning, before the refrigeration plant can be allowed to start chilling the primary water.

If the thermal response of the building is quicker, intermittent heating shows energy savings. With a two-pipe, non-changeover system the options are:

(1) Switch everything off at night but start the primary air fan and extract fan next morning at a time, related to outside air temperature, that will enable the system to bring the building up to temperature by the time the people arrive for work. The fresh air dampers are fully closed and the system delivers recirculated air at a boosted temperature to the induction units during the preheating period. The limit of about 50°C on the primary air temperature (see p. 79) still applies. When the boost period ceases, the system reverts to normal operation.

(2) Augment the primary air boost by circulating hot water through the secondary coils during the preheating period, taking due regard of the problems. In this way, high primary air temperatures are avoided.

Controls
Water-controlled systems in the past have generally used pneumatically operated two-port modulating valves or three-port mixing valves, with some preference for the former in order to take advantage of the reduction in secondary water flow under partial load (see Example 2.21). Self-acting valves have often proved a failure in the past for various reasons, one being the wide proportional band needed to work the valves, giving an unsatisfactory variation in room temperature. Recently, modulating solenoid valves have been accepted as a satisfactory alternative. Modulating air dampers, that vary the secondary airflow over the coils and are usually self-actuated from the primary air pressure in the induction units, are also used. Comparative cost studies suggest that an air-damper control system may be up to 5% cheaper than water control, taking account of the costs of induction units, automatic

controls, secondary piping, lagging and secondary pumping. No diversity factor may be applied to the secondary water flow if air dampers are used or three-port valves fitted. Secondary piping should be lagged and vapour-sealed on all systems, particularly four-pipe. One valve and thermostat is not always provided for each induction unit, so economy in capital cost is achieved by fitting a valve on each unit but slaving groups of, say, four valves from a common thermostat. If, after installation and commissioning, a rearrangement of partitions is done, the connexions between valves and thermostats can be modified farily easily, additional thermostats being bought if necessary, at the expanse of the tenant. Using one large valve and thermostat to control a group of several units is not as satisfactory since it lacks the flexibility to cope with partition rearrangement. Thermostats are best located behind recirculated air slots or grilles on the units with remote set-point adjustment at the sill. Positioning thermostats on partitions is undesirable because these are often moved at a later date, and locating them on external walls can introduce problems because surface temperatures are less than air temperatures in winter and vice-versa in summer.

Four-pipe systems

Units have the capacities of their heating and cooling coils controlled in sequence, with a no-capacity gap in between, either by water control valves or by air dampers. There is a tendency for air dampers not to close properly and so some secondary air is induced over both coils simultaneously, even though one is thought to be dampered off, and actual cooling and heating capacities not reaching rated values. Similarly, four-port valves, a pair of two-port throttling valves in a common valve body, and six-port vlaves, a pair of three-port valves in a common body, should be avoided as heat is conducted through the valve body from the hot to the chilled water, particularly in six-port valves where hot and cold water flow is continuous. A further objection to such multi-port valves is that, since clearances between valve discs and their seatings is small because of the deliberately compact construction, any scale or dirt in the water system prevents valves from closing fully and can cause endless difficulty with loss of performance.

The four-pipe system provides conditioned but unheated primary air at all times. There is, therefore, no cancellation of cooling by primary reheat and the problems sometimes experienced with two-pipe systems in selecting units for eastern and southern building faces (see Example 2.18) do not exist for the four-pipe version. Moving shadows across building facades present no difficulties and full heating and full cooling is available at all times. A wider range of set-point choice is possible at the thermostats and the response to load changes is quicker than with two-pipe units. Since no heating is used to cancel cooling, the system is economical to run. Four-pipe systems cost between 10% and 15% more than the equivalent two-pipe systems in terms of induction units, piping, lagging, pumping and controls. A four-pipe unit can be deeper than a two-pipe, occupying about 5% more floor area.

Unit location

The induction unit was initially designed for mounting beneath a window, blowing air upwards from the sill and recirculating room air through a grille in the front of the unit. A similar performance is achieved when an open slot, of at least 100 mm height and the full width of the secondary coil, at floor level replaces the front grille. However, other departures from these standard arrangements result in a reduction of performance. When any non-standard installation is proposed, tests on cooling capacity and air distribution should be done before the units are fitted on site in quantity. One unit per module is the usual arrangement but sometimes larger units are selected with sufficient capacity to cope with the gains in two modules, and for installation centrally beneath alternate windows. Partition rearrangement then introduces a problem since, for example, an office could comprise three modules, the two outer ones lacking an induction unit. A partial solution sometimes adopted is to select the units on the same basis but to position them centrally on the mullions so that the module on each side is then dealt with by half an induction unit. The objection to this is that acoustic privacy across the partition dividing a unit is not always certain. Therefore, it may be necessary to try and fit a barrier within the unit itself, between the nozzles and the secondary coil, obviously with great difficulty. Units have been mounted above suspended celings, freeing floor space. If the unit is mounted thus, horizontally, an access panel must be devised by the architect. Such a panel must be easily opened for maintenance; safely secured when not open; durable; easily cleaned; aesthetically pleasing. This combination of properties, however, is not always easily achieved.

A horizontal installation at high level could perhaps be accommodated in a clear ceiling space of about 250 mm, depending on the type of unit. Alternative arrangements are possible, with ingenuity, but any will suffer a loss of performance and the air distribution with a high level unit must always be tested to make sure that it will prove satisfactory.

Maintenance

Induction unit coils require lint screens to pick up floor dirt, and fibres from carpets, when they are floor-mounted. Such screens should also be fitted in high-level units because the air circulation pattern in the room carries dirt up to the ceiling. Also, lint screens, secondary coils and nozzles need cleaning every three to six months and if this is not done unit performance gradually declines, with dirt periodically ejected onto the window sill and into the room. Good quality filtration is recommended because, with time, dirt tends to build up within the unit, as it will with any air distribution system. In this respect, units with nozzles smaller than 3 mm seem to retain dirt more readily than do larger nozzles. Routine maintenance is also required for the automatic controls.

Noise from units

Selecting a quiet unit is insufficient guarantee of a quiet installation. Regenerated noise in the primary duct system will enter the unit, and hence the room, if the ducting has not been sensibly sized, constructed and installed. Its layout must also be such as to avoid the creation of turbulence. In particular, long and bent flexible connexions feeding units are a prime source of noise. Badly-made units may leak high pressure air from their casings and burrs on poorly moulded nozzles may generate unexpected noise. If the ductwork system has not been sized to achieve a natural balance, excessive pressure will be absorbed at the unit damper, giving unacceptable noise.

2.13 Fan coil systems

The supply of fresh air

As a means of air conditioning, particularly in tropical countries, fan coil systems have much in their favour, not least being the relatively small amount of time required for design. In the simplest and cheapest form of system the cooler coil in the unit receives chilled water at the lowest practical temperature and does both the sensible and latent cooling. Fresh air enters fortuitously through ill-fitting windows and condensate off the coil is drained to waste. A small improvement accrues if outside air, plus traffic noise and dirt, comes in through a purpose-made hole in the wall behind the unit, induced through the casing and mixed with recirculated air by the fan, prior to being blown over the cooler coil and delivered to the room.

A third possibility is to add a mechanical ventilation system that handles filtered and heated, as necessary, fresh air, ducted at low velocity to supply grilles located at high level on the corridor side of the room and blowing towards the windows. Mechanical extract is often through the light fittings, in the usual way. While this assists proper air distribution and removes noise and dirt from the fresh air, the fan coil units still run wet. In this connexion, if a changeover mode is used, wet and dirty unit coils may generate unpleasant smells, absorbed during the previous form of operation, as they dry out when hot water circulates.

The fourth and best option is to provide a cooler coil for dehumidification in the central air-handling plant and arrange for the fan coil units to run dry, doing only sensible cooling. The units will then cost more money because they will remove less sensible heat with the higher secondary chilled water temperature necessary to prevent latent cooling. This extra cost is partly offset by the sensible cooling contribution of the ducted air. As with the induction scheme, there is no need to install a piped, condensate drainage system. Any condensate formed during start-up, drains into an emergency collection tray beneath the cooler coil and is subsequently re-evaporated.

Heating

There is a problem in fan coil systems when heating with a two-pipe unit. In the UK climate, changeover designs are not a success but if, alternatively, the mechanical ventilation system is used to deliver warm air to cope with the heat loss, three difficulties arise: stratification of the warm air may occur in the vicinity of the high level supply grilles, with underheating in the occupied zones because the quantity of fresh air is likely to be small and its temperature, therefore, high; distributing a small amount of air at low velocity introduces a balancing problem at individual grilles and, while about $\pm 25\%$, may not matter very much for ventilation, it produces a serious variation in heating capacity; the best place to locate a source of heat is under the window, to deal with downdraughts from single glazing, local infiltration, and 'cold radiation', rather than at high level on the other side of the room. All this suggests the four-pipe, twin-coil unit as the correct choice for fan coil systems in temperate climates.

Fan coil unit capacity

Most fan coil units are available for horizontal or vertical mounting and provided with a metal casing for immediate installation, or are uncased when they are fitted behind or above joiners' or builders' work panels. Four-row coils are normal, all rows being used for cooling in two-pipe systems or three for cooling and one for heating in four-pipe versions. Manual selection for running the unit fans at high, medium or low speed is usual, and for applications in the UK it is customary to select units to match office loads at medium or low speed, but for hotel bedrooms selection is at low speed. Units in offices would normally be operated at a fixed speed after installation, without the option of an easy speed change, but in hotel bedrooms guests would have the chance to select a higher speed, giving greater-than-design capacity with a higher-than-design noise. In warmer climates a choice at high speed is often the rule, the greater noise levels being acceptable. As with cooler coils generally, total cooling is largely a function of entering wet-bulb temperature but when coils are chosen for sensible cooling only, the dry-bulb dominates. Commercial fan coil units, suitable for dealing with the loads in individual offices or hotel bedrooms, have cooling capacities from about 600 W to as much as 70 000 W, depending of course on the entering air state, with fans running at high speed and when fed with chilled water at entering temperatures between 11 °C and 4.4 °C. Air quantities vary but one typical manufacturer offers four unit sizes with fans handling 100, 150, 200 and 300 l s^{-1} of air.

Performances are usually shown in tables but catalogue information,

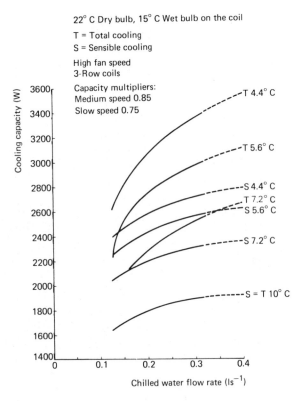

22° C Dry bulb, 15° C Wet bulb on the coil

T = Total cooling
S = Sensible cooling

High fan speed
3-Row coils

Capacity multipliers:
Medium speed 0.85
Slow speed 0.75

Figure 2.13   Performance of a typical fan coil unit with a three-row cooler coil for various entering water temperatures

particularly for sensible cooling, is seldom well-presented. However, as with induction units, sensible cooling capacity can be regarded as proportional to the difference between the entering air dry-bulb and the entering chilled water temperature, for a given water flow rate and fan speed. Selection to give an exact match between sensible and latent loads and corresponding fan coil capacities is rarely possible and, as long as the sensible gain is dealt with in a satisfactory way, this need not matter very much because of the relative unimportance of humidity in human comfort. Figure 2.13 shows performance curves, based upon technical information extracted from a manufacturer's catalogue, for the largest of the four fan coil units mentioned, with the fan running at high speed. The way in which the latent capacity falls off as the flow rate diminishes can be seen. For an entering water temperature of 7.2°C, for example, the sensible and total curves merge at a flow rate of about 0.16 l s⁻¹ when the thermal resistance of the water film within the tubes is great enough to ensure a surface temperature entirely above the entering dew-point. With a higher temperature, say 10°C, no latent cooling occurs at all for the entering air state of 22°C dry-bulb and 15°C wet-bulb (sling) quoted.

Example 2.22 Select a fan coil unit to deal with the design heat gains to a western module in the hypothetical office block. Assume that a central, mechanical ventilation plant delivers filtered but uncooled air to the modules at a rate of 1.3 $1s^{-1}$ m^{-2}, measured at the outside state, and that primary chilled water is available at 5.6°C.

Answer The fresh air delivered to the offices constitutes part of the load on the fan coil units. For the established outside and inside design states, the load on a western module is as follows:

$$\text{Fresh air total load:} \frac{(14.4 \times 1.3)}{1000 \times 0.8674} \times (55.36 - 43.39) \qquad = 0.258$$

$$\text{Fresh air sensible load:} \frac{(14.4 \times 1.3)}{1000} \times (28 - 22) \times \frac{358}{(273 + 28)} = 0.134$$

$$\text{Fresh air latent load:} \qquad\qquad\qquad\qquad\qquad\qquad \overline{0.124\,\text{kW}}$$

Sensible heat gain at 17.00 h sun time in July:	= 1837
Fresh air sensible load:	= 134
Total sensible load on fan coil unit:	= 1971 W
Latent heat gain at 17.00 h sun time in July:	= 134
Fresh air latent load:	= 124
Total latent load on fan coil unit:	= 258 W

The overall load on the unit is, therefore, $1971 + 258 = 2229$ W. Figure 2.13 shows that a typical fan coil unit, using three rows, has a sensible cooling capacity of about 2430 W at high speed or $0.85 \times 2430 = 2066$ W at medium speed when 0.2 $1s^{-1}$ of chilled water at 5.6°C is flowing. The total capacity is about 2730 W at high speed or 2320 W at medium speed and so the required room temperature could be achieved at medium speed. It is not uncommon for the total capacity of the fan coil unit to exceed the need and there is then a tendency for the room humidity to fall a little. However, this is usually not very important. For the eastern modules the sensible and latent components of the fresh air load will be less because the peak sensible gain occurs at 08.00 h sun time in July. However, a similar choice of fan coil unit, or one size smaller, is likely.

Example 2.23 Select a fan coil unit to deal with the design heat gain in the west module of the hypothetical office block assuming that a central mechanical system delivers dehumidified air at a rate of 30.65 $1s^{-1}$ to offset the latent gain, at a temperature of 14°C. Secondary chilled water at 11°C is available.

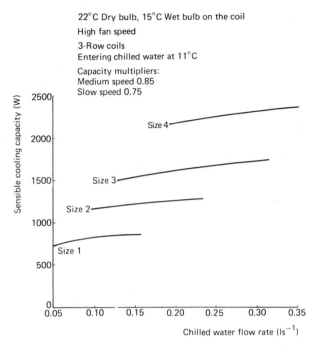

Figure 2.14   Typical sensible cooling performances of fan coil units

Answer From Equation (2.3) the sensible cooling capacity of the auxiliary air supply can be calculated as $30.65 \times (22 - 14) \times 358/(273 + 14) = 306$ W. Hence, the sensible duty on the fan coil unit is $1837 - 306 = 1531$ W. Figure 2.14 shows that a size 3 unit at high speed with flow rate of about $0.125 \, \text{s}^{-1}$ might be satisfactory. A better alternative might be a size 4 unit at slow speed, even if somewhat oversized.

The chilled water flow rates needed for a fan coil system are seen to exceed those for an induction system. For Examples 2.22 and 2.23 the rates were 0.2 and $0.125 \, \text{l s}^{-1}$, nominal, whereas the induction system in Example 2.21 needed about $0.1 \, \text{l s}^{-1}$. All figures may be subject to diversity factors, depending on how the system is controlled.

Noise

The noise mostly originates from the fan but sound power levels can vary according to the type of fan used, its bearings and mountings, the rigidity of the metal casing and the smoothness of airflow from the discharge grille. Manual changes in fan speed give variations in unit capacity according to the typical factors in Table 2.13, and refer to the units typified by Figures 2.13 and 2.14. It is possible to get sound power values from manufacturers and, when such

Table 2.13 Variations in unit capacity with fan speed

Unit	Low fan speed		Medium fan speed	
	Total capacity	Sensible capacity	Total capacity	Sensible capacity
1	0.90	0.89	0.81	0.79
2	0.90	0.88	0.80	0.77
3	0.85	0.85	0.75	0.74
4	0.85	0.80	0.70	0.67

information is used, the acoustic performance of a new unit, size 4, is as shown in Figure 2.15.

Controls
There are two basic ways of controlling unit capacity: cycling the unit fan and varying the chilled water flow rate. Cycling the fan from a thermostat behind the recirculation grille is the cheapest but least satisfactory method. Although adequate control is achieved by this method under tropical conditions, the variation in air movement and noise is seldom well-received in temperate

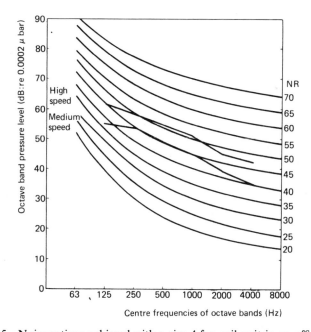

Figure 2.15 Noise ratings achieved with a size 4 fan coil unit in an office with zero room effect

climates. Water control, preferably by two-port modulating valves, is the best method although three-port valves also give good results.

No energy is saved by varying the fan speeds. Shaded pole motors with low power factors are used and speed reduction is achieved by dropping the supply voltage across a resistance. The nominal fan powers for the typical four fan coil units considered so far are 62, 78, 88 and 114 W, in order of unit size.

2.14 Chilled ceilings

The method of air conditioning by chilled ceilings has not proved particularly popular even though it is most economical to run, occupies no lettable floor area, requires no additional expenditure on joiners' work casings for terminal units, is silent in operation and includes an acoustic ceiling. Three possible explanations for this lack of application are: an apparently higher capital cost; some extra depth needed to accommodate the ceiling; and a comparative inflexibility in responding to partition rearrangement. However, insufficient credit is allowed for the acoustic celing and for the absence of joiners' work casings on terminal units. Secondly, as little as 200 mm is sufficient to accommodate the ceiling if, as is desirable, the auxiliary ventilation ducting is run above the ceiling in the central corridor, to feed side-wall grilles in the rooms. In any event, 200 mm is needed for a suspended ceiling with recessed light fittings. Thirdly, a suspended metal pan ceiling can carry chilled water pipes at 200, 300, 450 and 600 mm centres, to offer a fair degree of rearrangement possibilities.

Originally, chilled ceilings were provided by pipe coils embedded in the soffit of concrete floor slabs during building construction and finished with an appropriate rendering or plaster. Although this approach permitted pipe centres as close as 100 mm, with greater cooling capacity, capital costs were high and it has been replaced by an acoustic, aluminium pan ceiling, spring-clipped to pipes and suspended by short drop rods from the slab (Figure 2.16). The acoustic quality is given by perforations in the panels with a glass fibre blanket above the pipes, as shown in Figure 2.16, or glass fibre pads, encased in polythene bags, between the pipes. An auxiliary air handling plant is essential, to deliver filtered, cooled and dehumidified air through a low velocity ducting system to side-wall grilles or ceiling diffusers. Ceiling diffusers may not be suitable because the ceiling depth is not always enough to allow horizontally-flowing, ducted air to be turned smoothly into the diffuser necks and noise will result if there is an uneven distribution of air over the diffuser cones. The auxiliary air is enough for ventilation and, being mixed with recirculated air as necessary, deals with all the latent heat gains and some of the sensible heat gains in the treated rooms. The remainder of the sensible gain, and also any peripheral heat loss, is offset by the ceiling. Variations in sensible gain are met by thermostatic control over the flow rate of chilled water through the

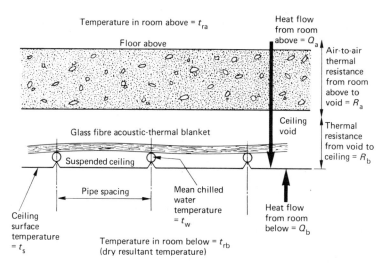

Figure 2.16 Section of a typical aluminium pan suspended ceiling showing heat flows, thermal resistances and temperatures

pipework, on a modular basis. For unfinned tube the thermal resistance of the inside water film is a comparatively small proportion of the overall, water-to-air, thermal resistance and it is, therefore, important that the water temperature is above the room dew-point at all times. Therefore, a secondary chilled water circuit is required and proportional plus integral control must be exercised over its flow temperature.

For the best results[8], the variable part of the heat gain should be dealt with by the thermostatically controlled capacity of the ceiling and the relatively constant or predictable portion of the gain by the constant or programmable capacity of the auxiliary air system. This is best illustrated for the case of a conditioned core area where the lights are on constantly and would be ideally covered by the cooling capacity of the air. The variable load is provided by the people and this is offset by the chilled ceiling. When using chilled ceilings for perimeter applications the part of the piping circuit nearest to the window wall can have a heating capacity. The piping circuit feeding the modular panels would be split so that the two or three pipes parallel to the wall are fed with LTHW in sequence with chilled water, whereas the remainder of the piping receives chilled water only.

An allowance should be made for the reduction in mean radiant temperature afforded by a chilled ceiling. Taking account of the surface temperatures of walls, Venetian blinds, the tubes and reflectors of the luminaires, the floor and the ceiling itself, the mean radiant temperature can be 1° to 2°C below the air temperature. Equating comfort with a dry resultant temperature of 22°C, implies an air temperature of 23°C and a mean radiant

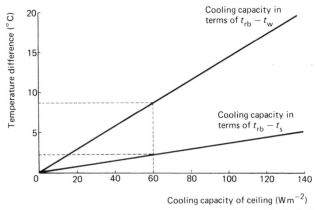

Figure 2.17   Typical capacity of an aluminium pan ceiling with chilled water pipes at 300 mm centres

temperature of 21°C, for example, which might be·typical of a west facing module in the hypothetical office block at 17.00 h sun time in July in the UK.

Typical catalogue data on the cooling performance of a metal pan chilled ceiling is shown in Figure 2.17 for pipe centres at 300 mm. The two lines give the difference between room air temperature (t_{rb}) and mean water temperature, (t_w) and between room air and ceiling surface temperature (t_s), respectively.

Example 2.24 Select a chilled ceiling with pipes at 300 mm centres to deal with sensible gains of 1837 W and latent gains of 134 W in a western module of the hypothetical office block.

Answer With a room dew-point of 11.3°C, corresponding to 22 C dry-bulb and 50% saturation, the lowest acceptable chilled water temperature is 11.5°C and, taking a water temperature rise of 3.3°C through a ceiling panel coil, the mean water temperature is 13.15 C. Thus, $t_{rb} - t_w = 22 - 13.15 = 8.85°C$ and the upper line in Figure 2.17 shows that the ceiling absorbs about 59 Wm^{-2}. The lower line shows that this is equivalent to $t_{rb} - t_s = 2.1°C$, so $t_s = 19.9°C$. The ceiling also absorbs some of the heat gain from the room above and this can be determined, assuming the thermal resistance between the void and the suspended ceiling (R_b) is 0.4 $m^2°CW^{-1}$ and calculating the resistance from the void to the room above (R_a). For the floor slab considered in Example 1.1 R_a is approximately 0.5 $m^2°CW^{-1}$ and the heat absorbed from above is, therefore,

$$(t_{ra} - t_s)/(R_a + R_b) = (22 - 19.9)/(0.5 + 0.4) = 2.3 \text{ W m}^{-2}.$$

This represents about 4% of the total ceiling capacity, in this case, but it could be more for a smaller value of R_b.

The sensible cooling capacity of the ceiling is thus $14.4 \times (59 + 2.3) = 883$ W, leaving $1837 - 883 = 954$ W to the auxiliary air supply system. With an off-coil state of 10°C dry-bulb, 9.7°C wet-bulb (sling) and assuming a medium velocity air distribution, the temperature rise by fan power and duct gain could amount to 3°C giving a supply temperature of 13°C. The auxiliary air requirement for a western module is then

$$\frac{954}{(23-13)} \times \frac{(273+13)}{358} = 76 \, l \, s^{-1}$$

which is more than enough to deal with the latent gain and provide the fresh air needed.

Exercises

1 If the plant considered in Example 2.8 handles 40% fresh air instead of one-sixth (16.67%), determine the lowest outside air state at which the refrigeration must run. Use the same assumptions and values as in Example 2.8, except for the fresh air amount. What is the lowest state onto the cooler coil?

(*Answer* 5.2°C dry-bulb, 3.205 g kg^{-1}; 15.3°C dry-bulb, 8°C wet-bulb)

2 Calculate the maximum cooling load for the hypothetical office block (see Section 1.1), assuming it is conditioned by a high velocity, perimeter-induction system with a low-velocity extract system and that its major axis is aligned east-west. Take the moisture content in August as 9.65 g kg^{-1}.

(*Answer* 1432 kW, 102.3 W m^{-2})

3 Using Tables 2.5 and 2.6, design a VAV ductwork distribution system alternative to that in Example 2.12 and Figure 2.7a, for the hypothetical office block. Assume that (a) the two service areas for ducts etc. are at the two short, windowless ends of the building and (b) the two service areas are within the main body of the building, on its major axis, each positioned one quarter of the way from the short end wall nearest to it.

4 Select fan coil units, using Figures 2.13 and 2.14, to match the loads of eastern modules in the hypothetical office block (a) with chilled water at 5.6°C at the units with 1.3 l s^{-1} m^{-2} of fresh air being supplied by a mechanical ventilation system and (b) with chilled water at 11°C at the units to do sensible gains only, 46.5 l s^{-1} of dehumidified air at 13°C being supplied to each module, by an auxiliary air system.

5 An acoustically hard office has the following room effect:

Mid octave-band frequency (Hz)	125	250	500	1000	2000	4000
Room effect (dB)	−1	−1	0	−1	−1	−1

The office is air conditioned by four VAV terminals, each handling 80 l s^{-1} with a duct pressure of 0.75 kPa under design load conditions but reducing to 20 l s^{-1} with 0.25 kPa for minimum sensible heat gains. Making use of Table 2.7

and a standard sheet for NR values (Figure A.2), determine the NR value likely in the room for (a) design conditions and (b) when the sensible gains are at a minimum.

(*Answer* (a) NR 51; (b) NR 26)

6 Repeat the calculations of Example 2.25 for an eastern module of the hypothetical office block.

7(a) A room has sensible heat gains of 2040 W by transmission, 1800 W from people, 4320 W from lights, 10710 W by solar gain through glass and latent gains of 1340 W, based on 28°C dry-bulb, 19.5°C wet-bulb (sling) outside and 22°C dry-bulb, 50% saturation inside. The treated room is 374.4 m³. The supply temperature is 14°C dry-bulb, the allowance for supply fan power and duct gain is 0.5°C and 10% by mass of the air supplied is from outside, the remainder being recirculated from the treated room. Using the psychrometric chart determine the supply air quantity and specific volume, the design states on and off the cooler coil, the design cooling load and the air change rate.

(b) Determine the outside air temperature at which the refrigeration plant can be switched off. What is the on-coil state immediately prior to switch-off? Assume that the inside state is 20°C dry-bulb, 34% saturation in winter at switch-off and that the differential on the switching thermostat is ±1°C. Ignore solar heat gains in winter but assume full gains from people and lights. Assume an outside state of −1°C saturated at switch-off.

(*Answer* (a) 1.891 m³s⁻¹, 0.824 m³kg⁻¹, on-coil: 22.6°C dry-bulb, 15.9°C wet-bulb, off-coil: 13.5°C dry-bulb, 12°C wet-bulb, 24.06 kW of refrigeration, 18.2 air changes per hour; (b) 7.4 − 2.0 = 5.4°C: 18.5°C dry-bulb, 10.8°C wet-bulb)

8 A condensing set using R 22 has a performance as follows when condensing at 40°C and using 4 cylinders:

Suction temperature (°C)	−10°	−5°	0°	+5°
Suction pressure (kPa)	219	261	309	362
Cooling capacity (kW)	57.9	77.3	99.8	126.5

The set is coupled to a direct-expansion cooler coil which cools air from 17°C wet-bulb to 10°C wet-bulb, for which the calculated duty is 100 kW of refrigeration. Plot the characteristic of the condensing set for 4 and 2 cylinders in coordinates of temperature (abscissa) and cooling capacity (ordinate). Also plot the characteristics for the cooler coil and determine the evaporating temperature and duty for 4 cylinders. In addition, determine the evaporating temperatures and duties for 2 cylinders when the entering wet-bulb falls to 13°C. Allow 1°C as corresponding to the pressure drop in the suction line. (*Answer* Evaporating temperature = 1°C, duty = 100 kW; evaporating temperature = 4°C, duty = 57 kW)

Symbols

c_p	Specific heat capacity	$\mathrm{J\,kg^{-1}{}^\circ C}$ or $\mathrm{kJ\,kg^{-1}{}^\circ C}$
c_s	Coefficient of discharge through a supply grille	—
c_d	Coefficient of discharge through a doorway	—
d	Relevant linear dimension, or grille depth	m
f	Free area ratio of a supply grille	—
g	Acceleration arising from the force of gravity, or	$\mathrm{m\,s^{-2}}$
	moisture content	$\mathrm{kg\,kg^{-1}}$ or $\mathrm{g\,kg^{-1}}$
g_p	Primary air moisture content	$\mathrm{kg\,kg^{-1}}$ or $\mathrm{g\,kg^{-1}}$
g_r	Room moisture content	$\mathrm{kg\,kg^{-1}}$ or $\mathrm{g\,kg^{-1}}$
g_s	Supply moisture content	$\mathrm{kg\,kg^{-1}}$ or $\mathrm{g\,kg^{-1}}$
H	Stack height, or	m
	sensible heat content of the air in a room at any time θ	kJ
H_o	Initial sensible heat content of the air in a room at time $\theta = 0$	kJ
$H(\theta)$	Sensible heat gain to a room expressed in $\mathrm{kJs^{-1}}$ for each $\mathrm{kgs^{-1}}$ of air supplied to it	$\mathrm{kJ\,kg^{-1}}$
h	Enthalpy, or	$\mathrm{kJ\,kg^{-1}}$
	doorway height	m
h_a	Air film heat transfer coefficient	$\mathrm{W\,m^{-2}{}^\circ C^{-1}}$
h_s	Specific heat content of air supplied to a room	$\mathrm{kJ\,kg^{-1}}$
k	Thermal conductivity	$\mathrm{W\,m^{-1}{}^\circ C^{-1}}$
M	Mass of air in a room	kg
n	Number of air changes after time θ	—
p	Static pressure	kPa or Pa
p_{at}	Atmospheric pressure	mbar
p_{ss}	Saturation vapour pressure	mbar
Q_s	Volumetric supply air flow rate	$\mathrm{m^3s^{-1}}$
Q_t	Volumetric air flow rate by combined effect	$\mathrm{m^3s^{-1}}$
q_p	Primary air flow rate	$\mathrm{m^3s^{-1}}$ or $\mathrm{ls^{-1}}$
R_a	Air-to-air thermal resistance between a room and the void under the floor slab but above the suspended ceiling.	$\mathrm{m^2{}^\circ C^{-1}W^{-1}}$
R_b	Air-to-surface thermal resistance between the void above a suspended ceiling and the ceiling surface.	$\mathrm{m^2{}^\circ C^{-1}W^{-1}}$
r_m	Thermal resistance of metal	$\mathrm{m^2{}^\circ C^{-1}W^{-1}}$
r_w	Thermal resistance of a water film	$\mathrm{m^2{}^\circ C^{-1}W^{-1}}$
S	Sensible/total heat transfer ratio, or	—
	sensible cooling duty	kW
T	Total cooling capacity, or	kW

	absolute temperature	K
t	Temperature	°C
t_p	Primary air temperature	°C
t_{ra}	Temperature in a room above a chilled ceiling	°C
t_{rb}	Temperature in a room beneath a chilled ceiling	°C
t_s	Mean surface temperature of a chilled ceiling	°C
t_w	Mean chilled water temperature in a chilled ceiling	°C
U	Thermal transmittance coefficient	$Wm^{-2}°C^{-1}$
u	Velocity	$m\,s^{-1}$
u_o	Wind speed	$m\,s^{-1}$
u_t	Velocity resulting from combined wind and stack effect	$m\,s^{-1}$
u_s	Supply air velocity	$m\,s^{-1}$
V	volumetric flow rate	$1s^{-1}$ or m^3s^{-1}
v	Specific volume	m^3kg^{-1}
w	Width of a doorway	m
θ	Time, or	s
	Temperature difference	°C
μ	Percentage saturation, or	%
	absolute viscosity	$kgm^{-1}s^{-1}$
ρ	density	$kg\,m^{-3}$
ϕ	Angle between the supply airstream leaving a grille and the vertical	degrees
(Nu)	Nusselt number	—
(Pr)	Prandtl number	—
(Re)	Reynolds number	—

References

(1) *CIBS Guide*, Volume C, 1970
(2) P. L. Martin and D. M. Curtis, *M-C Psychrometric Charts for a Range of Barometric Pressures* (in SI units), Troup Publications, 1972
(3) Jones, W. P. *Air conditioning Engineering*, 2nd edition, Edward Arnold Publishers, 1973
(4) Jones, W. P., Theoretical aspects of air conditioning systems upon start-up, *JIHVE*, **31**, September 1963, pp. 218–223
(5) ASHRAE Handbook and Product Directory, *Systems*, 1976
(6) Holmes, M. J., Designing variable air volume systems for room air movement, *HVRA Application Guide*, **1/74**
(7) Shataloff, N. S., High velocity dual duct systems for multizone installations, *Air Conditioning, Heating and Ventilating*, August 1964
(8) Jamieson, H. C. and Caland, J. R., The mechanical services at Shell Centre, *JIHVE*, **31**, 1963, p. 1

3
Applications

3.1 Principles

Since most plants operate at partial load for most of their life, the essential feature of good application is to choose a system with a capacity that can be satisfactorily controlled to match the full range of load variations expected, within the limits of the design brief. The nature of the load is also a very important factor. For example, a theatre auditorium with a large population is better suited by an all-air system that can easily provide the vast quantity of fresh air needed than by an air-water system which probably cannot. The size of the application also has a bearing on the choice of systems, e.g. small loads are dealt with more cheaply by direct-expansion, all-air systems than by water-chillers with air-water systems. In addition, it is important when a system serves different areas that all the rooms in the group treated should have similar patterns of use, so that the plant can be programmed to operate in an economical manner.

When choosing a system it is vital to select plant components that are suitable for each other and mutually compatible. It would be useless to couple a sophisticated and expensive automatic control system with a commercial, comparatively crude plant, for a tightly controlled, industrial application. The outcome would be a poor performance that is often wrongly blamed on the controls. The quality of the plant controlled must be on a par with the quality of the automatic control system if the best is to be obtained from both. By similar reasoning, it is uneconomical to select expensive plant and refined controls for a commercial, comfort conditioning application that could well be dealt with by equipment of lesser quality and price. The design calculations that precede system selection and the commissioning that follows its installation should be above reproach. Finally, the system must be commissionable, otherwise it will never work properly, no matter how appropriate otherwise for the job.

3.2 Office blocks

Air conditioning in office blocks has provided the stimulus for system design and application in recent years. Dirty, noisy, urban centres with high-rise, greenhouse buildings, have been where the market is and also where the capital has been available. Consequently a very large number of air-conditioning systems have been developed for this application and, therefore, which system to use is open to the designer's choice. The aesthetics of architectural inspiration and whim have given some variety in the design of window-wall facades and in the exploitation of the available site plan to maximise the lettable floor area produced for a given expenditure of capital, within the restraints of statutory obligation. However, two classes of office building have generally emerged: the narrow block, usually rectangular in form and having a central corridor 1.5 m wide, bounded by two usable peripheral strips of about 6 m width inboard from the windows: and, to a lesser extent in the UK, the deep plan building, often lacking an internal light well.

The first, narrow plan, epitomises the speculative development, with concrete floor slabs, fairly extensive single glazing and curtain walling. The modular construction concept involved has been associated with the provision of demountable internal partitions that allow the tenant to have many individual offices and to change the size and arrangement of them during the term of his tenancy, at his own, expense. Such a design aim has provoked the development of office air-conditioning systems that can offer flexibility in control and performance to cater for partition rearrangement, and has tended to require a controllable air-conditioning terminal in each module. Architectural and development philosophy has also influenced the size and cooling capacity of the terminal units themselves. For example, there is a small amount of evidence that a modular width of about 2.4 m is most economical in terms of unit selection, and capital cost, but this depends to a large extent on the amount of glazing and the level of illumination.

Latent gains in an office are relatively trivial with fairly good building construction in the UK, although this is not always the case in a tropical environment where a high outside moisture content and a poor building construction may give a latent load by infiltration, which dominates plant selection and performance. In Britain, the small latent heat gains derive, in almost equal proportions, from natural infiltration and the sparse population. Sensible gains come from air-to-transmission (T), people (P), electric lighting (L), solar gain through glass (S) and business machines (B). Example 1.8 showed these to be of the order of 12% for T; 10% for P; 20% for L; 55% for S; and 3% for B. Transmission gains and losses are regarded as being predictable since they are related to outside air temperature and are consequently often offset by compensated heating, e.g. the primary reheat schedule of a two-pipe induction system or the independent perimeter heating system often adopted with VAV schemes. Gains from lights are frequently fairly stable, once patterns of usage for the building have been established, and with block switching it ought to be possible to cut back zoned reheat to conserve energy, at least for part of the day, although this is not very often done. People and business machine gains also follow a common behaviour, since the use of the latter is related to the presence of the former. They should, therefore, have similar diversity factors applied to them and throughout the working day they ought not to present big variations in load. It must not be concluded from this that there is any case for abandoning individual thermostatic control for the modules. Generally speaking zone control, that is controlling all the units on one face of a building from one thermostat or from several averaging thermostats, has proved a failure. Solar gains are unpredictable in the UK and, for many buildings, significantly large. The designer must make sure that windows are adequately shaded as it is not possible to be comfortable in direct sunlight within a building, regardless of the temperature maintained by the air-conditioning system.

Of the many systems that have been explicitly developed to deal with offices, those that have proved most popular are nonchangeover, two-pipe, perimeter-induction; variable air volume with perimeter heating; and terminal heat reclaim units with auxiliary mechanical ventilation. Dual duct systems have generally trailed behind the field, for fairly obvious reasons. On an *ad hoc* basis, particularly for smaller buildings, individual offices and in the tropics, through-the-wall room air-conditioning units have been extensively and successfully used for individual offices. All these systems offer individual thermostatic control, usually on a modular basis, but not all provide the same flexibility in responding to load variations and in coping with partition rearrangement (see Chapter 2). Perimeter systems, generally, and induction systems, in particular, are best suited to dealing with a peripheral strip of 4.5 m width inwards from the window-wall, up to a maximum of 6 m.

For occupied areas beyond such treated peripheral strips, or 'core areas', the standard treatment in the past has been a low or medium velocity, constant volume, reheat system with one or more reheaters per floor, the number used depending on the number of tenancies anticipated by the letting arrangements. In more recent years, variable air volume has been applied to the core areas in deep plan buildings with the advantage of control and flexibility, referred to in Section 2.8, and with considerable success. Floor area cannot be conveniently occupied by any system intended for a core and so where induction and fan coil units have been chosen for such applications they are located at high level, which then causes difficulties of access and maintenance. The induction system is not intended for treating core areas and should not be so misapplied in this way.

For refurbished offices, air conditioning has been well-provided by two systems: terminal heat recovery units and four-pipe fan coil units. Both need an auxiliary, mechanical, ventilation installation.

For air conditioning in an office block, or anywhere else, to be a success a source of heat is required and this means that the boilers must be able to run throughout the summer as well as the winter. The only exception to this is in hot climates where buildings never suffer a heat loss, although it must be remembered that desert environments and locations at high altitudes have night-time temperatures that often sink to very low values and heating is still needed for comfort.

3.3 Hotels

The treatment for a hotel falls very clearly into two parts: that needed for the bedrooms and that necessary for the public rooms, the load characteristics between the two being very different.

In the bedrooms the load is somewhat similar to that in an office, with windows tending to be smaller and perhaps with external shading if balconies are provided. The electric lighting will probably be a good deal less, although some or all of it will be from tungsten lamps. A coloured television set is standard now in modern hotels with any pretension to luxury, liberating about 400 W when switched on. The design of bedrooms is usually for two people, twin single beds, or even twin double beds, being the most common furnishing. So sensible heat gains are in the region of 70 to 90 Wm^{-2} of floor area, say about 2000 W per bedroom, depending on the diversity factors allowed for lighting and television. Some rooms are likely to be occupied, with the television set on, at the time of peak afternoon sensible heat gain, although part, or all, of the lighting may be off. The standard fresh air allowance for a double bedroom is 25 $1s^{-1}$, on the assumption that this is exhausted to waste through the bathroom mechanical extract ventilation system.

Several systems of air conditioning have been used, with varying degrees of success. In a tropical environment a through-the-wall room air-conditioning unit can provide the welcome relief so necessary in a hot climate, without its excessive noise being regarded as a nuisance, but a more critical guest in a higher class hotel, or in Europe or America, might not be satisfied. Two-pipe fan coil units, frequently floor-mounted, are also used, in both temperate and warmer climates. They are operated as a changeover system if there is any need for winter heating and the changeover problems (Section 2.13) either do not exist or at least do not present a serious problem. With some designs, the fresh air is cooled and dehumidified by a central plant and delivered to the corridors, to find its own way through grilles or under-cut doors into the bedrooms for exhaust to waste via the bathroom extract ventilation system. With bathrooms generally located close to the entrance from the corridor the amount of fresh air supplied to the bedrooms is often only nominal. Corridors also tend to be over-cooled. Two-pipe and four-pipe induction systems have been used to condition hotel bedrooms, with mixed success. The induction system is really wrongly applied in these instances as units cannot be turned off and, except in the four-pipe case, there is not a quick enough response to the capacity changes sometimes demanded by the guest.

Terminal heat recovery units have also been used successfully in the UK, backed up by an auxiliary mechanical ventilation system providing filtered, and, when necessary, tempered, fresh air that is not cooled in summer, the terminal units in the bedrooms doing all the cooling needed. Units are usually located above the suspended ceiling in the bathroom, as is the fan coil unit shown in Figure 3.1. Although much quieter than through-the-wall room air-conditioners, terminal heat recovery units tend to be a little on the noisy side when the refrigeration compressor runs, unless encased in a special acoustic enclosure.

There is no doubt that the correct choice for hotel bedrooms is the four-pipe,

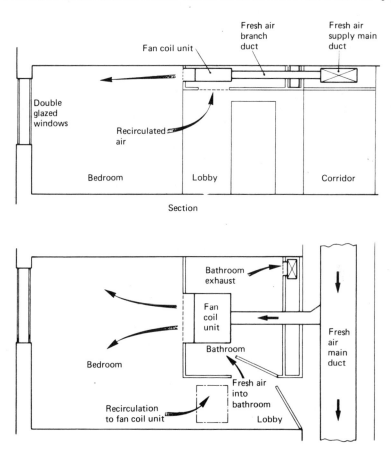

Figure 3.1   Section and plan of a typical four-pipe twin coil fan coil unit installation. Fresh air goes from the bedroom through the lobby into the bathroom. A condensate collection tray under the fan coil unit must be provided and drained to waste in the plumbing system

twin-coil, fan coil system with an auxiliary, low velocity, mechanical supply of filtered, cooled and dehumidified fresh air, ducted to the vicinity of the fan coil units and subsequently removed through the bathroom extract ventilation system. Figure 3.1 shows a typical method of installation. The fan coil units can run at low, medium or hish speed, by manual choice, with their selection made to cope with maximum design heat gains at low speed to give a noise level below NR 30 and as near as possible to NR 25. The unit can be switched off by the management when the room is unlet and the hotel guests can switch it off themselves if they wish. Furthermore, increased cooling or heating capacity can be rapidly obtained by switching to medium or even high speed operation if the penalty of a higher noise level is accepted. This facility of quick capacity change by switching fan speeds, coupled with the constant, simultaneous availability of full cooling and full heating by the four-pipe distribution to the twin coils, means that a wide range of settings is possible on the room thermostat and the system response to set point alterations or load fluctuations is very rapid. The whims of most room occupants can be accommodated, although if all guests chose to run their units at full capacity at the same time the central refrigeration or boiler plant might experience some difficulty.

Example 3.1 Suppose that a west-facing bedroom is of similar construction and dimensions to the modules in the hypothetical office block (Section 1.2) except that it is 3.6 m wide and contains only one window, which is double glazed to prevent the intrusion of traffic noise and is fitted with Venetian blinds between the panes of glass. The bedroom itself is 3 m deep with a further 3 m to cover the bathroom and lobby. Assuming 2 people are present, 400 W for a coloured television set and 300 W for lighting, determine the cooling load at 16.00 h sun time in July if air conditioning is by a four-pipe, twin-coil, fan coil system with an auxiliary supply of cooled and dehumidified fresh air at a rate of 25 ls^{-1}. No natural infiltration occurs.

Answer Referring to Example 1.8 and making the appropriate adjustments the following can be calculated:

		W
Glass:	=	65
Wall:	=	88
Solar gains through glass (see Table A.2):	=	497
Lights:	=	300
Television:	=	400
People:	=	180
Total sensible heat gain:	=	1530 W

This represents a specific gain of 71 Wm^{-2} over the total floor area of the bedroom, lobby and bathroom.

Example 1.9 showed that the latent heat gain is 100 W and, taking the outside and inside enthalpies as 55.36 and 43.39 $kJ\,kg^{-1}$, respectively, and assuming a specific volume of 0.8674 m^3kg^{-1} at the outside state, the fresh load can be calculated as

$$[0.025 \times (55.36 - 43.39) \times 1000]/0.8674 = 345 \text{ W}.$$

The auxiliary ventilation system will distribute air at low velocity and is, therefore, likely to have a fan total pressure of about 0.6 kPa with a temperature rise across the fan of 0.6°C. To allow for this and for duct heat gain, assume a rise of 2°C, giving a corresponding cooling load of $(0.025 \times 1000 \times 2 \times 358)/(273 + 28) = 59$ W. Section 2.13 shows that a large fan coil unit will liberate 114 W from its fan motor and so:

		W
Sensible gain:	=	1530
Latent gain:	=	100
Fresh air load:	=	345
Auxiliary supply fan and duct gain:	=	59
Fan coil unit fan power:	=	114
Total maximum cooling load:	=	2148 W

It is probable that the corridor would be supplied with cooled, dehumidified (reheated as necessary) fresh air from the auxiliary plant, imposing an additional cooling load.

Example 3.2 Calculate the cooling load imposed by the supply of 1.3 $1s^{-1}m^{-2}$ of cooled and dehumidified fresh air.
Answer
Fresh air load: $[0.0013 \times (55.36 - 43.39) \times 1000]/0.8674$ = 17.9
Auxiliary fan power and duct gain:
$$(0.0013 \times 2 \times 358 \times 1000)/(273 + 28) \qquad = 3.1$$

Total additional cooling load: = 21 Wm^{-2}

Table A.1 gives the solar gain through an east-facing window at 16.00 h sun time in July as 35 Wm^{-2}, which would make the solar component in Example 3.1, 68 W instead of 497 W. Table A.7 gives the equivalent temperature difference as 4.5°, making the wall gain 32 W instead of 88 W.

For the bedroom block as a whole it is possible, but not certain, that the maximum cooling load will occur during the period 14.00 h – 17.00 h sun time in July. A calculation survey using a computer will resolve this but the real problem facing the designer is in the allowance he must make for diversity factors on lights, television and people.

Example 3.3 Estimate a cooling load for the hypothetical building (Section 1.2) at 16.00 h sun time in July, supposing it to be the bedroom block of a hotel, and making use of the data and results in Examples 3.1 and 3.2.

Answer The number of bedrooms on each of the two long faces will be (86.4 × 12)/3.6 = 288. The diversity factors to adopt are entirely up to the judgement of the designer. In this case, assume values of 0.2 for people, 0.1 for lights and 0.05 for television sets. From Table A.7 the equivalent temperature differences for the roof, the north wall and the south wall are 15.5°, 3.4° and 17.2°C, respectively. The cooling load is then estimated to be:

West face (T + S): [288 × (65 + 88 + 497)]/1000   = 187.2
East face (T + S): [288 × (65 + 32 + 68)]/1000   = 47.5
Both faces (P + L + TV):
[576 × (0.2 × 180 + 0.1 × 300 + 0.05 × 400)]/1000   = 49.5
Roof: (86.4 × 13.5 × 1.1 × 15.5)/1000   = 19.9
North wall: (13.5 × 12 × 3.3 × 0.91 × 3.4)/1000   =   1.7
South wall: (13.5 × 12 × 3.3 × 0.91 × 17.2)/1000   =   8.4

Total sensible gain: = 314.2 kW
Total latent gain: (576 × 0.2 × 100)/1000   = 11.5
Fresh air load + auxiliary fan power and duct gain:
                    [576 × (345 + 59)]/1000   = 232.7
Fan coil units' fan power: (0.2 × 576 × 114)/1000   = 13.1
Corridor cooling load: (12 × 86.4 × 1.5 × 21)/1000   = 32.7

Total cooling estimate: = 604.2 kW

In this total the elements subjected to virtually guessed diversity factors, add up to 74.1 kW or about 12%. This comparatively small percentage reduces the risk associated with the guesses. For the hotel as a whole, the cooling load in the public rooms is very significant and it is not likely that these areas will be densely occupied at 16.00 h sun time in July, the bars and dining rooms being closed in the UK. A better time for assessing the maximum cooling load for the bedroom block might be 13.00 h sun time, to coincide with a peak of activity in the public rooms. In Exercise 1 this can be calculated as 469 kW, making the same assumptions for diversity.

The public rooms in a hotel comprise reception area and foyers, dining rooms, bars and a banqueting suite. The policy of many hotel developers is not to provide areas that fail to yield a revenue, so residents' lounges are rare in modern hotels, and, for the same reason, foyers and reception areas often include shops. Hotel designs vary enormously but a common practice is to house the public rooms in a three or four storey podium and to have a tower block of bedrooms above it, sometimes with a penthouse suite or a restaurant at the top.

The obvious characteristic of public rooms is a high population, so all-air systems are the correct choice for air conditioning. Three types are possible selections: multizone, constant volume reheat and, occasionally, double duct. The multizone system is the most popular because it takes full account of cooling load diversification and is comparatively cheap in first cost if the plants can be located fairly close to the areas treated in order to minimise duct runs. The double duct system might provide a good solution to a small part of the public areas if there exists a case for multiple, thermostatic control, say for a restaurant with alcoves for semi-private dining parties, but its use is rare because of its higher capital cost. The constant volume reheat system is really only acceptable for a single area where one heater battery could be controlled in sequence with the cooler coil, so that reductions in the heat gains would not be cancelled with reheating, otherwise no advantage could be taken of load diversity and the installed refrigeration capacity and capital cost would be large.

It makes sense to select a multizone unit to deal with a group of rooms sharing a common pattern of usage. Thus one unit would be chosen to treat the three or four bars in the hotel, another to condition the group of dining rooms, a third for the banqueting suite—which is often one very large room with one or more demountable partitions—and a fourth for the foyers and reception area. The first three of these groups would probably require to be conditioned at different times and the last might need air conditioning continuously. The administrative offices sometimes receive a supply of conditioned air from the reception plant and achieve individual thermostatic control with fan coil units. Sometimes they are only heated, with radiators, if they have openable windows. Shops can be treated in a similar way or merely provided with a supply of chilled water and be expected to make their own arrangements for conditioning. Another approach is to fit extract fans at the back of the shops which gives them second-hand air conditioning by drawing air in from the treated foyer or reception area. This is done with shopping centres.

Noise in public areas is never as critical as in the bedrooms but acceptable levels must be provided, i.e. NR 45 or NR 40, or lower, depending on the use of the space. Some hotels have conference facilities and in these cases the auditoria must have separate plants, for all-air systems that are acoustically compatible.

The location of plant has an important bearing on capital cost and the acoustics. The aim must be to minimise duct runs and avoid noise and vibration causing a nuisance within the treated areas or outside to the occupants of the adjoining buildings, although the latter may be less of a problem in the Middle East and the Gulf where noisy air-cooled condensers are the norm and are acceptable. For the typical tower block/podium arrangement mentioned, air-handling plant for the bedrooms and possibly the cooling towers would be on the roof of the tower, the multizone units for the public rooms would be on the roof of the podium, suitably disguised, or possibly in plant rooms inside the podium block itself, refrigeration and boiler plant would be in the basement. An alternative site for the cooling towers, giving shorter runs of cooling water piping, would be on the podium roof but screening the towers acoustically and visually, without affecting the airflow they need for their proper performance, can introduce problems.

The proportions of the public areas allotted to the various functions (bars, restaurants, etc.) differ among hotels, as also do the standards adopted for lighting and population densities. Furthermore, the ratio of bedroom area to public area depends on the commercial policy followed by the hotel operating group. It is consequently not easy to generalise about cooling loads in hotels in the way that one can about office blocks (see Table A.9). A similar situation exists for estimating the boiler power and often the best policy for a designer is to seek the advice of the chief engineer of the hotel group.

The results of a survey of 9 air-conditioned hotels in the UK, completed in the early 1970s, are shown in Table 3.1. The average ratio of private to public areas is 3.3 and the mean specific refrigeration load is 129 Wm^{-2}. Hotel number 9 is not far from the average and its design values of population density and power liberated by the electric lighting are given in Table 3.2, although the diversity factors applied to them are not known. The lighting is largely by tungsten filament lamps in the public areas.

With appropriate assumptions a cooling load for the complete, hypothetical hotel can now be estimated. The aim is to determine the maximum coincident sum of the cooling loads in the private and public areas and the proper way to do this is by calculating the combined load at hourly intervals, using a computer and making assumptions for diversity factors for lights and people. Without doing this though, the peak load in the public rooms can be judged to

Table 3.1 Comparison of air conditioning loads in hotels in the UK

Hotel	Public area (m^2)	Bedroom area (m^2)	Ratio of bedroom area to public area	Total cooling load (kW of refrigeration)	Specific refrigeration over the total treated floor area (Wm^{-2})
1	8500	14000	1.65	1758	78
2	1500	9340	6.23	2271	210
3	1000	3000	3.00	774	194
4	4425	13150	2.97	2532	144
5	2690	14950	5.56	1758	100
6	2700	5000	1.85		
7	2600	8000	3.08		
8	1000	2060	2.06		
9	1640	5290	3.23	1125	162

occur at lunchtime, or at dinner time in the evening, say at 2 pm or 8 pm, clock time, respectively. Consider a possible lunchtime load at 13.00 h sun time, for which the calculations in Exercise 1 yield a cooling load of 469 kW of refrigeration for the bedroom block, based on an outside enthalpy of 54.74 kJ kg^{-1} in July, at this time, determined from Equation (1.1), the outside design moisture content and psychrometric tables. Deciding on diversity factors for the population in the public rooms is difficult. If 2.87 is assumed to be the ratio of private to public areas then the public area associated with a bedroom block of 14 000 m^2 is 4878 m^2. If the restaurants are full (diversity factor = 1.0), the bars will be less full (diversity factor = 0.6, say) and the other public areas comparatively empty (diversity factor = 0.2, say). The banqueting suite, on the other hand, could well be fully occupied, but the committee room can be assumed to be empty, any occupants being at lunch. A similar line of reasoning cannot be easily applied to the lighting and it is possible that in some hotels the lights will be permanently on. However, at lunchtime in July it is reasonable to suppose there is some natural illumination through windows and that some of the lights will, therefore, be off intentionally, or off for maintenance. Hence, a factor of 0.8 can be assumed for all lights, except in the cloakroom and the banqueting suite, both of which can be assumed here to be internal rooms and have a diversity factor of 1.0. Allowing 90 W for sensible heat gains and 50 W for latent heat gains from people and taking the appropriate values from Table 3.2, the loads are as follows:

			People			Lighting		
Item	Floor Area (m^2)	Design population	Diversity factor	Sensible gain (kW)	Latent gain (kW)	Design load (Wm^{-2})	Diversity factor	Sensible gain (kW)
Bars	1220	678	0.6	36.6	20.3	75	0.8	73.2
Restaurants	1317	693	1.0	62.4	34.6	75	0.8	79.0
Banqueting	634	334	1.0	30.1	16.7	150	1.0	95.1
Reception	293	39	0.2	0.7	0.4	40	0.8	9.4
Committee room	49	(20)	0	0	0	—	0	0
Foyers	585	162	0.2	2.9	1.6	75	0.8	35.1
Administration	439	86	0.2	1.5	0.9	40	0.8	14.0
Cloakrooms	341	19	0.2	0.3	0.2	75	1.0	25.6
Totals	4878	2011		134.5	74.7			331.4

Example 3.4 Making use of the loads established above, for people and lights in the public areas and 469 kW of refrigeration for the bedroom block (Exercise 1), make an estimate of the cooling load for the whole hypothetical hotel building at 13.00 h sun time in July. Assume the public areas are in a two-storey podium of plan dimensions 87 m × 28 m, located beneath the bedroom block and with its major axis pointing north-south. Take the building construction to be similar to that of the bedrooms and assume 35% single glazing on its two long faces. Allow 12 ls^{-1} per person as a ventilation rate in

Table 3.2   Design values for population density and lighting power for a hotel in the UK

Item	Proportion of the total public area (%)	Design population density (m² per person)	Design lighting power Wm⁻²
Bars	25	1.8	75
Restaurants	27	1.9	75
Banqueting	13	1.9	150
Committee room	1	2.4	75
Reception	6	7.5	40
Foyers	12	3.6	75
Administration	9	5.1	40
Cloakrooms	7	18.3	75

Note. These figures must not be regarded as typical but only as an indication of possibilities

the bars, restaurants and banqueting suite and $5 \, \mathrm{l s^{-1}}$ elsewhere. There is no natural infiltration.

Answer From Equation (1.1) we can establish that $t_{13} = 27.4°C$ and from Tables A.7 and A.1 we can determine the equivalent temperature differences and the solar load through glass, respectively. The sensible heat gains are then calculated at 13.00 h sun time, in July, as follows:

		kW
Glass, east:	$[(0.35 \times 87 \times 6.6) \times 5.6 \times (27.4 - 22)]/1000 =$	6.1
Glass, west:	$[(0.35 \times 87 \times 6.6) \times 5.6 \times (27.4 - 22)]/1000 =$	6.1
Walls, north:	$[(28 \times 6.6) \times 0.91 \times -0.6]/1000$	$= -0.1$
Walls, south:	$[(28 \times 6.6) \times 0.91 \times 13.9]/1000$	$= 2.3$
Walls, east:	$[(0.65 \times 87 \times 6.6) \times 0.91 \times 8.4]/1000$	$= 2.9$
Walls, west:	$[(0.65 \times 87 \times 6.6) \times 0.91 \times 1.7]/1000$	$= 0.6$
Roof:	$[(87 \times 28 - 86.4 \times 13.5) \times 1.1 \times 8.9]/1000$	$= \underline{12.4}$
Subtotal:		$= 30.3 \, \mathrm{kW}$
Glass solar gains, east:	$(0.35 \times 87 \times 6.6) \times 60$	$= 12.1$
Glass solar gains, west:	$(0.35 \times 87 \times 6.6) \times 60$	$= 12.1$
People:		$= 134.5$
Lights:		$= \underline{331.4}$
Total sensible heat gains:		$= 520.4 \, \mathrm{kW}$
Total latent heat gain:		$= 74.7 \, \mathrm{kW}$

The contribution of the fan power will depend on the total supply air quantity which has not been calculated. However, a very rough approximation might be $10 \, \mathrm{l s^{-1} \, m^{-2}} \times 4878 \, \mathrm{m^2} = 48780 \, \mathrm{l s^{-1}}$. All the air distribution will be at low velocity so a reasonable estimate of fan total pressure is 0.625 kPa. Allowing 1.0°C per kPa, the approximate supply fan power load is, therefore, $(48.78 \times 0.625 \times 358)/(273 + 14) = 38.0 \, \mathrm{kW}$. Using the design populations the total fresh air quantity delivered is $(678 + 693 + 334) \times 12 + (39 + 162 + 86 + 19$

$+20) \times 5 = 22090 \text{ l s}^{-1}$. The fresh air load is, therefore, $[22.09 \times (54.74 - 43.39)]/0.822 = 305 \text{ kW}$.

An assessment must also be made of the contribution of the return air fan to the refrigeration load because not all the air is fresh. If a fan total pressure of 0.375 kPa is assumed for this fan its cooling load element will be $[(48.78 - 22.09) \times 0.375 \times 358]/(273 + 14) = 12.5 \text{ kW}$. Finally, duct heat gain to the supply air should be allowed for, say 1°C. This then represents: $48.78 \times 1 \times 358/(273 + 14) = 60.8 \text{ kW}$.

Summarising, the load is, therefore,

			kW
Public areas:	sensible gain:	=	520.4
	latent gain:	=	74.7
	supply fan power:	=	38.0
	extract fan power:	=	12.5
	duct gain:	=	60.8
	fresh air load:	=	305.0
Subtotal:		=	1011.4 kW
Bedroom block:		=	469.0
Total refrigeration load:		=	1480.4 kW

This represents a specific load of $1480\,400/(14\,000 + 4878) = 78.4 \text{ Wm}^{-2}$. This is at the lower end of the values in Table 3.1.

3.4 Residences and apartments

In a hot climate air conditioning is common and, in some instances, essential for living quarters, particularly for bedrooms where cooler conditions assist sleep and discourage insects. The approach has been to install through-the-wall, room air-conditioning units (see Section 2.3) on an *ad hoc* basis to meet the needs of individual rooms or dwellings. More refined treatments have been adopted for houses, generally using constant volume all-air systems with a single direct expansion cooler coil and a remote air-cooled condenser. One or more reheaters give temperature control, although a single thermostat in the corridor with one heater battery is often enough. Such systems are also used in apartment blocks, the advantage being in operation when a separate system is used for each apartment but the disadvantage is in accommodating the air-cooled condenser in a place with access to a plentiful supply of outside air. A variation for apartment blocks is to provide water-cooled units with multiple cooling towers on the roof and vertical flow and return cooling water mains to feed the self-contained units in each apartment. A third possibility is to install a central water-chilling plant and to distribute chilled water to each apartment for its air-handling unit. At the luxury end of the market the best approach is to treat the apartment block as a high class hotel and use a four-pipe, twin-coil, fan coil system with a common, low-velocity ventilation plant feeding filtered, dehumidified, tempered (in winter) air to each flat. Enough fresh air is delivered in this way to give either 25 l s^{-1} for each person normally present or enough to make good the mechanical extract ventilation, whichever is the greater. Such mechanical extract is essential and should take the form of 25 l s^{-1} from the bathroom and 20 air changes per hour in the kitchen. The fan coil units would be selected to meet the design heat gains and losses when running at slow speed and although the cooler coils would normally do sensible cooling only, condensate drain lines must be fitted and connected into the plumbing system, to cater for the odd occasion when many more than the design population is present. It is also desirable to provide smell removal, which can be done by a comparatively small unit, comprising an activated carbon and an electrostatic filter, handling a proportion of the recirculated airstream. A system for a luxury apartment must have: more than enough capacity to meet the design loads; quietness (NR 20 is the aim); a quick response to a manual resetting at a thermostat; plenty of fresh air; and system reliability. Each room, except the corridor, bathroom and kitchen, should have independent thermostatic control, in contrast to the simpler systems mentioned previously, where an entire house of two three bedrooms etc., is controlled on an average basis from a single thermostat in a corridor.

. In a temperate climate and in the UK, the same principles apply but the case for air conditioning is more difficult to make for this sort of application. The most compelling argument is for dwellings in urban environments where noise and dirt must be kept at bay with double glazing. Air conditioning then becomes a serious consideration, to prevent excessive rises in internal temperature when the windows must be kept shut. However, sensible gains are often less than for offices, with a much lower level of illumination and a smaller proportion of glazing in the walls. Mechanical ventilation, to give an adequate air change rate of, say, 10 per hour, is then a possible alternative. It costs a good deal less than air conditioning to buy and operate, and may give acceptable results although the client must expect an increase in room temperatures above the value outside during part of the summer.

3.5 Shopping centres

The design of air-conditioning systems for shopping centres in the UK is subject to two constraints:
(1) The economic pressures imposed by the need for the developer to pitch the amenities at a level that will command a rent local traders are willing to pay, whilst providing him with a satisfactory return on capital

(2) The desires of the local fire officer to ensure the safe escape of the people present in the event of a fire.

Shopping centre design has tended to follow an established pattern. Central malls are bounded by shopping units and are connected at large squares which become the focal points for aesthetic display, with fountains, exotic lighting, sunshine roofs and sometimes areas for rest fitted with benches and tables and provided with a light refreshment service. Most shopping centres are single-storey or have double height malls with shop units opening directly onto them at ground level and further shops at the first floor, fronting onto a balcony. Sometimes, however, the development is over two conventional storeys, with malls and shop units on each. For a shopping centre to be viable it is necessary that several nationally known chain stores take up important positions in the development, smaller concerns then being encouraged to cluster around them.

Lighting levels in the malls are at 200 to 400 lux but in the shop units they vary, with 500 lux being an average. It is common practice to include one or two supermarkets in a development and these have lighting levels that can be much higher, perhaps up to 2000 lux. The contrast ratio, shops to malls should not be greater than 5:1. The lighting will be provided in a variety of ways in the shops. Food shops, newsagents, chemists and the like will be lit by fluorescent tubes but boutiques, restaurants etc., will have spot lighting and tungsten filament lamps. Fluorescent tubes could produce 200 lux by liberating 15 to 20 Wm^{-2} of floor area, and 500 lux by 25 to 30 Wm^{-2}. Tungsten lamps will dissipate, on average, five times these amounts.

There is little well-established information on population densities in malls and shops. A study of the pattern of customer movement in a department store[1] suggested 2.5 to 1.0 m^2 per person over 60% of the gross floor area, the remainder being counter space. This corresponds to 4.3 to 1.7 m^2 per person over the gross area. Some supermarket operators use 3 m^2 per person. For the malls there is even less information but one suggestion[2] is 10 m^2 per person. Population densities vary enormously, Saturday being busier than any other day, with a peak at Christmas. A reasonable design basis is 3.3 m^2 per person for shop units and 10 m^2 per person for the malls.

The CIBS guide quotes a minimum fresh air allowance of $3 \, ls^{-1} \, m^{-2}$ for shops. For the population densities suggested, this corresponds to $9.9 \, ls^{-1}$ in the shops and $30 \, ls^{-1}$ in the malls, for each person. Both figures are in excess of the alternative CIBS recommended minimum values of 8 and $5 \, ls^{-1}$ for each person. The apparent inconsistency is of no real consequence because the usual supply rate to the malls is 5 to $6 \, ls^{-1} \, m^{-2}$, which is about enough, even when halved in winter for economy of operation.

The conventional design approach in the UK, and elsewhere, is rather different from that usually adopted for other air-conditioning applications. No attempt is made to calculate the supply air quantity needed to offset the heat gains in the malls and shops. Instead, roof-top units supply air to the malls at a rate of 5 or 6 ls^{-1} m^{-2} of floor area. Each shop unit has an extract fan, sometimes two-speed, that draws air from the malls through the shop and discharges it to waste. The shops, therefore, get second-hand air conditioning and are warmer than the malls in summer by about 2°C or more, depending on the activity in them. The tenant in the shop provides his own heating, usually electrical, but there is seldom much need for heating apart from early in the day because of the heat gain from lights, appliances and people. One or more roof-top units, each comprising a direct, gas or oil-fired heater battery, direct-expansion air cooler coil, in-built air-cooled condensing set and centrifugal supply fan (see Section 2.6) are mounted over the malls. They generally deliver air through a low-velocity ducting system to diffusers or side-wall grilles and handle an adjustable mixture of fresh and recirculated air. Extract is locally through a grille in the ceiling of the mall and it is commonly arranged to halve the amount of fresh air in winter, for economy.

This design approach appears to work quite well in the UK and in other parts of the world, where the climate in summer is not extreme. One important point, that cannot be over-emphasised, is the necessity of having conventional doors at the ends of the malls, as it is impossible to prevent the entry of cold draughts by attempting to pressurise the malls or by fitting an air curtain (see Section 2.11). Door heaters are desirable, even so, at the doors, to temper the inrush of cold winter air when they are opened to let people pass through.

A more expensive alternative, used predominantly in Canada and the USA, is to distribute chilled water and provide each shop with a piped-up air-handling unit as well as treating the malls. This assumes that the air-handling units in the shops will be used and a proper rent is charged. Each tenant provides a ducted air-distribution system for the shop at his own expense. A third possibility is to distribute clean, cooling water from a central cooling tower and plate heat exchanger complex to the shop units, in addition to conditioning the malls. The tenant then installs his own heating and his own water-cooled air-conditioning unit. Although cooling water distribution is cheaper than chilled water distribution, because no lagging is required, this approach does not seem to have been extensively adopted.

Large shops, department stores and supermarkets in shopping centres are invariably air conditioned by their own, independent systems and this must be remembered when planning the treatment for the rest of the centre.

The behaviour of fire and the production of smoke in shopping centres has been studied[3] and clear conclusions reached. Because the quantity of combustible material in a shop is large compared with that in a mall it is more likely that a fire will start in a shop, where a layer of hot gas and smoke will rapidly form beneath the ceiling and spread laterally till it reaches the walls of the shop, when the layer will thicken until it reaches the top of any opening through which it can escape. If there are no openings, or if they are too small, the layer of smoke will thicken downwards to below head level in the shop.

Except for large shops, greatly exceeding 1000 m^2 in floor area, the time taken for this to happen is seldom more than a minute or two. When hot, smoky gases escape through openings in the shop front into the mall, they rise and form a layer beneath the ceiling and then rapidly advance, at 1 m s^{-1} or more, towards the ends of the mall. When the end of the mall is open the smoke flows out at high level but local draughts and wind return large amounts back to the mall, where the lower levels are now filled with smoke returning with the cold air inrush to feed the fire. If the ends of mall are closed, the smoke doubles back on itself, again filling the lower reaches of the mall. Therefore, whether the ends of the mall are open or closed, it is rapidly clogged with smoke.

The aim of smoke control is to keep the mall free of smoke so that it can act as an escape route for people. Because of the speed with which smoke spreads, fusible links do not act quickly enough to be of any value in smoke control and smoke detectors must be used to sound an alarm. Ideally, to prevent smoke entering the mall from a fire in a shop, the air pressure in the mall should be 25 to 50 Pa above that in the shop. It may be impracticable with conventional building construction, to achieve this degree of pressurisation but the principle is that air should be supplied to the mall and extracted from the shop, and generally accepted design practice follows this. In the mall itself, the ceiling should be subdivided by downstanding screens into multiple smoke reservoirs, each of 1000 m^2 maximum area. The screens should be reasonable airtight, although small openings around pipes where they pass through the screens are acceptable, and not more than 60 m apart and of at least 1 m depth. Ideally, the screen should extend downward for at least one-third of the way from the ceiling to the floor. It is essential that each smoke reservoir has a natural smoke vent in the ceiling that can be opened to the atmosphere in the event of a fire. This is often done manually when the fire alarm sounds. Mechanical smoke relief systems are not liked because of their dependence on an electrical power supply and the risk of malfunction.

3.6 Supermarkets

There are three prime considerations when determining the heat gains: population density; electric lighting; open refrigerated cabinets.

Figures on population densities in chain stores and supermarkets are not too well-established but one study[1] suggests 1.7 to 4.0 m^2 per person over the gross floor area (Section 3.5). Another suggestion[4] is 3 m^2 per person over the gross floor area. The density varies with the front third having the heaviest load of people. With a conditioned state of 22°C dry-bulb and 50% saturation the heat output per person would be 100 W sensible and 60 W latent.

Since the object of a supermarket is sales, lighting to enhance the attractiveness of the goods on display is most important and illumination levels, mostly by fluorescent tubes, are in the range 1000 to 1500 lux. Extract light fittings should be used, to take away 40% to 50% of the heat liberated at the luminaires (see Section 1.6). For a typical lighting level of 1400 lux, the net gain to the conditioned space could be about 55 Wm^{-2}.

There are two types of open, refrigerated, display cabinet: that with a condenser at the bottom of the cabinet and that with a remote condenser, outside the conditioned space. In the former all the power used by the compressors is an extra load on the room and there is no benefit from the heat absorbed by the frozen food in the cabinets themselves. Stores with this type of display cabinet do not suffer from the underheating sometimes experienced by those having the other type. The second type of open refrigerated cabinet has a big impact on the air-conditioning load. All the heat gain to the cabinets is from the conditioned space and is, therefore, a credit, reducing the sensible heat gain because it is ultimately rejected at the remote condensers. This effect, plus the latent cooling also done at the cabinets, is very significant and must be taken account of when calculating the heat gains, the cooling load and the sensible/total ratio of the cooler coil performance in the central air-handling plant. Complaints sometimes arise[5] because cold air spills out of the cabinets and stratifies above the floor, to a depth of about 1 m. Air distribution can be arranged to deal with this effect, if extract grilles are located at low level, or even in the floor in front of the cabinets. Refrigerated cabinets with remote condensers remove heat from the sales area over 24 hours of the day and 365 days of the year, regardless of the room temperature; clearly, underheating is sometimes a difficulty, at unexpected times.

It is important to maintain humidity at or below 50% to minimise the effect of odours, which are less apparent at lower humidities, and to reduce the latent removal at the cabinets which results in a need for frequent defrosting, shortening the life of the product in the cabinet. High limit humidity control can thus be desirable and, if the sensible/total ratio of the cooler coil condition line is small, i.e. the slope of the condition line from the 'on' to the 'off' states is steep, this may be incompatible with maintaining a required room temperature of 20° to 22°C, unless reheat is used. There is then a good case for using condenser reheat. The simplest way of doing this is by directing hot gas from the compressor to the reheater instead of to the condenser, as required. If this is done the need to stabilise condenser pressure remains, as even when the reheater is being used it may not be able to reject enough heat. A more expensive approach that removes some of the refrigerant pressure control and oil return problems is to use a water-cooled condenser. When this is adopted, a plate heat exchanger is essential to ensure a supply of clean, warm, cooling water from the condenser to the reheater, dirty cooling water being circulated to the cooling tower on the other side of the heat exchanger when it cannot reject enough heat through the reheater.

Overall cooling loads vary from 90 to 120 Wm^{-2} of the total sales floor area, depending on the illumination level and the type of refrigerated cabinet used.

All-air systems of the constant volume, reheat type, preferably using variable proportions of fresh and recirculated air as dictated by the outside air state and an economical operation of the refrigeration plant, should be used. It is highly desirable to design the system to be as simple as possible to operate because the staff of the supermarket are not technically competent to do more than switch it on and off. With this in mind it is common to use air-cooled condensers, obviating the problems of corrosion, scaling and water treatment that would otherwise occur. It is also desirable to adopt heat reclaim techniques, if these are simple, to give economical system operation. Most air-handling plants and air-cooled condensing sets are roof-mounted, proper attention being paid to vibration isolation for the dynamic loads involved (see Section 7.26) and the risks of a noise nuisance to neighbouring properties.

Air distribution by low-velocity ducting should be arranged to deal with the possible spillage of air from refrigerated display cabinets, but sensible gains are not usually big enough to make the use of ceiling diffusers or side wall grilles or slots difficult. Because most of the load is near the entrance, 50% of the total supply air quantity should be delivered to the front third of the sales area. The entrance itself should be provided with a door heater to mitigate the worst effects of infiltration as customers pass through the doors in winter. More air should be supplied than is extracted, to achieve a small but unquantifiable positive air pressure within, and so discourage infiltration.

Example 3.5 A supermarket of dimensions 39 m long, 17.5 m wide, 3.785 m floor-to-ceiling height, is to be air conditioned at $22\frac{1}{2}°C$ dry-bulb, 50% saturation when the outside state is 28°C dry-bulb, 19.5°C wet-bulb (sling). The structural and solar heat gains amount to 25 kW, the population density is 3 m² per person and the illumination level is 1000 lux, obtained by the dissipation of 60 Wm⁻². Extract light fittings are to be used, returning 40% of the heat from the lights to the central air-handling plant. Open, refrigerated, display cabinets absorb 30 kW, of which 15% is latent[5], from the sales area and reject it to air-cooled condensing sets located outside the conditioned space. Natural infiltration amounts to one air change per hour. Determine the supply air quantity and the cooling load if an all-air system is to be used with low-velocity air distribution. State the quantity that ought to be supplied to the front third of the sales area.

Answer The heat gains can be calculated and summarised as follows:

		W
Structural and solar:		= 25000
People: $[(39 \times 17.5)/3] \times 100$		= 22750
Lights: $39 \times 17.5 \times 60 \times 0.6$		= 24570
Infiltration: $(39 \times 17.5 \times 3.785) \times (28 - 22.5) \times 0.33$		= 4690
Total gross sensible heat gain:		= 77010 W
Credit from refrigerated display cabinest: 0.85×30000		= 25500
Total net sensible heat gain:		= 51510 W

Latent gain from people: $[(39 \times 17.5)/3] \times 60$ = 13650

Latent infiltration gain: $(30 \times 17.5 \times 3.785) \times (10.65 - 8.632) \times 0.79$ = 4120

Total gross latent heat gains: = 17770

Credit from refrigerated display cabinets: 0.15×30000 = 4500

Total net latent heat gain: = 13270 W

Sensible/total ratio $= 51510/(51510 + 13270) = 0.8$

For low-velocity air distribution the fan total pressure is likely to be about 625 Pa, giving a rise of about 0.625°C across the supply fan. Assuming short duct runs, allow, say, 0.875°C for duct heat gain, making the total rise from the cooler coil to the conditioned space 1.5°C. An examination of the psychrometry suggests a suitable supply air temperature of 13°C (see Figure 3.2), assuming a four-row cooler coil will be used.

$$\text{Supply air quantity} = \frac{51.51}{(22.5 - 13)} \times \frac{(273 + 13)}{358} = 4.332 \text{ m}^3 \text{ s}^{-1} \text{ at 13 C.}$$

This corresponds to $(4.332 \times 3600)/(39 \times 17.5 \times 3.785) = 6$ air changes per hour, which is well within the capacity of conventional air distribution methods.

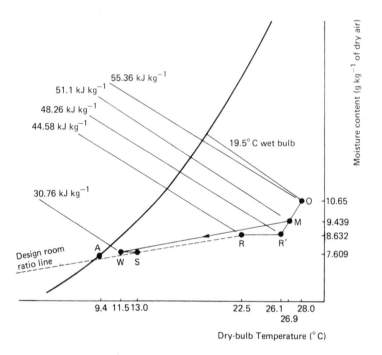

Figure 3.2   Psychrometry for Example 3.5

According to the CIBS Guide a good fresh air allowance would be $8 \, \mathrm{l \, s^{-1}}$ for each person, which is $[(39 \times 17.5)/3] \times 8 = 1820 \, \mathrm{l \, s^{-1}}$. This represents 42% of the supply air quantity, or $2.7 \, \mathrm{l \, s^{-1} \, m^{-2}}$ of floor area, which is well within the recommendations of the CIBS. This can be approximated to 40%, for simplicity.

Assuming that $1 \, \mathrm{l \, s^{-1} \, m^{-2}}$ of the air supplied to the supermarket is allowed to exfiltrate through the entrance, i.e. $0.682 \, \mathrm{m^3 \, s^{-1}}$. The amount mechanically extracted is then $4.332 - 0.682 = 3.65 \, \mathrm{m^3 \, s^{-1}}$ and of this $0.6 \times 4.332 = 2.599 \, \mathrm{m^3 \, s^{-1}}$ is recirculated under design conditions, the remainder being discharged to waste at the plant.

Since the heat picked up by the air extracted through the light fittings and returned to the plant is $39 \times 17.5 \times 60 \times 0.4 = 16380 \, \mathrm{W}$, it suffers a temperature rise of $[16.38 \times (273 + 13)]/(3.65 \times 358) = 3.6°C$. The recirculated air state is thus $26.1°C$ dry-bulb, $8.632 \, \mathrm{g \, kg^{-1}}$ and $48.26 \, \mathrm{kJ \, kg^{-1}}$ and the mixture state onto the cooler coil is as follows:

$$t_m = 0.6 + 26.1 + 0.4 \times 28 = 26.9°C \text{ dry-bulb}$$
$$g_m = 0.6 \times 8.632 + 0.4 \times 10.65 = 9.439 \, \mathrm{g \, kg^{-1}}$$
$$h_m = 0.6 \times 48.26 + 0.4 \times 55.36 = 51.1 \, \mathrm{kJ \, kg^{-1}}$$

The supply moisture content necessary is

$$g_s = 8.632 - \frac{13.27}{4.332} \times \frac{(273 + 13)}{856} = 7.609 \, \mathrm{g \, kg^{-1}}$$

The state off the cooler coil is therefore $11.5°C$ dry-bulb, $7.609 \, \mathrm{g \, kg^{-1}}$ and $30.76 \, \mathrm{kJ \, kg^{-1}}$. At the supply state the specific volume is $0.8201 \, \mathrm{m^3 \, kg^{-1}}$ and the cooling load is, therefore,

$$\frac{4.332}{0.8201} \times (51.1 - 30.76) = 107.4 \, \mathrm{kW}.$$

From the psychrometry (Figure 3.2) the apparatus dew point is $9.4°C$ and so the contact factor is $(26.9 - 11.5)/(26.9 - 9.5) = 0.88$. This is consistent with the assumption of a four-row coil, if the face velocity is low enough, say $2.2 \, \mathrm{m \, s^{-1}}$. The amount of air supplied to the front third of the sales area would be $0.5 \times 4.332 = 2.166 \, \mathrm{m^3 \, s^{-1}}$. The specific cooling load is $107\,400/(39 \times 17.5) = 157 \, \mathrm{W \, m^{-2}}$ floor area.

3.7 Department stores

A department store comprises a complex of different sales areas in which lighting levels vary considerably, population densities are different and internal heat gains from various appliances are possible. The air-conditioning treatment should therefore be subdivided among several plants, the duty of each being related to the load and application of the area treated. Although floor-mounted unitary equipment has been used in the past, it is not popular with store operators because of the valuable sales floor area occupied. Population densities tend to be high and it follows that all-air systems are favoured, generally located on the roof, but occasionally mounted at high level, above suspended ceilings in the sales area itself. Plant mounted at light level in an occupied area is difficult to get at and will not receive proper maintenance. It is much better to seek an outside location with easier access.

Although high-velocity air distribution has been used[6] to help accommodation of the ductwork, noise problems become a risk and the unavoidable, higher fan total pressures cause increased running costs and greater energy consumption. It is better to distribute air at conventional, low velocities, if at all possible. Department store layouts may be changed, from time to time, so the duct and plant design should be conservative, with enough flexibility and capacity built into them to permit any future reallocation of air quantities necessary for load revisions. The modern trend is to use packaged air-handling plant and this sets a practical limit on the area treated by one plant, which should correspond to a maximum supply air quantity of about 15 $m^3 \ s^{-1}$. Final air distribution can usually be through conventional slots, diffusers and grilles. It is good policy to use adjustable diffusers and grilles that allow modification of the air pattern, should this be necessary, to counter complaints of draughts or lack of air movement, particularly after a departmental layout rearrangement. Although several reheaters can be used with one air-handling plant, it is better to split the duty among several plants and have only one heater battery for each. In this way every plant can be economical in running cost, its heater battery being controlled in sequence with its cooler coil to conserve energy[7]. With sequence control it is necessary to introduce a high limit humidistat, set at 50%. Upon rise in humidity the heater battery is overridden but allowed to continue controlling temperature as a reheater, the cooler coil coming on to secure some dehumidification. When the humidity falls the system is permitted to return to its normal mode of control. Multizone systems have been used with success but variable air volume systems require a cautious approach because of the reduction in the fresh air quantity that may accompany a throttled air supply. Variable proportions of fresh and recirculated air should be provided for and it should be arranged that the balance of the supply and extract quantities between departments and from floor-to-floor is such as to avoid excessive air movement along escalators and through doorways.

Central boiler plant and water-chilling plant, located at basement level, are needed to distribute LTHW and chilled water to the air-handling units. While air-cooled condensers are simple to operate it is probable that the refrigeration load will be too big and cooling towers will be wanted.

In broad terms, the major sources of heat gain are the electric lights and the people. Some of the lighting will be by fluorescent tubes but some is likely to be by tungsten filament lamps with as much as five times the dissipation of heat for the same illumination. An overall figure of 60 Wm^{-2} has been suggested[8] with average population densities of 3 m^2 per person in the basement sales area, 4 m^2 per person on the ground floor and 6 m^2 per person on upper floors, compared with those given earlier[1] of 1.7 to 4.3 m^2 per person.

Certain areas have unique problems that merit particular attention. In a Beauty Salon the gains are from dryers and other appliances, in addition to lights and people. One person should be allowed for each basin and dryer, plus one member of staff for every four customers. A negative pressure is necessary in the salon to discourage smells from spreading to other parts of the store and for this reason a separate air-handling plant must always be used for this area. Fitting rooms are usually located around the perimeter of the sales floor and require supplementary heating, in particular if the floor overhangs the street or the car park and so gives an extra heat loss. Alterations rooms have higher heat gains because of steam irons used for pressing, and exhaust in their vicinity is sometimes a good policy, even to the extent of using hoods. At the same time, women sitting down at sewing machines must not feel draughts. Television and hi-fi display areas often suffer very heavy heat gains–a colour television set can liberate 500 W–so a proper allowance must be made, based on the number of sets on view and a diversity factor that is best agreed with the store operators. Local exhaust ventilation may be considered to reduce the worst effects of the heat gains. Lamp sales areas also have exceptionally high heat gains with radiant components that are not directly dealt with by air conditioning. Again, local exhaust may be useful. Entrances must receive extra heating to combat infiltration. Door heaters are the minimum provision and in some instances air curtains have been successful over much of the year (see Section 2.11), enabling the doors to be wide open at times, encouraging the entry of customers. Where possible, without compromising the design commercially, 10 Wm^{-2} may be added to the heat gains to cover an additional and unpredictable use of appliances over and above the other heat gains.

Fresh air allowances should follow the recommendations of the CIBS guide, i.e. 5 to 8 l s^{-1} for each person or 3 l s^{-1} m^{-2}, whichever is the greater.

3.8 Kitchens and restaurants

The essential principle of air distribution in kitchens and restaurants is to arrange for airflow from the restaurant into the kitchen in order to avoid the retention of food smells in the restaurant and the spread of odours to adjacent premises. The essential difference in treatment is that restaurants can be air conditioned to a comfort standard, whereas kitchens cannot. In kitchens there is a high proportion of radiant heat gain and the best that can be done is to cool the supply air to about 12° or 14°C, thus improving temperature conditions of as high as 45°C to about 30°C.

Restaurant loads are predominantly from people, with a population density of 1.8 to 2.0 m^2 per person and electric lighting, largely from tungsten sources, up to 75 Wm^{-2}. Odours from food, people and smoking must be diluted by using recommended fresh air supply rates[9] of from 5 to 8 l s^{-1} for each person. The type of restaurant influences the choice of inside design conditions, lower temperatures (22°C dry-bulb) being chosen for establishments with longer term occupancies, such as night clubs. In this connexion, it is worth noting that because of the high latent heat gain from people the room ratio line may have a steep slope, and maintaining 50% humidity with 22°C dry-bulb may not be a practical proposition with commercially available cooler coils and refrigeration plant. In such cases up to 60% is tolerable and should be the design aim; except during peak occupancy the humidity will be much lower than this. If a bar forms part of a restaurant, extract ventilation should be concentrated over the bar, to remove local smells and tobacco smoke.

Kitchens should have at least 20 air changes per hour of extract ventilation, removed mostly through hoods over the cooking equipment. Exhaust air quantities through hoods should be in accordance with the recommendations of the CIBS guide[9] with an absolute minimum air velocity of 0.3 m s^{-1} over the face of any hood. Hoods are ineffective with velocities less than this. Just as there is some extract from parts of the restaurant, such as the bar, remote from the kitchen, so there is often a need for the supply of air to parts of the kitchen, to supplement the air drawn from the restaurant. Such air must be filtered and tempered in winter and it should be cooled in summer as suggested, if this can be afforded. There should be no attempt to specify a condition to be maintained in the kitchen but it is most important to ensure that the balance of airflow is from the restaurant into the kitchen.

3.9 Auditoria and broadcasting studios

Auditoria may be roughly classified as cinemas, theatres and concert halls, in terms of the importance of noise control and the attention that must be paid to this in the design of the air-conditioning system. The sound production system in cinemas is sufficiently loud to make noise control of least importance among the three but in theatres audibility at all parts of the auditorium is critical and there must be no intrusive noise from the mechanical services. In concert halls audibility is even more important and background noise of any sort is unacceptable. The ASHRAE guide[5] quotes noise criteria that may be interpreted as NR 30 for cinemas and NR 20 for theatres and concert halls.

The major component of the load is from people in all these cases and it is evident that all-air systems are required. Low-velocity air distribution should be used because of the low noise levels necessary and because there is usually enough space to run ductwork. It is suggested[5] that 2 to 3 m^2 per person be allowed for pupulation density in the lobby spaces and 0.75 to 1.0 m^2 per person in the auditorium, referred to the total area including the aisles if a seat count is not possible. In cinemas and theatres the lights are off or dimmed, except when cleaning takes place and it is recommended[5] that 5 to 10% of the installed lighting power be taken for design purposes, coincident with the population load. Electric lighting is seldom a significant proportion of the heat gain in an auditorium of this sort, although in a convention hall this might not be the case.

The situation is quite different on the stage where lighting presents a most complex problem. Lights located around the proscenium can be dealt with by extract fittings that remove 40 to 50% of the heat liberated and return it to the central plant for discharge to waste or recycling, as appropriate. Over the stage itself the presence of movable scenery and the need for spot lighting raise difficulties; on the other hand, theatre-in-the-round, introduced as a break away from traditional stage/audience configurations, may have all its lighting in the auditorium, aiming largely at the stage and representing loads as high as 200 kW for a seating accommodation of 1400[10].

In assessing structural heat gains, advantage can be taken of stratification in high auditoria, if the air supply grilles are 1.5 m or more below the depth assumed to be occupied by the stagnant air. Such stratified air is assumed to suppress the natural convection component of the inside surface heat transfer coefficient, allowing heat gain by radiation only. This is then usually taken as 33% of the total strucutral gain.

An excellent survey of mechanical services in auditoria[10] shows that there are at least six effective possibilities for air distribution:

(1) Downward—air enters from ceiling diffusers and is extracted beneath the seats. This gives draghtless air movement but advantage cannot be taken of stratification. Supplementary heating is needed at the sides, where there is a heat loss and near emergency exits, in winter.

(2) Upward—air is supplied beneath the seats and extracted at high level. This is the best arrangement, in theory, because cooling air is delivered at the place where there is the major source of heat gain, i.e. from the people. Air has been successfully introduced in this way through perforations in the pedestals supporting the seats and also through specially designed perforated diffusers in the risers of the seating tiers. Careful design is essential and this technique of supply should never be used without a preliminary, full-scale, mock-up and a proper programme of test for the air distribution and the air temperatures involved. Draughts at the ankles are the risk and this is exaggerated by a large cooling temperature difference, room-to-supply.

(3) Front-to-rear—long-throw grilles or diffusers are needed and it is difficult to select these for a throw exceeding 10 m without producing too much noise. Taking advantage of stratification is possible if the supply grilles are sufficiently below the level of stratified air. Some variation of temperature and freshness is not unlikely over the length of the auditorium, in the direction of air throw.

(4) Front-of-stage-to-rear—air is blown from beneath the front of the stage to extracts at the rear of the hall. Similar considerations to (3) prevail. There must be a large distance between the stage and the first row of seats, if draughts are to be avoided there. A variant used in some of the early cinema installations was to extract the air on each side of the screen. When this is done supplementary heating is needed at the sides, where there is a winter heat loss.

(5) Rear-to-front—long-throw grilles are needed, with possible noise problems, and supplementary winter heating.

(6) Side-wall supply air with high level extract—this is a cheap arrangement in terms of ductwork but air distribution may not be adequate for the rear of the auditorium or the balcony.

A general comment on air distribution is that auxiliary supply and extract may be needed with any of the above systems at the back of the auditorium, above and beneath the balcony, to deal with vitiated, warm air that may stratify. It is sometimes claimed that air distribution over the large plan area of the auditorium can be helped by relying on the influence of the extract openings. However, it is only the momentum of the supply air that is significant in giving good air distribution[11] and the location of the extract openings is irrelevant in this respect.

The presence of the fly tower over the stage of a theatre introduces a large stack effect that is often apparent by the curtain billowing when it is lowered. There are often side stages and a rear stage in opera houses, and these require air conditioning or ventilation as well as having problems of air distribution.

The local authroity, also the licensing authority in the UK, the building regulations, the fire brigade and other municipal influences, must be consulted when the mechanical and electrical services are being designed. Significant restraints are often imposed by these authorities. For example, the Greater London Council require a minimum fresh air provision of 28 m³ per hour for each person in a place used for public entertainment, but this may be reduced to 14 m³ per hour if air conditioning is installed and the humidity does not exceed 55%. The same authority also requires that, with downflow air systems, the flow must be reversed, i.e. supply grilles becoming extract grilles, and vice-versa, in the event of a fire, to remove the smoke and so help people to escape from the auditorium.

Theatres and opera houses usually have 'crush bars' which are very densely occupied for fifteen minutes or so, once or twice during a performance, i.e. in the intervals. Heat gains from people are then very high indeed and local, temporarily boosted extract may be necessary to supplement the air conditioning. Where a concert hall or theatre forms part of a larger complex, incorporating restaurants, large foyers, bars, and so on, separate plants should be adopted for areas having similar patterns of usage, as for the public room in hotels (Section 3.3). The location of plant, particularly refrigeration machines and boilers, merits special care. On no account should they be in places where noise and vibration can be transmitted to the auditorium. The inside design conditions chosen for the auditorium, or other areas where long-term occupancy is the rule, should be those normally adopted, e.g. 22° to 23°C dry-bulb and up to 55%–60% humidity, in the UK. In entrance foyers, in the UK, it may be reasonable to design for a temperature half-way between that in the auditorium and that outside, bearing in mind that outside temperatures will fall as the time of the evening performance approaches.

Pre-cooling is sometimes advocated for the two or three hours preceding a performance to reduce the size of the installed cooling capacity necessary, but this does not always give good results, since temperatures at the start of a performance are too low and they rise to uncomfortably high values by its end. According to a survey[10], installed cooling capacities seem to be an average of 15 to 25 kW of refrigeration per 100 seats in European auditoria.

Television and broadcasting studios are very special cases indeed. Quite apart from the need to select quiet running plant, provided with adequate silencers and mounted on properly selected vibration isolators, the air distribution from the supply grilles or diffusers may cause far too much noise. The problem is made worse by the very high lighting loads, 300 Wm^{-2} being common in the UK, and as much as 600 Wm^{-2} in Europe. The studios often have very large floor-to-ceiling heights. There may be a subceiling, acting as a walk-way for maintenance and access to the lights supported from it. The space above this can be 5 to 6 m high and the space in the studio beneath it as much as 12 m. Extreme care must be taken with the design of the air distribution system. Air has been successfully supplied at high level above the suspended walk-way, to spread evenly over it and diffuse downward through it into the studio, giving 20 to 25 air changes, over its height of 12 m. All supply and extract ducting must be acoustically lined, minimum 50 mm thick, in addition to the silencers required at the plant. A maximum velocity is 2.5 ms^{-1} through the free area of grilles or slots and velocities in the ductwork must not exceed 3.5 ms^{-1}.

3.10 Museums, art galleries and libraries

Books, paintings and some other valuable articles are often made of hygroscopic materials that expand and contract with variations in the ambient humidity. Such movements eventually cause cracks and deterioration. Since humidity is temperature-dependent it follows that both should be controlled if the objects stored or on display are to be protected. Furthermore, the air-conditioning system must run continuously and must also have adequate stand-by features. Although natural daylight is preferred for viewing paintings, spotlights are sometimes used in art galleries, and these impose local radiant heat gains that exacerbate the thermal and hygroscopic movements referred to. Enclosing articles of value in glass-fronted cases is not always an answer as the cases breath as they undergo thermal expansion and contraction, possibly made worse by spotlights. One solution is to enclose very valuable objects in hermetically sealed cases filled with helium. Another approach is to feed a supply of conditioned air to each case and so keep it at a slight positive pressure in relation to the ambient air and in a controlled condition.

Apart from strucutural gains the load is from people and lights, the population density varying from an average of 10 m² per person to a possible occasional peak of 2 or 3 m² per person for special exhibitions, or for a social function. Lighting is unlikely to exceed 500 lux, produced by fluorescent tubes liberating 25 Wm^{-2} of floor area.

Atmospheric impurities in the outside air, notably SO_2, and even SO_3, are a danger to leathers, paper, textiles, wood and paint. Smoking is seldom permitted but, if allowed, will also damage these materials and many others. Filtration should, therefore, be aimed at removing these undesirable contaminants in both the outside and recirculated air.

All-air, low-velocity systems are the natural choice and if control over both temperature and humidity is demanded then constant dew-point plants with reheat are required. In many cases it is sufficient to keep the humidity reasonably constant at any value in the comfort zone, without paying too much attention to the precise value selected. Thus, 40% ± 5%, or 55% ± 5%, might be acceptable. It should be remembered that the first step to good control over humidity is good control over temperature.

3.11 Swimming pools

A swimming pool is intended for bathers and their comfort is best served, in the UK, by a water temperature of 27°C in the pool and the same air temperature above it. Air-conditioning a swimming pool hall to the comfort standards commonly accepted in this country for fully-clothed people is clearly out of the question. If the comfort of the spectators is a matter of concern they should be screened from the pool hall by vapour-tight glass partitions and conditioned by a separate, all-air plant. The pool hall itself must be ventilated and the following considerations apply in doing this:

The swimming pool complex
Pools in the UK are commonly built to three standards:
(1) County—25 m × 12.8 m, containing about 640 000 l
(2) National—33.3 m × 12.8 m, containing about 910 000 l
(3) Olympic—50 m × 17 m, containing about 2 270 000 l
A diving pit is assumed at one end, and a depth of 1 m at the shallow end. Teaching pools are much smaller, 12.8 m × 7.3 m, containing about 60 000 l and of a depth 600 to 700 mm. The rest of the accommodation generally provided includes changing rooms, toilets, showers and preclensing foot

baths, cafeteria, administrative offices and a plant room. Terraced seating is the rule along one side of the pool, to deal with 200 to 300 people but sometimes as many as 2000 people can be seated, along both sides of the pool[14].

Mechanical ventilation

Mechanical ventilation is essential and must run continuously. Its purpose is to keep the humidity within the pool hall to an acceptably low level in both summer and winter, to minimise the extent of condensation forming on cold surfaces in winter, to minimise the rise in air temperature in summer, to dilute the concentration of objectionable odours and to provide an adequate supply of fresh air. It is also often used to offset the winter heat loss. A study[12] of the consequences of adopting different ventilation rates indicates that $15\,\mathrm{l\,s^{-1}\,m^{-2}}$ of wetted surface area is not enough to prevent humidity from becoming too high at certain times of the year nor enough to prevent condensation streaming down single glazed windows. It is recommended that $20\,\mathrm{l\,s^{-1}\,m^{-2}}$ of wetted surface area be supplied[12]. This higher rate deals with the problem of high humidities for most of the year in the UK, except perhaps for the warmest summer weather. Condensation will still occur in winter on single glazing.

The evaporation rate, q_e, from the wetted surface areas can be calculated from

$$q_e = (0.0885 + 0.0779v)(p_w - p_s)\ \mathrm{W\,m^{-2}} \tag{3.1}$$

where v is the relative air velocity across the wetted surface in $\mathrm{ms^{-1}}$, p_w is the vapour pressure in Pa exerted by the water at its particular temperature, t_w, and p_s is the partial pressure in Pa of the water vapour in the air above the surface. There is some doubt as to the air velocity to choose but, for comfort conditions, $0.15\ \mathrm{ms^{-1}}$ is a reasonable value. If t_w as 27°C then p_w is 3564 Pa and, with $v = 0.15\ \mathrm{ms^{-1}}$, Equation (3.1) becomes

$$q_e = 357 - 0.1\,p_s \tag{3.2}$$

It is usual to take the wetted surface area as the pool surface plus 20% for the wetted surrounds, when using Equation (3.2) and when estimating the total supply air quantity.

Dressing rooms must be ventilated by a separate plant using 100% fresh air and giving 10 air changes per hour. Less than this rate is poor practice and 6 air changes per hour is totally inadequate for dealing with odours and helping to keep the floor dry. Pool halls and dressing rooms should be maintained at a slightly negative air pressure to discourage the migration of smells to adjoining premises.

The performance of a swimming pool hall in humidifying the ventilating air passing through it can be regarded as similar to that of an inefficient, steam-pan humidifier.

Example 3.6 A swimming pool measures 25 m long × 12.8 m wide and is maintained at a water temperature of 27°C. If the air in the pool hall is also at 27°C dry-bulb, when the outside air is at −1°C saturated, determine the humidity in the pool hall if it is ventilated at a rate of (a) 15 l s^{-1} m^{-2} and (b) 20 l s^{-1} m^{-2}. Assume 100% fresh air is used.

Answer

(a) The total supply rate of fresh air is $(1.2 \times 25 \times 12.8 \times 15)/1000 = 5.76$ m^3 s^{-1}, which will have a moisture content of 3.484 g kg^{-1}; from psychrometric tables, which shall be assumed to be expressed at a temperature of 27°C. From Equation (2.4) its latent cooling capacity can be calculated as

$$[5.76 \ (g_r - 3.484) \ 856]/(273 + 27) = 16.44 \ g_r - 57.26 \text{ kW} \tag{3.3}$$

The latent heat gain from the pool and its wetted surrounds, from Equation (3.2), is

$$[1.2 \times 25 \times 12.8 \times (357 - 0.1 \ p_s)]/1000 = 137.1 - 0.04 \ p_s \text{ kW} \tag{3.4}$$

Assuming different values for the percentage saturation (μ) in the hall with a dry-bulb temperature of 27°C, will give corresponding values for the moisture content (g_r) and the vapour pressure (p_s) of the air therein. Using Equations (3.3) and (3.4) latent cooling capacities and gains can be calculated. (b) With a supply rate of 20 l s^{-1} m^{-2} the total ventilation quantity is calculated as 7.68 m^3 s^{-1} and Equation (3.3) is modified to yield a new latent cooling capacity of

$$[7.68(g_r - 3.484) \ 856]/(273 + 27) = 21.91 \ g_r - 76.35 \text{ kW} \tag{3.5}$$

The calculation procedure may now be repeated, using Equations (3.4) and (3.5). The results for (a) and (b) can be tabulated as

μ (%)	g_r (g kg^{-1})	p_s (Pa)	Latent heat gain (kW)	Latent cooling capacity (kW) Ventilation rate (1 s^{-1} m^{-2}) 15	20
25	5.696	916.2	100.5	36.4	48.4
30	6.835	1097	93.2	55.1	73.4
35	7.974	1277	86.0	73.8	98.4
40	9.113	1459	78.7	92.6	123.3
45	10.250	1636	71.7	111.2	148.2

From this, a balance between gains and capacity occurs when for (a), μ = 37.5%; and for (b), μ = 33%.

If the relative velocity across the pool surface had been assumed to be doubled, at 0.3 ms^{-1}, Equation (3.2) would become

$$q_e = 399 - 0.11 \ p_s \tag{3.6}$$

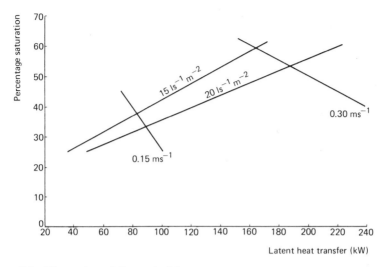

Figure 3.3   Illustration of Example 3.6

The cooling capacity Equations (3.3) and (3.5) are unaltered but the latent gain increases according to Equation (3.6). Figure 3.3 shows the answers to Example 3.6, and also that the humidity can rise to 59% if $15\ \mathrm{l\,s^{-1}\,m^{-2}}$ is supplied and to 53% if $20\ \mathrm{l\,s^{-1}\,m^{-2}}$ is delivered when the air velocity goes up to $0.3\ \mathrm{ms^{-1}}$.

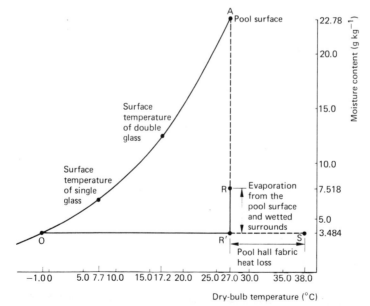

Figure 3.4   Psychrometry of pool hall ventilation in Example 3.6

If the hall suffered a heat loss of, say, 100 kW for an outside temperature of $-1°C$, and was ventilated at a rate of $20 \, 1s^{-1} \, m^{-2}$ then the supply air temperature necessary to offset the heat loss would be

$$t_s = 27 + \frac{100}{7.68} \times \frac{(273 + 27)}{358} = 38°C, \text{ from Equation (2.3).}$$

Figure 3.4 shows what might happen. Fresh air is warmed from $-1°C$ (state O) to 38°C (state S) and supplied to the pool hall, offsetting the heat loss and falling to 27°C (state R'). The air then flows over the pool surface and if this were infinitely long would attain 27°C saturated (state A). In fact, it is humidified by evaporation from the pool and the wetted surrounds to state R, at 33% and 27°C. It can be inferred that the pool has a humidifying efficiency of $[(7.518 - 3.484)100]/(22.78 - 3.484) = 21\%$, for a relative velocity of $0.15 \, ms^{-1}$.

Although using recirculated air is a possibility it is generally considered wiser to use 100% fresh air. Energy can be reclaimed from the exhaust air by the use of run-around coils[13] and transferred to the incoming fresh air (see Section 9.2).

Condensation

Taking the inside surface resistance of glass to be $0.123 \, m^2°C^{-1} \, W^{-1}$ and that outside to be $0.055 \, m^2°C^{-1} \, W^{-1}$, it can be estimated that the surface temperature of single glazing is $27 - [0.123/(0.055 + 0.123)](27 + 1) = 7.7°C$. With an air gap having a resistance of $0.178 \, m^2 \, °C^{-1} \, W^{-1}$ a similar calculation shows that the room-side surface temperature of double glazing is 17.2°C. Single glazing will stream with moisture all the time in design winter weather, particularly at night-time when outside air temperatures will drop below $-1°C$. Even if double glazing is used, condensation must be expected on the frames, if they are metal and do not include a thermal break. Condensation on roof lights and their frames, and even on roof beams too if they are steel and can reach a low temperature by conduction to outside, is also a possibility. This sort of condensation may escape notice and result in unexpected corrosion if a suspended ceiling conceals the roof. When suspended ceilings are fitted it is recommended that a branch duct should supply fresh air to the ceiling void, so pressurising it and discouraging the entry of humid, corrosive air from the pool hall.

Air distribution

Common sense should prevail in the location of supply openings, whose positions are much more critical for good air distribution than are those of the extract grilles. One of the best methods is to blow air upwards at the side walls and windows, particularly the latter where cold down draughts will be a problem otherwise.

Heat recovery

A pair of eight-row, run-around coils, with 320 fins per metre and a face velocity of about 2.5 ms^{-1} in the fresh and discharge air ducts will have a heat transfer effectiveness of about 50%. If such coils are used it is recommended that the coil in the discharge air duct should have copper tubes and fins, electro-tinned after manufacture. Some consideration should also be given to extra protection for the framework, which is normally made of galvanised mild steel. Thermal wheels will give much larger heat transfers and efficiencies, but at greater capital cost. It is not uncommon for the metallic fill of one type of thermal wheel to corrode quite rapidly, when handling swimming pool hall exhaust air. A further and most useful possibility for heat reclaim[13] is to use plate heat exchangers to transfer heat from the waste water leaving the showers to the cold feed for the HWS (hot water service) vessels.

Boiler power

The initial heating up of the water in the pool does not coincide with the demands for heating, ventilating and HWS. A reasonable basis for estimating the boiler power is to sum the heating requirements occurring simultaneously, as follows: fabric heat loss + fresh air load for ventilation + $\frac{1}{7}$°C h^{-1} for evaporative losses from the main pool + $\frac{2}{7}$°C h^{-1} for the evaporative losses from a teaching pool + the HWS load.

3.12 Bowling centres

For this competitive market, air conditioning has seldom been adopted in the UK, ventilation sufficing, but in warmer climates it is essential for the comfort of the spectators and bowlers. The major feature of the heat gain is the presence of large numbers of people in only a small part of the floor area, the lanes being unoccupied and, therefore, neither ventilated nor air conditioned, although air is sometimes exhausted above the pin setting machinery. Peak loads occur between 6 pm and 11 pm on weekdays and in the afternoon on public holidays and at weekends. Fresh air allowances should be generous to counter odours and smoking and 12 to 18 l s^{-1} per person is recommended.

Because only the area up to the foul line is treated, it is common to fit a curtain wall, sometimes transparent, coming down part of the way from the ceiling over the foul line to assist the separation between the conditioned and non-conditioned areas. It is important that this should not obscure the view of the spectators or the bowlers.

Although packaged units have been used, in the more competitive situations, the best air distribution and the best results are achieved with all-air systems, probably multi-zone to cater for the ancillary areas such as bars, cafeterias, etc., and low velocity ductwork. Air is commonly supplied from a duct running parallel to the foul line and blowing air from double deflection grilles at a height of no more than 3.7 m from the floor, towards the bowlers and spectators. No more than two lanes should be dealt with by one grille. Air is exhausted at the back of the spectator area and recirculation can be used provided that precautions are taken that it is not from contaminated areas such as the cafeteria or from the bar, where smells and smoke are likely to be pronounced. It appears[14] that in the United States, air change rates over the occupied area are between 10 and 15 per hour and that the supply air rate is between 215 and 270 l s^{-1} for each lane. Cooling loads lie in the range from 3.8 to 6.4 kW of refrigeration per lane.

3.13 Clean rooms

The presence of moisture, dirt and impurities in certain machinery, assembly and production work spoils the high quality of the finished product and it becomes necessary to control the contamination by arranging for the work to be done in a clean room, or at a clean work station. Contamination control is best achieved[15] in a clean room by adhering to the following five principles:
(1) Preventing particulate matter from entering the room
(2) Continuously purging the room of particles by providing a high air change rate
(3) Preventing particles from settling onto the product
(4) Restricting the generation of particulate matter within the room by the people present and their activity
(5) Arranging for the components dealt with, and the people handling them to be thoroughly cleaned, prior to entering the room.

It is claimed[16] that although well-designed clean room systems should prevent the entry of particles exceeding 0.5 μ in diameter, the main source of contamination is the activity of the work people themselves, who are continuously shedding skin, hair and clothing fibres. Initially clean rooms were air conditioned using conventional methods of air distribution with a high efficiency particulate air filter—the HEPA filter—introduced in about 1950. The HEPA filter is defined as having an efficiency of at least 99.97%, on a volumetric basis, for particles of 0.3 μ diameter, using the diocyte phthallate (DOP) test. Clean rooms conditioned in this way were often unsuccessful in keeping the particle count down to the desired level because of the turbulent nature of the air distribution which did not provide a self-cleaning facility. Small particles became permanently trapped and circulated in eddies in some parts of the room. It was also found that low levels of contamination were only possible after the activity in the room had ceased and the conditioning system run for some further considerable time. A resumption of the activity immediately raised the contamination level. It was clear that a satisfactory level of contamination control depended on more than the quality of the filtration and that a new approach to air distribution was needed. Laminar flow air distribution was introduced in 1960 and successfully achieved the low particle counts desired by providing a supply airflow without turbulence that gave a self-cleaning function and flushed out dust particles from all parts of the room.

Several standards of cleanliness have been proposed but that gaining general acceptance is Federal Standard 209a[17], with a modification, Federal Standard 209b[18]. These standards define the following three classes:

(1) Class 100—fewer than 100 particles ft^{-3} (3.53 l^{-1}) of size 0.5 μ or greater

(2) Class 10000—fewer than 10000 particles ft^{-3} (353 l^{-1}) of size 0.5 μ or greater or fewer than 65 particles ft^{-3} (2.29 l^{-1}) of size 5.0 μ or greater

(3) Class 100000—fewer than 100000 particles ft^{-3} (3530 l^{-1}) of size 0.5 μ or greater, or fewer than 700 particles ft^{-3} (24.71 l^{-1}) of size 5.0 μ or greater.

These definitions are based on statistical methods of particle count and some local deviations are to be expected. Temperature, humidity and air pressure must also be within specified limits for a given operation performed. Federal Standard 209b quotes various tolerances of which the most stringent is 72 $\pm$ 1°F (22.22 $\pm$ 0.56°C) and 40 $\pm$ 5% relative humidity. It is not uncommon to specify that a clean room should be at least 25 Pa (0.1 inches of water) above the ambient air pressure and, for a complex of several clean rooms, it is customary to stage the air pressure difference by about 12 Pa (0.05 inches of

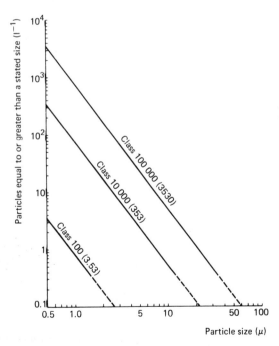

Figure 3.5   Particle size distribution for Federal Standard 209

water) from room to room. Figure 3.5 illustrates the distribution of particle sizes related to the three classes of Federal Standards 209a and b. There is also a Marshall Space Flight Centre Standard 246, developed at the same time as Federal Standards 209, but it is open to criticism because the distribution of particle sizes was not established and is regarded as inferior to them.

There are two forms of laminar flow clean room design: downflow and cross-flow, the former being the more effective but more expansive (primarily because more air is handled). With the downflow version the whole of the ceiling is covered with HEPA filters which introduce the air uniformly and produce laminar flow down to the floor. This consists of a grating behind which a washable, or throw-away, prefilter is supported by a wire mesh. The underfloor space serves for the distribution of cables etc. for the lighting and power requirements in the clean room. The supports for the floor grating must be designed to withstand the anticipated loads and to allow sections to be removed for servicing the prefilter units. The ceiling framework supporting the HEPA filters must be strong enough to withstand their weight when dirty, plus the force imposed by the maximum pressure drop across them. Because these filters occupy the space normally given to lights, surface mounted fluorescent tubes are often adopted and fitted along the lines of the filter frames, the laminar flow lines then separating to pass the tubes and reforming after them. As much as 1000 to 4000 lux is often needed at work bench level and is a major source of sensible gain in the room.

Figure 3.6 illustrates schematically how the air-conditioning system may be arranged for a downflow clean room. Primary and secondary fans are required

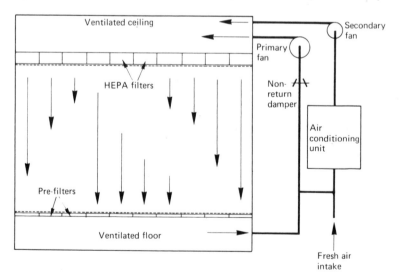

Figure 3.6　Schematic representation of an air-conditioning system for a laminar downflow clean room

(see also Section 3.16) and the-conditioning system should be able to maintain room conditions with the primary fan off. To do this proper account must be taken of the much reduced heat gain during non-working periods in the clean room when the main heat-producing equipment in it will be off. The air-conditioning system must have automatic controls of a quality allowing the necessary turn-down. Consideration should also be given to the influence of the reduced airflow rate on the air distribution in the room, remembering that a loss of laminar characteristics may not matter when there is no activity in the room.

With laminar flow there is little transfer of particles from one streamline to another and they tend to stay in a streamline until captured by a filter. Airflow is predictable and although laminar flow is partially disturbed by the presence of people and furniture, only clean air is present in the limited area of turbulence around an object and the streamlines reform after it, carrying away any contamination introduced by the object. The advantage of laminar downflow is complete isolation of every activity by the streamlines and so the lowest possible contamination level. The disadvantages are that more air is handled than with cross-flow and the costs of the room and its air-handling system are greater.

In cross-flow design, the whole of the smallest wall is covered with HEPA filters, due regard being paid to their support and protection from accidental damage on the room-side, usually by a protective screen over the filter. The opposite wall is usually the prefilter. Figure 3.7a illustrates a single crossflow arrangement and in Figure 3.7b we see a double cross-flow design, used when an unobstructed working space is wanted for 100 m or more. The chief advantages of cross-flow designs are that heavier floor loadings than with downflow systems are tolerable and costs are less. The disadvantages are that the standard of cleanliness changes across the room from 'white' at the supply wall through increasing shades of 'greyness' to the prefilter at the extract wall and so operations are not isolated, downstream being dirtier than upstream, even though laminar flow is maintained, because of the contamination introduced by people and their activities. It is, therefore, customary to grade the activities, and locate those needing the higher standards of cleanliness nearer to the supply wall. Because laminar flow stratifies, horizontal temperature gradients sometimes develop with heat-producing equipment, the heat from one item being carried to the next, downstream.

Duct systems should be well constructed of nonflaking and corrosion-resistant materials, preferably in stainless steel but aluminium is acceptable except in coastal areas. Circular section ducts are preferred to rectangular and they should be tested for leaks and sealed before acceptance. HEPA filters must be on the high pressure side of fans and as close as possible to the clean room itself. An increase of 100% in filter resistance, clean-to-dirty, is the usual basis for replacement and HEPA filters then last about 18 months, on average,

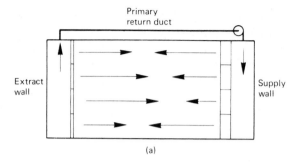

(a)

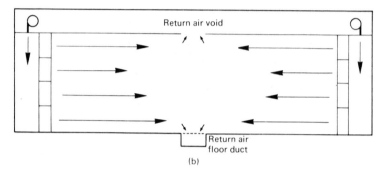

(b)

Figure 3.7a, Single laminar cross-flow. The secondary system is not shown; b, Double cross-flow. The secondary system is not shown

with final resistances sometimes as high as 2.5 kPa, if they are properly protected by prefilters. To keep a reasonably constant airflow through the clean room it is desirable to include a motorised, variable-position damper which is partially closed when the HEPA filter is clean and is gradually opened as it gets dirty, control being from a flow-sensing device in the ductwork at a carefully chosen position. The fan used should have a fairly steep pressure-volume characteristic curve at its point of rating, implying a backward curved impeller in a centrigual fan. It is very important to fit HEPA filters carefully so that dirty air cannot bypass them.

During construction of the room and installation of its air-conditioning system continual attention must be paid to cleaning and all dirt-producing activities must be carried out as far as possible from the clean room and plant. Conventional installation and construction procedures will not do. All air-handling units must be well cleaned and sealed before they leave the manufacturer's works; all openings in the duct system or plant must be sealed until required for use; after erection the ductwork itself must be thoroughly cleaned with an industrial vacuum cleaner and sealed until needed. Airflow should never be permitted though the system without the HEPA filter in place.

It ought to go without saying that similar standards of care and hygiene are essential in the construction and operation of the room itself, and achieving a high quality clean room standard depends on more than the efficiency of the HEPA filter.

Plant space is often at a premium and because compactness seldom goes hand-in-hand with quiet system operation or smooth air distribution across the face of coils, filters and duct sections, a good deal of ingenuity is often needed in designing the plant layout. Noise levels in the clean room must be considered and transmitted vibration can adversely affect the work being done in it.

The entrance to a laminar flow clean room should be protected by a hallway but if it is in a highly contaminated district an air lock is needed. Air showers are sometimes fitted in air locks and are needed with conventional air distribution clean room systems. They are intended to dust personnel before they enter the clean room and, to achieve this, high velocity jets of air impinge on the person in the air lock from opposite sides, at 70 to 150 km h^{-1}, in order to make the clothing flutter vigorously. Extract is through the floor and timed, interlocked doors ensure enough time is spent in the air shower to achieve adequate garment cleaning. Pass boxes are small air locks in the walls of the clean room through which tools, other equipment and materials may be passed.

It is considered[16] that clean rooms with laminar downflow can be successfully operated with air velocities as low as 0.25 ms^{-1} but values of 0.50 ms^{-1} are more typical.

Example 3.7 A clean room is proposed with dimensions 10 m long × 5 m wide × 3 m high. Illumination is 2000 lux at bench level, by the liberation of 90 Wm^{-2} of floor area from surface-mounted fluorescent tubes and four people are to work within the room. All surrounding rooms are maintained at 21°C dry-bulb, 45% saturation, which is also the state required in the clean room. Heat gains from equipment amount to 500 W. Calculate the supply air quantities needed for (a) a downflow laminar system and (b) a cross-flow laminar system. In each case determine the supply air temperature.
Answer Assume a velocity of airflow of 0.5 ms^{-1}.

Sensible heat gain $= (90 \times 10 \times 5) + (4 \times 90) + 500 = 5360$ W

(a) Downflow laminar system

Supply air quantity $= 0.5 \times 10 \times 5 = 25$ m^3 s^{-1}

Supply air temperature $= 21 - \dfrac{5.36}{25} \times \dfrac{(273 + 21)}{358} = 20.8°C$

Air change rate $= (25 \times 3600)/(10 \times 5 \times 3) = 600$ h^{-1}.

(b) Cross-flow laminar system

Supply air quantity $= 0.5 \times 5 \times 3 = 7.5$ m^3 s^{-1}

Supply air temperature $= 21 - \dfrac{5.36}{7.5} \times \dfrac{(273+21)}{358} = 20.41\,^\circ C$

Air change rate $= (7.5 \times 3600)/(10 \times 5 \times 3) = 180$ h^{-1}.

3.14 Hospitals

Hospitals in the UK have not always been fully air conditioned, except for new buildings in urban areas where ambient noise and atmospheric pollution necessitate having closed, double glazed windows[19]. Air conditioning has been restricted by economic considerations and has been confined to places where it was essential, e.g. operating theatres. Although balanced, mechanical ventilation has been used to limit the spread of smells from service areas, e.g. kitchens and places providing a source of odour or infection, wards have often relied on the natural ventilation afforded by opening windows. In warmer climates, on the other hand, the need for air conditioning is more apparent and it is claimed[5] that its provision in wards does not merely give comfort but is actually conducive to successful therapy and promotes a more rapid recovery by patients.

In the design of air conditioning or ventilating systems it is essential to restrict the dissemination of infection between different areas and to discourage the spread of smells. Four aspects of design help to achieve these aims:

(1) Different departments should be treated by independent systems

(2) A balance must be secured between the supply and extract air quantities to maintain a slightly negative or positive pressure in certain areas, according to the desire to limit the emission or admission of microbial infection and/or smells

(3) A relatively bacteria-free air quality should be achieved by adopting a proper standard of filtration efficiency

(4) Enough fresh air must be handled to dilute odours to an acceptably low level.

HEPA filters are effective in achieving a low bacteria count[15,16] by removing virtually all particles from the airstream down to one micron (1 μ) in size.[20] It is claimed[21] that the standards of fresh air supply recommended for hospitals are based on outdated and insufficient studies[22,23] but there is evidence[21] that as much as 80% of the air supplied can be recirculated from the treated space provided, of course, that it is properly filtered. The rates of fresh air supply recommended by ASHRAE are, nevertheless, quite satisfactory. CIBS, on the other hand, does not make recommendations directly but refers to the figures quoted in the various Hospital Building Notes, published by the Department of Health and Social Security. There is every reason to suppose that both these sources give satisfactory recommendations.

It is important that air washers, sprayed cooler coils, and the like, should not be used because they may be the focal points for the production and dissemination of microbial infection. When humidification is necessary it should be done by the injection of sterile, dry steam into the ducted airstream (see Section 3.15).

Although induction and fan coil systems have been used in hospitals, the presence of secondary cooler coils, emergency condensate trays and secondary filters or lint screens inside the treated space creates a harbouring place for microbes and possible source of infection. Of the air-water systems available, that best suited to hospital wards and similar areas, is the chilled ceiling, with an auxiliary air supply (Section 2.14). Through-the-wall room air conditioners are not really suitable because they also form local centres of potential infection and their use should only be regarded as a temporary expedient. All-air, centralised systems offer a good solution for hospitals generally, and of the three most apt, constant volume with reheat, double duct and variable air volume, the first two are likely to be the most expensive in both capital and running cost and the third the cheapest in these respects as well as the best. One favourable feature of the variable air volume system is its ability to run at low capacity and low noise levels with low energy consumption at night-time, when cooling loads are reduced and patients are sleeping in wards.

Hospitals must run for 24 hours each day and this imposes a need for a measure of stand-by in the refrigeration machines, air-handling units, pumps, boiler plant and air compressors for pneumatic controls. It is also necessary to have stand-by, diesel driven, electrical generators for at least the essential hospital services. Whenever stand-by plant is considered, it should always be chosen and installed in a way that will not allow it to deteriorate. Thus belted, running motors should be fitted as stand-by on fans, rather than motors that are static when on stand-by and will suffer bearing deformation by brinelling.

3.15 Operating theatres

Many operating theatres have been air conditioned using conventional methods of turbulent air distribution but, as with clean rooms (Section 3.13), this proves unsatisfactory in the prevention of airborne contamination. There are three sources of bacterial contaminants: the supply of air to the theatre; the surgical team; and the emissions of bodily vapours and organisms from the patient. To deal with these and to prevent turbulent air movement and convection currents from lifting pathogens, mixing them by entrainment with the supply air and depositing them on the patient, the best steps to take are as follows.

(1) Provide special body exhaust suits for the surgical team, with extract

openings at the crotch, armpits and nose, or body exhaust systems each comprising a face mask with a removeable transparent visor, a hood, and a gown of low permeability material from which air is exhausted under the hood and upward beneath the gown. Flexible hoses are attached to the backs of such body exhaust ensembles and a microphone is fitted in each face mask. Members of the surgical team are kept refreshed by the continuous flow of conditioned air and fatigue is diminished

(2) Provide an exhaust system at the operating table itself, for the removal of the emissions and organisms from the patient, in the vicinity of the wound.

(3) Provide a laminar downflow system of air distribution over the patient, the surgical team and the operating table, at a mean speed of between 0.3 and 0.4 ms^{-1} which is high enough to wash away any pathogens that may be deposited. It has been found[24] that velocities as high as 0.6 ms^{-1} are unsatisfactory because the exposed internal tissues of the patient are over-cooled and dried out by evaporation

(4) Provide terminal HEPA filters to remove virtually all dust particles above 0.3 μ in size. It is also necessary to install local exhaust in the vicinity of the anaesthetist to carry anaesthetic vapours away from him.

According to Green et al.,[20] airborne bacteria invariably attach themselves to dust particles and very small water droplets, 80% of the particles/droplets exceeding 2 μ in size and most of bacteria conveyed being of about 1 μ in size. Fungus cells and spores are in the range 3 to 20 μ and are not attached to carrier particles. Particles of size less than 0.3 μ play no significant part in conveying pathogens. It is general practice to use 100% fresh air because although it contains bacteria and other contaminants, these are seldom of the type (streptococci and staphylococci) that are major sources of wound infection.[25] Fresh air is thus very much better than recirculated air from operating theatres. It has been reported[26] that staphylococci thrive better in dry air (humidity less than 35%) and moist air (humidity greater than 65%), than at intermediate humidities. This evidence has been verified and extended[27] to claim that there is a general decrease in the life of many airborne microorganisms when the humidity lies between 20% and 45%. Earlier work[28] showed similar results and tendencies.

Typical operating theatres have plan dimensions of about 6 m × 6 m with floor-to-ceiling heights of approximately 3 m. It is impractical to use fully the downflow techniques of clean rooms over the whole of the area of the theatre and, in any case, an extract-ventilated floor poses structural porblems and is restrictive in theatre use. One approach[24] that is most effective in producing laminar downflow where it is wanted is to provide an enclosure of plan dimensions 3 m × 3 m within the theatre and surround the surgical team and patient with it; the supporting services team (anaesthetist, etc.) is in the theatre, outside the enclosure, which is air conditioned by conventional air distribution which uses 100% fresh air and HEPA filters. The enclosure comprises rigid, transparent, plastic, demountable panels, suspended from the ceiling or supported by four corner posts. The side panels are of modular construction, allowing openings with various dimensions to be provided in appropriate positions for the access of X-ray machines, etc. It is usually arranged that only the part of the patient that is being operated on is within the enclosure, the rest of the body, together with the anaesthetist, is outside. The laminar downflow of air escapes under the bottom edges of the enclosure, which do not reach to the floor, and prevents the inflow of bacterial contaminants. Members of the surgical team may leave the enclosure and later return, provided they put on a freshly sterilised body exhaust suit. Wrapped, sterile instruments can be passed from the outer theatre into the enclosure. Convection currents from lights over the table tend to spoil the laminar downflow. One solution to this is supporting the lights from the ventilating ceiling within the enclosure in a special way, and another is in having the lights outside the enclosure but with their beams directed through its transparent walls onto the patient.

A modification of the laminar downflow enclosure is to use partial walls[29] that do not extend very far down from the ceiling. The aim is to simulate the characteristics of the core of a freely flowing jet[30] over the surgical team and patient by restraining the natural expansion of the laminar downflow over a short distance. Apparently successful laminar downflow can be achieved at the table level provided that the airflow initially delivered is 20% to 25% more than would be handled by an enclosure extending to within 600 mm or so, of the floor. A possible disadvantage seems to be that entrainment of air from the outer portion of the theatre could contaminate sterile instruments stored outside the clean area. A third version[31], used in Scandinavia, encloses the clean, downflow area in an air curtain.

The conditions maintained within the laminar area, in the outer part of the theatre and in the ancillary rooms that complete the operating theatre suite, are $21 \pm 1\,^\circ$C and $50 \pm 5\%$ saturation with adjustable set points. It is worth providing humidity control in the vicinity of 50% not just because of the probable reduction in the life of bacteria, but because of the reduced risk of electrostatic discharges. At humidities less than about 40% the static charges which build up on non-conducting materials do not leak away to earth but accumulate and may give spark discharges, eventually with dangerous results if inflammable or explosive anaesthetic gases are used. It is also advisable to size the plant to be able to maintain $24\,^\circ$C for short-term, major surgery, if required.

The air-conditioning system should be all-air, constant volume, with multiple reheaters and sterile steam humidification, i.e., when injected the steam must not be wet. 100% fresh air should be drawn in through a louvred inlet located in a noncontaminated area. Intakes near ground level have the risk of introducing street pollution and the soil bacteria associated with gas gangrene. Three levels of filtration (Section 3.13) are desirable. It must be remembered that removing dust is not really synonomous with purifying the air of bacteria, even though the latter use dust as a carrier. Bacteria reproduce with great rapidity and the penetration of only a few through a filter can destroy the purity of the downstream air very quickly and extensively. Hence a prefilter, with the main object of protecting the air-conditioning plant from the grosser particles is the first line of defence. This should be followed by a high efficiency filter, say a bag filter, located on the discharge side of the fan to ensure that any air leakage thereafter is of clean air out of the system, rather than vice-versa. Finally, best quality HEPA filters should be fitted in the duct system, as close as possible to the supply air terminal outlets. These filters must be installed very carefully and great care taken that air cannot bypass them. Bacteria can live and multiply inside filters if the right conditions of humidity and temperature prevail[26]. Dirt held by the filter can contain sufficient organic matter to noutish bacteria. High humidity assists such bacterial growth. Unfortunately, air leaving a cooler coil is frequently in a nearly saturated state and, in this respect, some degree of reheat could sometimes be worthwhile, if such a problem were encountered, provided the economic and other penalties imposed by wasteful reheat are accepted. Fortuitous reheating by adiabatic compression at the fan and by duct heat gain may often be enough to lower the humidity. There is also the risk of capillary condensation within a filter[26] if the local humidity exceeds 70%. In spite of these potential hazards the fact remains that well-designed installations with multiple filtration and terminal HEPA filters feeding a laminar downflow air supply can successfully give average infection rates of 1.5%, or lower, to be compared with rates approaching 9% when conventional techniques of air distribution are used[24].

Microorganisms thrive on wet surfaces, particularly if these are lukewarm. Cooler coils, whilst indispensible, are therefore a potential source of airborne contamination and steps must be taken to ensure rapid and effective condensate drainage from them, with face velocities no greater than 2.25 ms^{-1} to ensure no liquid droplets are carried over. Eliminator plates are never 100% efficient and fitting them should never be regarded as a licence to tolerate carryover from a cooler coil. Air washers are particularly bad, as are sprayed cooler coils, because of the large amount of contaminated, recirculated water. Humidification should not be provided by water droplets at all, whether by direct aerosol injection or by spinning discs. It should only be done by the injection of dry, or slightly superheated steam, which will then be sterile and contain no water droplets. The humidifiers should be remote from the upstream side of any filter, but should always be followed by a filter because of the risk of microbial cultures forming in any patches of possible condensate in the subsequent ductwork. Ducting must be airtight and have provision made for cleaning and disinfection. Fumigation points should be provided for all plant and ducting. Circular ducts are preferred to rectangular ones and there should be no rough edges internally. Dampers are to be avoided.

Stand-by air conditioning plant should be provided for operating theatre suites. The extent and form of the stand-by is a matter of engineering judgement and economics but the aim should be to allow the operating suite to continue to function, without a loss of comfort or air purity, in spite of a failure of power from the electrical mains or a breakdown of a critical component in the air conditioning plant. This implies the need for a stand-by electrical generator, belted running motors on all fans and stand-by pumps in parallel. If water chilling plant provides refrigeration then the choice should lie between $2 \times 100\%$ or $3 \times 50\%$ plants with chilled water piped in series. If direct expansion plants are used the solution is not so easy. It is not good practice to oversize compressors because this promotes a tendency to undesirably low evaporating pressures with the likelihood of frosting on cooler coil surfaces and motor burn-outs, if hermetic or semi-hermetic compressors are used. The best solution is to provide $2 \times 100\%$ airhandling units and $2 \times 100\%$ associated, condensing sets. An alternative could be to use one air-handling unit fitted with a pair of 100% direct-expansion cooler coils, in series in the airstream, if the extra pressure drop can be tolerated, or in parallel in the airstream if sufficient space is available for this in the plant room and if tight shut-off dampers can be fitted to close off the coil not in use. Separate condensing sets would be piped up to the cooler coils. Hot gas valves should be installed to stabilize evaporating pressure and condenser pressure must also be regulated. (Section 2.3). If cooling towers are used, then $3 \times 50\%$ or $2\%100\%$ units should be selected, with their ponds interconnected.

Heat gains ought to be easily established. Lamps for operating tables run off 24 volts and liberate between 500 and 1000 W, as a rule. An additional 1000 W would constitute the gain from other lamps and appliances, and the surgical team would comprise between four and eight people.

3.16 Constant temperature rooms

The distinction between a constant temperature room and any other, more conventional, conditioned space is that temperature gradients, whether vertical or horizontal, cannot be tolerated outside specified limits. Thus if $21 \pm 1\,^\circ\text{C}$ is specified it means that nowhere in the room can the dry-bulb be otherwise. In conventional applications it is customary to supply air at about $8\,^\circ$ or $9\,^\circ\text{C}$ below the room temperature to offset sensible heat gains. Obviously, this is not acceptable for a constant temperature room. The supply temperature must be at the bottom end of the specified tolerance to maintain the room at the top end under design heat gains and vice-versa for design heat losses. It is impracticable to select a cooler coil to chill air through such a small range of temperature and so the method adopted is to use two plants: a secondary one, handling a small amount of air cooled and dehumidified in the normal way to cope with the design heat gains, and a primary plant circulating a much larger amount of unconditioned air to reduce the difference between room and supply temperature to the required value. Figure 3.8 shows such an arrangement. Alternative plant combinations, with less ducting, may suggest themselves and still fulfill the object of good mixing between the primary and secondary airstreams before they enter the room; for instance, the ceiling plenum itself might be used as a mixing chamber. The outside air introduced is enough to meet the ventilation needs and, if large, may require the use of pressure relief flaps in the room to aid natural exfiltration. Since the connexions between the primary and secondary duct systems are close together (points a and b in Figure 3.8) the ducted airflow pattern is stable. If a blow-through cooler coil is used in the secondary plant the full benefit of avoiding the temperature rise by fan power can be achieved and proper coil performance obtained if the fan discharge transition piece to the coil is straight, long and gentle, in order to give smooth airflow over the face of the coil.

It is important that the walls and floor of the room are well-insulated to ensure that surface temperatures seldom go outside the specified tolerance and that adequate vapour sealing is provided if there is a requirement for humidity control. Because the temperature difference between room and supply air temperatures is small, air distribution must be by a ventilated ceiling, wall or floor (see Section 3.13) since the air change rate will be so high. It is then

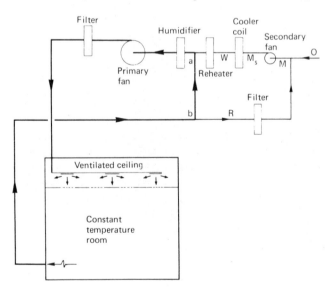

Figure 3.8   Schematic diagram of an air-conditioning system for a constant temperature room

vital that the ceiling plenum chamber be both properly lagged and vapour-sealed and that all structural holes, cracks and crevices, where pipes, ducts or conduits penetrate the enclosure, or where the building construction is poor, are positively sealed. Radiant gains from high temperature equipment within the room sometimes cause significant local temperature variations and these must then be screened. The location of the controlling thermostat is critical and a satisfactory position is often immediately behind the face of the extract grille. Unless careful attention is given to all these matters, particularly structural sealing, the installation will be a failure.

A constant temperature room is often required to be continuously conditioned and this means that some revision of the outside design state normally chosen for winter is necessary. It is suggested that in the UK a value of 5°C less than the conventional outside winter design temperature is appropriate.

Example 3.8 Two modules of the hypothetical office block (Section 1.2) have their windows blocked in and insulated and are to be used as a constant temperature room for which the sensible heat gains are 2000 W, the latent gains are 400 W and the heat loss is 3500 W, for inside conditions of $21 + \frac{1}{2}^\circ$C dry-bulb with $50 \pm 5\%$ saturation when the outside conditions are 28°C dry-bulb, 19.5°C wet-bulb (sling) in summer and -6°C saturated in winter. Three people are to occupy the room. Determine the necessary primary and secondary airflow rates, the maximum cooler coil refrigeration duty and the maximum reheater duty. The plant is to run continuously.

Answer First, the psychrometric considerations for the state to be maintained in the room must be established. The system will be designed so that 21.5°C is achieved under peak heat gain and 20.5°C when there is a maximum heat loss. Coupling this with $50 \pm 5\%$ means that a control rectangle must be drawn on the chart, i.e. the shaded area in Figure 3.9, if the tolerances of temperature and humidity are compatible, as they are in this case. Drawing a parallelogram is the wrong approach. If this was done one would be aiming to control the room at the point P (Figure 3.9) when heat gains were greatest, implying that if the sensible gains diminished there would be a temporary excursion to the left of P (shown by the arrow in the figure), taking the state outside the control domain specified, which is not acceptable in a constant temperature room. Note that it is not always possible to draw a rectangle, if the tolerances of temperature and humidity specified are incompatible. For example, for $21 \pm 2^\circ$C with $50 \pm 5\%$, drawing a control rectangle is impossible, as is shown in Figure 3.9 by the large broken-line parallelogram. The solution then is to tighten the temperature tolerance until the construction of a rectangle that has a practical proportional band of dew-point temperature control is possible.

The summer design room condition in the control rectangle is at the point

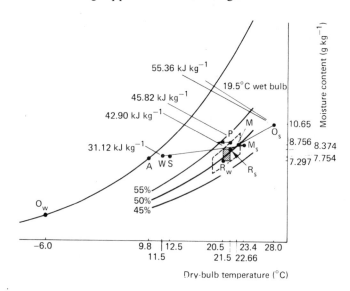

Figure 3.9   Psychrometry for Example 3.8

R_s, in the figure, at 21.5°C dry-bulb, a moisture content of 8.374 $g kg^{-1}$ (corresponding to 20.5°C and 55%) and an enthalpy of 42.90 $kJ kg^{-1}$. In winter the control point will be at R_w, namely, 20.5°C and 7.297 $g kg^{-1}$, corresponding to 21.5°C and 45%.

With an occupancy of 3 people the recommended fresh air allowance (CIBS guide) is 1.3 $1s^{-1} m^{-2}$ over a treated floor area of 28.8 m^2, equal to 37.44$1s^{-1}$ or 0.0443 $kg s^{-1}$ at the room state. A separate air-conditioning plant would be needed for the constant temperature room because it must run continuously, whereas the main plant serving the rest of the office block shuts down at night. An inspection of the psychrometric chart suggests that a suitable off-coil temperature might be 11.5°C, leading to the selection of a cooler coil with four or six rows. If a blow-through cooler coil is adopted for the secondary plant there will be no penalty of temperature rise from fan power, after the cooler coil. However, the primary fan is likely to be running at a fan total pressure of, say, 0.25 kPa, as a provisional estimate, giving a rise of 0.25°C across it. If we allow a further 0.75°C for duct heat gain, the secondary air would enter the conditioned room at 12.5°C, if it were unmixed with primary recirculated air.

The humid specific heat of air at the room state is $1.012 + 1.89 \times 0.008374$ $= 1.028$ $kJ kg^{-1}°C^{-1}$ and so, denoting the primary and secondary mass flow rates by $\dot{m}_p$ and $\dot{m}_s$, respectively, the following equation holds for air entering the conditioned room at a temperature of 20.5°C:

$$2.0 = (\dot{m}_p + \dot{m}_s) \times 1.028 \times (21.5° - 20.5°)$$

and so $\dot{m}_p + \dot{m}_s = 1.946$ $kg s^{-1}$. At the room state the specific volume is

$0.8455 \, \text{m}^3 \text{kg}^{-1}$ and so the volumetric flow rate is $1.645 \, \text{m}^3 \text{s}^{-1}$, representing an air change rate of $1.645 \times 3600/(28.8 \times 2.6) = 79.1$ per hour. This is clearly impossible to distribute with conventional diffusers or grilles, so a ventilated ceiling, or floor or wall, is essential, as expected.

If the primary air recirculated from the room were unmixed with secondary air, its supply temperature would be $21.5° + 0.25° = 21.75°C$, ignoring any duct heat gain as trivial since ambient air is likely to be at a temperature not much different from $21°C$. Therefore, $21.75 \, \dot{m}_p + 12.5 \dot{m}_s = 20.5(\dot{m}_p + \dot{m}_s)$, from which $\dot{m}_s$ is 13.5% and $\dot{m}_p$ 86.5% of the total supply mass flow rate. The secondary flow rate is therefore $0.135 \times 1.946 = 0.263 \, \text{kg s}^{-1}$. Of this $0.0443 \, \text{kg s}^{-1}$, or 16.8%, is from outside and 83.2% is recirculated. The mixed state (M) of the secondary air before it enters the fan will be

$$t_m = 0.832 \times 21.5 + 0.168 \times 28 = 22.6°C$$

$$g_m = 0.832 \times 8.374 + 0.168 \times 10.65 = 8.756 \, \text{g kg}^{-1}.$$

The secondary fan total pressure is likely to be about 0.75 kPa and so the mixed air will rise by $0.75°C$, giving a state (M_s), onto the secondary cooler coil of $t_{ms} = 23.4°C$, $g_{ms} = 8.756 \, \text{g kg}^{-1}$ and $h_{ms} = 45.82 \, \text{kJ kg}^{-1}$. Since only the secondary air delas with the latent heat gain in the room, the latent heat of evaporation of water can be taken as $2454 \, \text{kJ kg}^{-1}$ at $21.5°C$. Therefore,

$$0.400 = 0.263 \times (0.008374 - g_s) \times 2454$$

and so g_s, the moisture content of the secondary air after the cooler coil, is $7.754 \, \text{g kg}^{-1}$. Identifying state S, on a psychrometric chart as $12.5°C$ and $7.754 \, \text{g kg}^{-1}$, $1°C$ can be set back for primary fan power $(0.25°C)$ and secondary duct gain $(0.75°C)$ to state W $(11.5°C$ and $7.754 \, \text{g kg}^{-1})$. Joining W to M_s $(23.4°C$ and $8.756 \, \text{g kg}^{-1})$ by a straight line and projecting it to cut the saturation curve at A $(9.8°C)$ allows the approximate cooler coil contact factor to be determined as $(23.4 - 11.5)/(23.4 - 9.8) = 0.88$, suggesting a four-row or six-row cooler coil, depending on the face velocity. Incidentally, if a blow-through coil is used, it is imperative that the duct connexion from the fan discharge onto its face is such as to ensure smooth airflow over the coil.

From a chart or interpolating in tables, the enthalpy leaving the cooler coil is $31.12 \, \text{kJ kg}^{-1}$. The cooling load is thus $0.263 \times (45.82 - 31.12) = 3.87 \, \text{kW}$ of refrigeration. This should be checked as independently as possible. Therefore, noting that the secondary volumetric airflow rate, measured at the room temperature is $0.263 \, \text{kg s}^{-1} \times 0.8455 \, \text{m}^3 \text{kg}^{-1} = 0.222 \, \text{m}^3 \text{s}^{-1}$, the following can be calculated using Equation (2.3) where necessary.

		kW
Primary fan power:	$0.25° \times 1.645 \times 358/(273 + 21.5)$	$= 0.500$
Primary duct gain:		$= \ —$
Secondary fan power:	$0.75° \times 0.222 \times 358/(273 + 21.5)$	$= 0.202$

Secondary duct gain: $0.75 \times 0.222 \times 358/(273 + 21.5)$ $= 0.202$
Fresh air load: $0.0443 \times (55.36 - 42.90)$ $= 0.552$
Sensible heat gain: $= 2.000$
Latent heat gain: $= 0.400$

Total cooling load: $3.856\,\text{kW}$

which is in good agreement with the other result.

Proportional plus integral control should be used with a good quality hot gas valve and a hot gas header to control the temperature of the air leaving the direct-expansion cooler coil. The reheater should be controlled in a similar mode from a return air thermostat. For a plant of this small duty it would not be economically viable to vary the proportions of fresh and recirculated air to exploit the natural cooling capacity of the cold outside air in winter and so minimise running costs. Instead, minimum, fixed fresh air should be used with the refrigeration plant running throughout the year. This makes it more than ever necessary to stabilize condensing pressure. Humidification is best done with a dry steam injector, under proportional plus integral control, either from a central steam boiler or from a dry steam generator, probably energised electrically.

3.17 Computer rooms

A characteristic feature of the sensible heat gains is that the energy liberated by the computer units is so large as to dwarf the significance of the other components. Latent gains are also quite small and the slope of the room ratio line is therefore very flat. The size of the computer installation influences the design approach and, although it is hard to generalise, there is evidence that direct-expansion systems are cheaper and hence more appropriate when total cooling loads are less than about 175 kW of refrigeration, but chilled water may be a better proposition for duties exceeding this. There must be some overlap, of course, and the availability of water chillers with capacities as small as 15 kW of refrigeration makes the distinction between the use of the two forms of cooling somewhat blurred. The use of self-contained, incremental airconditioning units, actually located in the conditioned space, adds a further note of uncertainty about the dividing line between chilled water and direct-expansion, in computer air conditioning.

(1) **Direct-expansion systems of conventional type** With the smaller installations, although the sensible heat gains from the computer may still amount to a large proportion of the total, it is often possible to achieve conditioning with a fairly conventional system design: direct-expansion air cooling with an air, or water, cooled condensing set, either as a self-contained entity for the smallest schemes, or as a split system for larger duties. Ducting is

generally needed for air distribution to the grilles, or diffusers that can be used if the air change rate is less than about 25 per hour, as is likely with small duties. No separate extract fan is required and the system runs with about 5% fresh air as a fixed amount throughout the year. Since occupancy is small, little fresh air is necessary for ventilation but a small surplus of supply over extract is desirable to achieve a slight, but unspecified, positive pressure in the computer room. As a general rule it is misleading to quote this as a percentage of the air supply rate, e.g.5%, because exfiltration, and so pressurisation, depends on the tightness of the building structure. With high air change rates it may be impossible for 5% of the air supplied to exfiltrate and the room can then be regarded as part of the duct system with the airflow rate into and out of it coming to equilibrium at a value of less than the 100% design figure. The method of controlling temperature and humidity will depend on the tolerances acceptable to the computer manufacturers. These can be quite varied among the different makes, some accepting wide swings in temperature and humidity, as long as condensation does not occur. It is common to provide conditions that are comfortable for the occupants if the computer tolerances are broader than the comfort zone. Cycling the compressor motors or unloading cylinders, in sequence with a heater battery, from a return air thermostat may be an acceptable form of control in many cases, provided that the motor does not cycle more often than a safe, maximum number of times per hour—as few as, say, eight, for small hermetic machines. If the compressor motor continues to run, loading and unloading cylinders can generally be more frequent than the maximum number of motor starts, without harm. There is always the risk of frosting on the air cooler coil, with the ultimate consequence of motor burnout for hermetic compressors and, as discussed in Section 2.3, this is exacerbated by the use of larger fresh air quantities and may be made worse if humidification is not needed for the environment of the particular make of computer, because the wet-bulb temperature onto the cooler coil falls as winter operating conditions approach with a consequent lowering of the evaporating temperature. A check should always be made on the risk of such a situation developing and steps taken to pre-empt it by the use of a hot gas valve, which is not always possible with small, packaged units, by switching off the refrigeration plant when it is not needed, or perhaps by minimising the use of fresh air. An approach sometimes adopted successfully is to provide a small, separate, ventilation plant that handles filtered, tempered in winter, minimum fresh air and delivers it directly to the room, thus allowing the air-conditioning unit to deal with only recirculated air and achieving a fairly constant state onto its cooler coil. If this is done the sensible and latent components of the fresh air introduced must be added to the sensible and latent heat gains calculated for the room, to be dealt with by the air-conditioning unit. However the system is controlled it is essential to stabilise the condensing pressure, either by means of a liquid level back-up control or by modulating the condenser fan speed through a solid-state controller responding directly to condenser pressure. If a water-cooled condenser is used pressure should be controlled directly from the condenser by regulating the water flow rate through it. With larger installations, exceeding about 70 kW of refrigeration, an economic argument in terms of owning and operating cost, or present value, over the life of the plant, may possibly be made for the use of variable proportions of fresh and recirculated air quantities. In such a case the plant might run with minimum fresh air until the outside air temperature is cool enough to permit the refrigeration plant to be switched off. In this way the wet-bulb temperature onto the cooler coil and the cooling load is kept up until the switch-off temperature and the risk of frosting, compressor cycling and motor burn-out much reduced.

Controlling temperature by sequencing the capacity of the refrigeration plant and the heater battery, with a high limit humidity override to bring back part of the refrigeration capacity when needed for dehumidification, the heater battery continuing to control temperature by temporarily cancelling part of the cooling, may not be satisfactory in all cases. It can then be necessary to run the refrigeration plant to give a nominally constant temperature after the cooler coil, its evaporating temperature being regulated by a hot gas valve and header, and to control room temperature by reheating. Humidity control is achieved in its most stable form with a sprayed cooler coil, fitted with a good quality hot gas valve that can turn down to perhaps 5% of full load. The large thermal inertia of the mass of cold spray water in the recirculation tank under the direct-expansion cooler coil adds a high degree of steadiness to the control of air temperature off the coil. Variations in the on-coil state or in the evaporating temperature are damped. The big disadvantages of a sprayed coil are its capital cost and the maintenance problems it presents. Scaling and corrosion seem to combine to discourage its use in many instances. The alternative is to use steam injection. Adequate control over humidity is possible and, with a proper choice of humidifying equipment, scaling and corrosion problems are minimised. With steam injection it is important to inject the vapour into an airstream that can accept it: if the state of the air is near saturation initially little further moisture can be added and the injected steam will immediately form condensate.

(2) **Self-contained incremental units within the computer room** A natural development of small direct-expansion systems has been to package them with an external appearance and finish similar to that of the computer cabinets and to locate them in the computer room itself. Such packages commonly comprise one or more hermetic compressors, each with its own direct-expansion cooler coil and condenser, offering a nominal capacity in the range 10 to 60 kW of refrigeration for a state of 22°C dry-bulb, 15.3°C wet-bulb onto their evaporators, throwaway air filters, steam pan humidifier with a disposable inner surface to reduce the problems of scaling, forward curved

centrifugal fans, variable speed V-belt drives, drip-proof driving motors, reheaters using conventional media or hot gas, liquid receivers sized for low load operation and an automatic control system for temperature and humidity. Temperature control is effected from a thermostat positioned in the recirculated air stream within the cabinet which cycles one or more compressors in sequence with the heater battery. Modulating control over the reheat with the compressors running continuously can also be achieved. The risks of cycling the compressors too frequently should have been considered by the manufacturers. The injection of water vapour from the steam pan humidifier is often into some of the recirculated air which is arranged to bypass the cooler coil, thus avoiding the risks of condensation mentioned earlier. Humidity may be controlled by sequencing the steam pan humidifier with one of the compressors, overriding temperature control when necessary to achieve dehumidification.

Such packages come in various forms but manufacturers commonly offer four versions:

(a) An air conditioning unit with a remote air-cooled condenser. There are then the usual limitations on the lengths and vertical distances of the hot gas and liquid lines

(b) An air-conditioning unit with an in-built water-cooled condenser, fed from a remote cooling tower

(c) An air-conditioning unit with an in-built glycol-cooled condenser fed from a remote, forced draught heat exchanger, after the style of a motor car radiator. There are no limitations on the pipe runs and water treatment problems are avoided

(d) An air-handling unit fed with chilled water from a remote chilling plant.

Of these four, the glycol-cooled version is probably most popular and has certainly achieved effective results in reliability and control. One or more incremental packages, depending on the load, are located in the computer room and they may extract air from the room, at the top, condition it and discharge it into a floor void for subsequent delivery to the room through floor grilles or perforated panels, stategically positioned. Alternatively, the cabinets extract air from the room through grilles in their sides, condition it and discharge it upwards, through ducting into a ventilated ceiling. The downflow system is the more popular. Although a separate ventilating plant can be used to provide the fresh air needed, the incremental cabinets then doing all the load, both sensible and latent, it is not uncommon for the auxiliary ventilation system to be modified to cool and dehumidify the fresh air in summer, and vice-versa in winter. The plant then copes with the latent loads, transmission gains and losses, and perhaps also the gains from people and lights, leaving the incremental cabinets to do the sensible cooling associated with the computer load only. In this way the room and the various ancillary areas, such as tape stores, etc., can be kept conditioned through 24 hours, even when the computer plant is off. For the incremental cabinets to do sensible cooling their evaporating temperatures must be properly controlled at values high enough to avoid condensate forming on the cooler coils.

(3) **Chilled water systems** With larger installations, better flexibility, stand-by, control and running costs may be achieved by using chilled water from multiple, air- or water-cooled refrigeration plants. Two pumped chilled water circuits are necessary: a primary circuit delivering lower temperature water to the coils in the air-handling (ventilating) unit dealing with the latent loads and a secondary circuit feeding higher temperature chilled water to those cooler coils in the plant dealing with the computer loads and doing sensible cooling only. In this way, reductions in heat emission from the computers can be matched by reductions in the cooling capacity of the sensible cooling coils, instead of using wasteful reheat to cancel overcooling.

(4) **Air distribution** There are three possibilities of air distribution. If the air change rate is less than about 20 to 30 per hour, conventional side-wall grilles or ceiling diffusers may be used. If this rate is exceeded, a ventilated ceiling or floor is the only answer and in either case it cannot be too strongly stressed that the plenum chamber or void must be sealed and then properly lagged and vapour sealed. Failure to ensure this will cause the installation to be also a failure. The ventilated ceiling will usually consist of a mixture of live and dead tiles, unless the air change rate is very high, i.e. over about 200, when the whole of the ceiling will be live. The live tiles should be positioned over the items of computer equipment producing the heat gains but, since they are removable, it is always possible to reposition them during commissioning to get the best results. The argument in favour of a ventilated floor is that a floor void is needed in any case to accommodate cables feeding the computer cabinets and possibly other services. The raised floor usually consists of 600 mm square tiles, made of plywood faced beneath with a fire-retardant material, or die-cast steel. A variety of upper surface finishes is available, from vinyl to carpet. The minimum clear floor depth possible is about 75 mm, up to a standard maximum of about 500 mm. Clear depths greater than this are usually possible in non-standard forms, probably with cross bracing (stringers) underneath to give stability. Less than 100 mm clear space, after allowing for cables, is useless for supply ventilation. The same considerations apply for the throw and distribution of air in a floor void as in a ventilated ceiling (see Section 5.5). The tiles rest on supporting pedestals, very often without stringers, that allow the easy laying in of cables. Complete interchangeability, using suction cups for the simple removal of the tiles is usual, to accommodate rearrangement of computer cabinets which are fed with cables from underneath through specifically cut holes. It is possible to have steel or anodised aluminium grilles in the tiles for the supply of conditioned air, or the tiles may be perforated. Supply air grilles are often located around the perimeter of the room and should be sized for face velocites of about 1 ms^{-1}. Perforated tiles commonly

have 3 mm diameter holes at about 20 mm centres, giving 20% free area overall. Typical velocities through the holes are 3 ms^{-1}, with 0.6 ms^{-1} as a corresponding face velocity. Such air velocities are generally acceptable to people, with shod feet but bare legs, standing near the tiles or even on them. Placing tiles containing grilles near the peripheral walls tends to keep them out of the main avenues of foot traffic but perforated tiles are frequently positioned adjacent to the air inlet grilles in the lower parts of the computer cabinet side panels. Vertical temperature gradients of as much as 5°C over a floor-to-ceiling height of 3 m have been measured when supplying cooling air through perforated floor tiles into an unoccupied room, at the velocities mentioned. Such gradients usually disappear when the room is in normal use or can be corrected by increasing the velocity of air flow through the holes in the tiles. The upper limit of such an increase must be human comfort, which can only really be established on a subjective basis. Manufacturer's recommendations for sizing perforated tiles and grilles should be followed.

As with ventilated ceilings, sealing, lagging and vapour sealing the floor void is vital.

Exercises

1 Estimate the cooling load for the hypothetical hotel considered in Examples 3.1, 3.2 and 3.3 at 13.00 h sun time in July, making the same assumptions for diversity factors. Use Equation (1.1) and psychrometric tables to establish the outside enthalpy at 13.00 h sun time.   (*Answer* 469 kW of refrigeration)
2 For the hypothetical office block (Section 1.2) plot maximum cooling load against percentage glazing for a given orientation, and maximum cooling load against orientation for a given percentage of glazing. Make use of Table A.9 and assume a lighting load of 30 Wm^{-2} and a population density of 9 m^2 per person. Repeat the exercise for a lighting load of 20 Wm^{-2}
3 Repeat the calculations for Example 3.5 but assume the illumination in the supermarket is 1500 lux, the open refrigerated display cabinets absorb 40 000 W of total heat and the population density is 4 m^2 per person.

Symbols

g_m	Moisture content of mixed air	g kg^{-1}
g_{ms}	Moisture content of mixed air onto a secondary cooler coil	g kg^{-1}
g_r	Moisture content of room air	g kg^{-1}
g_s	Moisture content of supply air or of secondary air after a cooler coil	g kg^{-1}
h_m	Enthalpy of mixed air	kJ kg^{-1}
h_{ms}	Enthalpy of mixed air onto a secondary cooler coil	kJ kg^{-1}
$\dot{m}_p$	Mass flow rate of primary air	kg s^{-1}

158   Air Conditioning Applications and Design

$\dot{m}_s$ Mass flow rate of secondary air kg s^{-1}
p_s Partial pressure of water vapour in an air/water vapour mixture Pa
p_w Vapour pressure exerted by water at temperature t_w Pa
q_e Evaporation rate per unit area of wetted surface W m^{-2}
t_m · Dry-bulb temperature of mixed air   °C
t_s Dry-bulb temperature of supply air   °C
t_w Dry-bulb temperature of air leaving a cooler coil   °C
μ Percentage saturation   %

References

(1) Martin, P. L., A study of occupancy in chain stores, *JIHVE*, **33**, pp. 99–102, August 1970
(2) Stinson, R. G., Shopping centres HVAC, *Building Systems Design*, pp. 36–38, February 1970
(3) Hinkley, P. L., Some notes on the control of smoke in enclosed shopping centres, *Fire Research Note No.* 875, May 1971, Fire Research Station, Borehamwood, Herts
(4) Doone, R. E., Lighting and the integrated environment in multiple stores, *The Steam and Heating Engineer*, February 1971
(5) ASHRAE Handbook & Product Directory *Applications*, 1974
(6) Hattis, B. S., Air conditioning for shopping centres, *Heating Piping and Air Conditioning*, pp. 136–141, July 1964
(7) CIBS, *Building Energy Code*, Part 1, London, 1977
(8) Murphy, V., Department store air conditioning, *Buildings Systems Design*, pp. 41–43, February 1970
(9) *CIBS Guide*, Volume B, 1976
(10) Thornley, D. L., Auditoria—a review of present day HVAC practice, *JHIVE*, **37**, pp. 170–183, November 1969
(11) Jamieson, H. C., Presidential address, *JIHVE*, **27**, pp. 245, December 1959
(12) Doe, L. N., Gura, J. H. and Martin, P. L., Building services for swimming pools, *JIHVE*, pp. 261–286, December 1967
(13) Braham, G. D., Wise use of energy in swimming pool design, *The Heating and Ventilating Engineer*, pp. 6–8, December 1975
(14) Valerio, E. L., Air conditioning bowling centres, *Air Conditioning, Heating and Ventilating*, pp. 75–81, March 1959
(15) Austin, P. R., *Design and operation of clean rooms*, Business News Publishing Co., Detroit, Michegan, 1970
(16) Lieberman, A., *Contamination Effects Study*, ARF 3216–5, Chicago, Illinois, Armor Research Foundation, November 1962
(17) *Federal Standard* 209a, Clean room and work station requirements,

controlled environment, Office of Technological Services, Department of Commerce, Washington DC, 1966

(18) *Federal Standard* 209*b*, Office of Technological Services, Department of Commerce, Washington DC, 1973

(19) Hunt, E. L., Building engineering services at the new Charing Cross Hospital (Fulham), *The Building Services Engineer*, **44**, pp. 41–49, May 1976

(20) Green, V. M., Vesley, D., Bond, R. G. and Michaelson, G. S., Microbiological contamination of hospital air, I, Quantitative studies, *Applied Microbiology*, **10**, pp. 561–566, 1962

(21) Smith, R. M. and Rae, A., Odour and ventilation in hospital wards, *The Building Services Engineer*, **44**, pp. 265–271, March 1977

(22) Yaglou, C. P., Riley, E. C. and Coggins, D. I., Ventilation requirements, *ASHVE Trans.*, **43**, pp. 132–162, 1936

(23) Yaglou, C. P. and Witheridge, W. N., Ventilation requirements, *ASHVE Trans.*, **43**, pp. 423–436, 1937

(24) Howarth, F. H., The prevention of airborne infection during surgery, Proceedings of the International Symposium for Contamination Control, Swiss Federal Institute of Technology, Zurich, *Journal of the Society of Environmental Engineers*, Issue 55, pp. 31–33, October 1972

(25) Schicht, H. H. and Steiner, W., The contribution of air conditioning to asepsis in the operating theatre, *Sulzer Technical Review*, **4**, 1972

(26) Ma, W. Y. L., Air conditioning design for hospital operating rooms, *JIHVE*, pp. 165–179, October 1965

(27) Green, G. H., The effect of indoor relative humidity on absenteeism and colds in schools, *ASHRAE Trans.*, Part II, pp. 131–141, 1974

(28) Dunklin, E. W. and Puck, T. T., The lethal effect of relative humidity on airborne bacteria, *J. Experimental Medicine*, **87**, pp. 87–101, 1948

(29) Whyte, W., Shaw, B. H. and Bailey, P. V., An assessment of partial walls for a downflow laminar system, International Symposium for Contamination Control, London, 24 September 1974, *Journal of the Society of Environmental Engineers*, Issue 66, September 1975

(30) Bossers, P. A., *Die Lufthürung in Operationsräumen, Reinraumtechnik I*, Berichte des Internationalen Symposium für Reinraumtechnik, Zurich, Switzerland

(31) Allander, C. and Abel, E., Unterschung eines Enblassystems für Operationsräume, *Dechema Monogtaphie*, **69**, pp. 297–306, 1948

4

Water distribution

4.1 Pipe sizing

The basis of pipe-sizing is the Fanning equation:

$$\Delta H = \frac{4flv^2}{2gd} \tag{4.1}$$

in which ΔH is the head lost in metres of fluid flowing, f is a friction factor defined by Equation (4.2), l is the length of pipe, v is the mean velocity of flow, g is the acceleration arising from the force of gravity and d is the internal pipe diameter. Generally, waterflow in a pipe is turbulent and so Colebrook and White's formula applies:

$$\frac{1}{\sqrt{f}} = -4 \log \left[\frac{k_s}{3.7d} + \frac{1.255}{(\text{Re})\sqrt{f}} \right] \tag{4.2}$$

in which k_s is the absolute roughness of the pipe wall (in metres) and (Re) is the Reynolds number. Since pressure and head are related by

$$p = \rho g H \tag{4.3}$$

Equations (4.1) and (4.2) can be modified to yield an expression for the mass flow rate, M, in terms of the pressure drop per metre, Δp:

$$M = -4 \left[N_3 \Delta p d^5 \right]^{\frac{1}{2}} \log \left[\frac{k_s}{3.7d} + \frac{N_4 d}{(N_3 \Delta p d^5)^{\frac{1}{2}}} \right] \tag{4.4}$$

in which, using the notation adopted by the CIBS guide, $N_3 = \pi^2/32\rho$ and $N_4 = 1.255\pi\mu/4\rho$, μ and ρ being the absolute viscosity and density, respectively, of the fluid flowing.

Solving Equation (4.4) involves tedious computation and the CIBS guide publishes tables for the flow of low temperature hot water at 75°C in clean, medium grade, black steel pipes to BS1387:1967. However, chilled water flowing in pipelines is likely to be at about 7.5°C and cooling water at about 30°C. With lower water temperatures the kinematic viscosity increases and hence the Reynolds number reduces. Equation (4.2) shows that the friction factor increases as the Reynolds number falls, for a given pipe roughness. It follows that the rates of pressure drop for pipes carrying chilled water exceed

160

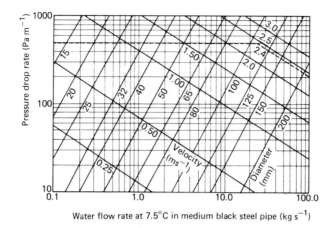

Figure 4.1   Pipe sizing chart for water at 7.5°C in clean, medium-grade, black steel pipes (reproduced by kind permission of Haden Young Ltd)

those quoted in the CIBS tables for the flow of LTHW. For equal mass flow at a velocity of 2.4 ms^{-1} the pressure drop rate at 7.5°C is about 30% greater than at 75°C over the range of pipe sizes from 25 to 200 mm.

Figure 4.1 is derived from Equations (4.1) to (4.4) and may be used to size pipes carrying chilled water at 7.5°C. It is suggested that the same figure also be used for sizing pipes carrying condenser cooling water at about 30°C. For such open circuits the dirtier pipework and greater surface roughness will take up the small margin in pressure loss.

The loss through most fittings is expressed as a factor, k, multiplying the velocity pressure. By means of Equation (4.3) substitution for ΔH in Equation (4.1) gives pressure loss in Nm^{-2}:

$$\delta p = \frac{2\rho f l v^2}{d} \tag{4.5}$$

The velocity pressure is $\frac{1}{2}\rho v^2$ and if k is unity the pressure lost through the fitting, δp, would be numerically equal to this:

$$\delta p = \tfrac{1}{2}\rho v^2 = (2\rho f l v^2)/d.$$

This can then be solved for the equivalent length of pipe, EL, to absorb one velocity pressure: $EL = d/4f$. EL can thus be established for any given pipe and tends to increase with rise in the Reynolds number. Tests have determined values of k for various fittings and the CIBS guide publishes a representative selection. The loss through a fitting can thus be expressed as so many metres of equivalent straight pipe.

Example 4.1 Determine the pressure drop past a 90° malleable, cast-iron elbow of 25 mm diameter for a flow rate of 0.5 kg s^{-1} at 75°C.

Answer From CIBS Table C4.12[1] for medium-grade, black steel pipe, the pressure drop rate for a flow of 0.5 kg s^{-1} in a 25 mm pipe is 345 Pa m^{-1}, by interpolation, and the *EL* is 1.1. From CIBS Table C4.36, $k = 0.8$, so the length of straight pipe with the same pressure loss as the fitting is $0.8 \times 1.1 = 0.88$ m and the actual loss is $0.88 \times 345 = 304$ Pa.

Notable among the fittings absent from the CIBS table is the strainer. Figure 4.2 shows the resistance to flow for brass and bronze, y-type strainers, based on data published by Spirax Sarco. We see that for a 200 mesh, 25 mm strainer with 0.5 kg s^{-1} flowing, the loss is about 3 kPa, which is a significant figure. As the strainer gets fouled its resistance increases towards infinity, ultimately stopping the flow.

As a general principle, pipe should be sized using velocities in the range 1 to 2 ms^{-1}, but because larger pipe, fittings and valves are much more expensive than the smaller sizes (see Figure 4.3), it is desirable to keep the water velocity high for the larger pipes, up to a maximum of about 2.4 ms^{-1}, set by the likelihood of excessive erosion, especially at elbows. On the other hand, smaller pipes carrying water at this speed have high pressure drops, leading to pumps with uneconomically large heads. The broken line in Figure 4.1 shows that it is suggested that pipes should be sized for 500 Pa m^{-1} until a velocity of 2.4 ms^{-1} is reached. After this, sizing should be at a reduced pressure drop rate but retaining 2.4 ms^{-1} as a limiting velocity.

Example 4.2 Size pipes to carry 1, 10, 30 and 50 kg s^{-1} of chilled water at 7.5°C, quoting the pressure drop rates and velocities.

Answer Using Figure 4.1 the following can be determined:

> 1 kg s^{-1},   32 mm diameter, 380 Pa m^{-1}, 0.95 m s^{-1};
> 10 kg s^{-1},   80 mm diameter, 500 Pa m^{-1}, 1.95 m s^{-1};
> 30 kg s^{-1}, 125 mm diameter, 360 Pa m^{-1}, 2.3   m s^{-1};
> 50 kg s^{-1}, 200 mm diameter,   87 Pa m^{-1}, 1.45 m s^{-1}.

If Table C4.12 had been used for water at 75°C, the following would have been obtained:

> 1 kg s^{-1},   32 mm diamater, 321 Pa m^{-1};
> 10 kg s^{-1},   80 mm diameter, 444 Pa m^{-1};
> 30 kg s^{-1}, 125 mm diameter, 329 Pa m^{-1}.

There is no entry for 200 mm pipe, but the pressure drop rates are less than for water at 7.5°C. The lines in Figure 4.1 for velocity and diameter should really be very shallow curves but are drawn straight, because of the small size of the diagram, without much loss of accuracy.

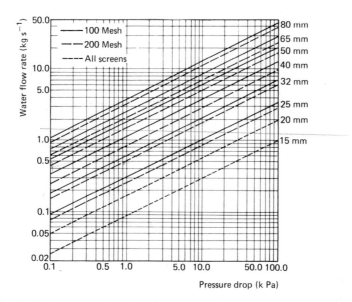

Figure 4.2   Typical pressure drop data for brass or bronze Y-type strainers with 200 mesh (after Spirax Sarco)

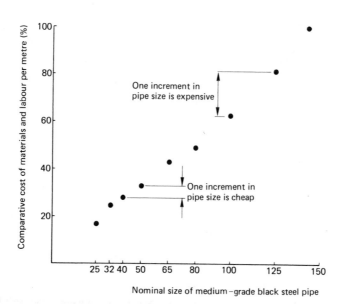

Figure 4.3   Comparative costs of medium-grade, black steel piping

4.2 The design of piping circuits

Most hydraulic circuits used in building services have an open water surface in them somewhere, but it is common practice to speak of a closed circuit when water is pumped in a continuous loop fitted with a connexion either to a feed and expansion tank (Figure 4.4a) or to pressurisation unit. An open system, on the other hand, involves water flowing under gravity from one level to another (Figure 4.4b) or its being pumped from a lower to a higher level (Figure 4.4c).

Nine important principles must be followed when designing pipe circuits.

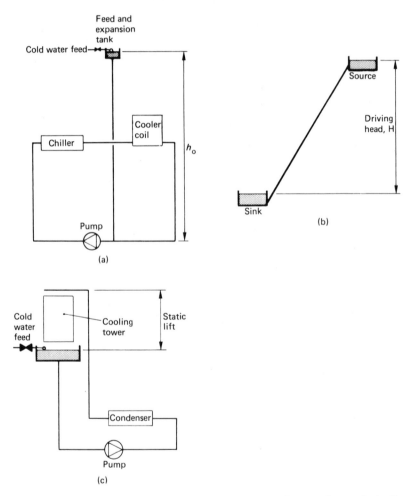

Figure 4.4a,   Closed pipe circuit connected to a feed and expansion tank; b, Open pipe circuit. Water flows under gravity from one level to another; c, Open pipe circuit. Water is pumped from a lower to a higher level

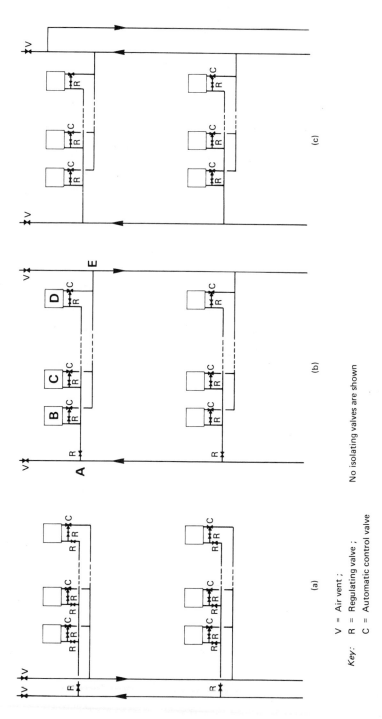

Key: V = Air vent ;
       R = Regulating valve ;   No isolating valves are shown
       C = Automatic control valve

Figure 4.5 Typical piping arrangements: a, Two-pipe; b, Two-pipe ladder with reversed return branches; c, Complete reversed return

(1) Centrifugal pumps must be always primed
(2) Cavitation must be avoided
(3) Air must not be drawn into the system
(4) All air must be vented from the system
(5) In open circuits, as much of the pipework as possible must be below the static water level
(6) All control valves must be below the static water level in open circuits
(7) Attention must be paid to position head
(8) Open vents, used when there is the risk of warmed water boiling, must not be located so as to discharge continuously into the feed and expansion tank
(9) The connexion from the feed and expansion tank must be made at a place such that the above principles are followed.

Chilled and cooling water circuits are invariably two-pipe, although in certain situations a one-pipe system is a possibility. Figure 4.5a shows a conventional two-pipe layout in which regulating valves are fitted to balance both branches and units. A two-pipe ladder with reversed-return branches is shown in Figure 4.5b, and this is very convenient for feeding induction or fan-coil units, the same pressure drop occurring for any horizontal branch, say **AE**, no matter which unit, **B**, **C**, or **D**, the water flows through. Fitting regulating valves at each unit is often unnecessary but regulation must still be provided for each horizontal branch. A complete reversed-return system is shown in Figure 4.5c. Theoretically, no regulating valves are needed at all but an extra riser is required, which makes the arrangement expensive, and so less popular.

4.3 Centrifugal pumps

When turning in the normal way, the backward-curved vanes on the impeller rotate the water and impart kinetic energy to it, directing the liquid outwards from the suction eye, over the vanes to the casing, where it flows away at high pressure. The kinetic energy of the water leaving the impeller, corresponding to its velocity head, is converted into potential energy, corresponding to its static head, either by a volute casing or by a diffuser casing. The former is the more usual design for pumps used in building services and with it most of the energy conversion takes place as the volute finally expands to the pump outlet. With the latter design it occurs between the diffuser vanes.

The total pump head, H, or pressure, p_t, is analogous to fan total pressure and is defined by

$$H = (H_d + v_d^2/2g) - (H_s + v_s^2/2g) \qquad (4.6)$$

where H_d and H_s are the static heads at pump discharge and pump suction, respectively, v_d and v_s being the corresponding velocities of water flow. Since $v^2/2g$ is velocity head, Equation (4.6) states that the total pump head is the difference between the total heads at pump discharge and suction, in accordance with Bernoulli's theorem. Total pump head is the total energy per unit weight of water flowing and, in the same way, the total pump pressure (see Equation 4.3) is the total energy per unit volume of water flow. It follows that the pump power imparted to the water by the impeller is defined by

$$W_p = \dot{m}gH = Vp_t \qquad (4.7)$$

in which W_p is the pump power, $\dot{m}$ is the mass flow rate of water and V is the volumetric flow rate. It follows also, from Equation (4.3), that the total pump pressure can be expressed as

$$p_t = (p_{sd} + 0.5\rho v_d^2) - (p_{ss} + 0.5\rho v_s^2) \qquad (4.8)$$

where p_{sd} and p_{ss} are the static pressures at discharge and suction, respectively.

The static pressure datum for a system is established by the connexion from the feed and expansion tank, if the circuit is closed, as in Figure 4.4a. In the case of an open circuit, such as in Figure 4.4c, the pond of the cooling tower is the feed and expansion tank and the static water level in it establishes the system datum pressure. If the feed and expansion tank has a water level at a height h_o above the centre-line of the impeller it imposes a static head of h_o, or a static pressure of $p_o = \rho g h_o$, on a closed circuit at the point of connexion, whether the pump runs or not. If the connexion is made at pump suction, $p_o = p_{ss}$ and this is the lowest static pressure in the system. When the connexion is at the pump discharge, $p_o = p_{sd}$ and this is the highest static pressure in the system. It is generally desirable to make the connexion at the pump suction in chilled water circuits so that there is no risk of cavitation (see Section 4.8) if a large pressure drop should occur across an item of plant elsewhere in the system.

Example 4.3

(a) A centrifugal pump delivers $7.6 \, \mathrm{l s^{-1}}$ through a closed pipe circuit and has suction and discharge connexions of 80 mm and 65 mm, respectively. The water level in the feed and expansion tank is 15 m above the centre-line of the impeller. Pressure gauges are fitted at suction and discharge and the connexion from the feed and expansion tank is at virtually the same position as the suction gauge. When the pump runs normally the discharge gauge indicates 250 kPa. Taking the density of water to be $1000 \, \mathrm{kg \, m^{-3}}$, determine the total pump pressure and power.

(b) Calculate the static pressure at pump suction if the connexion from the feed and expansion tank is at pump discharge.

Answer

(a) $V = 7.6 \, \mathrm{l s^{-1}} = 0.0076 \, \mathrm{m^3 \, s^{-1}}$.

The internal diameters of 80 mm and 65 mm medium grade steel tube are 0.08065 m and 0.06865 m, respectively (Table C4.2[(1)]). Hence, the area of the suction inlet is $0.005109 \, \mathrm{m^2}$ and that of the outlet is $0.003701 \, \mathrm{m^2}$. Therefore, $v_s = 1.488 \, \mathrm{ms^{-1}}$ and $v_d = 2.053 \, \mathrm{ms^{-1}}$; $h_o = 15 \, \mathrm{m}$, therefore $p_o = (1000 \times 9.81$

$\times 15)/1000 = 147.15$ kPa. Hence, $p_{ss} = 147.16$ kPa and $p_{sd} = 250$ kPa, and from Equation (4.8)

$$p_t = (250 + [(0.5 \times 1000 \times 2.053^2)/1000]) - (147.15 + [(0.5 \times 1000 \times 1.488^2)/1000])$$
$$= 252.11 - 148.26 = 103.85 \text{ kPa}.$$

From Equation (4.7)

$$W_p = 0.0076 \times 103.85 = 0.789 \text{ kW}.$$

(b) The same increases of static and total pressure occur across the pump but now $p_o = p_{sd} = 147.15$ kPa. Therefore,

$$p_{ss} = 147.15 - (250 - 147.15) = 44.3 \text{ kPa}.$$

It is to be noted that the influence of velocity pressure on the total pump pressure is small. It is often ignored and the difference in the readings of the gauges at discharge and suction taken as the pump pressure. For the above example, the total pump pressure would then have been taken as $250 - 147.15 = 102.85$ kPa. It is also to be noted that if the gauges are at different levels different readings are obtained and must be accounted for.

Example 4.4 The static pressure indicated by a gauge on the inlet side of a chiller is 100 kPa. The gauge on the outlet is mounted 1 m higher than that at the inlet and indicates 50 kPa. What is the drop of static pressure across the chiller?

Answer If the gauge at the outlet were lowered by 1 m, to bring it to the same level as the gauge at the inlet, the increase in position head imposed by the water level in the feed and expansion tank would be 1 m, corresponding to 9.81 kPa. Hence the pressure drop across the chiller is really $100 - 59.81 = 40.19$ kPa.

The mechanical efficiency, η, of a pump is the ratio of the rate of energy input to the water (Equation 4.7) to the power applied to the impeller shaft, W_s. Thus,

$$\eta = 100 \ W_p/W_s = 100 \ Vp_t/W_s \tag{4.9}$$

Since $p_t = \rho g h$, it follows that W_p is proportional to the density of the fluid and this may be significant when chilled brines or glycols are handled.

The difference $W_s - W_p$ arises from bearing losses, skin friction and turbulence within the pump, losses accompanying expansions and contractions and the energy losses incurred by the formation of eddies, all of which constitute losses of pump pressure between the places where this is measured at suction and discharge. There are also losses of pump capacity because of leakage between the impeller and its casing through the clearance spaces, and because of seepage through the gland.

Theoretical considerations of the relative velocities at entry to and exit from the impeller vanes show that a linear relationship exists for the static pressure developed and the volumetric flow rate. Figure 4.6 shows how the losses mentioned above combine to give a real curve, like an inverted parabola, very similar to the characteristic curve build-up of a centrifugal refrigeration compressor[2]. Although the actual shape of the curve is established by test results for a constant pump speed, its position on the $p - V$ coordinate system,

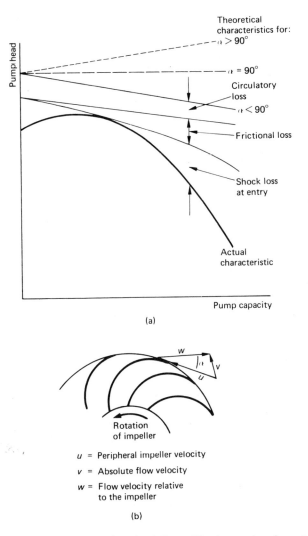

Figure 4.6   Build-up of a pump characteristic: a, Head capacity characteristics; b, Discharge velocity triangle

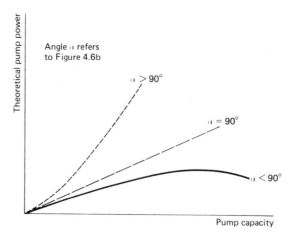

Figure 4.7   Power capacity of a pump

the pressure developed and the power absorbed are related by three pump laws:

$$V \quad \propto n \tag{4.10}$$
$$p_t \quad \propto n^2 \tag{4.11}$$
$$W_p \quad \propto n^3 \tag{4.12}$$

The last law is based on the assumption that the efficiency-volume curve is a fixed shape, for a given pump and impeller, independent of speed. It follows that the power absorbed at the pump impeller can also be plotted against the volumetric flow rate (Figure 4.7).

As with fans in duct systems, the actual duty of a pump-piping combination can only be determined from the intersection of the pump and system characteristics, on the same $p-V$ coordinates. A straightforward interpretation of Equation (4.5) assumes that the pipe friction factor, f, is a constant and that the pressure loss is proportional to the square of the velocity of water flow and hence to the square of the volumetric flow rate. This square law assumption fits the first two pump laws (Equations (4.10) and (4.11)).

Example 4.5 A piping circuit (Figure 4.8) carries 1 kg s^{-1} of chilled water and is of 32 mm nominal bore, medium-grade steel with a pressure drop rate of 380 Pa m^{-1} and an equivalent length of 1.6 m. Calculate the pressure loss in the system, assuming that pipe lengths without dimensions are negligible. The authority of the control valve is 0.3 and the losses of head through the cooler coil and the chiller are 1 m and 4 m, respectively. Gate valves are used for isolating purposes and malleable cast-iron 90° elbows are fitted where shown. *Answer* From Table C4.36 in the CIBS guide, $k = 0.7$ for an elbow and 0.2 for a gate valve. With a divergent tee having equal diameters on all branches, $k = 0.2$

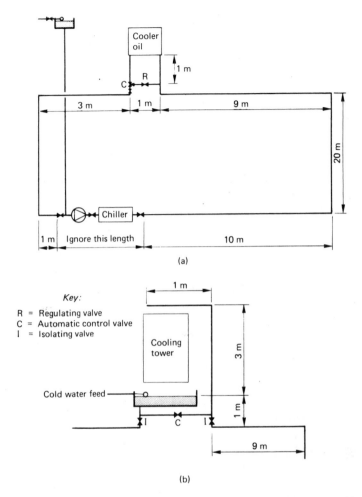

Figure 4.8 Closed and open piping circuits for Examples 4.5 and 4.6: a, Closed chilled water circuit; b, Open cooling water circuit

for straight-through flow. Adding dimensions given in Figure 4.8, the straight pipe length is $10+20+9+1+1+3+20+1 = 65$ m. The total equivalent length of pipe can now be calculated:

Straight pipe:	= 65
Elbows: $6 \times 0.7 \times 1.6$	= 6.72
Tee (branch to the coil): 0.2×1.6	= 0.32
Tee (connexion from the F & E tank): 0.2×1.6 =	0.32
Gate valves: $5 \times 0.2 \times 1.6$	= 1.6
Total equivalent length of straight pipe:	= 73.96 m

The authority of the control valve refers to the part of the circuit where variable flow occurs, namely, through the coil and local pipe connexions, the loss through the bypass being made equal to this by adjusting the regulating valve, R, during commissioning. Hence, the pressure loss through the control valve is:

$$\left(\frac{0.3}{1-0.3}\right)\left[\frac{2\times380}{1000}\text{ (for straight pipe)}+\frac{0.32\times380}{1000}\text{ (for the tee)}\right.$$

$$\left.+9.81\text{ (for the cooler coil, Equation (4.3))}\right]=4.58\text{ kPa}$$

The total pressure loss through the system may now be calculated:

Equivalent straight pipe: $73.96\times380/1000 = 28.10$
Chiller: $1000\times9.81\times4/1000$ $= 39.24$
Cooler coil: $1000\times9.81\times1/1000$ $= 9.81$
Control valve: 4.58
Total pressure loss: $= \overline{81.73}$ kPa

Assuming a coefficient of performance of 4, the condenser associated with the chiller, above, would probably need a cooling water flow rate of 1.25 kg s^{-1}. The rate of pressure drop for this flow in a 32 mm pipe exceeds the suggested limit of 500 Pa m^{-1} although not by much. Because of the fouling that inevitably occurs in open cooling water systems it might be wise to choose one pipe size larger, i.e. 40 mm. From Figure 4.1 it can be calculated that this size has a loss of about 250 Pa m^{-1}, with a velocity of about 0.91 m s^{-1}, using an internal diameter of 41.85 mm from CIBS Table C4.4. From CIBS Table C4.12, the equivalent length is 1.9 m.

Example 4.6 Using the modification to Figure 4.8a shown by Figure 4.8b, where an open cooling tower has been substituted for the cooler coil and assuming that a condenser with the same pressure drop replaces the chiller, calculate the total system loss for a flow rate of 1.25 kg s^{-1} in 40 mm nominal bore tube.

Answer Adding the modified piping dimensions in Figures 4.8a and b, gives 10 $+20+9+1+3+1+3+20+1 = 68$ m, beginning at the outlet from the condenser. The total equivalent length of pipe can now be determined:

Straight pipe: $= 68$
Elbows: $7\times0.7\times1.9$ $= 9.31$
Tees (past the tower bypass): $2\times0.2\times1.9$ $= 0.76$
Tee (connexion from the F & E tank): 0.2×1.9 $= 0.38$
Gate valves: $5\times0.2\times1.9$ $= 1.9$
Contraction leaving the cooling tower pond: $0.5\times1.9 =$ 0.95
Total equivalent length of straight pipe: $= \overline{81.30}$ m

Note that for the butterfly valve in the bypass to exercise effective control no water must flow over the tower when it is fully open. It follows that the loss of head across the butterfly valve, fully open, is 3 m, i.e. the static lift. However, in this case the bypass does not form part of the index circuit. The total system loss is, therefore

Equivalent straight pipe: (81.30 × 250)/1000   =20.32
Condenser: (1000 × 9.81 × 4)/1000   =39.24
Pressure loss corresponding to the static lift: (1000 × 9.81
× 3)/1000   =29.43
Total pressure loss: =88.99 kPa

When the pump stops, all the water in the system above the static water level drains back under gravity into the pond of the cooling tower.

Example 4.7 For the case in Example 4.6 determine the minimum necessary distance between the working water level and the overflow from the pond, assuming its plan area is 0.5 m^2.
Answer From Figure 4.8b, there is 4 m of 40 mm nominal bore tube above the water level. Taking the internal diameter of the pipe as 41.84 mm its water content is calculated as 0.0055 m^3. Hence, the bottom of the overflow must be at least 11 mm above the static water level, if wastage of water is to be avoided. This may not seem much but, if there is very little piping above the water level there will be very little drain back. Unfortunately, most cooling towers have shallow ponds that cannot accommodate much water and hence it is essential that the piping be designed as suggested, if wastage of water is to be avoided when the pump shuts down.

4.4 The interaction of pump and system characteristics

As with fan and duct systems, the only way of establishing the actual duty of a pump installed in a piping system is to plot the characteristics of both, using common pressure-volume coordinates. The characteristic curve for a pump having a given impeller and rotational speed is obtainable from the manufacturers and the system curve is determined by assuming a square law.

Example 4.8
(a) Assuming that a 1s^{-1} is numerically equal to 1 kgs^{-1}, plot the system pressure-volume characteristic curve and determine the actual duty achieved if a pump with the following performance for a speed of 24.17 rev s^{-1} is fitted in the closed circuit used in Example 4.5.

1s^{-1}	0.2	0.4	0.6	0.8	1.0	1.2	1.4	1.6
kPa	82	83	83.5	84	83.7	82.2	80.7	76.8

(b) Plot the system characteristic curve for the open circuit used in Example 4.6 and determine the duty obtained if the same pump is used.

Answer

(a) Assuming a square law relationship between pressure loss and water flow rate, the system has the following characteristic:

$1 s^{-1}$	0.2	0.4	0.6	0.8	1.0	1.1	1.2	1.3
kPa	3.3	13.1	29.4	52.3	81.78	99	117.8	138.2

This is plotted in Figure 4.9, with the data for the pump. An intersection occurs at point A and it can be seen that the duty obtained is about that wanted, $1.0 \ 1s^{-1}$ at 81.8 kPa.

(b) With the open system, enough pressure must be developed to lift the water by 3 m before any flow occurs at all, although thereafter a parabolic system law may be assumed, as before. Example 4.6 shows that the total system loss is 88.99 kPa but that of this, 29.43 kPa is ascribed to the static lift. The loss through the rest of the system for a flow rate of $1.25 \ 1s^{-1}$ is therefore 59.56 kPa and it is this figure that must be used with the square law assumption. The following may be calculated:

$1 s^{-1}$	0	0.2	0.4	0.6	0.8	1.0	1.25	1.4
Loss in pipe, etc. (kPa)	0	1.5	6.1	13.7	24.4	38.1	59.56	74.7
Static lift (kPa)	29.43	29.43	29.43	29.43	29.43	29.43	29.43	29.43
Total system loss (kPa)	29.43	30.93	35.53	43.13	53.83	67.53	88.99	104.13

Plotting this on Figure 4.9 shows that the intersection with the pump curve now occurs at point B and the duty is only about $1.18 \ 1s^{-1}$. This is not enough.

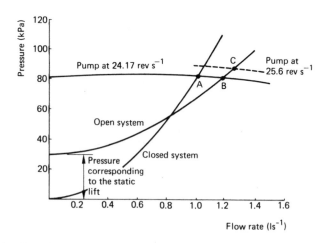

Figure 4.9   Closed and open pumped circuits for Example 4.8

If the pump were belt-driven, it might be possible to speed it up, by changing the pulleys, in accordance with the pump law given by Equation 4.10:

Speed required $= 24.17 \times 1.25/1.18 = 25.6$ rev s^{-1}.

The pump would then have the characteristic shown by the broken line in Figure 4.9, the intersection would be at point C and the desired duty of 1.25 l s^{-1} obtained.

If the pump were driven directly from its motor, changing speed would not be a practical proposition. The solution then is to use a larger impeller, within the same volute if this is possible. Another law of pump performance is that the flow rate is directly proportional to the impeller diameter, at constant pump speed and fluid density, and so this could be used to size a new impeller. If it is not possible to do this, because of the size of the pump casing, a larger pump must be chosen, its impeller diameter being selected to give the duty wanted.

4.5 Variable flow systems

When a constant water flow rate can be ensured through boilers and chillers, by means of primary and secondary circuits, two-port throttling valves may be adopted to regulate the capacities of heater batteris and cooler coils in the secondary system. In fact, with larger installations it is highly desirable that variable flow be used so that full advantage may be taken of load diversity, the sizes of the mains and pumps being reduced and running costs minimised. Although such two-port valves will be sized for a pressure drop when fully open that gives an authority of between 0.2 and 0.4, pressures throughout the system will change as the valves modulate independently to match load changes and, at low flow rates, the pressure drop across the few valves remaining open will be exceedingly large.

Example 4.9 Figure 4.10 shows a simplified secondary pipe circuit feeding five cooler coils from a primary main in which the pressure is constant at 1 kPa, there being no significant drop between X and Y, nor between Y and Z. Pipes for which a dimension is not shown are of negligible length and the loss through fittings is ignored. The design water flow rate is 0.2 l s^{-1} through each cooler coil, with a corresponding pressure drop of 0.5 kPa. An automatic, motorised, modulating valve (C1, C2, etc.) is fitted in the flow line to each coil. (a) Calculate the total pump pressure and the pressures at pump suction and discharge, assuming that the index run is through control valve C5, which is sized for an authority of 0.3.
(b) If all control valves, except C5, are fully closed, calculate the pressure that this remaining open valve must absorb if it is to pass its design flow rate. For simplicity it is assumed that the pump used has a flat, horizontal characteristic.

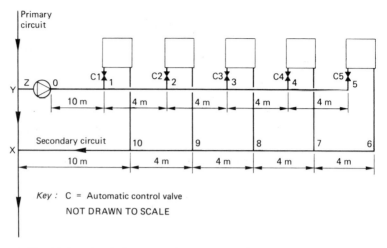

Figure 4.10   Piping circuit for Examples 4.9 and 4.10

Answer

Item	Flow rate ($1\,s^{-1}$)	Size (mm)	Pressure drop rate ($kPa\ m^{-1}$)	Length (m)	Pressure drop (kPa)
0–1	1.0	32	0.380	10	3.80
1–2	0.8	32	0.250	4	1.00
2–3	0.6	32	0.150	4	0.60
3–4	0.4	25	0.270	4	1.08
4–5	0.2	20	0.250	4	1.00
0–5					7.48
6–11					7.48
Cooler coil					0.50
Subtotal					15.46

(a) For an authority of 0.3,

0.3 = (valve loss)/(valve loss + loss in rest of system)

Hence, valve loss = $(0.3 \times 15.46)/(1.0 - 0.3)$ = 6.66 kPa, and the total system loss = 6.66 + 15.46 = 22.12 kPa.

If a pump is selected to deliver $1\,1s^{-1}$ with a total pressure of 22.12 kPa then, when installed where shown in Figure 4.10, the pressure at pump suction, Z, will be 1.0 kPa and that at pump discharge, 0, will be 23.12 kPa.

(b) When only $0.2\,1s^{-1}$ is flowing through the circuit to the index unit, the pressure loss through the piping can be assessed by assuming a square law as a reasonable approximation for Equations (4.2) and (4.5), without reference to

Figure 4.1. For example, if the pressure loss in section 0–1 is 0.380 kPa m^{-1} when 1.0 l s^{-1} is flowing then it is $0.380 \times (0.2/1.0)^2 = 0.0152$ kPa m^{-1} when 0.2 l s^{-1} is flowing. Hence the pressures at various points, numbered throughout the system, may be determined:

Item	Flow rate (l s^{-1})	Pressure drop rate (kPa m^{-1})	Length (m)	Pressure drop (kPa)	Pressure at a point in the system (kPa)
0					23.12
0–1	0.2	0.0152	10	0.152	
1					22.968
1–2	0.2	0.0156	4	0.062	
2					22.906
2–3	0.2	0.0167	4	0.067	
3					22.839
3–4	0.2	0.0675	4	0.270	
4					22.569
4–5	0.2	0.2500	4	1.000	
5					21.569

Flow conditions in X–7 are similar to those in 0 to 4, giving a pressure drop of $23.12 - 22.569 = 0.551$ kPa. Hence, since the pressure at X is 1 kPa, it must be 1.551 kPa at 7. The loss from 7–6 is 1 kPa, the same as for 4–5, and the loss through the coil is 0.5 kPa, for 0.2 l s^{-1} flowing. The pressure on the coil side of the index valve, C5, is therefore $1.551 + 1 + 0.5 = 3.051$ kPa. So the index valve must absorb $21.569 - 3.051 = 18.518$ kPa and will be almost closed if it is to pass only 0.2 l s^{-1}. Apart from the stress imposed on the valve the amount of stem movement available for full control of the water flow is very much reduced and control will tend to degenerate from proportional to two-position, probably with noticeable water noise and mechanical juddering.

Figure 4.11 shows how the pressure to be absorbed by the index valve will increase from 6.66 kPa under design full load conditions to 18.518 kPa at the partial duty considered above.

It is worth considering here the meaning of the system characteristic curve. Any piece of pipe, or any fitting or item of plant, has a system characteristic that has nothing to do with the pump which may be connected to it. The system characteristic shows the relation between the flow rate through the pipe, or other item, and the pressure loss, in accord with the equations mentioned, especially Equations 4.4 and 4.5. However, for simplicity, it is common to adopt a square law, pressure loss proportional to flow rate squared, without introducing much error, on the assumption that turbulent flow is occurring. As soon as any change in the system is made, for example by partially closing a control valve, it becomes an entirely different system and has

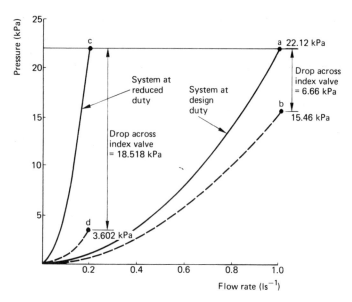

Figure 4.11   System curves with variable flow

quite a different characteristic. Thus the curve (a) in Figure 4.11 depicts the flow-pressure loss relation for the system as designed and balanced, by regulating valves at each cooler coil in addition to the control valves shown in Figure 4.10, to pass a total of $1.0 \, \text{l s}^{-1}, 0.2 \, \text{l s}^{-1}$ flowing through each coil. If the index valve is removed and replaced by a short piece of frictionless pipe, its new system characteristic is shown by curve (b). Curve (c) shows the system when all the valves are shut except at the index coil, which continues to pass $0.2 \, \text{l s}^{-1}$, under its own, local, thermostatic control. Similarly, curve (d) is for the system passing $0.2 \, \text{l s}^{-1}$ to the index coil only, but assuming that the index control valve has been removed. To produce these curves the starting points for the application of a square law were: (a) $1.0 \, \text{l s}^{-1}$, at 22.12 kPa, (b) $1.0 \, \text{l s}^{-1}$ at 15.46 kPa, (c) $0.2 \, \text{l s}^{-1}$ at 22.12 kPa and (d) $0.2 \, \text{l s}^{-1}$ at 3.602 kPa ($= 22.12 - 18.518$).

Example 4.10 Plot pressure against position in the system for curves (a) and (c) in Figure 4.11 and also for the case when all control valves are partly closed under thermostatic control to pass $0.1 \, \text{l s}^{-1}$ each.

Answer Pressure through the system when it is passing $0.2 \, \text{l s}^{-1}$ has been tabulated in answering Example 4.9(b) and this can be plotted to show the pressure distribution in the system described by curve (c). The results from example 4.9(a) can be used to establish pressure throughout the other two systems:

Item	Flow rate (ls⁻¹)	Pressure drop (kPa)	Pressure (kPa)	Flow rate (ls⁻¹)	Pressure drop (kPa)	Pressure (kPa)
0			23.12			23.12
0–1	1.0	3.8		0.5	0.95	
1			19.32			22.17
1–2	0.8	1.0		0.4	0.25	
2			18.32			21.92
2–3	0.6	0.6		0.3	0.15	
3			17.72			21.77
3–4	0.4	1.08		0.2	0.27	
4			16.64			21.50
4–5	0.2	1.00		0.1	0.25	
5			15.64			21.25
Z			1.00			1.00
Z–10	1.0	3.8		0.5	0.95	
10			4.8			1.95
10–9	0.8	1.0		0.4	0.25	
9			5.8			2.20
9–8	0.6	0.6		0.3	0.15	
8			6.4			2.35
8–7	0.4	1.08		0.2	0.27	
7			7.48			2.62
7–6	0.2	1.00		0.1	0.25	
6			8.48			2.87

These results are plotted in Figure 4.12. Whilst pressures at pump suction

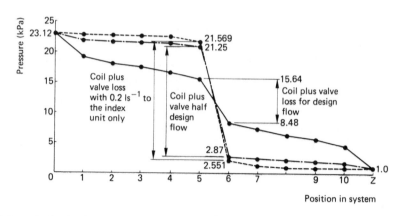

Figure 4.12   System pressure distribution with variable flow

and discharge remain constant, those elsewhere in the system vary considerably as the flow rate changes. It is to be noted that the pressure at pump discharge is constant because a flat, straight-line, pump characteristic was assumed. In a real case there would be some variation as the point of intersection with the system curve shifted up or down the curved pump characteristic.

Figure 4.12 shows that, whilst the pressure absorbed across the index valve is 6.66 kPa ($= 15.64 - 8.48 - 0.5$) for design duty, it rises to 18.518 kPa ($= 21.569 - 2.551 - 0.5$) as the flow falls to $0.21\,\mathrm{s}^{-1}$. To ease this situation there are three possibilities: reducing pump speed; bypassing water across the coil circuit; throttling flow at pump discharge. The first solution is the best in theory and is commonly used on large installations where the penalty of the extra capital cost for the speed control device or the variable speed motor is more than balanced by the saving in running cost over the system life (see Section 8.4). As an alternative to a variable speed motor a variable speed hydraulic coupling can be used. It seems[3] that variable couplings have a maximum drive efficiency of about 95% and this reduces proportionately as the transmitted speed falls. Using this property with the third pump law (Equation (4.12)), it can be verified that the power absorbed by the drive is proportional to the square of the speed ratio and so

$$W_{p2} = (W_{p1}/0.95) \times (n_2/n_1)^2 \tag{4.13}$$

Pressure changes in the variable flow piping circuit are used to regulate the flow control devices mentioned. The best approach seems to be to choose a pair of places, one in the flow and one in the return, about two-thirds of the way from the pump towards the index unit, and measure the differential pressure. For the circuit shown in Figures 4.10, 4.11 and 4.12, one pressure-sensing probe might be located at position 3 in the flow and the other at 8, in the return. It is good sense to provide places for pressure-sensing proves in about three different pairs of locations, between two-thirds and three-quarters of the way to the index unit, to allow some repositioning on site during commissioning, in the event that the first choice is not the best. Under design flow conditions the sensor at 3 would measure 17.72 kPa and that at 8 a value of 6.4 kPa, giving a differential of 11.32 kPa. If nothing were done, the pressure at 3 would rise to 22.839 kPa and that at 8 would fall to 1.281 kPa, providing a differential of 21.548 kPa. Supposing that a reasonable proportional band for the pressure sensors were 5 kPa, then the differential could rise to $11.32 + 5 = 16.32$ kPa. This variation in pressure difference is needed to tell the pump to reduce speed or to open a bypass valve across the coil circuit, i.e. between section 0–1 in the flow and X–10 in the return).

If a throttling valve is used in the main at pump discharge, not as much power is saved at reduced flow as with pump speed reduction. Firstly, the overall design pump pressure must be greater so as to give the main throttling valve a reasonable authority and, secondly, the product of the pressure drop across this valve and its volumetric flow rate (Equation (4.7)) represents a loss of power.

4.6 Pump types

The centrifugal pump with a volute casing is the type most commonly used for building services and, among the many styles available, one method of classification is according to the drive arrangement:

(1) Integral canned rotor—the impeller is fixed to the shaft of the rotor, which revolves in a rotor can filled with water. The stator and the electrical connexions are outside the rotor can and, since the pump shaft does not emerge from the casing, there is no need for a shaft seal to limit water leakage. Such pumps are common in domestic heating installations and, if they are light enough in weight, may be fixed directly in the pipe-line without additional support. Otherwise, they are floor-mounted. Such pumps must never be used in chilled water lines because condensation then occurs on the electrical connexions and causes continual difficulties.

(2) Direct-coupled—the motor shaft is coaxial with and attached to the impeller shaft through a flexible coupling, both motor and pump being mounted on a common base-plate. Difficulties in shaft alignment are sometimes experienced and a shaft seal is necessary to limit leakage from the pump casing.

(3) Close-coupled—the motor and pump are separate but the impeller is mounted on an extension of the motor shaft. There is consequently no possibility of misalignment but motor noise can be transmitted directly into the piping system. Although the pump has no bearings as those of the motor serve for both, a shaft seal is needed.

(4) Belt-driven—vee-belts and pulleys provide the drive connexion between the pump and its motor, the whole assembly being fixed on a common base-plate. A shaft seal is necessary.

Modifying the pump performance is done by changing the impeller in cases (2) and (3), by altering the pulleys in case (4) and by electrical methods for case (1).

That part of the pump where the impeller shaft passes through the casing is formed into what is called a stuffing box, containing either a packed gland or a mechanical seal. The former contains replaceable, asbestos string or the like, lubricated with graphite grease or something similar. A screwed top to the gland may be tightened to control seepage but some leakage is desirable to give shaft lubrication and cooling at the gland. The packing is replaced when worn. If there is a negative pressure at the pump suction air can be drawn into the system and to prevent this occurring a lantern ring may be fitted to divert a small amount of water from the pump discharge to the gland. A mechanical seal comprises a spring-loaded labrynth of carbon-ceramic or carbon-stainless steel faces, through which there is virtually no leakage but which may offer some difficulty in replacement should this be necessary. Both types of seal can be used for water temperatures up to 100°C but beyond this special arrangements for materials and cooling are needed. For mechanical seals in particular, the working pressure and temperature are critical to performance and cooling water from an external source must be supplied when they operate above 100°C. It is essential that the piping system is properly flushed out before a pump with a mechanical seal is run and all seals must be provided with flushing connexions to keep the seal interfaces free from contamination. Mechanical seals should only be fitted to pumps that are of suitable design, namely, those with short, stiff shafts having adequate bearings. Mechanical seals must not be regarded as bearings. Seal faces will be damaged if the pump runs without water, even as a momentary dry run, when the electrician tests the direction of rotation, is sufficient to cause serious damage and render the seal useless.

Other aspects of classification are according to construction: horizontal or vertical impeller shafts, split casings which facilitate impeller changes, cleaning and maintenance, single or double suction impellers, single or multi-stage, self-priming, etc.

4.7 Margins and pump duty

Few systems suffer because the pump is slightly oversized since it is nearly always possible to reduce capacity by changing impellers or speeds, but many are in difficulties if their resistance has been underestimated. If a serious underestimation has been made and no margin added, it may not always be possible to get the desired duty by altering the impeller or the speed and an entirely new and larger pump may be needed. If any margin is added to the flow rate, to cover a design uncertainty or for any other reason, then a corresponding allowance must be made to the system resistance, in accordance with Equation (4.5). Using the binomial approximation this means that a small increase in the flow rate must be accompanied by a doubled increase in the system resistance. Furthermore, there is the likelihood that the system will not be installed exactly as it was designed; almost certainly the actual installation will be more complicated and hence will offer a greater resistance to flow. It is, therefore, suggested that 5% be added to the design flow rate, that 10% be added to the calculated resistance, and that a further resistance addition, as estimated for the particular difficulty of the job in question, or 5%, whichever is the greater, be made to cover installation variations.

In general, a pump should be chosen so that the design flow rate occurs at a steeply falling part of the pressure-volume characteristic and at a near peak on the efficiency-volume curve. The virtue of this is that changes in system resistance will give small variations in the flow rate, which is most desirable with open systems where continuous fouling occurs.

4.8 Dissolved gases and cavitation

The solubility of a gas in water is given by Henry's law:

$$c = H p \qquad (4.14)$$

where c is the concentration of the gas in water at a given temperature, H is a constant and p is the partial pressure of the gas. Hence the mass absorbed is directly proportional to the partial pressure of the gas and, since its volume is also proportional to this, it follows that water at a given temperature will absorb a constant volume of a given gas. Table 4.1 gives the volumetric solubilities of some common gases in water at various temperatures.

Table 4.1   Volumetric solubilities of gases at different temperatures[4, 5]

Gas	Volume of gas absorbed per unit volume of water			
	0°C	20°C	50°C	100°C
Air	0.032	0.02	0.0125	0.012
Nitrogen	0.026	0.017		0.0105
Oxygen	0.053	0.034	0.021	0.0185
Carbon dioxide	1.87	0.96	0.5	0.26
Hydrogen	0.023	0.02		0.018
Ammonia	1250.0	70.0		0
Chlorine	5.0	2.5		0
Hydrogen disulphide	5.0	2.8		0.87

It must be emphasised that the relevant pressure in Equation (4.14) is the partial pressure of the gas. Consequently when the partial pressure of the air above water at 100°C is 101.325 kPa, the total pressure over the water will be 202.65 kPa because water at 100°C in equilibrium with its gaseous phase also exerts a vapour pressure of 101.325 kPa. Only under such circumstances will 0.012 volumes of air be dissolved in one volume of water at 100°C. The corollary is that, since water at 100°C and under a total pressure of 101.325 kPa exerts this as its saturated vapour pressure, it can contain no dissolved air at all.

Example 4.11 Determine the volume and mass of air that could be dissolved in 1 m³ of water at 20°C if the ambient atmosphere is at 20°C dry-bulb, 50% saturation and 101.325 total pressure.

Answer Table 4.1 shows that 0.02 volumes are dissolved. The partial pressure of the air in the ambient atmosphere is $101.325 - 1.182 = 100.143$ kPa (from

CIBS tables of psychrometric data). From the same source, taking the density of dry air at 101.325 kPa and 20°C as 1/0.8301 = 1.2047 kg m^{-3} the mass of dissolved air can be deduced as $(0.02 \times 1.2047 \times 100.143)/101.325 = 0.0238$ kg m^{-3}.

When water flows through a piping system air will tend to come out of solution as the pressure drops and as the temperature rises. The air pockets so formed restrict the area available for the flow of water and so increase the pressure drop rate, the net result being that less water is delivered. The release of air in this way is not sudden and it appears[5] that the amount coming out of solution depends on the time the water flow in the pipe is subjected to the conditions that favour its production.

The restricting effects of air pockets are reduced as the velocity of flow increases. Higher velocities help to break up bubbles into smaller sizes and to scour out the pockets themselves. In general, air is carried along with water when velocities exceed 0.6 ms^{-1}[6] for pipes up to 50 mm. It is recommended[7] that above this the minimum velocity to make the system self-purging should be that corresponding to a pressure drop rate of 75 Pa m^{-1}. Thus for 150 mm pipe at 75 Pa m^{-1}, the minimum velocity should be about 1 ms^{-1}. Much higher minimum velocities are required to convey air along downward sloping piping, and as much as 3 ms^{-1} is suggested by some authorities[6] as necessary although such high speeds are usually to be avoided because of the risks of erosion of the pipe walls.

A distinction must be drawn between the amount of air dissolved in water and the amount that can come out of solution under changes of pressure and temperature, the latter being not easy to predict. It has been suggested[5] that as little as 10% of the quantity theoretically possible actually comes out of solution.

Example 4.12 Cooling water at a rate of 1.25 1s^{-1} enters a condenser at 27°C and leaves at 32°C. If the initial pressure of the water is 99 kPa and the drop through the condenser is 39 kPa, determine the mass of dissolved air that could, theoretically, come out of solution.

Answer Interpolating in Table 4.1 at temperatures of 27°C and 32°C, 0.0182 and 0.017 volumes of air, respectively, could be dissolved in one volume of water. If the air came out of solution at entry to the condenser, its pressure would be 99 kPa and, since dry air at 27°C and 101.325 kPa has a density of 1/0.85 = 1.176 kg m^{-3} (from CIBS tables of psychrometric data), its density at 99 kPa would be $(1.176 \times 99)/101.325 = 1.149$ kg m^{-3}. So the mass of air in solution at entry to the condenser could be $0.0182 \times 1.149 = 0.0209$ kg m^{-3}. At exit from the condenser, the air, if it came out of solution, would have a temperature of 32°C and a pressure of $99 - 39 = 60$ kPa. The density of dry air at 32°C and 101.325 kPa is 1/0.8642 = 1.157 kg m^{-3}. Hence at 32°C and 60 kPa its density is $(1.157 \times 60)/101.325 = 0.685$ kg m^{-3}. So the mass of air that could be dissolved in the water leaving the condenser is $0.017 \times 0.685 = 0.0116 \, \text{kg m}^{-3}$. Hence, the theoretical mass of air that might be released as the water flows through the condenser is $(0.0209 - 0.0116) \times 0.00125 = 0.000011625 \, \text{kg s}^{-1}$. If this air were liberated at 60 kPa, the pressure prevailing at the condenser outlet, it would correspond to a volumetric flow rate of $(1000 \times 0.000011625)/0.685 = 0.017010 \, 1 \, \text{s}^{-1}$, i.e. the percentage of air in the water, by volume, would be $(0.017 \times 100)/1.25 = 1.4\%$. However, only one-tenth of this might actually be present.

With an open system using a cooling tower or air washer the air is thoroughly aerated, but in closed systems the water is not necessarily saturated with air. There are, however, other sources of free air bubbles, such as: improper venting during filling; air leakage into the system through pump glands, valve glands or poorly made joints, if these are in parts of the piping where the pressure is subatmospheric; the formation of a vortex at the outlet from a tank, particularly from the pond of a cooling tower.

Any permanent feature of a tank, not necessarily close to the outlet, may impart a rotational component to the water flowing past it; this input of energy is continuous and so the rotational movement is self-sustaining and causes the formation of a whirlpool in the water, above the outlet from the tank. Transient disturbances of the water surface produce eddies that are not self-sustaining and play no part in establishing the vortex at the outlet. The funnel of air at the centre of the whirlpool extends into the outlet pipe, its tail thinning and eventually breaking, to form bubbles that are tnrained by the water and conveyed through the system. As much as 10% of the outlet flow can be air[8], in extreme cases.

Discouraging the formation of a vortex at an outlet seems to be possible[8] by taking one or more of the following steps: minimising the rotational flow leading to the outlet; using a larger area of outlet; increasing the depth of the water; locating the outlet near a vertical tank wall; intercepting the tail of the whirlpool by placing a baffle beneath the surface, near the outlet (Figure 4.13).

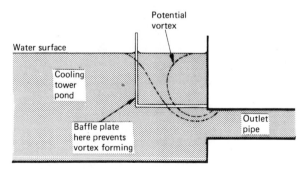

Figure 4.13   Prevention of a vortex formation by interception of its potential tail with a suitably positioned baffle plate near the outlet

None of these steps necessarily prevents swirl being established in the outlet pipe. This can best be prevented[8] by inserting cruciform guide vanes in the pipe, some two or three diameters downstream from the outlet. The length of the vanes should be at least one outlet diameter. Although swirl can be removed in this way, a good deal of turbulence remains in the water and the presence of guide vanes alone cannot prevent a vortex forming in the tank.

To see some of these seemingly insignificantly small percentages in perspective, consider a pipe of radius R and length $2R$, containing n bubbles, each of radius r. The percentage by volume occupied by the bubbles is $200\,n\,r^3/3R^3$. For the case of a 50 mm tube, containing 1% of free air in the form of 5 mm diameter bubbles, $n = 3 \times 25^3/(200 \times 2.5^3) = 15$, but if the bubbles are only 0.5 mm in diameter, there are 15 000 of them.

There is very little published information concerning the effect of free air on the performance of centrifugal pumps. However, Stepanoff[9] shows the results of some tests done by Siebrecht[10], a version of these being shown in Figure 4.14. It seems that pump pressure, efficiency and power are all diminished by the presence of free air in the impeller. Taking a flow rate of 50 ls^{-1} as an example, Figure 4.14 shows that the presence of 2% free air reduces the pump pressure developed by about 3% from 189 kPa to 183 kPa. Further along the curve, where it is falling more steeply at 70 ls^{-1}, the effect is more pronounced, and the presence of 2% free air causes a drop of 11% from about 167 kPa to about 148 kPa. According to one view[12] the presence of 5% by volume of free air corresponds to a 20% drop in pump speed. Any free air in a system is undesirable.

Although the term is sometimes used also to denote the formation of

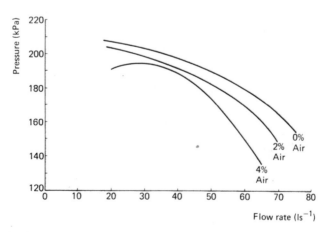

Figure 4.14   An approximate interpretation of Siebrecht's results[9] showing the effect of free air admitted into the pump suction

bubbles of gas, cavitation is really quite a different phenomenon and occurs when the pressure in a fluid falls to a value less than the saturation vapour pressure, p_w, corresponding to the local fluid temperature. If water flowing along a pipe at an initial pressure p_1 suffers a frictional pressure loss to a lower pressure, p_2, then if p_2 is less than p_w some of the water will flash to steam, producing bubbles of vapour that are carried along with the water. If these bubbles subsequently enter a region of higher pressure, say in the passages of the pump impeller, they suddenly collapse with considerable noise and set up pressure waves in the water that cause mechanical damage to the impeller and pipe wall, termed cavitation erosion. Prandtl[11] postulated that cavitation was favoured by the presence of gas bubbles and dissolved air. More recently[13], Pearsal considers that the presence of submicroscopic gas bubbles might be the nucleii needed to give cavitation at pressures exceeding the vapour pressure. Apparently[13], prepressurised, de-aerated, pure water may be subjected to considerable tension of up to 300 atmospheres, without cavitation occurring, in the absence of nucleii. It is certain that cavitation is responsible for much severe damage to pump impellers, appearing as deep pitting on the blades. Moreover, it is accompanied by a pronounced fall in pump performance, affecting both head and efficiency, and this forms the basis of determining what is known as the net positive suction head (NPSH) required by the pump manufacturers. NPSH is defined[14] as the total inlet head plus the head corresponding to atmospheric pressure, minus the head corresponding to the vapour pressure, the total inlet head being the sum of static, position and velocity heads at the inlet section of the pump.

As water flows from the suction flange into the pump it suffers a significant fall of pressure before the impeller starts to impart energy and so raise its pressure again. This loss of energy, defines the lowest absolute pressure that is possible at the suction flange if cavitation is to be avoided. The only pressures that can be easily measured are those indicated by the gauges at the suction and discharge flanges. It is not possible, unfortunately, to measure the lowest pressure within the impeller and this can only be inferred from other observations. Several methods may be adopted to measure the NPSH required but that currently most popular is to reduce the head at the suction flange until a 3% reduction in the pump head is observed. It is clear from this that cavitation has already commenced some time earlier and it follows that, even if the NPSH required by the manufacturer is just barely provided, there will still be cavitation, and possible damage from cavitation erosion, occurring within the pump. The inception of cavitation and its extent depends upon how far the operating pump efficiency is from its maximum efficiency, reinforcing the dictum that pumps should always be chosen to work at their point of peak efficiency. Grist[15] recommends that the NPSH available should exceed the NPSH required, measured on a 3% basis by the manufactures and termed NPSH (3%), by a factor, f,

$$NPSH_{available} = f\,NPSH(3\%) \tag{4.15}$$

as given in Table 4.2.

Table 4.2 Recommended factors for applying to the NPSH required

Percentage of the flow rate at peak efficiency	30–49	50–79	80–110	111–125
f		9	6	3	12

Thus the NPSH available should desirably be at least three times that required by the manufacturers, even when the pump is working at the flow rate that gives maximum efficiency. The value of the NPSH required rises rapidly as the flow rate increases (Figure 4.15). NPSH available is defined by

$$NPSH_{available} = H_{at} + H_z - H_w \tag{4.16}$$

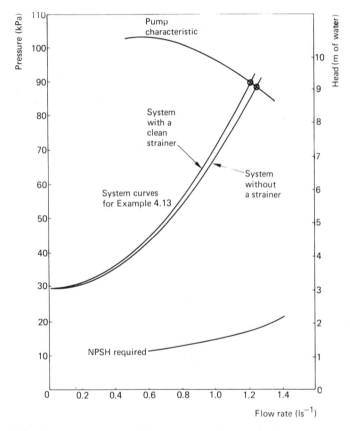

Figure 4.15   Pressure-volume and head-volume characteristic curves for a typical centrifugal pump, with the corresponding NPSH required

if the feed and expansion connexion is at the pump suction and by

$$\text{NPSH}_{\text{available}} = H_{at} + H_z - \Delta H_p - H_w \qquad (4.17)$$

if the connexion is upstream of the suction branch, where H_{at} is the head corresponding to the atmospheric pressure acting on the open surface in metres of the fluid handled; H_z is the position head represented by the vertical distance of the open surface above the centre-line of the pump suction branch; ΔH_p is the friction and entry loss between the feed and expansion connexion and the pump suction branch in metres of the fluid handled; and H_w is the head corresponding to the vapour pressure of the fluid.

Example 4.13 Using the appropriate information from Example 4.6, but with the assumption that a 200 mesh, 32 mm strainer is fitted in the suction line between the pond and the pump, determine the flow rate and the likelihood of cavitation occurring with water at 27°C. Take the atmospheric pressure as 101.325 kPa and the density of water as 1000 kg m^{-3}. Assume that the centre-line of the pump suction branch is 1 m below the surface of the water in the pond. The pump used has the characteristic performance shown in Figure 4.15.

Answer First the loss in the suction line and the new overall system loss must be established. Referring to Example 4.6 and Figures 4.8a and b shows that, on the suction side of the pump, for a flow rate of 1.25 kg s^{-1}:

Length of straight pipe:	= 25.0
Elbows: $3 \times 0.7 \times 1.9$	= 3.99
Tee (past the cooling tower): 0.2×1.9	= 0.38
Tee (connexion to the feed and expansion tank): 0.2×1.9	= 0.38
Gate valves: $2 \times 0.2 \times 1.9$	= 0.76
Contraction leaving the pond: 0.5×1.9	= 0.95
Original subtotal:	= 31.46 m
Original pressure loss: $(31.46 \times 250)/1000$	= 7.865
Loss through a clean strainer (from Figure 4.2):	= 5.0
Revised suction loss:	= 12.865
Original total system loss:	= 88.99
Loss past a clean strainer:	5.0
Revised total system loss:	= 93.99 kPa

The revised system characteristic performance can now be established, assuming a square law:

Flow rate (kg s^{-1})	0	0.2	0.4	0.6	0.8	1.0	1.2	1.25
Loss in pipe etc. (kPa)	0	1.65	6.61	14.87	26.44	41.32	59.50	64.56
Static lift (kPa)		29.43	29.43	29.43	29.43	29.43	29.43	29.43	29.43
Total system loss (kPa)	29.43	31.08	36.04	44.30	55.87	70.75	88.93	93.99

In Example 4.8 the system characteristic performance without a strainer was calculated, so both system curves may be plotted (Figure 4.15) and it can be seen that, whereas the duty was 1.25 kg s^{-1} without a strainer it is a little less at 1.21 kg s^{-1} when a clean strainer is fitted and for this a NPSH of about 1.7 m H_2O is required.

Referring to CIBS tables, $p_w = 3.564$ kPa at 27°C and, calculating the revised loss in the suction line as $12.865 \times (1.21/1.25)^2 = 12.05$ kPa, it can now be determined that

$$H_{at} = (101.325 \times 1000)/(1000 \times 9.81) = 10.33 \text{ m}$$
$$H_z = 1.00 \text{ m}$$
$$\Delta H_p = (12.05 \times 1000)/(1000 \times 9.81) = 1.23 \text{ m}$$
$$H_w = (3.564 \times 1000)/(1000 \times 9.81) = 0.36 \text{ m}$$

Hence, from Equation 4.17:

$$\text{NPSH}_{available} = 10.33 + 1.0 - 1.23 - 0.36 = 9.74 \text{ m } H_2O.$$

The critical value of ΔH_p in the suction line is $10.33 + 1.0 - 0.36 - 1.7 = 9.27$ m H_2O and this corresponds to a pressure drop of $(1000 \times 9.27 \times 9.81)/1000 = 90.94$ kPa.

When the strainer gets dirty this sort of pressure drop is a possibility. It is generally a bad principle to put a strainer, or any other significant resistance, on the suction side of a pump, because of the risk of cavitation. For this reason condensers and chillers, which invariably do have a significantly large pressure drop, always have their pump arranged to discharge into them and never to suck from them.

4.9 Temperature rise across pumps and heat gain to pipes

The rate of energy input to the water flowing through a pump, given by Equation (4.7), causes a small temperature rise. If c is the specific heat capacity of water, then

$$\dot{m}c\Delta t = \dot{m}gH = Vp_t = \dot{m}p_t/\rho$$

whence $\Delta t = gH/c$ or $p_t/\rho c$. If 60% is taken as the typical pump efficiency and it is assumed that half of the wasted 40% enters the water, the remaining 20% being dissipated to the surroundings, a fractional efficiency of 0.8 can be used to give the actual rate of energy input to the water. Inserting values of 4178 J kg^{-1}°C^{-1} for c, 9.81 ms^{-2} for g and 1000 kg m^{-3} for ρ, approximate expressions are obtained as follows:

$$\Delta t = 0.003°\text{Cm}^{-1} \text{ of pump head} \tag{4.18}$$

$$\Delta t = 0.0003°\text{C kPa}^{-1} \text{ of pump pressure} \tag{4.19}$$

Example 4.14 A pump develops a pressure of 94 kPa, corresponding to 9.61 m of water. Determine the temperature rise across the pump.

Answer From Equations (4.18) and (4.19)

$$\Delta t = 0.003 \times 9.61 = 0.029°\text{C or}$$
$$\Delta t = 0.0003 \times 94 = 0.028°\text{C}$$

Heat gain to insulated piping carrying chilled water has received little attention and data is scanty, one reason probably being that the loads imposed by the heat gain are only a very small proportion of the total cooling load. Table 4.3 gives some approximate heat gains. The figures refer to a temperature difference between the surface of the pipe beneath the lagging and an ambient temperature of about 30°C, but it is common to assume, without much error, that the difference between the chilled water temperature and the ambient air temperature may be used. The figures are not likely to be more accurate than $\pm 10\%$ and they do not include the gains to fittings, valves, etc., which might account for an additional 10%, or even more, in plant rooms.

Example 4.15 Determine the temperature rise accruing from pump power and heat gain to the chilled water pipes used in the circuit for Example 4.5. Take the thickness of the insulation to be 40 mm, the chilled water flow temperature to be 6.5°C, the return temperature to be 12°C and the ambient air temperature to be 30°C.

Answer The total pump pressure calculated in Example 4.5 was 81.73 kPa and 65 m of 32 mm pipe was involved. The temperature rise across the pump is given by Equation (4.19):

$$t = 0.0003 \times 81.73 = 0.025°\text{C}.$$

Table 4.3 Heat gains to insulated piping

Nominal pipe size (mm)	15	25	32	40	50	80	100	150	200	250	300
Nominal thickness of lagging (mm)	40	40	40	40	40	40	45	45	50	50	50
Heat gain per metre of pipe run (Wm^{-1} C^{-1})	0.203	0.238	0.274	0.309	0.354	0.491	0.525	0.696	0.797	0.968	1.121

Note. The thermal conductivity of the lagging is assumed to be about 0.043 Wm^{-1}C^{-1}.

From Table 4.3, the heat gain is $0.274 \text{ Wm}^{-1}\text{°C}^{-1}$. If the mean chilled water temperature is 9.25°C the heat gain to the piping is $0.274 \times 9.25 \times 65 = 164.7$ W. With a flow rate of 1 kg s^{-1}, this corresponds to a rise in the temperature of the water of $164.7/(4718 \times 1) = 0.035$°C.

To bring these answers into perspective they should be looked at as percentages of the total cooling load:

$$\Delta t \text{ for the pump power} = 0.025 \times 100/5.5 = 0.45\%$$
$$\Delta t \text{ for pipe gain} = 0.035 \times 100/5.5 = 0.64\%$$
$$\text{Total } t = \overline{1.09\%}$$

Therefore, any margin to cover pump power and heat gain to the pipes is of the order of 1%.

Exercises

1 A closed piping circuit has a resistance of 50 kPa. If the water level in the feed and expansion tank is 40 m above the centre-line of the pump suction, to which the cold feed is connected, determine the heads and pressures that would be indicated by gauges positioned at (a) 0.5 m below pump suction and (b) 1.5 m above pump discharge.

(*Answer* (a) 40.5 m, 396 kPa; (b) 43.9 m, 429 kPa)

2 A closed water piping system comprises 130 m of straight pipe of 50 mm nominal bore, 16 elbows $(k = 0.7)$, two tees $(k = 0.2)$ and 6 gate valves $(k = 0.2)$. Given that $f = 0.0048$, calculate the equivalent length of straight pipe that will absorb one velocity pressure and determine the total equivalent length of straight pipe.

(*Answer* 2.6 m; 163.2 m)

3 If the system in **2** handles 3 kg s^{-1} and includes a chiller having a pressure drop of 40 kPa, determine the system pressure drop using Figure 4.1 for the friction loss in pipework.

(*Answer* 107 kPa)

4 If, for the circuit used in **2** and **3**, the cold feed is located at the pump suction but 20 m of straight pipe and the chiller precede this point of connexion, determine the NPSH available at the pump suction given that the water level in the feed and expansion tank is 15 m above the centre-line of the pump suction and the water temperature is 10°C. If the NPSH required is 6 m, establish whether cavitation will occur within the pump. Take atmospheric pressure as 101.325 kPa.

(*Answer* 5.33 m; yes)

Symbols

EL   Equivalent length   m

H	Head or total pump head, or Henry's constant	m
H_{at}	Head of fluid handled corresponding to atmospheric pressure	m
H_d	Static head at pump discharge	m
H_s	Static head at pump suction	m
H_w	Head of fluid handled corresponding to its vapour pressure at a particular temperature	m
H_z	Position head corresponding to a distance z	m
ΔH	Head lost	m
ΔH_p	Head of fluid handled corresponding to the pressure loss in a suction line.	m
M	Mass flow rate	$kg\,s^{-1}$
R	Pipe radius	m
(Re)	Reynolds Number	—
V	Volumetric flow rate	m^3s^{-1} or $l\,s^{-1}$
W_p	Pump power	W
c	Concentration of a gas in water	—
d	Internal pipe diameter	m
f	Friction factor	—
g	Acceleration arising from gravity or the specific force due to gravity in the earth's field	$m\,s^{-2}$ $N\,kg^{-1}$
h_o	Static head imposed on an open surface of fluid	m
k	Friction factor for pipe fittings	—
k_s	Absolute roughness of a pipe wall	m
l	Length of a pipe	m
$\dot{m}$	Mass flow rate	$kg\,s^{-1}$
p	Pressure	$N\,m^{-2}$ or Pa or kPa
p_{at}	Atmospheric pressure	$N\,m^{-2}$ or Pa or kPa
p_g	Gauge pressure at a pump	$N\,m^{-2}$ or Pa or kPa
p_s	Static pressure corresponding to h_o	$N\,m^{-2}$ or Pa or kPa
p_{sd}	Static pressure at pump discharge	$N\,m^{-2}$ or Pa or kPa
p_{ss}	Static pressure at pump suction	$N\,m^{-2}$ or Pa or kPa
p_t	Total pump pressure	$N\,m^{-2}$ or Pa or kPa
p_v	Vapour pressure	$N\,m^{-2}$ or Pa or kPa
r	Radius of a bubble	m
n	Number of bubbles	—
n	Rotational speed of a pump	$rev\,s^{-1}$
p_w	Vapour pressure of water	$N\,m^{-2}$ or Pa or kPa
p	Partial pressure of a gas	$N\,m^{-2}$ or Pa or kPa
v	Mean velocity of water flow	$m\,s^{-1}$
v_d	Mean water velocity at pump discharge	$m\,s^{-1}$
v_s	Mean velocity of water at pump suction	$m\,s^{-1}$

Δp	Specific pressure loss per metre of pipe length	$N\,m^{-3}$ or $Pa\,m^{-1}$
δp	Pressure loss	$N\,m^{-2}$ or Pa or kPa
ρ	Density of a fluid	$kg\,m^{-3}$

References

(1) *CIBS Guide*, Volume C. 1970

(2) Jones, W. P., *Air Conditioning Engineering*, 2nd Edition, Edward Arnold Publishers, 1973

(3) Etheridge, R., Variable speed pumping, *The Building Services Engineer*, **44**, A45, Sept 1976

(4) Walker, W. H., Lewis, W. K., McAdams W. H. and Gilliland E. R., *Principles of Chemical Engineering*, McGraw-Hill Book Company, 1967

(5) Crocker, S. and King, R. C., *Piping Handbook*, McGraw-Hill Book Company, 1967

(6) Miller, D. S., *Internal Flow Systems*, Volume 5, BHRA Fluid Engineering Series, 1978

(7) ASHRAE, *Handbook of Fundamentals*, 1977

(8) Denny, D. F. and Young, G. A. J., *The Prevention of Vortices and Swirl at Intakes*, Publication SP 583, BHRA, VIIth Congress of the IAHR, Lisbon, July 1957

(9) Stephanoff, A. J., *Centrifugal and Axial Flow Pumps*, 2nd Edition. John Wiley and Sons, New York, 1967

(10) Siebrecht, W. Untersuchungen uber Regelung von Kreiselpumpen, *Z Ver deut Ing*, **74**, p. 87, 1930

(11) Prandtl, L., *Essentials of Fluid Dynamics*, Blackie and Sons, London, 1953

(12) *Experiments with Air in Centrifugal Pumps*, BHRA Publication No. RR 465

(13) Pearsall, I. S., *Cavitation*, M & B Monograph ME/10, Mills & Boon, London, 1972

(14) BS 5316: Part 1, *Acceptance Tests for Centrifugal, Mixed Flow and Axial Pumps; Class C Tests*, 1976

(15) Grist, E., *Net Positive Suction Head Requirements for Avoidance of Unacceptable Cavitation Erosion in Centrifugal Pumps, Cavitation*. A Conference arranged by the Fluid Machinery Group of the I Mech E, Heriot-Watt University, Edinburgh, pp. 153–162, Sept 1974

5
Air distribution

5.1 The free isothermal jet

The behaviour of an air jet that is discharged into a large room at the same temperature has been well studied[1, 2, 3, 4, 5] and is best described in terms of four sections of its length:

(1) For a short distance, up to about four equivalent diameters from the plane of the outlet, its centre-line velocity is constant

(2) Over the succeeding four diameters of length a transition to turbulent flow occurs and in this zone the centre-line velocity, v_x, is inversely proportional to $\sqrt{x}$, where x is the distance from the plane of the outlet

(3) After this, turbulent flow is fully established and the influence of inertial forces predominates. For the next 25 to 100 equivalent diameters of jet length v_x is proportional to $1/x$. This is the zone of most interest

(4) Finally, at the end of the turbulent zone, v_x diminishes rapidly to less than 0.25 ms^{-1} and the pattern of air movement is unpredictable, viscous forces being dominant and quite small influences enough to produce random and transient changes.

Within the third zone the following empirical equation may be used to determine v_x, for most practical purposes:

$$v_x = K'Q/[x\sqrt{(A_g c_d R_{fa})}] \tag{5.1}$$

in which K' is a constant of proportionality (see Table 5.1), Q is the volumetric airflow rate, A_g is the gross area of the outlet, c_d is its coefficient of discharge which varies from 0.6 for sharpedged orifices to 1.0 for circular openings with well-rounded edges, and R_{fa} is the ratio of free to gross area for the outlet.

Table 5.1 Values of the proportionality constant for Equation (5.1)

	Values of K'	
Type of opening	$v_o = 4$ to 8 ms^{-1}	$v_o = 2$ to 4 ms^{-1}
Round or square openings	7.0	5.7
Rectangular, free slot $(R < 40)$	6.0	4.9
Grilles $(R_{fa} > 0.4)$	5.7	4.7

195

In Table 5.1, R is the aspect ratio of the opening (breadth/height) and v_o is the effective velocity of the jet over the section of the vena-contracta when issuing from a sharp-edged orifice, or the average velocity of discharge through an open-ended duct, as given by

$$v_o = v_c/(c_d R_{fa})$$ (5.2)

where v_c is the nominal mean velocity through the area of the orifice or the open-ended duct.

The typical profile over the cross-section of a free isothermal jet in the third zone is in the form of a bell-shaped curve for velocity against distance through the jet section. Although the maximum velocity, v_x, lies along the centre-line of the jet the mean velocity over its section is only about 20% to 30% of this. The throw of a jet, for comfort conditioning, is usually defined as the value of x for which v_x equals 0.25 ms^{-1} and thus, on average over the cross-section of the jet, the mean residual velocity is only about 0.05 to 0.075 ms^{-1}. One criterion adopted for the throw is that v_x should reach 0.25 ms^{-1} when $x = L$, L being the distance from the outlet to the opposite wall, or to the end of the throw of a jet coming from another supply opening, opposite. Sometimes the distance down the opposite wall, or vertically downward from the point of meeting with the oncomimg jet, to the occupied zone (1.8 m from floor level) is included as part of the throw.

An isothermal jet in free space expands naturally with an included angle of between 20 and 24°, air being entrained around its periphery, momentum conserved and its mean velocity consequently reducing. Because the jet is at the same temperature as the room air generally, no buoyancy forces are present and only the natural expansion of the jet can produce air movement in the room, the tendency being that room air wafts slowly towards the supply opening and the periphery of the jet. The concept of drop is really only relevant when the jet is colder than the room air and, therefore, falls in a trajectory towards the occupied zone, under gravitational influences. The intention is then to deliver the jet from its outlet at a velocity and temperature that will decay to 0.25 ms^{-1} and room temperature by the time the occupied zone is reached, but such nonisothermal behaviour has not yet been fully investigated.

Most research has been done on the behaviour of free jets entering large rooms but, in the practical case, air is discharged from openings so as to flow along adjoining ceilings or up nearby walls, taking account of the Coanda effect, which is that the frictional loss between the jet and the surface with which it is in contact creates a pressure difference across the section of the jet that tends to press it to the surface, countering any downward buoyancy forces and delaying the drop into the occupied zone. The proximity of the ceiling to a side-wall grille or a diffuser is thus a significant feature of the selection of proprietary distribution terminals.

Example 5.1 A 300 mm diameter nozzle with $R_{fa} = 1.0$ and $c_d = 1.0$ delivers a horizontal jet of air into a very large room. Assuming that K' (Equation (5.1)) is 7.3, determine the centre-line velocity at a distance of 9 m from the nozzle if the initial air velocity is 5 ms^{-1}.

Answer

$Q = A_g v_o = (0.3^2 \pi/4) \times 5 = 0.0707 \times 5 = 0.3535 \ m^3 s^{-1}$

From Equation (5.1) $v_x = (7.3 \times 0.3535)/[9\sqrt{0.0707}] = 1.1 \ ms^{-1}$.

5.2 The free nonisothermal jet

The behaviour of air jets issuing from outlets at temperatures other than that of the ambient air is complicated. Koestel[6] has proposed that the drop, y, of a jet flowing horizontally from an opening of diameter D_o, at a mean initial velocity v_o, may be calculated for a horizontal distance, x, from the outlet by the equation

$$\pm\frac{y}{D_o} = 0.065\left(\frac{x}{D_o}\right)^3\left(\frac{t_r - t_o}{273 + t_r}\right)\left(\frac{gD_o}{v_o^2}\right) \tag{5.3}$$

where t_r and t_o are the room and initial jet temperatures, respectively. The coefficient of proportionality for the jet, $K = K'/1.13$, has been taken as 6.5 in this equation, corresponding to $K' = 7.3$.

Example 5.2 For the case of Example 5.1 determine the drop at $x = 9$ m, if $t_r = 22°C$ and $t_o = 12°C$. Take g as 9.81 ms^{-2}.

Answer From Equation (5.3),

$$y = 0.3 \times 0.065\left(\frac{9}{0.3}\right)^3\left(\frac{22-12}{273+22}\right)\left(\frac{9.81 \times 0.3}{5^2}\right) = 2.1 \ m$$

Koestel's equation makes certain simplifying assumptions, notable among which is that the slope of the jet trajectory should not be too great. This would seem to limit its practical use but, nevertheless, reasonable agreement with experimental results has been reported[6].

Koestel[7] has also studied the maximum downward throw, x_{max}, of warm air discharged from a nozzle and he proposes that

$$\frac{x_{max}}{D_o} = \sqrt{3.4\left(\frac{273 + t_d}{t_o - t_r}\right)\left(\frac{v_o^2}{gD_o}\right)} - 2.85 \tag{5.4}$$

Example 5.3 Determine the maximum downward throw of a jet at an initial temperature of 40°C into a room at 20 C, for the conditions of Example 5.1.

Answer From Equation (5.4)

$$x_{max} = 0.3\left[\sqrt{3.4\left(\frac{273+40}{40-20}\right)\left(\frac{5^2}{9.81 \times 0.3}\right)} - 2.85\right] = 5.5 \ m$$

An approximate relationship between jet temperature and velocity, for the horizontal, nonisothermal case, is given by

$$\frac{t_o - t_r}{v_o} = \frac{t_x - t_r}{v_x} \tag{5.5}$$

where t_x is the mean temperature of the jet at a distance x from the outlet.

5.3 Side-wall grilles

Laboratory studies[8] suggest that the path of a horizontal, nonisothermal jet is best described in terms of the Archimedean number, (Ar), defined for a room by

$$(\text{Ar}) = g(t_w - t_o)D_h/(T_r u_r^2) \tag{5.6}$$

in which t_w is the temperature of the heated surfaces in the room, T_r is the absolute room temperature, u_r is a fictitious mean air velocity through the cross-section of the room and D_h is its mean hydraulic diameter, defined by $D_h = 2BH(B+H)$, B and H being the breadth and height of the room, respectively.

Further laboratory studies[9] have attempted to use the Archimedean number to establish a design procedure for the selection of side-wall grilles. The method proposed, however, usually yields a supply air quantity that requires a larger temperature difference, room-to-supply, for offsetting the sensible heat gains than would be determined by the practical considerations of psychrometry. The method is not recommended and it is better to adopt conventional, commercial procedures for selecting the necessary supply air temperature and to use Equation (2.3) to calculate the supply air quantity, following this by a grille selection from a manufacturer's catalogue.

The cheapest way of supplying air to a conditioned space is very often by side-wall grilles rather than by ceiling diffusers. For the distribution to be effective the pressure drop along the duct in which the grilles are fitted should be small compared with the drop across the grille and its associated dampers and vanes, in order to assist balancing and sizing the duct by static regain helps. It is very important to ensure smooth airflow from the duct normally into the face of the grille if the anticipated throw, drop, spread and noise level are to be achieved.

Values of throw to a terminal velocity of 0.25 ms^{-1} for a typical grille located near a flat ceiling and fitted with opposed-blade dampers and two sets of direction-control vanes are given in Table 5.2 for sizes from a commercial range. Figure 5.1 shows a plot of the throw against the volumetric flow rate for the full range of sizes available. The following conclusions can be drawn.

(1) For a given grille size, corresponding to a part of the curve, the throw is approximately proportional to the volumetric flow rate

(2) The throw is more sensitive to changes in the flow rate at the lower volumes

Table 5.2 Values of throw to a terminal velocity of 0.25 ms⁻¹ for grille sizes from a commercial range

Available sizes of grilles with nominal dimensions in mm

Velocity through the free area (ms⁻¹)	NR (dB)	Pressure drop across opposed-blade dampers and grille (Pa)			Size A 406×102, 305×127, 254×152 Flow rate (ls⁻¹)	Throw to a terminal velocity of 0.25 ms⁻¹(m)			Size B 457×102, 356×127, 305×152, 203×203 Flow rate (ls⁻¹)	Throw to a terminal velocity of 0.25 ms⁻¹(m)			Size C 508×102, 406×127, 356×152, 254×203 Flow rate (ls⁻¹)	Throw to a terminal velocity of 0.25 ms⁻¹(m)			Size D 610×102, 457×127, 406×152 Flow rate (ls⁻¹)	Throw to a terminal velocity of 0.25 ms⁻¹(m)		
Vertical vane setting ( )		0	22.5	45		0	22.5	45		0	22.5	45		0	22.5	45		0	22.5	45
1.5	21	2	3	4	47	5.5	4.3	2.7	54	5.8	4.6	3.0	66	6.7	5.5	3.4	73	7.0	5.5	3.4
2.0	21	4	5	7	64	6.4	5.2	3.4	73	7.0	5.5	3.4	87	7.6	6.1	3.7	99	7.9	6.4	4.0
2.5	21	7	8	12	80	7.3	5.8	3.7	82	7.6	6.1	4.0	109	8.2	6.7	4.3	123	8.8	7.0	4.6
3.0	21	9	11	16	97	7.9	6.4	4.0	111	8.5	6.7	4.3	130	9.1	7.3	4.6	146	9.8	7.9	4.9
3.5	26	13	14	22	113	8.5	6.7	4.3	130	9.1	7.3	4.6	151	9.8	7.9	4.9	172	10.7	8.5	5.2
4.0	30	17	19	29	127	9.1	7.3	4.6	146	9.8	7.9	4.9	175	10.7	8.5	5.2	196	11.3	9.1	5.5
5.0	36	27	30	45	160	10.1	7.9	5.2	184	11.0	8.8	5.5	217	11.9	9.4	6.1	245	12.5	10.1	6.4
6.0	42	39	44	66	193	11.3	9.1	5.5	222	12.2	9.8	6.1	260	13.1	10.4	6.4	295	13.7	11.0	7.0

Note. All grilles are assumed to be fitted with opposed-blade dampers and two sets of manually adjustable direction-control vanes. Noise ratings are for fully open dampers with smooth, uniform airflow at right angles to the plane of the grille. Room effect is taken as zero (see Section 7.8). Vane settings of 22.5° and 45° increase the NR value by 1 and 7 dB, respectively.

In practice, it is very likely that higher NR values will be experienced because airflow is seldom smooth into a grille face and because most grilles have partially closed dampers in order to achieve the correct airflow rate

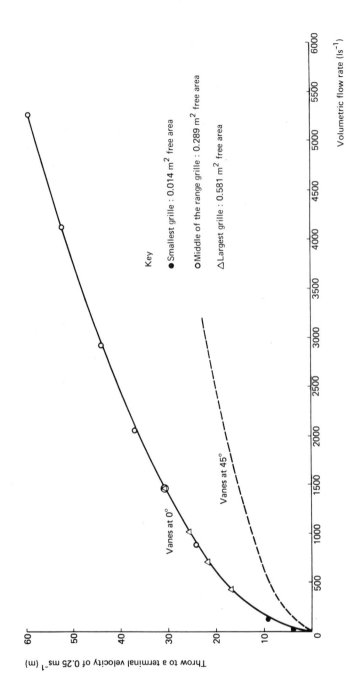

Figure 5.1   Relationship between flow rate and throw for a typical commercial range of side-wall grilles with vertical vanes set at 0°. The throw for a setting of 45° (90° included angle) is about half of this value. Appropriate for room-to-supply air temperature differences from 8°C to 13°C

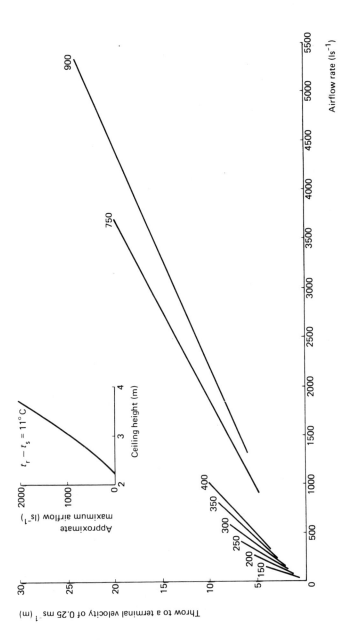

Figure 5.2 Overall performance of a range of sizes of a typical commercial circular ceiling diffuser. Sizes are nominal neck diameter in mm. Manufacturers' catalogues should always be referred to for specific cases

(3) A shorter throw can be achieved for a given total flow rate by using several small grilles rather than be a few large ones.

Furthermore, if the throw for grilles with their vertical vanes set at the 45° position (90° included angle) is plotted, as shown by the broken line in Figure 5.1, the throw is seen to be about half that obtained for the 0° vane setting, with vertical vanes parallel.

Data are sparse on the best separation, z, between grilles but one manufacturer suggests:

$$z = 0.20 \ x, \text{ if the vanes are set at } 0° \tag{5.7}$$
$$z = 0.25 \ x, \text{ if the vanes are set at } 22.5° \tag{5.8}$$
$$z = 0.30 \ x, \text{ if the vanes are set at } 45° \tag{5.9}$$

When the grille is adjacent to a wall, half the above values of z should be taken as the minimum allowable distance from the wall.

Some general principles of grille selection are:

(1) A side-wall grille near a ceiling gives a longer throw than a square or circular ceiling diffuser

(2) The effective use of grilles is limited to air change rates of less than about 20 per hour, with conventional ceiling heights

(3) Stagnant air pockets may form if the air change rate is less than approximately 4 per hour, corresponding to specific supply rates of $3 \, \mathrm{l \, s^{-1} \, m^{-2}}$

(4) The drop may be excessive, in the nonisothermal case, if the discharge velocity through the free area is below $0.2 \ \mathrm{ms^{-1}}$

(5) The upper edge of the grille should be within 300 mm of the ceiling.

Example 5.4 Select suitable side-wall grilles for the supply of $0.4 \ \mathrm{m^3 s^{-1}}$ to a room of size 7.2 m wide × 7.5 m long × 2.6 m high. The grilles are to be mounted in the wall that is 7.2 m wide and the height of the occupied zone is 1.8 m.

Answer The air change rate is $(0.4 \times 3600)/(7.2 \times 7.5 \times 2.6) = 10.2$ per hour, so side-wall grilles can be used. Required throw $= 7.5 + (2.6 - 1.8) = 8.3$ m. Figure 5.1 shows that a single grille would give a throw of about 17 m with its vanes at 0°, or 8.5 m with them at 45°, suggesting that 2 or even 3 grilles may be suitable. Table 5.2 shows that two grilles of size C can be used to give the desired throw with their vanes set at between 22.5° and 45°, which gives about NR 32, plus from 1 to 7 dB, depending on the vane setting. Supposing the vanes must be opened to 45° to get the throw with draughtless distribution then the desirable minimum separation between the grilles is $z = 0.3 \times 8.3 = 2.49$ m, according to Equation (5.9). If the widest grille of size C is chosen, i.e. 508 mm × 102 mm, the minimum total width of wall required will be $2 \times (2.49 + 0.508) = 5.996$ m, which is less than the 7.2 m available, and is satisfactory.

If 3 grilles are chosen, each handling $133 \ \mathrm{l \, s^{-1}}$, a possibility is size B. Then, from Table 5.2 the required throw could be obtained with the vanes set at between $0°$ and $22.5°$, with a probable noise level of about NR $26 + 1$ dB for the diverging vanes. From Equation (5.8) the minimum permissible separation is $z = 0.25 \times 8.3 = 2.075$ m. Selecting the widest grille, 457 mm $\times$ 102 mm, means that a distance of $3 \times (2.075 + 0.457) = 7.596$ m, which exceeds the available wall width of 7.2 m, and so 3 grilles is not possible, unless a smaller width is chosen, say 305 mm $\times$ 152 mm.

Consider the maximum possible air change rate that can be handled. The principle is to find a grille in the maker's catalogue that gives the desired throw of 8.3 m with the largest possible volumetric flow rate, ignoring considerations of noise. Because throw is roughly proportional to flow rate and a $45°$ vane setting halves the throw, the catalogue must be searched for the narrowest grille that will give a throw of 8.3 m with its vanes at $45°$, which gives a grille of 254 mm $\times$ 254 mm, handling 431 ls^{-1} (not shown in Table 5.2). From Equation (5.9), it can be calculated that the minimum separation is $0.3 \times 8.3 = 2.49$ m and so the maximum number of grilles that can be fitted in the 7.2 m wall is $7.2/(0.254 + 2.49) = 2.62 \simeq 2$. The air change rate is then $(2 \times 0.431 \times 3600)/(7.2 \times 7.5 \times 2.6) = 22.1$ h^{-1}. If the room had had a wall long enough to accommodate 3 grilles, i.e. $3 \times (0.254 + 2.49) = 8.232$ m, then the maximum possible air change rate would have been $(3 \times 0.431 \times 3600)/(8.232 \times 7.5 \times 2.6) = 29$ h^{-1}. This confirms the earlier statement that sidewall grilles are unsuitable for air change rates exceeding about 20 h^{-1}, since one manufacturer's grille is much the same as another's.

Manufacturers' tests show that the drop of an airstream depends on the air quantity as well as the temperature difference, a conclusion not readily inferred from Equation (5.3). It follows that the risks of drop may be minimised by using many small outlets rather than few large ones. The inset in Figure 5.2 gives an approximate relation between drop and airflow rate for one particular type of adjustable, circular, ceiling diffuser. The relationship varies considerably with different types and reference should always be made to manufacturers' data for specific cases. For side-wall grilles, the risk of drop can be reduced by adjusting the horizontal vanes to curve the airstream towards the ceiling, if the top edge of the grille is more than 300 mm below it.

5.4 Ceiling diffusers

Circular ceiling diffusers distribute a radially expanding airstream over the ceiling that rapidly entrains air and gives a very good pattern of air movement in the room. Temperature differences of up to $14°C$ for cooling can usually be safely adopted with conventional ceiling heights, provided the diffusers are properly selected. Table 5.3 gives a selection of performance details for a commercial, circular ceiling diffuser with adjustable cones, and Figure 5.2 shows the overall performance for the complete range of sizes available for the type.

Table 5.3 Performance of a commercial circular ceiling diffuser with adjustable cones

| Mean neck velocity (m s⁻¹) | Total pressure drop (Pa) | Nominal size of ceiling diffuser (mm) | | | | | | | | | | | |
| | | 150 | | | 200 | | | 300 | | | 400 | | |
		Flow rate (ls⁻¹)	Radius of diffusion (m)	NR (dB)	Flow rate (ls⁻¹)	Radius of diffusion (m)	NR (dB)	Flow rate (ls⁻¹)	Radius of diffusion (m)	NR (dB)	Flow rate (ls⁻¹)	Radius of diffusion (m)	NR (dB)
2.0	5	38	0.9		66	1.2		149	2.1		264	2.7	
2.5	8	47	1.2		83	1.5		184	2.4		330	3.4	22
3.0	12	57	1.5	23	99	2.1	24	222	3.0	26	396	4.0	27
3.5	16	66	1.8	28	116	2.4	29	260	3.4	31	462	4.6	33
4.0	21	76	2.1	32	132	2.7	34	297	4.0	35	529	5.2	37
4.5	27	85	2.1	35	149	3.0	37	333	4.6	39	595	6.1	40
5.0	33	94	2.4	39	165	3.6	40	370	4.9	42	661	6.7	44
6.0	47	111	3.0	44	198	4.0	46	444	5.8	48	793	7.9	49

If the diffuser is mounted in an exposed duct the quoted radius of diffusion, to a terminal velocity of 0.25 ms^{-1}, must be multiplied by 0.7. A room-to-supply air temperature difference of 11 °C for cooling is assumed and the NR values in dB are based on a room effect of zero. It should be noted that many makers quote NR values on the assumption of an 8 dB room effect.

It is claimed by some manufacturers that any pattern of air discharge from horizontally across the ceiling to vertically downwards is possible by adjusting the relative cone positions in the diffuser. Another view is that any distribution pattern between these two extremes is unstable and, at best, only transient. A small difference of pressure, inside to outside, across the cone of air will cause it to collapse to one or other of the two stable positions, on the ceiling or blowing vertically downwards.

As for all other air distribution terminals the makers' published data is for ideal conditions of installation and assumes smooth, uniform airflow normal to the plane of the cones with no upstream volume control damper. To achieve the tabulated performance these ideal conditions must prevail but they are only obtained with great difficulty in many actual installations and the presence of any turbulence in the neck of the diffuser will cause a departure from the expected behaviour, particularly from the NR value. Matters can be helped by having the longest possible straight duct feeding into the diffuser neck. Short lengths, which are the result of insufficient space above the suspended ceiling, are notorious for giving turbulent airflow into the diffuser cones and so causing noise. Projecting the diffuser neck into the duct itself makes things worse. The presence of proprietary volume control dampers in the diffuser neck often upsets the airflow enough to generate objectionable noise. It is best to use aerofoil section turning vanes, of short chord width, to assist smooth entry from the duct main to the branch feeding the diffuser and to size the main by static regain, if at all possible. The neck velocity should be as low as possible, consistent with the desired throw. Where dampers must be used to balance airflow they should be located as far away from the diffuser cones as is practicable.

Example 5.5 Select circular ceiling diffusers from Table 5.3 for the distribution of 0.4 m^{3}s^{-1} of air in the room considered in Example 5.4.
Answer Using a single, centrally-placed diffuser means that the throw should not exceed $3.6 + (2.6 - 1.8) = 4.4$ m. Reference to Table 5.3 shows that the choice is a size of 400 mm, 4.0 m radius of diffusion and NR 27.

The practical difficulties of accommodating a large number of closely-located diffusers in a ceiling and the problems of ducting air to them in the void above, limit the air change rates that can be handled to a maximum of about 30 per hour, although more than this can be delivered in some instances. Not all manufacturers offer diffusers with neck velocities as low as 2.0 ms^{-1} (Table 5.3), a common minimum is often 3.0 ms^{-1}, and this provides a further limitation on the maximum practical air change rate.

Square ceiling diffusers have performances that are similar to circular ones but the plan size of the square cones influences the throw for a given neck velocity. Thus, a diffuser of 200 mm square neck and a plan size of 300 mm square will deliver 99 l s^{-1} with a radius of diffusion of 3.4 m but the throw will be only 2.1 m when fed into a 600 mm square.

Linear slot diffusers are often used because they can be unobtrusively integrated with a suspended ceiling. They are commonly available in lengths up to about 2 m, greater distances needing several sections and shorter ones being cut to length on site. From 1 to 10 parallel slots may be combined in a single diffuser and arranged to blow in the same direction or outwards in opposing ways. The blow can also be directed vertically downwards, for spot cooling, although this is unlikely to give comfort under more normal conditions. It is essential that the duct connexions recommended by the diffuser manufacturer be followed and if good results are to be obtained, i.e. quiet, draughtless air distribution, the air velocity through the section of the plenum chamber or duct feeding the slots should be less than that through the slots themselves.

If a tapered duct is used to feed the slots, Koestel and Young[10] propose the following:

$$\cot \theta = A_s\, c_d/A_d \qquad (5.10)$$

in which θ is the angle between the linear diffuser and the airstream issuing from it, A_s is the area of the slot in the diffuser and A_d is the cross-sectional area of the duct feeding the diffuser, at its upstream end.

The performance of a selection of commercial linear diffusers is given in Table 5.4 and the approximate performance over the entire range is shown in Figure 5.3. Generally speaking linear diffusers have a shorter throw than side-wall grilles but a longer one than circular or square diffusers. Outlets, like circular diffusers, that entrain air rapidly have short throws and rapid

Table 5.4   Performance of commercial linear ceiling diffusers

Total pressure loss (Pa)	Number of slots in diffuser								
	1			3			5		
	Flow rate (ls^{-1} m^{-1})	Throw (m)	NR (dB)	Flow rate (ls^{-1} m^{-1})	Throw (m)	NR (dB)	Flow rate (ls^{-1} m^{-1})	Throw (m)	NR (dB)
1	12	1.2		37	3.4		62	4.8	
4	25	2.6		74	5.8		124	7.3	19
9	37	3.4	21	112	7.0	29	186	9.1	32
16	50	4.6	30	149	8.2	38	248	10.4	41

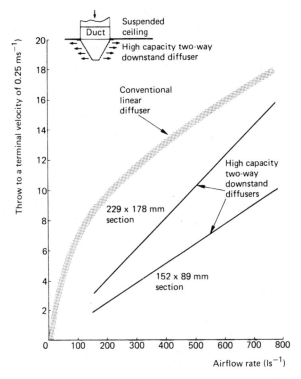

Figure 5.3 Typical performances of ranges of conventional and high capacity linear diffusers. The numbers of slots in a conventional linear diffuser does not affect the throw

temperature equalisation, room-to-supply, and can, therefore, handle rather more air changes per hour than outlets like side-wall grilles which have longer throws. Linear diffusers lie in between these.

Example 5.6 Select linear diffusers from Table 5.4 for the distribution of 400 ls^{-1} of air in the room considered in Example 5.1. Locate the diffuser in the centre of the ceiling parallel to the 7.2 m room dimension.
Answer The required throw is $7.5/2 + (2.6 - 1.8) = 4.55$ m, to a terminal velocity of 0.25 ms^{-1}. The specific airflow rate is $400/7.2 = 56 \, ls^{-1} \, m^{-1}$. Figure 5.3 shows that a throw of about 4.6 m will not be exceeded with this rate. Table 5.4 shows that a 3-slot diffuser could be used, interpolating between throws of 3.4 and 5.8 m.

A high capacity version of the linear diffuser is available for applications demanding a higher air change rate than can be conveniently handled by conventional air distribution terminals, and it is an alternative to a ventilated ceiling for duties up to about 40 air changes per hour. Figure 5.3 shows its triangular, downstand section and that the air is delivered parallel to the ceiling in opposing directions from a pair of perforated faces. Airflow must be smooth and uniform into the diffuser for good results. The performance lines for the two available sizes (152 mm × 89 mm and 229 mm × 178 mm, base and height, respectively) do not coincide, unlike the performance curve for conventional linear diffusers, where the sizes within the range overlap.

Example 5.7 Determine the air change rate that can be supplied through high capacity, downstand, two-way diffusers, using the performance lines in Figure 5.3, to the room used in Example 5.1.
Answer With the diffusers in the centre of the ceiling, parallel to the 7.2 m dimension, the tolerable throw is 4.55 m, as calculated earlier. Figure 5.3 shows that the larger diffuser will permit a delivery of about 225 l s^{-1} m^{-1}. The air change rate is, therefore, $(0.225 \times 7.2 \times 3600)/(7.5 \times 7.2 \times 2.6) = 42$ air changes per hour.

5.5 Ventilated ceilings

Although ventilated ceilings can be used for air change rates from about 7 h^{-1} upwards, they are unsuitable for small duties and only come into practical application for rates exceeding about 25 h^{-1}, where conventional air distribution terminals become difficult to select for draughtless conditions. Proprietary ceilings are available that will satisfactorily distribute from 30 to 520 l s^{-1} m^{-2} of live tile area with static pressures in the ceiling from 3 to 37 Pa, depending on the type of tile selected. When unavoidable, it is sometimes possible to locate extract grilles in the ceiling itself but this is the least favoured position and it is much preferred to position them at low level in the walls, or in the floor. If the whole of the ceiling is made live air distribution can be poor, particularly with a low air change rate, and it is even possible to get the downward flow of air moving obliquely across the room to a low-level extract point, giving draughts in part of the room and stagnant conditions elsewhere[11]. The secret of good distribution is to achieve turbulent mixing, above the occupied zone, between the down-moving cold air and the rising, warm, convection currents. This is often done by making only part of the ceiling live, the live tiles being positioned over the major sources of sensible heat gain, e.g. computer cabinets. There is then ample opportunity for entrainment and good mixing.

In computer room applications many of the cabinets have in-built fans that forcibly eject air upwards, ensuring turbulent mixing with the down-coming air and it is then possible, and often essential, for a very much larger proportion of the ceiling to be live. It is generally not feasible to use 100% of the gross ceiling area because of the presence of light fittings and perhaps downstand beams

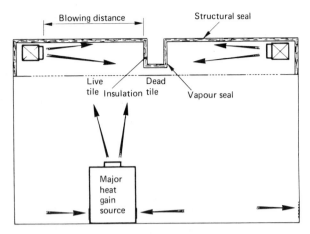

Figure 5.4   Air distribution for a ventilated ceiling

above the ceiling and these dead areas must be subtracted from the gross area to establish the maximum useable net ceiling area. Air change rates as high as $250\,h^{-1}$ have been successfully used with extract grilles at low level in the walls, but with rates up to $600\,h^{-1}$, as in clean rooms (Section 3.13) it may be necessary to use the whole of the floor area as an extract grille when laminar downflow is wanted.

To get good distribution beneath the ceiling it is first essential to arrange for good air distribution above it by introducing the air to the ceiling plenum chamber through a rudimentary duct system with a number of dampered outlet spigots blowing air horizontally across the top of the suspended ceiling (see Figure 5.4). Large ceiling plenum chambers must be divided into zones by downstand barriers from the soffit of the slab. Such zones should not exceed $500\,m^3$ and should be of fire-resistant material. The exit velocities from the supply spigots should not be greater than $5\,ms^{-1}$ and the spigots ought to be as far above the suspended ceiling as possible, otherwise there is the risk that air may be entrained upward through the live tiles in the vicinity of the spigot. Access tiles are required near the spigots for damper adjustment during commissioning.

The exact design of the ceiling must be left to the manufacturer but a guide to safe blowing distances, based on manufacturers' literature, is given in Table 5.5.

There is a risk that small holes in the thicker (10–15 mm) non-metallic ceiling tiles may block with dirt, after a period of use. To minimise this risk it is recommended that the air handling plant includes a bag filter with a minimum efficiency of 60% on Test Dust No. 1 (BS 2831:1971) and a prefilter having an efficiency of 95% according to Test Dust No. 2.

It cannot be too strongly emphasised that the chamber above the ventilated ceiling must be properly sealed, insulated and vapour-sealed. If there are cracks or openings in the structure of the plenum chamber the system will be an abject failure because the conditioned air will leak away. If the soffit of the slab and the four side-walls, together with any downstand beams, are not properly insulated, and vapour-sealed, heat gains, or losses, will nullify the effectiveness of the installation. It should be remembered that the temperature difference across the structure of the chamber is greater than usual, when calculating heat gains, because the air in the plenum is at about 14°C, instead of the more usual value of 22°C for conventional heat gains. A further cogent reason for insulating the slab, side-walls and beams is to isolate them thermally from the air temperature in the chamber. Otherwise the thermal inertia of the building structure will upset the response of the control system. For example, if a computer is switched off at weekends but the room is kept at 20°C, the supply air temperature to the plenum chamber above the ceiling will also be at about 20°C and the whole of the slab, side-walls and beams will have attained this temperature by start-up time on Monday morning. The outer 75 mm, or so, of the slab, etc. must then be cooled down to the required supply air temperature when the system then begins to try and meet the computer heat gains. It may be some time before the system is achieving good control again.

Table 5.5   Safe blowing distances for a ventilated ceiling

Clear depth of the ceiling plenum chamber (mm)	Safe blowing distance from a supply spigot (m)	
	Parallel to the joists or downstand beams	At right angles to open-web trusses and joists
120–150	6.0–7.5	4.0–5.5
150–210	7.5–9.0	5.5–6.0
210–250	9.0–12	6.0–8.5
250–300	12–15	8.5–10.5
300–450	15–17	10.5–11.5
450–750	17–18	11.5–13.0
750–1000	18–20	13.0–14.0
>1000	20–23	14.0–16.0

(Reproduced by kind permission of Haden Young Ltd.)

Example 5.8 If the lower 75 mm of the concrete slab over a ventilated ceiling is at a temperature of 21°C determine the time taken for it to reach a value of 15°C if the air is supplied to the plenum chamber at a constant value of 14°C. Assume Newtonian cooling occurs and the slab has a specific heat capacity of 0.85 kJ kg^{-1} °C^{-1} and a density of 2150 kg m^{-3}. Take the heat transfer coefficient at the surface of the slab as 9.5 Wm^{-2} °C^{-1}.

Answer Newtonian cooling is defined by:

$$\theta = \theta_o \, e^{-K/t} \tag{5.11}$$

where θ is the temperature of the material above a datum at time t, θ_o its initial temperature above the datum and $1/K$ is the time constant of the material, defined by:

$$\frac{1}{K} = \frac{\text{Heat stored in the material (J kg}^{-1})}{\text{Steady-state heat flow through the material (J kg}^{-1})} \tag{5.12}$$

The value of the heat transfer coefficient is virtually independent of the air velocity across it for the velocities likely to be encountered. Considering 1 m² of the slab Equation (5.12) can be used to establish the structural time constant:

$$1/K = (0.075 \times 2150 \times 850)/(9.5 \times 3600) = 4 \text{ hours}$$

$$\theta_o = 21° - 14° = 7°C \text{ and } \theta = 15° - 14° = 1°C$$

and so, from Equation (5.11):

$$1 = 7 \, e^{-t/4} \text{ and } t = 7.8 \text{ hours.}$$

5.6 Ventilated floors

Ventilated floors were dealt with in some detail towards the end of Section 3.17, which should be referred to.

5.7 The influence of obstructions on airflow

Accurate information for predicting the behaviour of an airstream upon encountering an obstruction is not available but Holmes and Sachariewicz[12] have proposed a simple method for an approximate assessment. It is based on experimental results for airflow from a slot across a ceiling that meets a nearby, parallel, downstand beam. Both the beam and the slot extend over the full ceiling width and the influence of temperature is said to be negligible.

When an airstream moves over a surface and meets a barrier, such as a downstand beam or a light fitting (see Figure 5.5) it may behave in one of three different ways:

(1) The airstream may closely follow the contours of the barrier. This happens if the distance from the slot to the barrier, x_d, exceeds $8x_c$, where x_c is a critical distance that can be obtained approximately from Figure 5.6. To use the figure the nominal height of the slot, h, is determined by assuming that the total pressure drop across the slot equals the velocity pressure of the airstream emitted from it. The downstand dimension of the barrier is d.

(2) The airstream may permanently separate from the ceiling, at the beam,

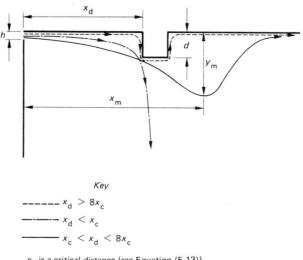

Key

$- - - - - - x_d > 8x_c$

$- \cdot - \cdot - x_d < x_c$

$——— x_c < x_d < 8x_c$

x_c is a critical distance (see Equation (5.13))

Figure 5.5   Behaviour of an airstream encountering an obstruction

and flow downwards into the occupied zone. This happens when $x_d < x_c$. (3) The airstream may leave the ceiling at the beam but return to it on its downstream side. This happens if $x_c < x_d < 8x_c$. The maximum, vertical separation of the centre-line of the airstream from the ceiling, y_m, can be determined approximately from Figure 5.7.

Example 5.9 A continuous slot along the full distance of the cornice at one end of a room is 7.2 m wide and delivers 400 $1s^{-1}$ across the ceiling towards a continuous, downstand beam of 80 mm square section, parallel to the slot and 1.5 m distant from it. The total pressure drop through the slot is 10 Pa and the floor-to-ceiling height is 2.6 m. Assess the probable behaviour of the airstream. *Answer* Total pressure drop = velocity pressure, by assumption. Therefore,

$$10 = 0.6 \, v_c^2$$

$$v_c = 4.082 \text{ ms}^{-1}.$$

Nominal slot area = 0.4/4.082 = 0.098 m², and nominal slot height, h, = (0.098 × 1000)/7.2 = 13.6 mm.

$$d/h = 80/13.6 = 5.88$$

From Figure 5.6, $x_c/h = 90$, and $x_c = 1.22$ m. $x_d < 8 \times 1.22$ m, therefore the airstream will not follow the contours of the beam. $x_d > 1.22$ m, therefore the

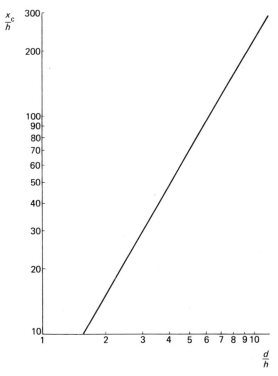

Figure 5.6   Relationship between critical distance and beam depth when an airstream follows the contours of the beam (after Holmes & Sachariewicz[12])

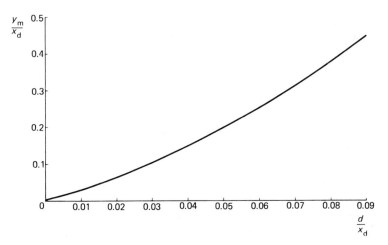

Figure 5.7   Maximum separation of an airstream from the ceiling on its downstream side (after Holmes & Sachariewicz[12])

airstream will return to the ceiling after a temporary excursion from it beyond the beam.

$$d/x_d = 0.08/1.5 = 0.0533$$

Therefore, from Figure 5.7

$$y_m/x_d = 0.22 \text{ and so } y_m = 0.33 \text{ m}.$$

Remembering that the airstream expands and that it is the centre-line that is 330 mm below the ceiling, it is prudent to add 300 or 400 mm to the generally accepted value of 1.8 m for the height of the occupied zone. In this example, the centre-line of the airstream is 2.27 m from the floor and it is therefore probable that no discomfort will be felt in the occupied zone, near the beam.

The velocity of the airflow on the downstream side of the beam is difficult to predict with certainty. Holmes[12] stated that 'very large, low-frequency fluctuations in velocity were experienced in the flow downstream of the barrier which made mean readings difficult to obtain'. When the air supply opening does not extend over the full width of the ceiling but the downstand obstruction does, the critical distance, x_c, is increased and the method is not strictly applicable except with caution. It can only be regarded as giving a rough indication of behaviour. When the obstruction is less wide than the slot, the critical distance is decreased and the method may be applied to give approximate results. It is claimed[12] that when the span of the obstruction is less than half the span of the slot, the effect of barrier can be ignored, provided that $x_d > x_c$.

5.8 Extract air distribution

Extract air distribution has been considered in Section 1.6 when extract light fittings were dealt with and needs little further comment, except to reiterate that the location of the extract opening has virtually no effect on air distribution in a room.

5.9 Air distribution performance index [13,14]

It has been established[15] experimentally that if the effective draught temperature, t_{ed}, lies between $-1.7°C$ and $+1.1°C$ and the velocity is below 0.35 ms^{-1} then a large majority of the occupants in a room are likely to be comfortable. Effective draught temperature is defined by

$$t_{ed} = (t_x - \bar{t}_r) - 7.65 (v_x - 0.152) \tag{5.13}$$

where t_x is the local air temperature in °C, $\bar{t}_r$ is the mean room temperature in °C and v_x is the local air velicity in ms^{-1}. The air distribution performance index (ADPI) is the percentage of positions in a room where measurements of the effective draught temperature lie between $-1.7°$ and $+1.1°$ and v_x is less than 0.35 ms^{-1}. The ideal would be an ADPI of 100% but, generally speaking, a value of 80% meets the most critical standards of comfort.

The ASHRAE handbook[15] quotes characteristic room lengths, related to a terminal velocity of 0.25 ms^{-1} for all terminals except linear diffusers where 0.5 ms^{-1} pertains. These lengths are the horizontal distances from the air outlet to the nearest wall or obstruction, or half-way to the nearest outlet blowing in opposition and if they are taken to be values of throw, the ADPI will be at a maximum. Measurements leading to the determination of an ADPI would only be relevant in the occupied zone.

Symbols

A_d	Cross sectional area of a duct	m^2
A_g	Gross area of an outlet	m^2
A_s	Area of a slot in a linear diffuser	m^2
(Ar)	Archimedean number	—
B	Breadth of a room	m
D_h	Mean hydraulic diameter of a room	m
D_o	Diameter of an opening	m or mm
H	Floor-to-ceiling height in a room	m
K	Coefficient of proportionality	—
K'	Constant of proportionality	—
L	Length of a room or a horizontal distance from an outlet to the opposite wall	m
Q	Volumetric airflow rate	$m^3 s^{-1}$ or $l s^{-1}$
R	Aspect ratio of an opening (b/h)	—
R_{fa}	Ratio of free to gross area of an outlet	—
T_r	Absolute room temperature	K
b	Breadth of an opening	mm or m
c_d	Coefficient of discharge of an outlet	—
d	Vertical dimension of a downstand obstruction in a ceiling	mm or m
g	Acceleration arising from the force of gravity	$m s^{-2}$
h	Height of an outlet	mm or m
t	Time	s or h
t_o	Initial temperature of a nonisothermal jet	°C
t_r	Room temperature	°C
$\bar{t}_r$	Average room temperature	°C
t_w	Temperature of the heated surfaces in a room	°C
t_x	Mean temperature of an air jet at a distance x from an outlet or local air temperature	°C

u_r Fictitious mean air velocity through the cross-section
of a room $m s^{-1}$
v_c Nominal mean velocity through the area of an orifice
or an open-ended duct $m s^{-1}$
v_o · Effective velocity of an air jet over the section of the
vena-contracta or the average velocity through an
open-ended duct. $m s^{-1}$
v_x Centre-line velocity in an air jet at a horizontal distance
x from an outlet or local air velocity $m s^{-1}$
x Distance horizontally from an outlet m
x_c Critical distance of an obstruction from an air supply
slot m
x_d Distance of an obstruction from an air supply slot m
y Vertical drop of the centre-line of a non-isothermal jet
below the horizontal centre-line of an outlet mm or m
y_m Maximum vertical separation of the centre-line of an
airstream from a ceiling mm or m
z Separation between adjoining side-wall grilles mm or m
θ Angle between a linear diffuser and the airstream
flowing from it or temperature above a datum   angular
degrees
or $^\circ C$
θ_o Initial temperature above a datum $^\circ C$

References

(1) Farquharson, I. M. C., The ventilating air jet: Part I, *JIHVE*, **19**, p. 449, 1952.

(2) Frean, D. H. and Billington, N. S., The ventilating air jet: Part II, *JIHVE*, **23**, p. 313, 1955.

(3) Parkinson, J. T. L. and Billington, N. S., The ventilating air jet: Part III, *JIHVE*, **24**, p. 415, 1957.

(4) Tuve, G. L., Air velocities in ventilating jets, ASHVE research report no. 1476, *ASHVE Trans.*, **59**, pp. 261–282, 1953.

(5) Koestel, A., Herman, P. and Tuve, G. L., Comparative studies of ventilating jets from various types of outlets, ASHVE research report no. 1404, *ASHVE Trans.*, **56**, p. 459, 1952.

(6) Koestel, A., Paths of horizontally projected heated or chilled air jets, *ASHVE Trans.*, **61**, pp. 213–232, 1955.

(7) Koestel, A., Computing temperatures and velocities in vertical jets of hot or cold air, *ASHVE Trans.*, **60**, pp. 385–410, 1954.

(8) Müllejans, H., *Uber die Ähnlichkeit der nichisotherm Strömung und den Wärmeübergang in Raümen mit Strahllüftung, Forschungsberichte des*

Lauds Nordrhein-Westfalen, Nr 1656, Westdeutscher Verlag-Koln und Opladen, 1966

(9) Jackman, P. J., *Air Movement in Rooms with Side-wall Mounted Grilles—a Design Procedure*, HVRA Laboratory Report No. 65, 1970

(10) Koestel, A. and Young, C. Y., The control of airstreams from a long slot, ASHVE research report no. 1429, *ASHVE Trans.*, **57**, p. 407, 1951.

(11) Rydberg, J., *Introduction of Air to Perforated Ceilings*, HVRA Translation No. 45, June 1962

(12) Holmes, M. J. and Sachariewicz, E., *The Effect of Ceiling Beams and Light Fittings on Ventilating Jets*, HVRA Laboratory Report No. 79, 1973

(13) Miller, P. L., and Nash, R. T., A further analysis of room air distribution performance, *ASHRAE Trans.*, **77**, Part II, p. 205, 1971

(14) Nevins, R. G. and Miller, P. L., ADPI—an index for design and evaluation, Australian refrigeration, *Air Conditioning and Heating*, **28**, No. 7, p. 26, 1974

(15) ASHRAE, *Handbook of Fundamentals*, 1977

6
Plant location and space requirements

6.1 Plant location

The art of plant location is to minimise the lengths of piping and ductwork that link the plant with ancillary components or terminal units, while ensuring proper performance[1]. The implications of this are seen by considering some common examples.

Cooling towers
Because copious quantities of outside air are essential and its free flow to and from the tower must not be compromised by the proximity of neighbouring structures, the best location for a cooling tower is often on a roof. Towers should be sited on the prevailing upwind side of any flues, to minimise the risk of cooling water contamination and the pond water level must always be sufficiently above the suction branch of the cooling water pump to keep it primed at all times (see Section 4.8). If need be, the tower should be erected on stilts.

Air-cooled condensers
Similar considerations apply about airflow through air-cooled condensers, with the additional constraint that the practical maximum length of the refrigerant lines leading to the compressor and evaporator is often about 15 m. Furthermore, when evaporators are above condensers there is the risk that the loss of static head in the rising liquid line may cause flashing to vapour before the expansion valve is reached.

Refrigeration plant
Where the roof can bear the dynamic loads imposed during operation and there is no risk of noise and vibration transmission to the building, the proper precautions being taken (see Sections 7.12, 7.20 and 7.26), refrigeration plant can be successfully erected on roofs. There is then the advantage that the lengths of cooling and chilled water pipelines to cooling towers and air-handling units are minimised. Nevertheless, the problems of roof installation are sometimes misunderstood or underestimated by engineers and architects and it is frequently better to put water-cooled water-chillers in the basement on

a solid foundation, where noise and vibration will pose fewer difficulties. In the UK it is not permissible to have refrigeration plant in the same room as the boilers because of the inflammable or toxic nature of the refrigerants generally used.

Air-handling plant
With smaller plant using direct-expansion air-cooler coils the restrictions on the lengths of refrigerant lines, as with air-cooled condensers, apply but with larger plant having chilled water cooler coils there is no such restraint on location. Air-handling plants can be put at basement level but this is usually a poor choice because space must then be found for the vertical duct mains needed for supply air up the building, extract air downwards, discharge air upwards if discharge to waste locally is impossible, and fresh air down the building if a local outside air inlet is out of the question. On the other hand, when plant is on the roof only two vertical ducts are required: for supply and extract air. With high-rise buildings the cost of duct-work and the space it occupies can be minimised by putting air-handling units in a plant room on an intermediate floor, specially intended and constructed for the purpose. Between ten and sixteen storeys above and below can be conveniently dealt with.

6.2 Cooling tower space

Broadly speaking, towers of the same type occupy the same volume, per kW of refrigeration, when working under the same conditions, although induced draught towers tend to need more space than forced draught towers, particularly at the lower end of the range of duties. Data published in catalogues suggest a range of specific volumes required for commercially available induced and forced draught towers: 3 to 4 m³ per 100 kW for the former and 2 to 3 m³ per 100 kW for the latter.

Shapes, heights and types of cooling towers differ and there is consequently less correlation between specific plan area and refrigeration load, (Figure 6.1). Small towers are less efficient than larger ones and induced draught versions require more space than forced draught. Generalisation is not as easy as with specific volumes but it can be inferred that forced draught towers require from 0.6 to 0.8 m² per 100 kW, whereas induced draught need between 1.0 and 1.5 m² per 100 kW, for loads over about 1000 kW of refrigeration. Increasing the ambient wet-bulb from 20°C, assumed for Figure 6.1, to 25.6°C means that the specific plan area rises by about 15% for the induced draught type and by about 20% for the forced draught tower.

As well as the plan area of the tower itself, a walkway space of at least 1.5 m must be provided all round, for maintenance, and, in addition, sufficient extra plan area must be allowed for free airflow into the tower. The total plan area is

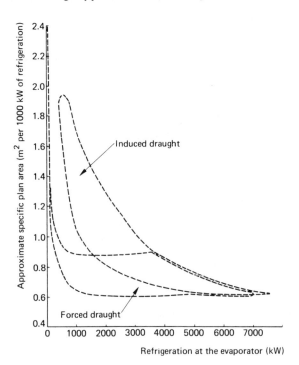

Figure 6.1 Comparative approximate plan areas occupied by typical commercial cooling towers. Based on 20°C wet-bulb (screen) and water cooled from 32.2°C to 26.7°C

unlikely to be less than twice the plan area of the tower alone; for a provisional estimate of the plan area needed it is suggested that 5 m² plus 2.5 m² per 100 kW of refrigeration be allowed.

6.3 Air-cooled condensers

Horizontally arranged condenser soils are always to be preferred to vertical coils because the vagaries of wind effect can then be ignored. Since air-cooled condensers are multi-row, finned-tube, heat exchangers the volume occupied is much less significant than the plan area, which depends on the refrigerant used, e.g. R12 needs slightly more than R22, where the duty lies in the commercial range of sizes available and the temperature difference between the condensing refrigerant and the ambient air. However, Figure 6.2 shows that the approximate specific plan area required is from 2.5 to 5.0 m² per 100 kW for duties exceeding about 100 kW of refrigeration, but below this the requirement increases to 8 m² per 100 kW, or more, of refrigeration. At least twice these plan areas should be allowed for preliminary planning purposes.

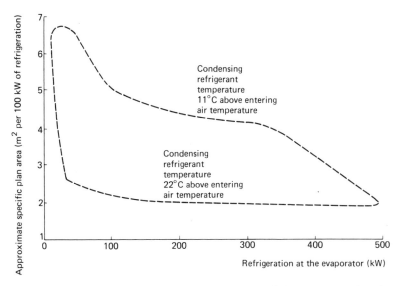

Figure 6.2   Comparative approximate plan areas occupied by a range of typical commercial air-cooled condensers with horizontal coils and vertical induced air flow. Temperature difference between condensing refrigerant and entering air taken as 11°C at the upper boundary and as 22°C at the lower

6.4 Water chillers

Figure 6.3 shows the results of a survey of manufacturers' literature for typical, commercial, centrifugal and screw chillers. The specific space allowance includes 1 m all round for access, plus tube withdrawal space at one end. Curve A is for a commonly used hermetic, centrifugal machine with a single shell to house condenser and evaporator tubes and the motor-compressor assembly mounted on top. Curve C is for machines having separate condenser and evaporator shells and their hermetic compressors positioned alongside. The end of the curve, for the larger duties, includes open centrifugal machines intended to be driven by steam turbines. Curve B is for a middle range, single shell, hermetic, centrifugal machine that is shorter than the others but somewhat wider. The broken line is for screw compressors, which tend to be rather longer but narrower, than centrifugals. Reciprocating chillers are used in the lower span of duties, i.e. less than about 550 kW of refrigeration, and in general, use more space. They are not shown in Figure 6.3, but can need as much as 10 m² per 100 kW of refrigeration, for small duties.

The specific space requirements given in Figure 6.3 are the bare minimum for the machines. Additions must be made to cover the height of concrete bases and antivibration mountings, and overhead clearance is essential to accommodate large diameter, lagged chilled water and unlagged cooling water

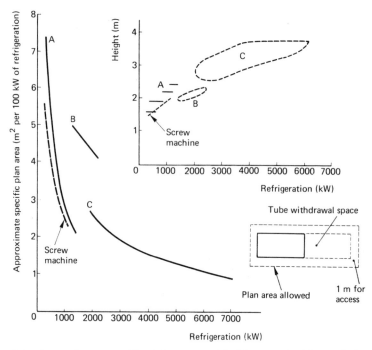

Figure 6.3   Approximate specific plan areas and heights required by typical commercial centrifugal and screw water chillers

pipes. Piping connections also have to be made at the ends and pumps are usually located nearby, often with stand-by. Switchgear and controls occupy space as well. Furthermore, the cooling duty is frequently shared among several machines to give a measure of stand-by capacity. To cover all these items it is recommended that, at the preliminary formative design stage, i.e. before any layout drawings are prepared, an allowance of 8 m^2 plus 8 m^2 per 100 kW of refrigeration be made, for centrifugal and screw machines. Thus, for a cooling load of 1000 kW, the provisional estimate of space would be $8 + 8 \times 1000/100 = 88$ m^2 of plan area. For reciprocating chillers it is recommended that manufacturers' dimensions be obtained before any estimate of the space needed is done.

Finally, it is fatal to underestimate the clear height required in plantrooms, of any sort. Figure 6.3 shows that up to 4 m can be needed. Less than 3.5 m often results in difficulties.

6.5 Air-handling plant

Commercial, packaged, air-handling units occupy between 0.4 and 0.1 m^2 per m^3 s^{-1} of air delivered and their heights are from 0.5 to 2.0 m over the range of duties from 0.5 to 20 m^3 s^{-1}, the better quality, quieter units requiring more space and being higher than those that are cheaper and noisier. Individual, forward-curved, centrifugal fans need from 0.06 to 0.03 m^2 per m^3 s^{-1} of air, over a similar span of airflow rates.

Air-handling plantrooms may accommodate a packaged air-handling unit for supply air; an extract fan and motor set; ducts for supply, recirculated, discharge and fresh air; silencers; duct-mounted heated batteries; controls; switch-gear; pumps and lagged pipes. The ducts are large and of a complicated shape, usually having to cross over one another, and plant is best erected on concrete plinths. Taking account of these factors and of the need for enough space to give access for maintenance suggests that, for preliminary planning purposes, it is wise to allow 12 m^2 plan area plus 13 m^2 per m^3 s^{-1} of air handled, with a clear internal height of 2.7 m plus 0.1 m per m^3 s^{-1} of airflow, up to a maximum of 4.5 m.

6.6 Systems

With one exception[2] little information giving details of the space occupied by different systems has been published. Table 6.1 gives typical space requirements for the mechanical plant of air-conditioning systems as a percentage of the treated area. Some latitude is necessary when interpreting

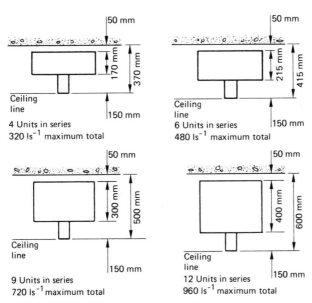

Figure 6.4 Ceiling space requirements for a variable air volume system with variable area linear slots and the possibility of partitions running along the slots, independent temperature control being retained in the offices on each side (see Section 2.8 and Figure 2.7)

Table 6.1   Typical space requirements for the mechanical plant of air-conditioning systems

System	Total area of plant space as a percentage of treated floor area	
	From Swain et al.[2]	Suggested allowance
Terminal heat-recovery units, plus ducted fresh air	—	5
Perimeter-induction	4.5	5
Fan coil units, plus ducted fresh air	4.5	5
Chilled ceiling, plus ducted fresh air	5.1	5
Single duct, all-air, low or high velocity	5.9	7
Dual duct, high velocity	6.5	8

the data, bearing in mind the figures relating space occupied with plant duty. The tabulated information is perhaps best used for comparative purposes, the actual plan area needed depending greatly on the system design and the building shape and size.

The clear ceiling space required by different systems is a function of the disposition of the terminal units, grilles or diffusers, their selection and the ductwork arrangement. Suggestions are given in Table 6.2.

Putting induction units above suspended ceilings is really a misapplication (see Section 3.2) and although successful results have been achieved, air

Table 6.2   Clear ceiling space requirements of different air-conditioning systems

System	Clear ceiling space needed (mm)
Chilled ceiling, plus ducted fresh air fed from side-wall grilles in a bulkhead	120●
Variable air volume (see Figure 6.4)	370–600
Ceiling-mounted induction units	450
Ceiling-mounted fan coil units	500
Chilled ceiling, plus ducted fresh air fed from ceiling diffusers	500□△
Ceiling-mounted terminal heat-recovery units	550
Dual duct feeding ceiling diffusers	600
Minimum return air space (Section 1.6)	150

● More clear space must be allowed if pipes have to cross over one another

□ Smooth air flow into the necks of the diffusers is essential if quiet operating conditions are to be achieved. More than 500 mm may, therefore, be needed to secure this.

△ Reducing the ceiling space to a minimum for this type of diffuser, or any system using ceiling diffusers, is inviting noise problems

Table 6.3 Floor area needed by terminal units of air-conditioning systems

Terminal unit	Floor area occupied as a percentage of the total treated floor area
Perimeter-induction, conventional	1.3–2.8
Perimeter-induction, low silhouette	1.6–2.7
Fan coil	1.3–2.0
Terminal heat-recovery	1.5–2.1

distribution patterns and unit capacities cannot be determined from catalogue data but must always be established by tests in a full-scale mock-up of the building module.

The plan area occupied by terminal units should be determined by actually using dimensional details of the units, properly laid out on architect's drawings. However, Table 6.3 gives an indication of the floor area used up. The actual floor area required by the units depends on the building design, the sensible heat gains and the unit selection in the commercial range available. Four-pipe induction units are at the upper end of the range quoted in Table 6.3 but four-pipe fan coil units do not seem to need significantly more space than two-pipe units, a split four-row coil with three rows for cooling and one for heating, is no bigger than an ordinary four-row coil which is used entirely for cooling.

6.7 Duct space

At a very early stage in the design process an estimate must often be made of probable space to be occupied by the ductwork. It is never wise to underestimate space requirements at the conceptual phase and Table 6.4, therefore, lists conservative suggestions for the supply air quantities needed for office blocks. Generalisation for other applications is best made by means of a

Table 6.4 Supply air quantities required for office blocks with different air-conditioning systems

System	Specific supply air quantity $(\text{ls}^{-1}\,\text{m}^{-2})$
Perimeter induction	3.25
Variable air volume	8.5
Double duct	12.5
Ducted, uncooled, fresh air for a fan coil system	1.3
Ducted, cooled and dehumidified air for a fan coil system	3.0

rough estimate of the sensible heat gain and the use of Equation (2.3), bearing in mind that the choice of conventional air distribution terminals (Chapter 5) is limited to about 25 air changes per hour or $12.5 \, \text{ls}^{-1} \, \text{m}^{-2}$. The figures in Table 6.4 refer to the total treated floor area, i.e. the modular area plus the area of the central corridor.

6.8 Miscellaneous items

Although air conditioning is often regarded as merely comprising refrigeration plant and cooling towers, etc. with systems of air and water distribution to deploy cooling capacity, there are other mechanical services that must be provided for an air-conditioned building if it is to be habitable. Table 6.5 gives the approximate plantroom space required for most of these other servies, spedifically applied to office blocks. The designer must use his judgement if he wishes to refer the data to different applications. The figures in Table 6.5 include an allowance for maintenance and, where relevant, tube withdrawal or burner removal.

Plantrooms should be of rectangular shape with a plan aspect ratio of 2:1. An excessive departure from this, an unusual shape, or the presence of columns, will increase the area needed. An air conditioned building seems to require between 5 and 15% of the treated floor area as space for the plant of the

Table 6.5   Approximate plantroom space required for the services provided for office blocks

Item	Approximate space needed	Suggested minimum clear height
Boiler	9 m² per boiler + 3 m² per 100 kW of boiler power	3.9 m
Oil tanks:		
1 tank	10 m² + 2.9 m² per 100 kW of boiler power	3 m + 0.1 m per 100 kW, up to 4 m maximum
2 tanks	15 m² + 2.9 m² per 100 kW of boiler power	3 m + 0.1 m per 100 kW, up to 4 m maximum
HWS (hot water service) storage:		
Vertical vessels:		
1 vessel	3.5 m² + 1.65 m² per 1000 l	3.5 m + 0.25 m per 1000 l
2 vessels	6 m² + 1.65 m² per 1000 l	3.5 m + 0.25 m per 1000 l
Horizontal vessels:		
1 vessel	7 m² + 3.5 m² per 1000 l	2.5 m + 0.1 m per 1000 l
2 vessels	10 m² + 3.5 m² per 1000 l	2.5 m + 0.1 m per 1000 l
CWS (cold water service) storage:	9 m² + 1.5 m² per 1000 l	2.2 m
	or	
	9 m² + 0.75 m² per 1000 l	3.5 m

(Reproduced by kind permission of Haden Young Ltd.)

mechanical services and vertical shafts to house pipes and ducts. Small buildings need more plant space than large ones, proportionally.

Example 6.1 Make a preliminary estimate of the plantroom floor area that should be allocated for air conditioning the hypothetical office block considered in Chapter 1, assuming the following:
System—two-pipe, non-changeover, perimeter induction
Refrigeration load—1742 kW (Example 1.11)
Boiler power—1500 kW
HWS—7000 1
CWS—84 000 1, to cover domestic needs and the storage required at present by most water boards in the UK for cooling towers, i.e. half a day's usage or four hour's consumption, whichever is the greater.
Answer
(1) Air-handling plant (see Table 6.4 and Section 6.5)—$3.25 \times 14\,000/1000$ $= 45.5 \text{ m}^3 \text{ s}^{-1}$. A duty of $45.5 \text{ m}^3 \text{ s}^{-1}$ would be too much for a single plant and well beyond the range of packaged plants. Four packages would probably be chosen, each to handle $11.4 \text{ m}^3 \text{ s}^{-1}$.
Plant area needed: $4(12 + 13 \times 11.4) = 641 \text{ m}^2$
Clear height required: $2.7 + 0.1 \times 11.4 = 3.84 \text{ m}$
(2) Refrigeration plant (see Section 6.4)—two machines each of 871 kW capacity would probably be selected.
Plant area needed: $2(8 + 8 \times 8.71) = 155 \text{ m}^2$
Clear height required: 3.5 m
(3) Cooling towers (see Section 6.2)—assume two towers, each for 871 kW of refrigeration.
Plant area needed: $2(5 + 2.5 \times 8.71) = 54 \text{ m}^2$
Clear height required: difficult to say with certainty, but probably wise to allow 5 m.
(4) CWS (see Table 6.5)—assume the lower height tanks are desirable.
Plant area needed: $9 + 1.5 \times 84 = 135 \text{ m}^2$
Clear height required: 2.2 m
(5) Boilers (see Table 6.5)—assume two boilers are to be provided.
Plant area needed: $2(9 + 3 \times 7.5) = 63 \text{ m}^2$
Clear height required: 3.9 m
(6) HWS (see Table 6.5)—assume two vertical vessels.
Plant area needed: $6 + 1.65 \times 7 = 18 \text{ m}^2$
Clear height required: $3.5 + 0.25 \times 3.5 = 4.5 \text{ m}$
(7) Oil tanks (see Table 6.5)—assume two equal tanks.
Plant area needed: $15 + 2.9 \times 15 = 58 \text{ m}^2$
Clear height required: $3 + 0.1 \times 15 = 4.5 \text{ m}$
(8) Duct space for vertical primary air ducts (see Section 6.7 and Table 6.4)—assume plant on the roof and a vertical distribution system for the primary air,

feeding two units on each side of the dropper. One dropping duct, therefore, deals with four modules on each floor, and handles a maximum duty of

$$\frac{12 \text{ floors} \times 4 \text{ modules} \times (6.75 \times 2.4) \text{ m}^2 \times 3.25 \text{ l s}^{-1} \text{ m}^{-2}}{1000} = 2.527 \text{ m}^3 \text{ s}^{-1}.$$

If the duct is sized conservatively with a maximum velocity of 15 ms^{-1}, the duct area needed is 0.1685 m^2 and this can be provided by a spirally-wound, circular duct of 475 mm diameter. It would be wise to call this 500 mm and then, allowing 50 mm of lagging, the overall diameter is 600 mm. This must be housed in a square enclosure of 700 mm cross section, allowing 50 mm clearance. Assuming the ducts will be sized by static regain, to ease air balancing, the size of a vertical dropper is unlikely to reduce in size as it goes down the building. There will be nine droppers on each face of the building and so the floor area occupied by the primary air ducting will be $2 \times 9 \times 0.7 \times 0.7 \times 12 = 106$ m^2.

(9) Extract ducts—these must relieve the whole of the primary air to waste or for recirculation and must be sized for conventional velocities. Choosing a conservative velocity of 6 ms^{-1} the total cross sectional area of duct needed will be $(14\,000 \text{ m}^2 \times 3.25 \text{ l s}^{-1} \text{ m}^{-2})/(1000 \times 6) = 7.583$ m^2.

This area will be used up on every floor since the ducts will be in builders' work and therefore unlikely to change section as they rise through the building. The total floor area occupied will then be $12 \times 7.583 = 91$ m^2.

To summarise, therefore,

	m^2	% of total area
Air-handling plant:	641	4.6
Refrigeration plant:	155	1.1
Cooling towers:	54	0.4
CWS tanks:	135	1.0
Boilers:	63	0.5
HWS vessels:	18	0.1
Oil tanks:	58	0.4
Vertical primary air ducts:	106	0.8
Extract ducts:	91	0.6
	1321 m^2	9.5%

This estimate is liberal, as it should be in the conceptual stage of a design.

References

(1) Jones, W. P., The why and when of air conditioning—planning and building design, *RIBAJ*, **77**, pp. 363–365, August 1970
(2) Swain, C. P., Thornley, D. L. and Wensley, R., The choice of air conditioning systems, *JIHVE*, **32**, pp. 1–41; 307–320, 1964

7

Applied acoustics

7.1 Simple sound waves

Sound consists of progressive wave trains, each comprising a series of alternate compressions and rarefactions travelling past a point in an elastic medium such as air, water, or a building material. In a simple imaginary case, a point source of sound, e.g. a very small pulsating balloon, imparts energy to the ambient air at a rate defining its sound power and produces an expanding, spherical, travelling wave system that is nondirectional. An alternative simple illustration is a reciprocating piston at the end of a tube, producing a directional plane wave train, moving along the axis of the tube (Figure 7.1). The distance between the crests is the wavelength, λ, the speed of propagation is c (344 ms^{-1} in air at 22°C) and f is the frequency, defined by

$$f = c/\lambda \qquad (7.1)$$

Real wave trains are more complicated and contain a large number of tones, not necessarily related harmonically. When a sound consists of many frequencies that are harmonically-related, the prime frequency is called the first or fundamental harmonic and the others the second, third, etc. Simple, rotating objects such as the impellers of centrifugal compressors, tend to produce harmonically-related wave trains, but random sources like air turbulence do not. Most plant items generate a complicated wave train with perhaps a few, discernible harmonics imposed on an aperiodic background.

7.2 Simple wave equations

In a wave train, the variation of sound pressure about the mean barometric pressure, at any time t, and distance x from the sound source, can be expressed by

$$p(x, t) = P \cos k(x - ct) \qquad (7.2)$$

where k is a constant termed the wave number and equals $2\pi/\lambda$ and P is the maximum amplitude of the pressure. When a forward-travelling wave (see Figure 7.1) is reflected from a nonabsorptive surface, a backward-travelling wave is produced, which is expressed by

$$p(x, t) = P \cos k(x + ct) \qquad (7.3)$$

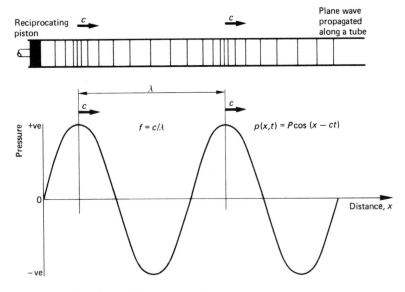

Figure 7.1   A directional plane wave train

The combined acoustic field in the tube is then expressed by

$$p(x,t) = P\cos k(x-ct) + P\cos k(x+ct)$$
$$= 2P\cos kx \cos 2\pi ft \qquad (7.4)$$

This is the equation for a standing wave (Figure 7.2). At a distance from the source, $x = 0$, $p(0,t) = 2P\cos 2\pi ft$ and the sound pressure varies from $+2P$ to $-2P$ with time. This is also true for distances $x = \lambda/2$, λ, $3\lambda/2$, etc., defining areas of permanent sound in the tube. On the other hand, at distance $x = \lambda/4$ from the source, $p(\lambda/4,t) = 2P\cos k\lambda/4 \cos 2\pi ft = 2P\cos \pi/2 \cos 2\pi ft$, which always equals 0, regardless of the value of t. The same is true for distances $x = 3\lambda/4$, $5\lambda/4$, etc., defining places of permanent silence along the axis, alternating with the areas of permanent sound.

Standing waves are characteristic of sound fields in any enclosure with reflecting or partially-reflecting surfaces when the waves from the acoustic source contain harmonics.

7.3 Root mean square pressure

Since both positive and negative pressures are the same to a listener and both contribute in equal measure to the sound power, measurement must be done in a way that avoids cancellation. This is achieved by measuring the square of the pressures and taking the square root of the average. Thus the measured indication of the strength of a sound is the root mean square pressure (p_{rms}).

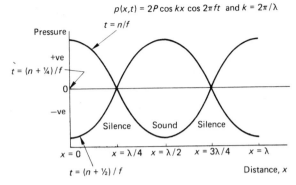

$$p(x,t) = 2P \cos kx \cos 2\pi ft \text{ and } k = 2\pi/\lambda$$

Figure 7.2 A standing wave

Since, at any time, the average of a cosine squared is half the amplitude of the cosine (Figure 7.3)

$$p_{rms} = P/\sqrt{2} = 0.707\,P \tag{7.5}$$

7.4 Intensity, power and pressure

If the molecules in a progressive wave train vibrate with a velocity u, it can be shown that $u = p/\rho c$ for a plane wave train, where ρ is the density of the air and p is defined by Equation 7.2. By substitution, therefore,

$$u = \frac{P}{\rho c} \cos k(x - ct) \tag{7.6}$$

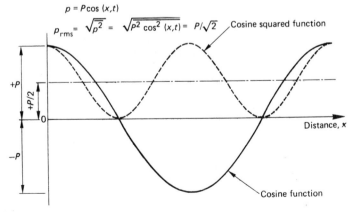

Figure 7.3 Cosine squared function obtained from a cosine function

The intensity (I) of a sound is defined as the sound power (W) per unit area of wavefront and, for a spherical wave train, this is

$$I = W/4\pi r^2 \tag{7.7}$$

It can also be shown that the intensity is the product, pu, and hence, at any instant

$$I = \frac{P^2}{\rho c} \cos^2 k(x - ct)$$

$$= \frac{P^2}{\rho c}[\tfrac{1}{2} + \tfrac{1}{2}\cos 2k(x - ct)] \tag{7.8}$$

There is an analogy with fan power for $I = pu$. The volumetric flow rate per unit area corresponds to u, and the fan total pressure corresponds to p, implying the product corresponds to fan power per unit area.

Since the average of a cosine function with respect to time, at any place, is zero we can see that the average intensity is

$$I_{av} = \frac{P^2}{2\rho c}$$

$$= \left[\frac{P}{\sqrt{2}}\right]^2 \frac{1}{\rho c}$$

$$= p_{rms}^2/\rho c \tag{7.9}$$

from equation (7.5).

For a spherical wave train an analysis of the propagation yields

$$p(r, t) = \frac{P'}{r}\cos k(r - ct) \tag{7.10}$$

Therefore, p is inversely proportional to r, the radial distance from the source, by analogy with the circumferential stress in a thin-shelled boiler, and P' is a pressure amplitude factor. Equations (7.7) and (7.9) show that the sound power is proportional to the square of the sound pressure, and so

$$W = \frac{4\pi r^2 p_{rms}^2}{\rho c} \tag{7.11}$$

which is the expression for the sound power in a spherical wave train. The expression ρc is termed the characteristic resistance of the medium and for air at 22°C and 101.325 kPa barometric pressure it has a value of 406 N s m^{-2}.

Example 7.1 The peak sound pressure in a spherical wave train, measured 2 m from the source, is 2 Pa. Determine the root mean square pressure, the average intensity and the sound power.

Answer $P = 2$ Pa, $c = 406$ N s m^{-2} and $r = 2$ m, therefore,

$$p_{rms} = P/\sqrt{2} = 2/\sqrt{2} = 1.4142 \text{ Pa}$$
$$I_{av} = p_{rms}^2/\rho c = 2/406 = 0.004926 \text{ Wm}^{-2}$$

$$W = 4\pi r^2 p_{rms}/\rho c$$
$$= 4\pi \times 2^2 \times 1.4142^2/406 = 0.2476 \text{ W}$$

7.5 Decibels

Because of the vast range of values considered, linear measurement scales are not used to express acoustic pressure, intensity and power, logarithmic scales to base 10 being used instead. In each case the logarithm used is the ratio of the measured quantity to a reference quantity. Although, strictly speaking, such ratios are dimensionless, their logarithms are termed bels or, when one-tenth of the size for convenience, decibels.

Sound pressure level (L_p) is defined in terms of the ratio of the squares of the root mean square pressures:

$$L_p = \log (p^2/p_{ref}^2) \text{ bels}$$
$$= 20 \log (p/p_{ref}) \text{ dB} \tag{7.12}$$

In this equation the subscript 'rms' is dropped, for convenience, as it will be for the majority of the following text. The reference pressure adopted by international agreement is 2×10^{-5} Pa, regarded as the threshold of hearing for a healthy young adult. The use of the word level implies, in an acoustic context, the use of a reference value and for this reason the reference value should always be stated, although this principle is not always followed in practice or where usage makes the matter clear. For example, Equation (7.12) should have the expression 're 2×10^{-5} Pa' added to it.

Example 7.2 Determine the sound pressure level at a distance of (a) 2 m and (b) 4 m from the source mentioned in Example 7.1.

Answer
(a) At $r = 2$ m, $P = 2$ Pa and $p_{rms} = 1.4142$ Pa; $p_{ref} = 2 \times 10^{-5}$ Pa

$$L_p = 20 \log 1.4142/(2 \times 10^{-5}) = 96.99 \text{ dB:re } 2 \times 10^{-5} \text{ Pa.}$$

(b) At $r = 4$ m, $p_{rms} = 1.4142 \times \frac{2}{4} = 0.7071$ Pa

$$L_p = 20 \log (0.7071/(2 \times 10^{-5}))$$

$$= 20 \left[5 + \log \frac{0.7071}{2} \right] = 90.97 \text{ dB:re } 2 \times 10^{-5} \text{ Pa.}$$

This is an important result, showing that doubling the distance from a source of sound in a direct, free field reduces the sound pressure level by about 6 dB. This is not true for the reverberant field which tends to develop in a room some distance from the acoustic source.

Sound power level (L_W) and sound intensity level (L_I) are defined by international agreement in relation to 10^{-12} W and 10^{-12} Wm^{-2}, respectively:

$$L_W = 10 \log (W/W_{ref}) \text{ dB:re } 10^{-12} \text{ W} \qquad (7.13)$$
$$L_I = 10 \log (I/I_{ref}) \text{ dB:re } 10^{-12} \text{ Wm}^{-2} \qquad (7.14)$$

Example 7.3 Determine the sound power level and the sound intensity level at a distance of (a) 2 m and (b) 4 m from the source mentioned in Example 7.1.
Answer
(a) At $r = 2$ m, $P = 2$ Pa and $p_{rms} = 1.4142$ Pa

$$\begin{aligned}
L_W &= 10 \log (W/W_{ref}) \\
&= 10 \log (0.2476/10^{-12}) \\
&= 10 \log (0.004926/10^{-12}) \\
&= 113.94 \text{ dB:re } 10^{-12} \text{ W}
\end{aligned}$$

and

$$\begin{aligned}
L_I &= 10 \log (I/I_{ref}) \\
&= 10 \log (0.004926/10^{-12}) \\
&= 10(12 + \log 0.004926) \\
&= 96.92 \text{ dB:re } 10^{-12} \text{ Wm}^{-2}
\end{aligned}$$

(b) At $r = 4$ m

$$L_W = 113.94 \text{ dB:re } 10^{-12} \text{ W, as before}$$

$$I = \left(\frac{2}{4}\right)^2 \times 0.004926 = 0.0012315 \text{ Wm}^{-2}$$

$$\begin{aligned}
L_I &= 10 \log (0.0012315/10^{-12}) \\
&= 10(12 + \log 0.0012315) \\
&= 90.90 \text{ dB:re } 10^{-12} \text{ Wm}^{-2}
\end{aligned}$$

It can be shown that $L_I \simeq L_p$ by considering Equations (7.7) and (7.9): $I = W/4\pi r^2 = p^2/\rho c$, where the rms subscript for pressure has been dropped. Then,

$$\begin{aligned}
L_I &= 10 \log (p^2/\rho c I_{ref}) \\
&= 10 \log \left(\frac{p^2}{p_{ref}^2}\right)\left(\frac{p_{ref}^2}{\rho c I_{ref}}\right) \\
&= L_p + 10 \log (p_{ref}^2/\rho c I_{ref}) \text{ dB}
\end{aligned}$$

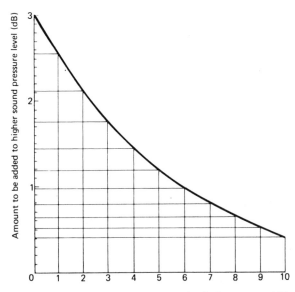

Figure 7.4   Addition of sound pressure levels from two sources

The second term approaches zero as ρc approaches (p_{ref}^2/I_{ref}). Since at 101.325 kPa and 22°C it equals 0.13 dB, which is almost immeasurable, $L_1 = L_p$ for all practical purposes.

When two levels in dB are added a straightforward arithmetical addition cannot be followed. Instead the levels must be converted to bels, the antilogarithms taken, the numbers produced added, the logarithm of the sum taken and the result converted to decibels.

Example 7.4 Determine the sound pressure level in dB resulting from the addition of two sources, each of 20 dB:re 2×10^{-5} Pa.
Answer 20 dB = 2 B; antilog 2 = 100. Hence 2 B + 2 B becomes 200. Therefore, log 200 = 2.301 B = 23.01 dB: re 2×10^{-5} Pa.

In the same way, 2 B + 2 B + 2 B becomes 300 with a logarithm of 2.477 B. Thus, the addition of two equal sources gives a combined level about 3 dB higher than either and the addition of three, a level 5 dB higher, and so on. The same approach can be adopted for the addition of unequal sources and the results of doing this are shown in Figure 7.4.

7.6 Sound fields and absorption coefficients

Large rooms are those of most concern in air-conditioning applications because they are defined acoustically as having dimensions many times larger than the wavelength of concern. Using Equation (7.1) gives the figures shown in Table 7.1.

Table 7.1 Values of frequency and wavelength

f (Hz)	63	125	250	500	1000	2000	4000	8000
λ (m)	5.33	2.67	1.33	0.67	0.33	0.17	0.08	0.04

Unfortunately, simple calculations cannot be used for large rooms and statistical methods must be adopted instead. There are two sound fields to consider: near a source the field has a directional quality but further away this direct field decays (see Example 7.2) and multiple reflections from the room surfaces (see Equations (7.2), (7.3) and (7.4)) produce a background reverberant field which swamps the direct field. The reverberant field strength may be described by the mean of the square of the sound pressure, averaged with respect to distance, or by the mean intensity, in the vicinity of the point of measurement.

Sound waves meeting a surface will not be reflected with the same amplitude if the surface has a sound-absorbing quality. Such a quality is expressed by the sound absorption coefficient (α) which has at least three forms:
(1) Coefficient for a given angle of incidence (θ):

$$\alpha_\theta = \frac{\text{Sound energy absorbed by the surface}}{\text{Sound energy incident on the surface at an angle } \theta}$$

(2) Statistical coefficient:

$$\alpha = \frac{\text{Sound energy absorbed by the surface}}{\text{Sound energy incident on the surface when the field is perfectly diffuse}}$$

(3) Sabine coefficient (α_{sab}): this is measured in a laboratory and requires a nearly perfect, diffuse field with a large specimen of the material being tested laid on the floor (10 to 12 m^2 in Europe, 6.7 m^2 in USA). It is to be noted that a diffuse field is one in which, at any point of measurement, the net flow of acoustic energy is independent of direction.

A random incidence coefficient, similar to (2) and (3) may be obtained theoretically from the normally incident coefficient, α_n, which is a special case of α_θ. Values of α_n can be obtained more readily than values of α_{sab}, since a much smaller specimen is used and located at the end of a tube in which an exploration of the standing waves set up yields the desired information. Values of α and α_{sab} are often very similar, except for occasional, inexplicable anomalies. Values of α_{sab} are often merely written as α. Figure 7.5 shows how α varies with frequency for some common materials, although it is misleading

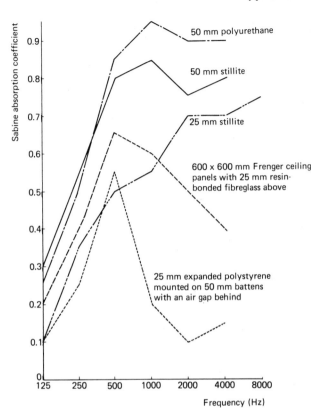

Figure 7.5 Variation of the sabine absorption coefficient with frequency for some common materials

since it conceals a certain amount of information because the method of mounting the material greatly influences its characteristics. For example, the presence of a 50 mm air gap behind the polystyrene panels improves their acoustic absorption properties, and the peak at 500 Hz is not necessarily a feature of the material–in all probability it is the result of mounting the panels on battens spaced at 600 mm intervals (see Table 7.1). Tuning effects of this kind are not uncommon. There is a further example in the case of the Frenger ceiling tiles which may owe part of the peak at 500 Hz to the dimensions of the panels (600 mm square).

The term noise reduction coefficient (NRC) is sometimes used, being the average of α_{sab} over 250, 500, 1000 and 2000 Hz. More often, the average absorption coefficient, $\bar{\alpha}_{sab}$, must be calculated as follows, to establish the acoustic quality of the room:

$$\bar{\alpha}_{sab} = \frac{S_1\alpha_{sab_1} + S_2\dot{\alpha}_{sab_2} + \dots S_n\alpha_{sab_n}}{S} \tag{7.15}$$

where S is the total room surface area and equals $S_1 + S_2 + \ldots S_n$, the sum of the individual surface elements, having absorption coefficients $\alpha_{sab_1}, \alpha_{sab_2}, \ldots \alpha_{sab_n}$. Sound-absorbing objects, such as people and furniture, must be included in the calculation but because such objects are often of ill-defined area they are generally given a value of $S\alpha_{sab}$, in units termed sabines, for inclusion in the numerator of Equation (7.15). Some typical values are given in Table 7.2.

No modification is made to the value of S when using the values given in Table 7.2 for objects, and the room constant, R, is then defined by

$$R = \frac{S\bar{\alpha}_{sab}}{(1 - \bar{\alpha}_{sab})} \tag{7.16}$$

Table 7.2 The sound-absorption of objects in a room

Object	Sound absorption ($S\alpha_{sab}$) (sabines)					
	Frequency (Hz)					
	125	250	500	1000	2000	4000
Desk or table	0.01	0.02	0.02	0.04	0.04	0.03
Upholstered chair	0.11	0.18	0.28	0.35	0.45	0.42
Clothed person	0.17	0.36	0.47	0.50	0.50	0.46
Glass-fronted cabinet	0	0.01	0.01	0.02	0.02	0.02
Wooden door	0.15	0.20	0.10	0.10	0.10	0.10

7.7 Octave bands

The human ear can, at best, detect changes of frequency over a spectrum between 20 and 20 000 Hz. Since the energy of most sounds is distributed over part or all of this range, a spectral analysis is necessary to describe the nature of a noise. Because the response of the human ear is more logarithmic, to base two, than linear, an octave scale is used to divide the spectrum so that successive frequencies are doubled, the span between them denoting octave bands: 62.5 to 125 Hz, 125 to 250 Hz, and so on, usually up to 8000 Hz, for most practical purposes. The mid-frequency, f_c, in each band equals $\sqrt{f_1 \times f_2}$, where f_1 and f_2 are the extreme frequencies of the band. The sound pressure level in a band is termed the octave band level.

An octave band analyser does not always yield sufficient information for engineering needs and so one-third octave bands are also used. Whereas with an octave band the frequency bands could be represented by 2^n and 2^{n+1}, with a one-third octave band they would be given by 2^n and $2^{n+1/3}$, the mid-frequency still being the root of their product. The narrower the frequency band adopted, the less the sound pressure level in it: for instance, three equal sound pressure levels of 40 dB in contiguous one-third octave bands are added to give 45 dB in a whole octave band (see Section 7.5 and Figure 7.4).

When a source of sound radiates acoustic energy into a room it does so over the audio range of frequency and, since the absorption coefficients of the surfaces are frequency-dependent, it is necessary to analyse the noise of the source in octave, or one-third octave, bands. The resultant sound pressure level in the room can then be established with respect to the octave bands and some idea formed of the subjective quality of the sound field in the room.

7.8 Room effect

If a steady source of sound exists in a room the sound waves will suffer multiple reflections from the surfaces and, provided there are no highly absorptive areas, a complicated pattern of standing waves will be established, constituting the reverberant field. The energy lost by absorption at the surfaces equals the input by the source and the waves travel with equal probability in all directions.

In such a field the concept of energy density, per unit volume, D_r, is useful[1.7]. The average intensity over a small area in the field is the rate of energy flow through it at speed c, expressed in Wm^{-2} of $Js^{-1}m^{-2}$. Dividing the intensity by the speed of sound then gives the average energy density in Jm^{-3},

$$D_r = I_{av}/c = p^2_{av}/\rho c^2 \tag{7.17}$$

If a small area δS, within the field, is considered, half the sound waves will, on average, enter one side of it and half the other, at various angles of incidence, θ. Any particular wave, with intensity I, may be resolved in a direction normal to the surface to yield an expression $I \cos \theta \delta S$ for the energy flow rate into one side of the surface. Over the solid angle subtended by this side the average value for such an expression is $\frac{1}{2}I \delta S$. Since, statistically, the average energy flow through one side of a surface in the field is also half that through both sides, the average energy flow through the surface in one direction only is $\frac{1}{4}I \delta S$. From Equation (7.17), the flow of power through one side of a surface can be expressed as $\frac{1}{4}D_r c \delta S = \frac{1}{4}I_{av} \delta S$. If the surface has an absorption coefficient α, the power loss from the reverberant field is $\frac{1}{4}D_r c \alpha \delta S$. If the power output from the source is W, then after each complete reflection of sound waves has occurred on the room surfaces, the power absorbed by them, on average, is $W\bar{\alpha}$ where $\bar{\alpha}$ is the average absorption coefficient for all the room surfaces. The remaining power, $W(1 - \bar{\alpha})$ is what the source contributes to the reverberant field and is balanced by the power flow expression referred to all the surfaces in the room, of area S, having an average absorption coefficient $\bar{\alpha}$. Thus $\frac{1}{4}D_r c \bar{\alpha} S = W(1 - \bar{\alpha})$ and the energy density in the reverberant field can be expressed as

$$D_r = \left(\frac{4W}{c\bar{\alpha}S}\right)\left(\frac{(1 - \bar{\alpha})}{\bar{\alpha}}\right) \tag{7.18}$$

Equations (7.7) and (7.9) give an expression for the sound pressure in the direct field at distance r from the source:

$$p^2 = \frac{\rho c W}{4\pi r^2}$$

If the source is in the centre of a large open space it is radiating all its energy into a sphere and it is said to have a directivity factor, Q, of unity. If it is in the middle of a large flat ceiling its energy is radiated into a hemisphere and Q has a value of 2. Values of 4 and 8 correspond to sources of sound located in the junction of a ceiling and wall, and in a corner, respectively. Strongly directive sources, which beam the sound, can have factors exceeding 8.

At a point in the direct field, distant r from the source, $I = QW/4\pi r^2$ (Equation 7.7) and from Equation (7.9)

$$p^2 = \rho c Q W / 4\pi r^2 \tag{7.19}$$

At any point, sound pressures in the direct and reverberant fields can be added and so, from Equations (7.16), (7.17), (7.18) and (7.19) an expression for the combined mean square sound pressure is obtained:

$$p^2 = \frac{\rho c Q W}{4\pi r^2} + \left(\frac{\rho c^2 4 W}{c \bar{\alpha} S}\right)\left(\frac{(1-\bar{\alpha})}{\bar{\alpha}}\right)$$

$$= \rho c W \left[\frac{Q}{4\pi r^2} + \left(\frac{4}{\bar{\alpha} S}\right)\left(\frac{(1-\bar{\alpha})}{\bar{\alpha}}\right)\right]$$

$$= \rho c W \left(\frac{Q}{W\pi r^2} + \frac{4}{R}\right)$$

where $\bar{\alpha}$ is used instead of $\bar{\alpha}_{sab}$.

$$L_p = 10 \log \frac{\rho c W}{(2\times 10^{-5})^2}\left(\frac{Q}{4\pi r^2} + \frac{4}{R}\right) \text{ dB:re } 2\times 10^{-5} \text{ Pa}$$

and since $(2\times 10^{-5})^2/\rho c \simeq 10^{-12}$, numerically,

$$L_p = 10 \log \frac{W}{10^{-12}} + 10 \log\left(\frac{Q}{4\pi r^2} + \frac{4}{R}\right) \text{ dB:re } 2\times 10^{-5} \text{ Pa}$$

$$= L_w + 10 \log\left(\frac{Q}{4\pi r^2} + \frac{4}{R}\right) \text{ dB:re } 2\times 10^{-5} \text{ Pa}$$

Figure 7.6 shows a graphical representation of the sound field in a room with a source of noise radiating acoustic power from a point at one side. Immediately next to the source anomalous and inconsistent readings are often obtained but, after the ill-definable area of this near field, the far field is established. This comprises the direct field and the reverberant field, as shown in Figure 7.6.

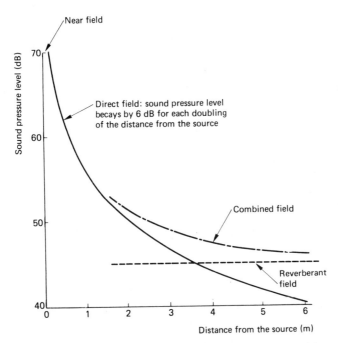

Figure 7.6 Graphical representation of the sound field in a room with a source of noise radiating acoustic power from a point at one side

Example 7.5 A double module office has dimensions 4.8 m wide × 2.6 m high × 6.0 m deep. One wall (2.6 m × 4.8 m) contains two windows of total area 7.92 m² and the opposite wall contains a door of 1.61 m² area. A single air-conditioning terminal unit is located in the centre of the ceiling. Making use of the information given, establish the room effect in each octave band from 125 to 4000 Hz. Take r as 1.769 m, the distance between the measuring microphone and the terminal unit.

The furnishings and statistical absorption coefficients are as follows:

		Absorption coefficients at the mid-octave bands					
Item	Area (m²)	125 Hz	250 Hz	500 Hz	1000 Hz	2000 Hz	4000 Hz
Carpet and underlay	28.8	0.05	0.25	0.50	0.50	0.60	0.65
Plastered walls	46.63	0.03	0.03	0.02	0.03	0.04	0.05
Curtains	0.99	0.05	0.15	0.35	0.55	0.65	0.65
Acoustic ceiling	28.8	0.25	0.70	0.85	0.85	0.85	0.40
Door	1.61	0.19	0.25	0.12	0.12	0.12	0.12
Window	7.92	0.10	0.07	0.04	0.03	0.02	0.02

Two people are present and the total absorptions of the occupants and furniture are as follows:

Absorption units at the mid-octave bands

Item	125 Hz	250 Hz	500 Hz	1000 Hz	2000 Hz	4000 Hz
Hard-topped desk	0.01	0.02	0.02	0.04	0.04	0.03
Two soft chairs	0.22	0.36	0.56	0.70	0.90	0.84
Two hard chairs			0.03	0.04	0.08	
Two people	0.34	0.72	0.94	1.04	1.00	0.92
Glass-fronted bookcase	0.01	0.02	0.02	0.04	0.04	0.03

Answer It should be noted that because the terminal unit is in the centre of the ceiling the diversity factor, Q, is 2.0, and the component of the direct field can be evaluated as follows:

$$Q/4\pi r^2 = 2/(4 \times \pi \times 1.769^2) = 0.051$$

From the tabulated information above it can be calculated that:

$$S = 114.75 \text{ (including curtains)}$$

and

Mid-octave bands	125 Hz	250 Hz	500 Hz	1000 Hz	2000 Hz	4000 Hz
$\Sigma A\alpha$	11.19	29.87	40.67	41.25	44.62	33.56
$\Sigma A\alpha$ + absorption units = total absorption	11.77	30.99	42.24	43.11	46.68	35.38
$\bar{\alpha}$ = total absorption/S	0.103	0.270	0.368	0.376	0.407	0.308
$(1 - \bar{\alpha})$	0.897	0.730	0.632	0.624	0.593	0.692
$R = S\bar{\alpha}/(1 - \bar{\alpha})$	13.18	42.44	66.82	69.14	78.76	51.07
$4/R$	0.303	0.094	0.060	0.058	0.051	0.078
$Q/4\pi r^2$	0.051	0.051	0.051	0.051	0.051	0.051
$4/R + Q/4\pi r^2$	0.354	0.145	0.111	0.109	0.102	0.129
$L_W - L_P$ (dB)	-4.5	-8.3	-9.5	-9.6	-9.9	-8.9

Therefore, it can be seen that even a very soft room only gives a room effect of between 4 and 10 dB. It is unrealistic to quote sound pressures levels to fractions of a decibel since they cannot be measured that accurately. A hard room, however, can give positive values for the room effect.

If the room effect is known a given sound power level for a terminal unit can be added to it to yield the sound pressure level likely in the room at the position considered. Alternatively, a reverse procedure may be followed. If the desired sound pressure level in each octave band is known, the room effect can be subtracted from it to give the maximum acceptable sound power level in each octave band for the terminal unit.

7.9 Noise criteria and ratings

The response of the human ear to sound is frequency-dependent and various indices have been proposed to express this subjective quality. One of the

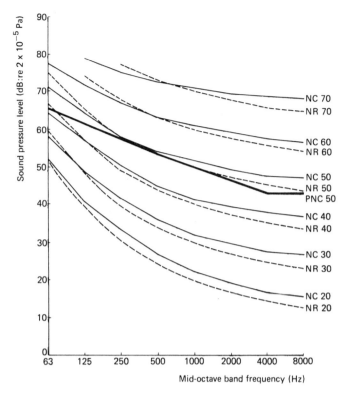

Figure 7.7 NC and NR curves with a single PNC curve superimposed

earliest was the concept of loudness level, expressed in phons and defined as the sound pressure level of a pure tone at 1000 Hz, presented centrally in front of the listener, that seems equal in magnitude to the tone at the frequency considered. A slightly different index, the perceived noise level (expressed in PNdB), and also the effective perceived noise level (expressed in EPNdB), adopts a band of noise between 910 and 1090 Hz as a reference and is commonly used to express the annoyance value of steady noises, particularly aircraft.

An attempt to define noises of subjectively equal loudness level indoors, has led to noise criterion (NC) curves, originally proposed by Beranek in 1957[1]. These refer to steady noises and specify acceptable band levels, usually between 63 and 8000 Hz. Since then, the improved standards of preferred noise criteria (PNC) curves have been put forward by Beranek (1971)[2]. Developments in Europe induced Kosten and Van Os (1962)[3] to suggest noise rating (NR) curves and these are gaining some acceptance internationally. Although based on the idea of the acceptability of a noise to listeners, equations have been derived for the curves and they can therefore be used beyond the range of human hearing if need be. Interpolation can also be done. Figure 7.7 shows NC and NR curves with a single PNC curve superimposed. There does not seem to be a great deal of difference between NC and NR values and, given the subjective nature of the curves and the practical difficulties of exact measurement, they can probably be regarded as the same (see Figures A.1 and A.2 in the Appendix, p. 317).

7.10 Traffic noise and windows

Traffic noise varies considerably with its density, the gear ratios used to climb the inclines and the distance from the listener. In an attempt to define traffic noise a quantity L_{10}, has been proposed. This is the arithmetic mean hourly value of the sound pressure level in dBA (see Section 7.23), at a distance of one metre from the building facade, that is exceeded for ten per cent of the time between the hours of 6 a.m. and midnight. It is termed the 18 hour value of L_{10}. Values of 55 dBA for general offices and 45 dBA for private offices, inside the building, are suggested as reasonable. More than 60 dBA leads to considerable complaint. Clearly, the attenuation given by the windows is highly significant (Table 7.3).

Table 7.3 The attenuation given by different windows

Window type	Mean attenuation over 160–3150 Hz (dB)
Ordinary single, openable, without weatherstrip	20
Fixed or openable, single, with weatherstrip	25
Sealed, double-glazed unit	30
Weatherstripped, openable, double, with 200 mm air gap	40
Weatherstripped, openable, double, with 400 mm air gap and sound absorbant reveals	45

7.11 Privacy of speech

The Preferred Speech Interference Level (PSIL) has been developed as an indication of the intelligibility of speech in a noisy environment. It is defined as the arithmetic mean of the sound pressure levels in the three octave bands having mid-frequencies of 500, 1000 and 2000 Hz. Table 7.4 gives the level corresponding to a communication reliability of 60% for words and numbers, out of doors. For example, if two people are 1.8 m apart a PSIL of 70 dB will mask more than 40% of their conversation, even if they are shouting. However, if they are 0.60 m apart, it needs 80 dB to achieve the same effect.

Masking noise may be deliberately introduced in open-plan offices, at times, to achieve a level of privacy. Such noise should lie within an acceptable

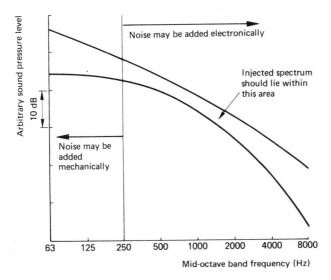

Figure 7.8   Recommended methods and spectrum for injecting noise (after Beranek[2])

spectrum, although it may be provided by mechanical air-conditioning equipment and, at, the higher frequencies, by electronic devices. However, the designer does not have the freedom to offer a carelessly noisy system. Beranek has suggested that the injected noise ought to lie within the pair of curved lines shown in Figure 7.8.

Typically acceptable levels for steady background noise, according to Beranek, are: concert halls NR10–20; private offices NR30–40; large offices NR35–45; general offices NR40–50; computer rooms NR45–55.

In quiet rooms, it is only possible to achieve privacy if intruding noises are excluded and this is best done by having massive walls, extending up above the suspended ceiling and sealed tightly to the soffit of the slab. Any break in the wall negates the isolating effect of its mass and it is therefore necessary to

Table 7.4 The preferred speech interference level (PSIL)

Distance between two people (m)	PSIL (dB)			
	Normal speech	Raised voice	Very loud speech	Shouting
0.3	68	74	80	86
0.6	62	68	74	80
1.2	56	62	68	74
1.8	52	58	64	70

provide well-fitted packing around ducts and pipes where they pass through a wall or partition. For ducts, their walls may offer less acoustic impedance than does the partition penetrated and it then becomes necessary to reduce the flanking path so provided by covering the duct with a dense material and possibly also lining it with a sound-absorbing quilt.

7.12 Sound transmission through building structures

The equipment working inside a plant room sets up a reverberant field which loses energy continuously through the walls, roof and floor (Section 7.8). Further, the direct fields in the vicinity of the plant items also impart energy to the surfaces nearby and, also, some sound waves travel directly from the equipment through the building material. These effects excite the plant room structure, producing compression and shear waves in it that combine to make the surfaces bend, periodically, in various modes and harmonics. Such structural flexures produce sources of acoustic radiation on the outer surfaces of the plant room.

To reduce the transmission of sound through the plant room surfaces, one first step might be to lower the strength of the reverberant field within by covering the inner surface with sound-absorbing material. This is seldom the most effective approach, although it may sometimes help, in conjunction with other measures. The first and most important step is always to construct the plantroom walls, roof and floor, of massive materials. Theory suggests that the mass law transmission loss for homogeneous panels should be 6 dB per doubling of mass but experimental evidence indicates about 5 dB, which is the figure usually taken.

In practice, a sound reduction index (R) is measured for a building material and BS 2750:1956 specifies how this should be done, according to

$$R = L_1 - L_2 + 10 \log (S/A) \text{ dB:re } 2 \times 10^{-5} \text{ Pa} \tag{7.20}$$

in which L_1 and L_2 are the sound pressure levels in the rooms on each side of the specimen, S is its area and A is the total number of absorption units in the receiving room. The sound transmission loss (R) may be used as an alternative term for the sound reduction index and defined in terms of mean squared sound pressures, $|p_1|^2$ and $|p_2|^2$, in the transmitting and receiving rooms, respectively:

$$|p_2|^2 = \frac{\tau S}{A} |p_1|^2 \tag{7.21}$$

leading to a concept of τ, the sound transmittance coefficient. The sound power entering a room through a partition is then directly proportional to the product τS, in m². BS 661:1969 defines the sound reduction index as

$$R = 10\log 1/\tau \text{ dB:re } 2 \times 10^{-5} \text{ Pa} \tag{7.22}$$

Given an experimental value of R, τ and hence τS can be deduced by Equation (7.22). Thus the overall value of R for a parallel combination of building elements can be calculated.

Example 7.6 A $6.0 \text{ m} \times 2.6 \text{ m}$ partition, constructed of Thermalite blocks 100 mm in thickness contains a door, $2.0 \text{ m} \times 0.9 \text{ m} \times 62 \text{ mm}$ thick, fitted with a rubber gasket. Determine the overall average sound transmission loss.
Answer From Table 7.5 the average values of R for the partition and the door are 41 dB and 30 dB, respectively. Using Equation (7.22), the following may be calculated:

Item	R (dB)	$1/\tau$	τ	S (m^2)	τS (m^2)
Partition	41	12590	7.9428×10^{-5}	13.8	109.65×10^{-5}
Door	30	1000	100×10^{-5}	1.8	180×10^{-5}
Total				15.6	289.65×10^{-5}

$$\text{Therefore, } \bar{\tau} = \frac{289.65 \times 10^{-5}}{15.6} = 18.567 \times 10^{-5}$$

and $\bar{R} = 10\log 1/\bar{\tau} = 37.3$ dB

The presence of a hole or a crack in a wall significantly reduces its transmission loss. For the case of a hole or a slit, the diameter or width of which is large compared with the thickness of the wall, $\tau \simeq 1.0$. This is usually the case for open windows, provided that the opening is a large percentage of the total window-wall area. When the opened window is 10% or less of the total area, the loss is generally taken as 10 dB. If the width of the hole is not small in comparison with the wall thickness, τ has a value of less than 1.0. For a slit width of from 5 mm to 25 mm, in a 50 mm thick wall, or door frame, the value of τ lies between about 0.1 at 2000 Hz and about 1.0 at 125 Hz. A reasonable average for is 0.3 speech frequencies. τ can have a value of greater than 1.0, at low frequencies.

An approximate equation, proposed by Cook and Chrzanowski[4] gives a value for the mean transmission loss in accordance with the mass law mentioned earlier:

$$\bar{R} = 13 + 14.5\log m \text{ (dB)} \tag{7.23}$$

where m is the mass of the barrier in kg m^{-2}.

When acoustic energy travels through a medium some of it is dispersed in damped vibrations of the material and so its stiffness is important. Preferably, most building materials, with natural frequencies of 5 to 20 Hz, should be limp, like lead. However, when a sound wave passes through different, successive media, especially an air gap in a solid structure, it encounters discontinuities

Table 7.5 Average values of *R* for various objects

Item	Mass (kg m⁻²)	Approximate transmission loss (R) (dB)						
		Mid-octave frequency (Hz)						
		Av	125	250	500	1000	2000	4000
6 mm plywood glued to both sides of 25 mm × 75 mm studs at 400 mm centres; 75 mm thick	12	24	16	18	26	28	37	33
18 swg corrugated steel sheet	21	24	30	20	22	30	28	31
Glass fibre board; 50 mm thick	26	30	27	23	27	34	39	41
6 mm plywood glued to both sides of 25 mm × 75 mm studs at 400 mm centres plus 12 mm plasterboard nailed to each side; 99 mm thick	32	40	26	33	39	46	50	50
Heavy wooden door plus rubber gasket around edges; 62 mm thick	61	30	30	30	24	26	37	36
Common brick; 100 mm thick	187	44	30	36	40	50	54	60
Thermalite block; 110 mm thick	200	41	27	33	40	44	56	57
Breeze block, plastered both sides; 125 mm thick	205	42	27	33	40	50	57	56
Common brick, plastered both sides; 135 mm thick	220	45	31	36	41	51	55	61
Cavity wall, 2 × 110 mm brick plus 2 × 12 mm plaster plus 50 mm air gap plus butterfly ties	407	29	29	40	45	62	72	84
Reinforced concrete; 150 mm thick	366	46	37	42	47	51	56	60
Reinforced concrete; 200 mm thick	488	48	38	44	49	54	58	62
Reinforced concrete; 300 mm thick	732	50	39	46	51	56	60	63
3 mm glass in a light frame	7	21	15	15	20	23	29	27
3 mm glass in a heavy frame	7	23	14	20	22	28	30	30
2 × 3 mm glass sheets plus 50 mm air gap	14	33	19	24	29	39	48	53
2 × 3 mm glass sheets plus 100 mm air gap	14	37	19	25	37	45	51	53
6 mm plate glass in a heavy frame	17	26	16	21	27	29	29	37
10 mm plate glass in a heavy frame	25	29	21	26	31	32	32	39
16 mm plate glass in a heavy frame	42	32	23	28	33	31	38	45

and a reflection occurs at each interface, constituting an extra transmission loss. Table 7.5 shows that a pair of 3 mm glass sheets, separated by a 50 mm air space, have a mean loss of 33 dB whereas a single 6 mm sheet only gives 26 dB. The greater the width of the air gap the better; less than about 100 mm is seldom worthwhile.

To prevent noise travelling through a floor it is sometimes uneconomical to thicken the slab to increase its mass. Instead it is often better to use a more conventional structural slab and to float a floor on top of it. The floating floor should cover the entire floor area and frequently comprises 100 mm of concrete, reinforced as necessary, resting on pads of resilient material to give an air space of about 50 mm. The air space is often filled loosely with sound-absorbing material. The conventional housekeeping concrete pads, anti-vibration mountings and inertia blocks are still very necessary and rest on top of the floating floor. Resilient material is placed around the edge of the floating floor to isolate it from the walls and it is most important that the floor be laid properly, under competent supervision, to make sure there are no solid bridges across it to the building structure.

7.13 Sources of noise in mechanical systems

No single element in a mechanical system fails to contribute to the production or transmission of noise. The plant itself generates noise, ducts and pipes help to distribute it about the building, the air and water flowing create further noise and, finally, the terminal units in the rooms provide their quota. Even silencers can produce more noise than they are supposed to remove, under some circumstances. It is clearly necessary to know something of the noise-generating characteristics of the components in a system.

7.14 Fan noise

When air passes over a fan blade a pressure gradient is developed across it that is uniform if laminar flow occurs, generating little noise. This case seldom prevails in practice and the airstream is not laminar but separates in a random way from the curvature of the blade, forming eddies in a fluctuating pattern with vortices that are shed from the trailing edge. With centrifugal fans, vortices may also be formed at the leading edges of the blades. Noise over a wide spectrum is produced, its power depending on fan selection, efficiency, size and speed. Further noise is created by turbulence within the casing and matters may be aggravated by obstructions at the fan outlet or inlet and also by ill-conceived or badly installed duct connexions. Although it does not seem possible to relate fan efficiency directly with noise, some approximate generalisations can be made. A given fan will be noisier if it works at a higher fan total pressure or if it handles more air. Further, fans with higher discharge velocities tend to be noisier than those with lower. With axial flow fans, tip clearance should be minimal since much of the noise generated is at the blade tips. Reducing fan capacity by throttling at a damper produces noise. It is better to use variable inlet guide vanes, if these are properly constructed, or variable pitch blades in the case of axial flow fans. It is possible to overdo the attempt to specify a quiet fan. If the manufacturer is restricted in terms of impeller diameter, tip speed, outlet velocity and efficiency, he may find it impossible to offer a fan that will operate on the stable part of its characteristic where pressure increases with volume reduction.

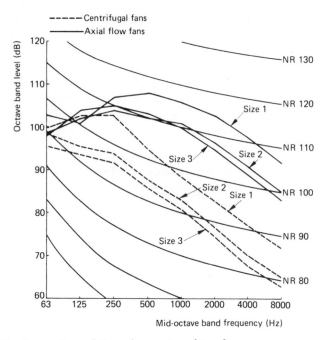

Figure 7.9   Comparison of the noise spectra of two fans

The scroll of a centrifugal fan is designed like an involute, its radius of curvature increasing with the angle turned through from the cut-off. Consequently, the static pressure in the casing increases from the cut-off to the fan discharge but there is a sharp fall in static pressure as the cut-off is passed again. The result is that noise is produced here at the blade-passage frequency.

Nonaerodynamic noises are generated by out-of-balance impellers; bearings, particularly ball or roller; driving motors, giving noises largely of magnetic origin that are notably bad with single phase motors of more than the smallest size. Couplings and vee-belt drives seldom cause complaint, if properly selected.

Figure 7.9 compares the noise spectra of two fans, each selected to deliver 2830 ls^{-1} at a fan total pressure of 0.623 kPa. It can be seen that the axial flow fan is the noisier and this emphasises that its selection and installation requires care. It is not merely a matter of fitting silencers but also of ensuring that noise does not break out through the flexible couplings and is not radiated objectionably from the casing. Silencers should be bolted directly onto the flanges of axial flow fans at both ends, the flexible couplings being fitted at the extremes of the silencer-fan-silencer combination. Radiation from the casing may be dealt with by installing the fan in a plant room with walls having adequate sound reduction indices. All holes in the walls, etc. must be made good with grout and the annular holes where ducts and pipes pass through the walls tightly plugged with fibreglass, asbestos rope, or similar material. It is often acoustically fatal to locate a fan above a suspended ceiling, even if silencers are fitted. A partial remedy for such a difficult situation is to cover the fan casing completely with a layer of sound-absorbing material and, most important, to put a layer of heavy, barrier matting on top. The covering must be done very carefully, with 75 mm lap joints for the outer barrier mat. Leaving small gaps in the coverage will nullify the effort and expense. A further, if expensive remedy is to install a massive subceiling, suspended from resilient hangers. Again it is important that there is no gap around the edges and that the ceiling is free from holes or cracks.

7.15 Noise in ducts

Ducts should be sized for the lowest practicable velocities and bends and fittings designed to give smooth airflow with the minimum of turbulence. The characteristic roar from turbulent airflow is very difficult to remove after a duct system is installed. It is not easy to lay down hard and fast rules but Tables 7.6 and 7.7 suggest maximum air velocities and quantities for high velocity systems in comfort applications.

The acoustic power emitted by the fan is partly absorbed by the silencer, reduced in intensity by being spread over wavefronts of increasing area as the

Table 7.6 Maximum air velocities for high velocity system

Volume of air handled (ls^{-1})	Maximum velocity ($\mathrm{m\,s}^{-1}$)
100	9.0
100–500	11.5
500–1500	15.0
1500–3000	19.0
3000	20.0

Table 7.7 Maximum air quantities for a high velocity system

Duct diameter (mm)	Maximum volume (ls^{-1})
Flexible ducting	
75	40
100	90
Rigid ducting	
75	45
100	100

duct system branches out, augmented by locally generated noise at fittings, further augmented by turbulence at the air distribution terminal and slightly reduced in the lower frequencies by an end reflection when the air finally enters the room. Some attenuation is provided by the unlined duct system as the duct walls are excited to vibrate and bends also give a loss by reflection, but these effects, together with the end reflection at the terminal opening are somewhat unpredictable and comparatively small. It is usually best to ignore any benefit from them. The terminal unit itself may have some added sound-absorbing material to deal with residual noise.

The starting point in the assessment of the silencing to be provided is the fan, and an accepted method of measuring its noise is set out in BS 848: Part 2, on fan noise testing. The test method yields sound power levels at the mid-octave frequencies from 125 to 4000 Hz. It is important to note that the test uses good inlet and outlet duct connexions and up to 5 dB should be added to the test results to cater for disturbed airflow in a real case. The sound power levels in the inlet and outlet duct connexions are of most interest and it is these in-duct levels that are most often quoted. Since sound pressure level is almost equal to sound intensity level (see Section 7.5), differing only by $10 \log [p_{ref}^2/\rho c I_{ref}]$, sound level intensity can be calculated. Multiplying by the duct cross-sectional area gives the in-duct sound power level.

An approximate formula for the overall sound power level generated by ducts and fittings is

$$I_w = C + 10 \log A + 60 \log v \, (\text{dB}) \tag{7.24}$$

in which C is a constant related to the type of fitting, A is the minimum cross-sectional area of the fitting and v is the maximum velocity. The formula is said to be roughly correct for a range of velocity from 10 to 30 ms^{-1}, according to the CIBS guide[5]. The same source tabulates values for C and gives corrections to be applied to yield sound power levels at the mid-octave frequencies. Thus, the value of C is -10 for a straight duct, 0 for a conventional bend, i.e. aspect ratio ≤ 2, throat radius $\geq$ half the width, and $+10$ for a square-mitred bend with turning vanes, i.e. closely spaced, short-radius, single skin. In each case the mid-octave band corrections are given as -2, -7, -8, -10, -12, -15 and -19 dB, respectively, over the range of 125 to 8000 Hz.

Example 7.7 Using the above data and Equation (7.24) calculate the sound power level produced by a square-mitred bend fitted with short-radius, closely spaced, single skin turning vanes if the section is 300 mm square and the velocity is (a) 10 ms^{-1} and (b) 30 ms^{-1}.
Answer From Equation (7.24)
(a) $L_w = 10 + 10 \log (0.3 \times 0.3) + 60 \log 10 = 60 \, \text{dB}$
(b) $L_w = 10 + 10 \log (0.3 \times 0.3) + 60 \log 30 = 88 \, \text{dB}$

Hence, applying the quoted corrections the octave band analysis is

Overall L_w	125 Hz	250 Hz	500 Hz	1000 Hz	2000 Hz	4000 Hz	8000 Hz
(a) 60 dB	58 dB	53 dB	52 dB	50 dB	48 dB	45 dB	41 dB
(b) 88 dB	86 dB	81 dB	80 dB	78 dB	76 dB	73 dB	69 dB

It is to be noted that large radius turning vanes in high velocity ducts can produce pure tones, of objectionable strength, generated by vortices formed when the airstream breaks away from the vanes.

Tie rods in ducts produce noise at a frequency given by

$$f = 0.2 \, v/d \ \text{(Hz)} \tag{7.25}$$

where d is the rod diameter and v the velocity of airflow. The noise produced is much amplified by tuning effects when f equals $nc/2D$, n being an integer, c the velocity of sound and D the transverse duct dimension.

7.16 Silencers

The attenuation of noise in ducts lined with sound-absorbing material has been the subject of a lot of experimental and theoretical research. No simple, accurate expression is possible but some acceptance has been gained for Sabine's equation, despite the severe restrictions on its use:

$$\frac{R}{L} = 1.052 \frac{P}{A} \alpha^{1.4} \ \text{(dB m}^{-1}) \tag{7.26}$$

where R/L is the attenuation per unit length of duct, P is the duct perimeter, A its cross-sectional area and α the sound-absorption coefficient (statistical or Sabine) for its lining. Sabine originally referred it to frequencies between 128 and 2048 Hz, for ducts of dimensions from 225 to 450 mm with aspect ratios of 1:1 to 2:1. It is evident from the form of the equation that the duct shape should provide a large perimeter for a given cross-sectional area. It is at the perimeter of each wavefront, where it meets the sound-absorbing material, that acoustic energy can flow out of the wave train and attenuation occur. For this reason, proprietary silencers often take the form of an array of splitters, covered with sound-absorbing material and offering multiple, parallel paths to the wavefronts, with a large value of P/A. The thicker a sound-absorbing material the better its ability to absorb low-frequency components. Less than 25 mm is scarcely worth bothering with and splitters are usually from 50 to 200 mm in thickness. At the very least they should be covered with a scrim to minimise erosion but the most desirable cover is perforated metal, not least because of the extra structural strength it gives when being man-handled on site.

Low-frequency noise is not very directional, but high-frequency components do tend to travel in straight lines and follow the laws of reflection from surfaces. For this reason it is possible for high-frequency noise to 'beam' straight through a silencer, between splitters. To deal with this, one proprietary

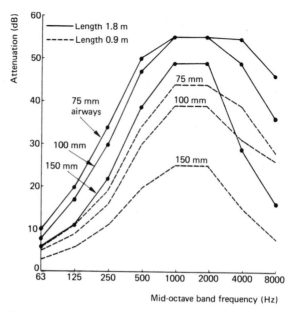

Figure 7.10   Comparison of the performance of two typical silencers with different airway widths

silencer has curved pathways between the splitters, ensuring high-frequency reflections from the sound-absorbing surfaces. Typical silencers achieve some selectivity over the spectrum by varying the thickness of the splitters and the spacing between them. Air turbulence occurs at entry and exit and to minimise this the ends of the splitters are often streamlined. Figure 7.10 shows typical silencer performances; all of them have splitters 100 mm thick but each has a different airway width: 75, 100 and 150 mm. As expected, a width of 75 mm gives the best performance and a silencer 1.8 m long is nearly twice as effective as one of 0.9 m. The cross-sectional area and the air pressure drop are influenced by the splitter configuration. Excessively high velocities and pressure drops should not be adopted in an effort to economise in the space occupied. All silencers generate some noise, half of which travels downstream and half upstream. For the silencer to be useful it must absorb significantly more noise than it produces. Note that according to Equation (7.24), each doubling of the airflow velocity adds 18 dB to the self-generated noise. Not all silencers use splitters; for axial flow fans, lined circular ducts are used, with or without coaxial pods of sound-absorbing material. Other silencers can be purpose-made to provide a bend for the airflow and give extra silencing by reflection. Yet another possibility is to construct silencers with resonant chambers, tuned by design to absorb sound selectively at particular frequencies.

As a general guide it is suggested that self-generated noise is not likely to be troublesome if the face velocity is less than 7 ms^{-1}, the velocity through the airways is less than 15 ms^{-1} and the air pressure drop does not exceed 0.75 Pa. Special consideration, beyond these suggestions, must be given to low-noise areas such as television studios, etc.

Example 7.8 By means of Equation (7.26) estimate the attenuation likely in the range 125 to 4000 Hz for a silencer 1200 mm wide × 600 mm high × 1800 mm long, fitted with five splitters, parallel to the 600 mm dimension, each 100 mm thick to form six, equally-spaced airways 100 mm apart. Assume the lining is stillite with absorption coefficients as shown in Figure 7.5.

Answer If each splitter is 100 mm wide it may be assumed that this is equivalent to a 50 mm thick lining for each airway of cross-sectional dimensions 100 × 600 mm.

$$\frac{P}{A} = \frac{0.6 + 0.6 + 0.1 + 0.1}{0.6 \times 0.1} = 23.33$$

for one airway or for several airways in parallel. *L* is 1.8 m and by Equation (7.26) $R = 1.052 \times 23.33 \times 1.8 \; \alpha^{1.4} = 44.18 \; \alpha^{1.4}$. The results can, therefore, be tabulated as follows:

f (Hz)	125	250	500	1000	2000	4000
α	0.30	0.53	0.80	0.84	0.75	0.80
R (dB)	8	18	32	35	30	32

Figure 7.10 shows that at the corresponding frequencies the attenuations for a proprietary silencer of a similar type are 8, 18, 30, 47, 55 and 55 dB. This seems to confirm that the Sabine equation underestimates attenuation at the higher frequencies.

It is no good installing a silencer if the noise from the plant breaks out of the duct before the silencer and re-enters after it. Silencers should therefore be bolted directly onto the plant item, the flexible coupling being after the combination, or be fitted in the duct where it leaves the plant room, butting tightly against the wall. Running ducts through places where the noise level is high should be avoided, otherwise break-in may nullify the effect of the silencer. Covering the duct is effective in minimising break-in and break-out.

Table 7.8   Sound reduction index (*R*)

	Sound reduction index (*R*) (dB)							
	Frequency (Hz)							
	63	125	250	500	1000	2000	4000	8000
Bare duct	3	10	17	22	28	33	38	40
Duct plus cover	18	24	30	34	38	42	45	45

The rules for the cover, i.e. mass, discontinuity, homogeneity, still apply but it is worth noting that an 18 gauge steel duct of 1.2 mm nominal thickness, lagged with 25 mm of glassfibre and covered with a hard-setting cement plaster, trowelled smooth, may give a fairly good sound reduction index (R) (Table 7.8), provided that at least 20 mm of hard-setting cover is used. Lack of uniformity in the thickness of the cement finish nullifies the effect.

7.17 End reflection

When a wave train encounters a change in the impedance of its acoustic path, a reflection occurs (see Section 7.2 and Figure 7.2). A change in the section of a duct, as at the entry to a plenum chamber, or at the terminal diffuser delivering air to a room are instances of impedance variations that produce significant end reflections, mostly in the lower frequencies. The square root of the area of the opening or of the duct cross-sectional area is an approximate index of the attenuation occurring in this way, although this depends also on the shape of the opening or duct, its position at entry to the chamber or room, and the sound-absorption properties of the surfaces of the latter. Figure 7.11 illustrates typical end reflections and shows that these are most effective at the lower frequencies. Even so, it is the low frequency components of system noise that are the most difficult to deal with. For example, the broad spectrum noise produced by air turbulence often has objectionable peaks at 125, 250 and 500 Hz.

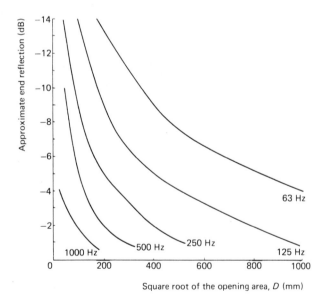

Figure 7.11   Typical end reflections

7.18 Duct branches

When a duct divides into branches so does the wavefront and it is usually assumed that the acoustic energy is distributed accordingly. If the main duct after the branch has a cross-sectional area a_1 and the area of the branch is a_2, then the attenuation in the main, because of the loss of acoustic energy down the branch, is given by

$$R = 10 \log \left[\frac{a_1}{a_1 + a_2} \right] \text{(dB)} \qquad (7.27)$$

Example 7.8 If $2830\,\mathrm{l\,s^{-1}}$ flows down a duct and is distributed equally between a pair of ducts each conveying the air at $7.5\,\mathrm{ms^{-1}}$, determine the branch attentuations.

Answer $a_1 = a_2 = \dfrac{2.830}{7.5} = 0.377\,\mathrm{m^2}$ and from Equation (7.27)

$$R = 10 \log \left[\frac{0.377}{0.377 + 0.377} \right] = -3\,\mathrm{dB}.$$

Although it is common to ignore the natural attenuation of unlined ductwork, which is really because of break-out, the effect of branches is considerable and should not be ignored.

Example 7.9 A centrifugal fan has an in-duct sound power level as given by the curve for size 2 in Figure 7.9 and is directly connected to a silencer 1.8 m long with properties of attenuation as in Figure 7.10 for 75 mm airways. If the air quantity is ultimately distributed by successive branchings amongst 8 subducts of equal area before being delivered through a side-wall grille having an area of 0.16 m², determine the sound power level emitted at the grille. If the grille supplies air to a room similar to that forming the basis of Example 7.5, determine the noise level therein. Use Figure 7.11 to establish the end reflection.

Answer The square root of the area of the supply grille is 400 mm and this is used in Figure 7.11 to find the end reflection. The first branching produces 2 subducts and gives 3 dB attenuation for each, since they are of equal area. The second branching gives 4 subducts and a further 3 dB. The third provides the 8 duct branches and another 3 dB. The following can now be tabulated.

Frequency (Hz)	63	125	250	500	1000	2000	4000	8000
Sound power level at fan outlet	99	96	94	88	83	77	70	65
Attenuation from silencer	−10	−20	−34	−50	−55	−55	−54	−46
Subtotal	89	76	60	38	28	22	16	19
Branches attenuation	−9	−9	−9	−9	−9	−9	−9	−9

Subtotal	80	67	51	29	19	13	7	10
End reflection	−9	−5	−2	0	0	0	0	0
Sound power level entering room	71	62	49	29	19	13	7	10
Room effect		−4	−8	−10	−10	−10	−9	—
Sound pressure level in room:	71	58	41	19	9	3	—	10
L_p values for NR 50	75	66	58	54	50	47	45	44
L_p values for NR 40	67	57	49	44	40	37	35	33

If the 63 Hz component is ignored, the level in the room is NR 40.

7.19 Noise from pumps and pipes

The major component of pump noise is the blade passage frequency but the noise output is related in practice to the pump speed. Pumps that operate against a high head must run at a high speed and those running at 47.5 rev s⁻¹ (2850 rpm) are undoubtedly much noisier than at 23.8 rev s⁻¹ (1425 rpm). The former often consitute a major noise source in plant rooms and are to be avoided.

Water flow in pipes is generally turbulent and, therefore, generates some noise[6]. Fortunately, tube walls are massive and rigid, so noise radiation from them is seldom a problem, provided that the water is free of air and velocities are not too high. Pipes with rough and corroded internal walls tend to create more noise than do smooth bores but noise-production in air-free water is not the criterion of velocity. The limit is generally set at 2.4 ms⁻¹ for constant flow to minimise erosion in the tubes, especially at the heels of elbows. The commonest source of noise in pipes arises from the air present in improperly vented systems. Bubbles are conveyed by the water and cause a characteristic tinkling at modest velocities, or a broader spectrum, whiter noise at high velocities. Cavitation can also occur in systems when the static head is insufficient for the prevailing temperature, and is another origin of noise, particularly at the pump, which may give a pronounced roar when cavitation is well-established. Quieter running pumps can be obtained by selecting an impeller diameter that is only about 85% of the maximum impeller diameter, in the process using a larger pump to achieve the duty, and paying the small extra cost for a dynamically balanced electric driving motor.

7.20 Refrigeration plant

Sound power levels for refrigeration compressors are difficult to obtain because of the intrusion of noise from auxiliary plant, notably pumps. However, it has been established[7] that compressor noise is dominant within 1 m of the machine, allowing representative sound pressure levels to be

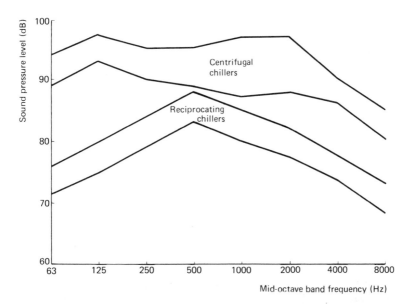

Figure 7.12   Comparison of the sound pressure levels of centrifugal and
reciprocating chillers

measured. When assessing the transmission of noise through floors and walls
that are near to the compressor, such values should be used without correction,
but at distances greater than 3 m from the machine the reverberant field is
fairly constant at about 5 dB less than the sound pressure levels measured
within 1 m.

Hermetic and open-drive, centrifugal and reciprocating chillers, over the
range from 135 to 14 000 kW (40 to 4000 tons of refrigeration), show no
significant correlation between sound pressure level and machine size, but
centrifugal compressors running at partial load produce some 3 dB more noise
than at full duty. Open-drive machines are approximately 5 dB louder than
hermetics. Figure 7.12 shows the results of a survey of 34 centrifugal and 14
reciprocating chillers, available in the North American market. Reciprocating
compressors are clearly quieter than centrifugals and reach a peak at 500 Hz,
probably arising from piston stroke frequency or its harmonics. The
centrifugal spectrum is more uniform and flatter, although noisier. The
broadening between 500 and 4000 Hz is caused by the larger, open-drive
compressors.

Some sound power levels have been measured and Figure 7.13 compares a
single-stage, semi-hermetic chiller with speed-increasing gear and a semi-
hermitic, screw machine. Each plant has a nominal refrigeration capacity of
1370 kW. The screw machine is up to 20 dB quieter than the centrifugal at full
load and we also see that the centrifugal generates more noise, mostly at

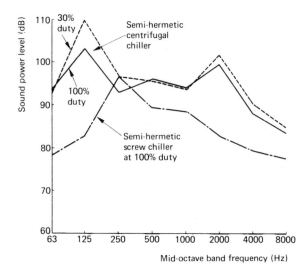

Figure 7.13   Comparison of the sound power levels of a single-stage, semi-hermetic chiller with speed-increasing gear and a semi-hermetic, screw machine

125 Hz, when its duty is turned down to 30 percent. This is a chacteristic of centrifugals but not of screws.

7.21 Cooling towers and air-cooled condensers

A straightforward comparison of in-duct sound power levels for two cooling towers, one with an axial flow fan and the other with a centrifugal chosen for the same duty from the same manufacturer (Table 7.9), verifies that the forced-draught centrifugal arrangement is much the quieter.

Table 7.9   Comparison of in-duct sound power levels for two cooling towers

	Sound power level (dB)					
Cooling tower	Frequency (Hz) 125	250	500	1000	2000	4000
With axial flow fan	100	99	95	93	89	83
With centrifugal fan	88	85	81	75	69	63

Whether the fan is inside or outside the tower casing and the type of tower itself, also have some bearing on the noise created, as the comparative sound pressure levels, measured on the same basis, show (Figure 7.14). There is little to choose among them, except that the ejector tower, which has no fans, relying

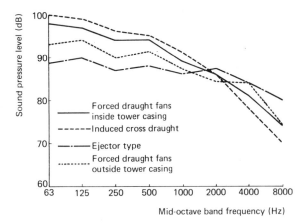

Figure 7.14   Comparative sound pressure levels for various cooling towers

on the water jets to induce the airflow, is significantly quieter at the low frequencies. Air-cooled condensers have the reputation of being noisy but this is because they generally use axial flow or propeller fans. The greatest nuisance to the surroundings is sometimes caused by the intermittent operation of condenser or cooling tower fans under automatic control, particularly at night-time. Solid-state speed controllers on air-cooled condensers make significantly more noise when they reduce the speed of the fans. One other cause of noise from colling towers is water dripping from the fill into the pond. This can be partly overcome by fitting screens beneath the fill to break up the pattern of drips.

Silencing towers after the event is a difficult and expensive business. It is better to select a quiet tower initially. Screening can be effective, 20 dB(A) being achieved with barriers of surface density 10 to 20 kg m^{-2}, but as much as 10 dB(A) is possible with as little as 5 kg m^{-2}.[8] The screen obtains its results by casting an acoustic shadow and it is pointless to try for more than about 20 dB(A) because of diffraction effects. Barriers should be homogeneous and as close as possible to the source of noise, remembering the need for adequate airflow paths into the tower or condenser.

7.22 Terminal units

These can be separated into three classes: mechanical units, high-velocity air terminals and low-velocity air diffusers or grilles, roughly in order of noisiness. In the first class, air-cooled, self-contained, 'unit conditioners' or 'window units' are undoubtedly the noisiest but differences of price and quality are reflected in the sound created. Water-cooled units are invariably quieter than air-cooled. In the same class, fan coil units can be very much quieter, particularly if selected for operation at medium or low speed, when they can then fall into the lowest noise category.

High-velocity terminals selected to deliver large quantities of air at high pressure will be noisier than those chosen for reduced duties. This feature is to the advantage of variable air volume units (see Figure 7.15) which operate for much of the time at a partial load and consequently at much less than their design noise level. High-velocity terminals always radiate some noise from their casings and are often located above suspended ceilings that scarcely impede the flow of noise into the conditioned space beneath at all. The presence of a silencer in the low-velocity side of the terminal does nothing to prevent such radiation.

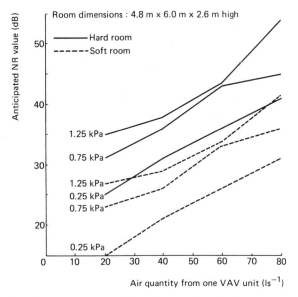

Figure 7.15   Relationship between NR value and duty for a VAV terminal unit

The sound power levels claimed for low-velocity air distribution devices always assume smooth, uniform airflow from a silent duct system into the cones of the diffuser or the bars of the grille. This is a most unlikely situation in reality. The presence of a damper disturbs the airflow over the cones or bars and more noise than anticipated is generated. Further, airflows are frequently distorted before entering the terminal by the duct system and it follows that the noise levels claimed should never be taken at their face value. Caution in selection is advisable. Regardless of the sound produced at the terminal, turbulent airflow noise in a poorly-designed duct system feeding it may give additional noise.

7.23 Measurement of sound

Sound pressure level is measured by means of a sound level meter which comprises microphone, preamplifier, filters, amplifier, rms rectifier and indicating meter. An undamped measurement is often difficult because the needle on the meter oscillates rapidly as the sound pressure level fluctuates; it is usually easier to damp the response of the meter and so give averaged values over a short time period.

There are four types of microphone: crystal, condenser, electret and dynamic, of which the first two are the most commonly used. The cheaper and more rugged crystal microphone relies on the piezo-electric effect of a crystal placed against a diaphragm, where small changes of air pressure strain the atomic lattice of the crystal, generating a proportional voltage. The condenser microphone has greater acoustic sensitivity. Alterations in sound pressure deflect a diaphragm and produce variations in the capacitance with an adjacent plate. A constant charge is usually maintained on the capacitor assembly so that the voltage output varies with the change in capacity, that is, with change in sound pressure. All microphones, especially condenser instruments, need careful treatment.

Measurements should never be made close to a strongly absorbing or reflecting surface and microphones used in moving airstreams must be shielded from the airflow to avoid the irrelevant noise from the air turbulence.

The purpose of the filter in the meter is to simulate the subjective response of the human ear. An A-weighted network includes filters that modify the output signal to the meter, according to frequency, in such a way that there is a high degree of correlation with speech interference levels, loudness level (see Section 7.9) and NC, PNC or NR levels. In a rough and ready way, an NR value is about 7 dB less than the dB(A) value. It follows that sound pressure levels in dB(A) are most useful. B-weighted networks are seldom used and the C network gives a flat response. Other weightings are useful for special purposes.

Where measurements in dB(A) are not sufficiently accurate or informative, a frequency analyser must be used, in conjunction with a sound level meter, to yield an octave band or even a one-third octave band analysis.

7.24 Vibration transmission

Because of imperfect construction and balance, rotational and reciprocating machines impose oscillatory, out-of-balance forces on their mountings, producing linear, rocking, rolling and yawing movements. If simple harmonic motion, giving only linear, vertical displacements is assumed, elementary analysis leads to some convenient, if optimistic, answers. When a resilient mounting of stiffness k, is placed between the machine and the supporting building structure, the ratio of the force transmitted through the mounting to the force imposed on it by the machine is termed the transmissibility (τ) of the mounting and, ignoring damping effects, is defined by

$$\tau = 1/[1 - (f/f_o)^2] \tag{7.28}$$

whence, as a useful alternative,

$$f_o = f\sqrt{\tau/(1 + \tau)} \tag{7.29}$$

in which f is the frequency of the imposed force and f_o is the natural frequency of the mounting, defined by

$$f_o = 15.8/\sqrt{d} \tag{7.30}$$

where d is the static deflection in mm of the machine at rest on its mountings. Since the static deflection depends on the stiffness of the mounting, i.e. the force needed to give a unit static deflection, it follows that the choice of suitable mountings depends on the static deflection, this requiring to be large if low frequencies are involved.

Example 7.10 Out-of-balance forces have frequencies of (a) 100 Hz and (b) 50 Hz. What static deflection must be specified for the resilient mountings in each case, to give a transmissibility of 0.005?
Answer
(a) Using Equation (7.29) $f_o = 100\sqrt{0.005/1.005} = 7$ Hz and from Equation (7.30) $d = 249.6/49 = 5$ mm.
(b) Similarly, $f_o = 50\sqrt{0.005/1.005} = 3.5$ Hz and $d = 249.6/12.25 = 20$ mm.

Resonance occurs when f/f_o equals unity. If a machine runs continuously under this condition, successive amplitudes of vibration increase until there is a mechanical failure or damping forces restrict further amplitude increases. When a machine starts, its speed builds up and it passes through the resonant frequency of the mountings. If the run-up time is short, resonance is only a transient effect but with slow accelerations it may be necessary to introduce extra damping to minimise resonant amplitudes.

There is the risk of a beat frequency developing when two machines, running at slightly different speeds, are connected, as by a pipe between a chiller and its pump. The beat frequency is the difference of the component frequencies and may be near to the natural frequency of the link.

7.25 Damping

When a mass, m, freely supported on a resilient mounting, is displaced vertically by an amount, y, from its position of equilibrium, it will oscillate indefinitely with a frequency, f_o, and maximum amplitudes $\pm y$, in the absence of damping forces. In practice, air resistance and the internal friction of the material of the mounting will reduce the movement, which will eventually cease. The reduction may be helped by adding external damping, as by a dash pot in which the viscous resistance to the flow of oil through an orifice retards the movement, but it does not follow that the oscillations will always then occur. If c is the damping force per unit of velocity, oscillations will only take place when $c/m < 4\pi f_o$; above this the movement is dead beat and decays slowly to zero without oscillation. The value $c_o = 4\pi f_o$ is the critical damping force per unit of velocity and the fraction c/c_o is termed the damping ratio, D.

If forced vibrations of frequency f are imposed on a damped, resilient mounting, a new expression for the transmissibility can be derived from elementary theory:

$$\tau = \sqrt{\frac{1 + 4D^2(f/f_o)^2}{[1 - (f/f_o)^2]^2 + 4D^2(f/f_o)^2}} \tag{7.31}$$

Example 7.11 A machine at rest on a damped, resilient mounting gives a static deflection of 25 mm. If the damping factor is 0.25 and the machine runs up slowly from rest to a normal operating frequency of 25 Hz, determine (a) the transmissibility as the machine passes through resonance and (b) the transmissibility at normal running.
Answer
(a) $(f/f_o) = 1$ at resonance and so from Equation (7.31)

$$\tau = \sqrt{\frac{1 + 4 \times 0.25^2}{0 + 4 \times 0.25^2}} = 2.24$$

(b) From Equation (7.30) $f_o = 15.8/\sqrt{25} = 3.16$ Hz and from Equation (7.31)

$$\tau = \sqrt{\frac{1 + 4 \times 0.25^2 \times (25/3.16)^2}{[1 - (25/3.16)^2]^2 + 4 \times 0.25^2 \times (25/3.16)^2}} = 0.07$$

In general, a damping factor greater than zero reduces the transmissibility for $f/f_o < \sqrt{2}$, but increases it for $f/f_o > \sqrt{2}$, (Figure 7.16).

7.26 Anti-vibration mountings

Pads or mats in compression, synthetic or natural, ribbed or studded rubber, glassfibre, cork, felt, etc., are used for dealing with high frequencies where static deflections are less than about 5 mm. It is essential that they are uniformly and correctly loaded, as underloading gives insufficient static deflection and overloading causes distortion and spoils resilient properties. Rubber-in-shear fittings may be used for comparatively small loads with static deflections up to

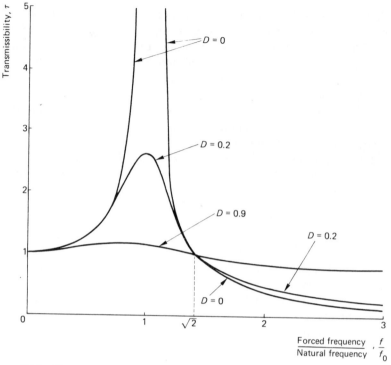

Figure 7.16   The effect of damping factor upon transmissibility

about 8 mm. They are affected by ageing, oil or other solvents, and temperature. Internal damping factors are of the order of 0.03.

Helical steel springs must be used when static deflections greater than 8 mm are desired. Since they have relatively low stiffness and hence large static deflections they tend to be unstable if badly installed or subjected to lateral movement. They have very little internal damping and transmit high frequencies unattenuated. It is therefore customary for proprietary spring isolators to incorporate levelling screws, to be fitted with rubber snubbers to restrict excessive lateral and vertical movement, especially during run-up or run-down, and to be provided with synthetic rubber pads for attenuating the high frequencies.

Machines and their anti-vibration mountings should be located on level plinths, or housekeeping pads, 100 mm or more in thickness. The resilient mountings must be positioned to carry equal loads and the machine lowered carefully onto them, so that lateral displacements of the mountings or torsional forces on them, are avoided. The machine base-frame should then be levelled, using shims if necessary.

It is important that there are no rigid bridges, e.g. by electrical conduit, across the anti-vibration mountings. Flexible couplings with lower stiffnesses than the mountings should be fitted in duct and conduit. Flexible couplings in pipes on each side of a pump or a chiller are largely a waste of time as they become rigid and ineffectual under hydraulic pressure. It is much better to bolt the pipe directly to the machine flanges and to use Victaulic couplings for the pipe joints to take up any vibrational movement; such joints can accommodate from 1°, for large pipes, to 5°, for small pipes, of angular displacement. The pipes themselves should be supported by spring hangers with a static deflection of at least 25 mm for a distance of about 30 m, horizontally, from the machine. In this way they will attenuate any transmitted noise and vibration. Thereafter, conventional pipe brackets may be used. It should be noted that unrestricted heavy valves or other fittings may impose a rotational force on pipework with victaulic joints. The valves or fittings then tend to rotate into a stable position, hanging down beneath the pipe.

Pumps should be either bolted down rigidly to floors with solid ground beneath, with their pipe connexions as above, or, otherwise, fitted on a strong, rigid, steel base-frame, loaded with concrete to form a substantial inertia block and mounted on steel springs.

When two machines are coupled, e.g. a fan, belt-driven from a motor, it is essential that they are both mounted on a common steel base-frame and that this is supported as a whole by anti-vibration fittings. The lowest frequency component in the pair should be used for the selection of the resilient mountings. In this connexion it is bad to fit a stand-by motor, that is normally not running, on a common base frame with the running plant, as transmitted vibrations will cause bearing damage by brinelling. When stand-by motors are used they should be belted up to the fan, for example, and driven, along with the fan, by the duty motor.

Inertia blocks are very desirable. They are often provided by filling with concrete the space within the steel channel base-frame, to which the machine is bolted and to which the resilient mountings are fitted. The increased mass so provided lowers the centre of gravity of the assembly and so adds stability, increases the static deflection on the mountings, reduces the amplitude of movement, reduces the transient disturbances as the machine runs up or down, and minimises the bad effects of any unequal loading on the resilient mountings caused by imprecise knowledge of the weight disposition in the machine itself. Ideally, the centre of gravity should be below the upper surface of the anti-vibration mountings and for this reason they are often fitted on extension members from the upper part of the inertia block.

With fans, in particular, it is sometimes possible for a reactive movement to occur which means the fan base tilts upon start-up. This may be minimised by the addition of a heavy inertia block and a lengthening of the base frame in the direction of reaction. Alternatively, the assembly can be designed to have a reverse tilt that is corrected when the fan runs.

Locating anti-vibration mountings on a suspended floor may yield unpredictable results. The natural frequency of the resilient mountings should be as far as possible from the natural frequency of the floor, which itself is difficult to predict. The approximate natural frequency of a concrete floor slab is the shorter span in metres divided by 600. The safest plan is to use large static deflections, never less than 30 mm, for large machines such as refrigeration compressors. Lightweight floors and cantilevered slabs are very likely to cause trouble and mounting dynamic loads on them is to be avoided. When machines are located on suspended floors it is wise to position them close to load-bearing walls and columns. Better still, they should be entirely off the floor, supported on resilient mountings fixed to steel channels or joists which are in turn supported by load-bearing walls or columns. Even so, there is the risk of noise penetrating the slab and passing to spaces beneath. Table 7.10 suggests suitable static deflections for various locations and different dynamic loadings. In spite of the suggestions made in Table 7.10, it is best to locate boilers and refrigeration plants in basements, on solid non-suspended floors with ground beneath. The same should apply, as far as possible, to pumps.

Table 7.10　Suitable static deflections for various locations and different dynamic loadings.

	Static deflections (mm)			
Dynamic load	Basement	6 m span	9 m span	12 m span
Centrifugal chillers	6	25	44	62
Reciprocating compressors:				
8.3 to 12.5 Hz	25	38	62	69
Above 12.5 Hz	25	25	38	62
Packaged boilers	6	6	25	44
Pumps up to 7 kW	9	9	25	25
Pumps above 7 kW	9	25	38	62
Cooling towers:				
Below 8.3 Hz	9	9	44	62
Above 8.3 Hz	9	9	25	44
Floor-mounted fans and air-handling units:				
Up to 7 kW; 3–8.3 Hz	9	44	44	44
Up to 7 kW; above 8.3 Hz	9	25	25	38
Up to 27 kW; 3–8.3 Hz	9	62	62	88
Up to 27 kW; above 8.3 Hz	9	44	44	62
Above 27 kW; 3–8.3 Hz	9	62	88	127
Above 27 kW; above 8.3 Hz	9	44	62	88

Exercises

1 Evaluate the room effect in dB in each octave band from 125 to 4000 Hz for an acoustically hard room of the same dimensions as in Example 7.5. Take the same absorption coefficients for the walls, window and door. Use the following coefficients for the hard floor and ceiling:

Frequency (Hz)	125	250	500	1000	2000	4000
Floor	0.02	0.04	0.05	0.05	0.10	0.05
Ceiling	0.03	0.03	0.02	0.03	0.04	0.05

Assume two people are present measuring the sound pressure levels, the terminal unit is in the middle of the room and that $r = 1.769$ m.

(*Answer* -0.2, -1.0, -0.3, -1.0, -2.5, -2.0 dB)

2 If the room in Exercise 7.1 is fitted with a variable air volume terminal having a sound power level of

Frequency (Hz)	125	250	500	1000	2000	4000
dB:re 10^{-12} W	10.0	11.0	16.5	25.0	32.0	35.5

determine the NR level in the room, with the aid of Figure 7.6.

(*Answer* Approximately NR 38)

3 A wall 4.6 m long × 2.7 m high has a mean sound transmission loss of 45 dB. If a door of dimensions 0.9 m × 2.1 m having a loss of 31 dB is fitted in the wall, what will be the overall loss? (*Answer* 38 dB)

Symbols

A	Cross-sectional area	m^2
	Total number of absorption units	m^2
C	Constant	
D	Damping ratio	
	Transverse duct dimension	m
D_r	Energy density in a reverberant field	Jm^{-3}
I	Intensity of a sound	Wm^{-2}
I_{av}	Average intensity of a sound	Wm^{-2}
L	Duct length	m
L_p	Sound pressure level	dB
L_1	Sound intensity level	dB
L_w	Sound power level	dB
P	Maximum sound pressure in a wave train	Pa
	Duct perimeter	m
P'	Pressure amplitude factor	m Pa
Q	Directivity factor	
R	Sound reduction factor	dB
	Sound transmission loss	dB
	Room constant	dB

	Attenuation in a duct	dB
S	Surface area in a room	m^2
W	Sound power	W
a	Cross-sectional area of a duct	m^2
c	Speed of sound	$m\,s^{-1}$
	Damping factor per unit velocity	$N\,s\,m^{-1}$
d	Rod diameter	m
	Static deflection	mm
f	Frequency	Hz
f_c	Mid-frequency of an octave band	Hz
f_o	Natural frequency	Hz
k	Wave number	m^{-1}
m	Mass	kg
	Surface density of a wall or barrier	$kg\,m^{-2}$
n	Integer	
$p(x, t)$	Sound pressure at distance x and time t	Pa
$p(r, t)$	Sound pressure at distance r and time t	Pa
p_{rms}	Root mean square sound pressure	Pa
r	Radial distance	m
	Distance in a direct field from a sound source	m
t	Time	s
u	Particle or molecule velocity	$m\,s^{-1}$
v	Maximum air velocity	$m\,s^{-1}$
x	Distance	m
y	Vertical displacement	m
α	Sound absorption coefficient	
	Sabine absorption coefficient	
	Statistical absorption coefficient	
α_{sab}	Sabine absorption coefficient	
$\bar{\alpha}_{sab}$	Average sabine absorption coefficient	
α_θ	Sound absorption coefficient at a given angle of incidence	
α_n	Sound absorption coefficient at normal incidence	
θ	Angle of incidence	
λ	Wavelength	m
ρ	Air density	$kg\,m^{-3}$
τ	Sound transmission coefficient	
	Transmissibility	

References

(1) Beranek, L. L., Revised criteria for noise in buildings, *Noise Control*, **3**, pp. 19–27, 1957
(2) Beranek, L. L., *Noise and Vibration Control*, McGraw Hill, 1971

(3) Kosten, C. W. and Van Os, G. J., Community reaction criteria for external noises, *Proc. Conf. Control of Noise*, HMSO, London, 1962
(4) Harris, C. M., *Handbook of Noise Control*, McGraw Hill, 1957
(5) CIBS Guide, *B*-12 *Sound Control*, Volume B, 1970
(6) Rogers, W. L., *Trans. ASHVE*, **60**, p. 411, 1954
(7) Blazier, W. E., *Chiller Noise: Its Impact on Building Design*, ASHRAE Semi-annual meeting, New Orleans, January 1972
(8) BRS Digest No. 153, *Motorway Noise and Dwellings*, May 1973
(9) Osborne, W. C., *Fans*, Pergamon Press, 1966

8
Economics

8.1 Capital costs

Generalisation about capital costs is difficult because the options available to the designers of buildings and services are so many that an accurrate correlation with design parameters is not easy. Nevertheless, the cost of mechanical services in $£ \, m^{-2}$ of treated floor area has been extensively used for budget price indications and proved of some value with office blocks but of less worth in other applications. Alternative cost indicators, measured per unit of

Table 8.1 Percentage contribution of the components of a system to its total cost

	Percentage of the total capital cost for various systems				
Component	Two-pipe perimeter induction	Double duct	Fan coil plus ducted air	Fan coil plus local air	Low velocity ducted air
Refrigeration plant and cooling towers	19.1	16.3	20.7	23.6	18.4
Air-handling plant and controls	7.6	13.7	7.4	2.1	17.7
Pumps	1.1	0.5	0.6	1.4	0.5
Pipe etc.	5.5	1.8	5.7	6.5	2.1
Insulation on pipes and plant	4.5	1.5	7.3	8.3	1.4
Ducts, insulation, diffusers and grilles	23.0	44.6	27.0	14.3	51.5
Terminal units	21.6	8.5	22.2	33.3	
Individual control on terminal units	8.3	4.0	inc.	inc.	
Air compressors and accessories	0.5	0.4			
Boilers	2.6	3.3	3.1	3.6	2.8
Electrical wiring and switchgear	6.2	5.4	6.0	6.9	5.6
Total	100.0	100.0	100.0	100.0	100.0

These figures were determined[3] by costing comparative designs for a hypothetical office building of about 14 200 m^2 treated floor area

installed refrigeration capacity and per unit of supply airflow rate are also useful at times.

Whichever approach is adopted its accuracy is significantly affected by the following building features: total treated floor area; building shape; type of glazing and shading; proportion of glazing in the facade; illumination level and the heat dissipated by electric lights; population density; and, for office blocks, the width of the module. The U-values of the structural elements in the fabric are generally of less importance, except in the case of low rise-buildings having large plan areas, e.g. hypermarkets, where the thermal transmittance of the roof is significant. The thermal mass of the building structure also plays a part, notably in reducing the impact of solar gains through glass when it is large. The choice of system[1,2] and the way it is designed are major influences on capital cost. It is evident that taking account of all the factors is a hindrance to the accurate preparation of indicative costs. However, if the total cost of a system is broken down to show the percentage contributions of its elements, the influence of design changes on the overall cost can be seen but, because of the many ways of grouping the component costs, an exact consensus of opinion cannot be obtained. Tables 8.1 and 8.2, based on references (1) and (2),

Table 8.2 Percentage contribution of the components of a system to its total cost

| Component | Percentage of the total capital cost for two systems over a treated floor area of | | | |
| | 6000 m² | | 15 000 m² | |
	Four-pipe perimeter induction	VAV plus perimeter heating	Four-pipe perimeter induction	VAV plus perimeter heating
Refrigeration plant, cooling towers and pumps	7.88	8.70	7.03	7.10
Air-handling plant and silencers	13.69	17.41	13.68	15.64
Chilled water pipe and insulation	14.42	3.96	13.90	3.47
Cooling water pipe	2.15	1.95	1.66	1.61
LTHW pipe, insulation and pumps	11.61	5.32	9.85	4.65
Ductwork, insulation, grilles and diffusers	17.99	43.89	18.45	50.21
Terminal units	10.20		14.20	
Automatic controls	8.25	5.78	8.08	5.66
Boilers, flues and gas installation	4.45	3.96	3.72	3.04
Space heating	3.56	3.12	4.04	3.30
Electrical supplies to control panels and plant	2.60	2.60	2.28	2.45
Water treatment	1.19	1.04	1.14	0.93
Fire detection	2.01	2.27	1.97	1.94
Total	100.00	100.00	100.00	100.00

These figures are based on reference (2) and are for two systems not covered by Table 8.1

illustrate such cost analyses. It should be noted, however, that it is always difficult to know exactly what comprises the cost of each component without access to the details.

The results of statistics collected for office blocks[4] within the range of $1000\,\mathrm{m^2}$ to $10\,000\,\mathrm{m^2}$ of treated floor area and with refrigeration loads between 110 and 150 $\mathrm{Wm^{-2}}$ are given as comparative figures in Table 8.3, the two-pipe perimeter induction system being taken as unity.

Table 8.3 Relative costs of various systems

Approximate relative costs of various systems					
Two-pipe perimeter induction	Four-pipe perimeter induction	Fan coil plus ducted air	VAV plus perimeter heating	Dual duct	Low velocity ducted
High	1.3	1.5	1.4	1.5	1.7	1.45
Average	1.0	1.15	1.1	1.1	1.35	1.35
Low	0.7	0.8	0.8	0.7	1.0	1.25

Note. The two pipe perimeter induction system has been taken as having unit cost, from which the relative costs of the other systems have been calculated

The figures in Table 8.3 do not necessarily compare like systems. For instance, a low velocity ducted system from a central plant, perhaps with simple zoned control, does not provide the same quality of air conditioning as do the other four systems listed. Further, accommodating extensive low velocity duct runs poses serious problems in an office block, where space is at a premium. In the case of systems using terminal units, which are usual in office air conditioning, the number of units per module is a major influence on the capital cost and also, of course, on the options for partition arrangement open to the tenant (Sections 2.8 and 2.12).

For applications other than offices, low velocity ducted systems are often a good solution and Table 8.4, based on similar statistical evidence[4], suggests

Table 8.4 Relative costs of systems for different applications

Approximate relative costs of systems for various applications				
Public rooms in hotels	Theatres etc.	Hospitals	Restaurants	Factories
High	1.5	1.4	4.3	1.5	1.3
Average	1.1	1.0	2.9	1.1	0.9
Low	0.7	0.7	1.5	0.7	0.5

Note. The costs are related to a unit cost for the perimeter induction system in Table 8.3

comparative costs, the ratios again being related to unity for the perimeter induction system in Table 8.3.

Attempts have been made[1, 2] to relate capital costs to treated floor area but the results have not always shown good correlation, mainly because of the weightings imposed by the many different features of the building and services design. The conclusion of an analysis[2] of the costs for twenty different buildings was that an accurate correlation was impossible on this basis. Figure 8.1 shows the results of some attempted correlations, based on reference (1).

Quoting an absolute value for capital costs is not of lasting use in a time of variable inflation. Figure 8.2 shows a graph of the probable inflationary movement of the capital costs of air conditioning, making use of published statistics[5]. If we take the two pipe perimeter induction system as a standard, the cost quoted[1] for a building of about 14 000 m^2 floor area in 1964 was about £16.68 m^{-2}. From Figure 8.2 this would become about £76 m^{-2} in 1977 and Table 8.3 then shows that the cost of a two-pipe, perimeter induction system in 1977, for a treated area of about 14 000 m^2 probably lay between about £53 m^{-2} and £99 m^{-2}, even though, strictly speaking, the table is for areas less than this. Similarly, Table 8.3 suggests that a variable air volume system might cost between £53 m^{-2} and £114 m^{-2}. A knowledge of the inflation indices would give the budget costs for subsequent years.

8.2 Energy consumption

Energy consumption falls into two parts: the thermal energy used in burning fossil fuel for heating and the electrical energy used to drive the mechanical plant or, occasionally, used for heating. Making an accurate estimate is virtually impossible at the design stage because the actual consumption will depend greatly on the manner of system operation. Nevertheless, estimates are often necessary, even if for no other reason than to compare the performances of two different, competing systems on the same basis, at the conceptual stage. CIBS[6] proposes a way of calculating the mean, annual power required by a building and its services, representing the total energy consumption divided by the total number of hours in a year (8760). This method[6] goes to some lengths to assess the contribution of casual gains by solar radiation through windows and by electric lighting, both of which reduce the energy requirement for heating if the system is thermostatically controlled in an appropriate way.

The energy used by burning fuel

The energy used by burning fuel depends on the type of system. Any four-pipe design will take full credit for casual gains whereas other systems, such as the two-pipe, non-changeover, perimeter induction, may not. Although the more involved technique[6] may be adopted, the traditional method is the use of degree days[7]. For any given day when the average temperature is less than a

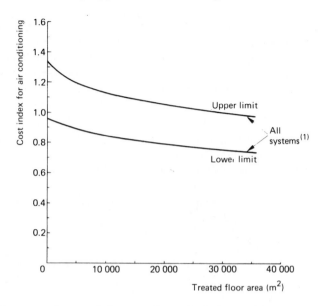

Figure 8.1 Approximate relative costs for various air conditioning systems against treated floor area. For example, the two-pipe non-changeover perimeter-induction system might lie along a mean curve between the two boundary curves

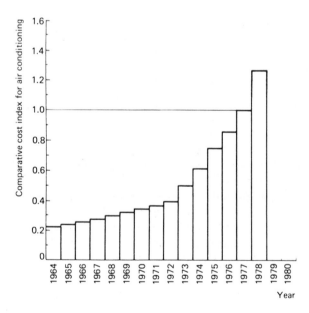

Figure 8.2 Inflationary trends in the construction industry

chosen base temperature, the number of degree days is the difference between the base temperature and the mean temperature. Degree days are summed over the heating season to give a measure of the heating energy requirement.

Before estimating the consumption of fuel energy the design boiler power must be determined. It will be the greater of:

(a) The design fabric heat loss, including natural infiltration, plus a margin for warming up the building structure during the preheat period, in the case of intermittent operation or

(b) the design fabric heat loss, including natural infiltration, plus the fresh air load (because of the air introduced mechanically from outside), plus the HWS load.

Usually, (b) exceeds (a). The fabric heat loss plus the fresh air load, Q'_h, is calculated by

$$Q'_h = U'(t_r - t_o)/1000 \text{ (kW)} \tag{8.1}$$

where t_r and t_o are the inside and outside design temperatures, respectively and

$$U' = (\Sigma AU + nV/3) \text{ (W}^\circ\text{C}^{-1}) \tag{8.2}$$

where A is an element of area of the building envelope, U is its thermal transmittance coefficient, n is the number of fresh air changes per hour, natural and/or mechanical, and V is the volume of the treated space.

The number of degree days to a base temperature of 15.5°C is compiled by the Gas Council for various parts of the UK and Table 8.5 lists the twenty-year averages up to and including 1977, for the Thames Valley area.

Table 8.5 Average number of degree days over a period of twenty years in the Thames Valley

Month	Jan	Feb	Mar	Apr	May	Jun	Jul	Aug	Sep	Oct	Nov	Dec	Total
Number of degree days	349	304	285	199	113	49	24	26	55	132	256	336	2128

In practice, degree days are usually quoted in the UK to a base temperature of 15.5°C, it having been argued in the past[8,9] that this is the highest outside temperature for which heating is needed. If a higher base temperature is to be used the number of degree days to the base 15.5°C may be increased by about 12% for each degree above 15.5°C by inference from reference (7). A more involved method[10] may be adopted if greater accuracy is thought worthwhile.

If the heating system operates under thermostatic control and the influence of casual gains is ignored then the average usage factor, F, over the year is given by

$$F = D_{15.5} \times 24 \times f/(8760(t_r - t_o)) \tag{8.3}$$

wherein $D_{15.5}$ is the total number of degree days in the year to the base 15.5°C and f is a correction factor to cover the period of occupancy; the mode of operation, continuous or intermittent); the class of building structure[7]; and the base temperature adopted. The mean annual boiler power is then:

$$\bar{Q}_h = F Q'_h \ (kW) \tag{8.4}$$

If the boiler efficiency is η, expressed as a fraction, then the total fuel energy consumption over a year is

$$H = (\bar{Q}_h \times 8760 \times 3600)/(1\,000\,000\ \eta) - G \ (GJ) \tag{8.5}$$

where G represents the casual gains.

Example 8.1 Estimate the probable heat energy requirement for the hypothetical office block (Section 1.2), assuming it to be conditioned by a two-pipe, non-changeover, perimeter induction system with primary air scheduled to maintain a room temperature of 20°C. Also assume location in London, heavy-weight structure, 9 hour day, 5 day week, intermittent operation, gas-fired boiler, fresh air supply rate of 1.3 $1s^{-1}m^{-2}$ and an average natural infiltration rate of 0.75 air changes per hour. Ignore heat flow through the ground floor slab.

Answer

$\Sigma AU = 0.5(86.4 \times 3.3 \times 12 \times 2)0.91 + (13.5 \times 3.3 \times 12 \times 2)0.91$
$+ 0.5(86.4 \times 3.3 \times 12 \times 2)5.6 + (86.4 \times 13.5)1.1$
$\quad = 24530 \ W°C^{-1}$

$n = 0.75 + \dfrac{0.0013 \times 86.4 \times 13.5 \times 12 \times 3600}{86.4 \times 13.5 \times 2.6 \times 12} = 2.55$ per hour

$\dfrac{nV}{3} = \dfrac{2.55 \times 86.4 \times 13.5 \times 2.6 \times 12}{3} = 30933 \ W°C^{-1}$

From Equation (8.2)

$U' = 24530 + 30933 = 55463 \ W°C^{-1}$

and from Equation (8.1)

$Q'_h = 55463(20 + 2)/1000 = 1220 \ kW$

A reasonable assumption for the mean seasonal boiler efficiency is 78%[11] and from the CIBS guide the following factors can be determined: 9-hour day, 1.005; 5-day week, 0.85; intermittent operation, 0.95. An induction system as defined will ignore casual gains and attempt to maintain 20°C through its open loop, primary reheat schedule. Therefore, 20°C should be selected as the base temperature for degree days. However, during the summer outside temperatures less than 20°C are most likely to occur during the night, when the system is off. Therefore, the number of degree days for the nine months from September to May, inclusive should be taken. $D_{15.5} = 2029$ for this period

(Table 8.5). The degree day correction factor is $(1+0.12(20-15.5)) = 1.54$ and thus the overall correction factor, f, is $1.005 \times 0.85 \times 0.95 \times 1.54 = 1.25$. Then from Equation (8.3)

$$F = (2029 \times 24 \times 1.25)/(8760 \times (20+2)) = 0.316$$

and from Equation (8.4) $\bar{Q}_h = 0.316 \times 1220 = 385.5 \text{ kW}$

and from Equation (8.5) the total annual heat energy used is

$$H = 385.5 \times 8760 \times 3600)/(1\,000\,000 \times 0.78) = 15586 \text{ GJ}$$

The specific heat energy consumption, per unit of treated floor area is $15586/(86.4 \times 13.5 \times 12) = 1.11 \text{ GJ m}^{-2}$. (This is a simplification: the fabric loss plus reheat from the off-coil state yields a smaller answer.)

It is to be noted that a variable air volume system with perimeter heating, compensated against outside air temperature on an open loop, would use heat energy to the same extent, no account being taken of casual gains and any overheating being cancelled by the supply of cool air. If a four-pipe induction or fan coil system were used casual gains would reduce the heat energy consumption because of the mode of thermostatic control over the units, heating capacity being in sequence with cooling capacity. For casual gains, Table 1.2 gives diversity factors for people throughout the year, but as regards lighting it is reasonable to assume a factor of 1.0 for, say, the winter months, November to February, and to apply the tabulated diversity factors for the remaining months. The heating benefit from solar gains is a much more complicated matter and is difficult to establish, although an attempt to do so is possible[6]. It is particularly hard to assess because of the uncertainty concerning the benefit of simultaneous solar and other gains and the possibility of undesirable overheating. For business machines an overall diversity factor of 0.75 might be assumed, although perhaps this is a slight overestimation.

Example 8.2 Repeat Example 8.1, assuming a four-pipe perimeter induction system is used. With 50% of the two long, outer facades glazed the corresponding proportion of the inner faces is 64% and the benefit from solar gains can be estimated[6] as approximately 18.5 Wm^{-2} of glass over the east and west faces for a heating season of 150 working days.

Answer Using mean diverxity factors from Table 1.2 with the restriction mentioned for lights, and referring to Section 1.2 as necessary, the casual gains are

People: $\dfrac{(86.4 \times 13.5 \times 12)}{9} \times \dfrac{90 \times 0.75}{1000}$ $= 105.0 \text{ kW}$

Lights: $\left[\dfrac{(86.4 \times 13.5 \times 12) \times 25}{1000}\right]\left[1 \times \dfrac{4}{12} + 0.775 \times \dfrac{8}{12}\right]$ $= 297.4 \text{ kW}$

Business machines: $\dfrac{(86.4 \times 13.5 \times 12) \times 5}{1000} \times 0.75$ $= \underline{52.5 \text{ kW}}$

Total: 454.9 kW

Solar: $\dfrac{(0.5 \times 86.4 \times 3.3 \times 12 \times 2) \times 18.5}{1000}$ $= 63.3 \text{ kW}$

The occupied period per year is $(5 \times 52 - 8$ statutory holidays$) \times 9 = 2268$ hours. People, lights and business machines are regarded as providing a useful gain over the whole of the occupied period, i.e. $2268 \times 454.9 \times 3600/10^6 = 3714$ GJ. The solar gains are only regarded as useful[6] over the winter heating season of 150 days and hence their contribution is $63.3 \times 150 \times 9 \times 3600/10^6 = 307.6$ GJ. The total casual gains are $G = 308 + 3714 = 4022$ GJ and the mean annual heat energy used is, from Equation (8.5) and Example 8.1, $H = 15586 - 4022 = 11564$ GJ. The specific heat energy requirement per unit of treated floor area, is $11564/(86.4 \times 13.5 \times 12) = 0.83$ GJ m^{-2}.

The electrical energy used to drive mechanical plant
The electrical energy used clearly depends on the type of system and the way it is designed. The energy consumed may be estimated by listing the items of plant that use electricity, their maximum absorbed powers and their utilisation factors. The products of such powers and factors are summed to yield the average annual electrical power likely to be required.

Example 8.3 If the hypothetical office building (Section 1.2) is treated by a two-pipe, non-changeover, perimeter induction system, estimate the likely annual electrical energy consumption. Assume the following.
Primary fan duty (see Example 2.20): 43470 l s^{-1}; 2 k Pa fan total pressure; 85% fan efficiency; 90% motor and drive efficiency; 114 kW power absorbed
Extract fan duty: 43470 l s^{-1}; 0.25 kPa fan total pressure; 75% fan efficiency; 90% motor and drive efficiency; 16 kW power absorbed
Primary chilled water pump duty: 65 l s^{-1}; 200 kPa; 65% pump efficiency; 89% motor and drive efficiency; 22.5 kW power absorbed
Secondary chilled water pump duty: as primary pump duty
Cooling water pump duty: 90 l s^{-1}; 200 kPa; 65% pump efficiency; 90% motor and drive efficiency; 31 kW power absorbed
Cooling tower fan power: 15 kW absorbed
Installed boiler power: 1800 kW.
LTHW primary pump power: 3 kW absorbed.
LTHW secondary pump power: 3 kW absorbed.
Forced draught fan power: 6 kW absorbed.
Water chiller capacity: 1742 kW of refrigeration (see Example 1.11).
Refrigeration compressor motor power: 370 kW absorbed.
Answer Utilisation factors express the actual hours that an item of plant runs

as a fraction of the total number of hours in a year (8760) and some typical values have been published[6]. Reasonable estimates can be made here for most of the items, remembering that the total occupied time for the building is 2268 hours, so plant items that run continuously during occupied hours will have a utilisation factor of $2268/8760 = 0.26$. In the case of items needed for preheating, i.e. primary and exhaust fans and LTHW pumps, an addition of, say, $1\frac{1}{2}$ hours a day for 150 days can be made to cover boost operation in the heating season. Their factors then increase to $2493/8760 = 0.28$. An assumption for the forced draught fans is difficult but since their contribution is comparatively insignificant any error will be small, so a factor of 0.2 can be assumed. The factors for the refrigeration compressor, cooling tower fans and cooling water pump are always contentious but studies [6,12] suggest that a factor based on 1000 equivalent full-load running hours would not be unreasonable, for the UK, i.e. $1000/8760 = 0.11$. Table 8.6 shows all this data.

Table 8.6 Annual average electrical power in a hypothetical office block

Item	Maximum power (kW)	Utilisation factor	Annual average power (kW)	(kW)	Percentage (%)	(%)
Primary fan	114.0	0.28	31.92		33.00	
Extract fan	16.0	0.28	4.48	36.40	4.62	37.62
Primary chilled water pump	22.5	0.26	5.85		6.05	
Secondary chilled water pump	22.5	0.26	5.85	11.70	6.05	12.10
Refrigeration compressor	370.0	0.11	40.70		42.07	
Cooling water pump	31.0	0.11	3.41		3.52	
Cooling tower fans	15.0	0.11	1.65	45.76	1.71	47.30
LTHW primary pump	3.0	0.28	0.84		0.87	
LTHW secondary pump	3.0	0.28	0.84		0.87	
Forced draught fans	6.0	0.28	1.20	2.88	1.24	2.98
Total				96.74		100.00

The total annual electrical energy used is, therefore, $96.74 \times 8760 \times 3600 \times 10^{-6} = 3051$ GJ or 0.22 GJ m^{-2} of treated floor area.

8.3 Electrical and thermal energy used by VAV systems

Electrical and thermal energy used by VAV systems is a function of sensible heat gain; fan total pressure; the proportional band of the pressure sensor used to regulate the position of the inlet guide vanes or change the blade pitch angle of the centrifugal or axial flow supply and extract fans (see Section 2.8 and

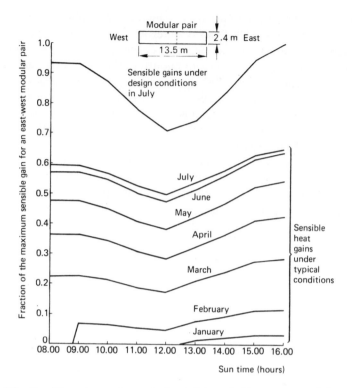

Figure 8.3   Sensible gains under typical conditions (taking account of diversity factors on lights, people and business machines, daily variations in outside temperature and cloud cover) compared with maximum design conditions. Other months show similar patterns. Note 50% of the outer facade is glazed

Figure 2.8); the turn-down of the VAV terminals; and the fan efficiency. Estimating the probable energy consumption of the fans depends in the first place on assessing the variation in sensible heat gains, not for summer design weather but for typical weather during the occupied hours for each month of the year. This estimation is able to be done by a computer and such a study for the hypothetical office building, modified to have U-values of 0.5 and 0.3 $Wm^{-2}°C^{-1}$ for the walls and roof, respectively, to conform with the Building Regulations[13], yields the results shown in Figure 8.3. It was assumed for this that air handling plants fed both faces of the building from common ducts in order to take full advantage of the variation in the solar load. Account was taken of cloud cover[14] and mean daily variations of outside temperature. A diversity factor of 0.88 was applied to heat gains from people, lights and business machines. Table 8.7 gives calculated values of the typical sensible heat gains for each hour of the day and each month of the year, as fractions of the maximum sensible gains, occurring at 16.00 to 17.00 h sun time in July, for a modular pair having east and west facing windows in the hypothetical office block with 50% of its two, long, outer facades glazed. The fractions may then be interpreted as airflow factors.

Table 8.7 Typical sensible heat gains for a modular pair having east and west-facing windows in an office block with a major building axis pointing north-south

	Heat gains expressed as a fraction of the maximum sensible gain, occurring between 16.00 and 17.00 h sun time in July								
Month	Sun time (h)								
	08.00	09.00	10.00	11.00	12.00	13.00	14.00	15.00	16.00
January	0	0	0	0	0	0.015	0.024	0.034	0.034
February	0	0.069	0.064	0.052	0.048	0.078	0.093	0.112	0.114
March	0.224	0.225	0.212	0.186	0.173	0.210	0.240	0.275	0.285
April	0.363	0.363	0.342	0.306	0.284	0.325	0.365	0.411	0.426
May	0.474	0.475	0.450	0.408	0.382	0.423	0.470	0.522	0.542
June	0.570	0.570	0.544	0.500	0.473	0.513	0.561	0.615	0.636
July	0.593	0.591	0.567	0.525	0.500	0.538	0.581	0.631	0.649
August	0.583	0.583	0.560	0.519	0.494	0.532	0.576	0.627	0.646
September	0.466	0.468	0.452	0.423	0.406	0.441	0.476	0.515	0.529
October	0.278	0.283	0.279	0.266	0.261	0.292	0.314	0.339	0.346
November	0	0.099	0.104	0.106	0.112	0.135	0.146	0.157	0.158
December	0	0	0.005	0.010	0.017	0.036	0.044	0.052	0.052

Example 8.4 Determine the electrical energy consumption of a VAV system used to air condition the hypothetical office building, given that the maximum simultaneous sensible heat gains are 1135.7 kW (Example 1.11) and that four air-handling plants are to be used, delivering air at 13.5°C from common ducts to both glazed faces. Make use of the data in Table 8.7 and the fan curves in Figure 8.4. Take the fan total pressures of the supply and extract axial flow fans as 1.0 and 0.25 kPa, respectively. Assume the minimum allowable static pressure at a VAV terminal is 180 Pa and the proportional band of the pressure sensor regulating the blade pitch angles is 100 Pa. Assume also that the VAV units will turn down to a minimum of 25% of design airflow.
Answer

$$\text{Maximum total supply air quantity} = \frac{1135.7}{(22-13.5)} \times \frac{(273+13.5)}{358} = 106.9 \text{ m}^3\text{s}^{-1}$$

Air quantity per plant $= 26.7 \simeq 27 \text{ m}^3\text{s}^{-1}$

If the static pressure sensing probe is assumed to be located in a position along the index run, probably two-thirds to three-quarters of the way from the fan, where it senses representative changes of pressure as the volume handled changes and, further, that the proportional band of the pressure sensor gives a

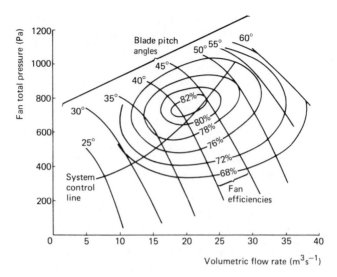

Figure 8.4   Characteristic curves for a typical axial flow fan with controllable blade pitch. The system control line is the characteristic curve for the system using a square law for the system resistance plus a linear relationship between the pressure sensed by the sensor regulating the blade pitch angle and the volume flowing

linear relationship between volumetric flowrate and pressure sensed, a square law can be applied to the rest of the system and pressure/flow values for a system characteristic or control curve can be calculated (Table 8.8). It should be noted that in the duct feeding the index VAV unit the design air velocity is likely to be not more than about 2.5 ms^{-1} and that the velocity pressure is therefore trivial, static pressure being virtually the same as total pressure, particularly at reduced flow rates. As the static pressure measured at the sensor rises from 180 Pa, for the design flow, the blade pitch angles on the supply and extract fans are reduced in unison.

The final column in Table 8.8 is plotted in Figure 8.4 to form the pressure/volume control curve for the system as it throttles at the VAV unit terminals. From the intersections of the fan curves, at various blade pitch angles, with the system control line flow rates can be read off, $\dot{v}$, fan total pressures, p_t, and efficiencies, η. The absorbed fan power at each flow rate, W_f, is then given by

$$W_f = \dot{v}p_t/\eta \tag{8.2}$$

With the simplifying assumption that the motor efficiency is constant at 90%, the electrical power absorbed at various flow rates can be calculated (Table 8.9).

Table 8.8 Pressure/flow values for a system characteristic or control curve

Flow rate		Total pressure loss (Pa)		
%	m^3s^{-1}	Duct system	VAV terminal	System plus terminal
100	27.0	820	180	1000
90	24.3	664	193	857
80	21.6	525	207	732
70	18.9	402	220	622
60	16.2	295	233	528
50	13.5	205	247	452
40	10.8	131	260	391
30	8.1	74	273	347
25	6.75	51	280	331

Referring to Table 8.7 for the airflow factors and remembering that the minimum factor is 0.25, the absorbed powers from Table 8.9 can be used to determine the electrical energy used in kWh, and hence in MJ, for each hour of the day in each month of the year. Thus for 10.00 h sun time in May the airflow factor is 0.45 and so, interpolating for 45% in Table 8.9 it can be established that the power absorbed is 8.05 kW and the energy consumed between 09.30 and 10.30 h is 8.05 kWh or 29.0 MJ. Table 8.10 summarises such calculations.

Since the extract fan is of the same type and controlled in the same way, in unison with the supply fan, one can assume, for simplicity, that the energy it uses is proportional to the design fan total pressure, i.e., that it equals 58.24 × 0.25/1.0 = 14.55 GJ, annually. The energy consumed by all fans is thus 4 (58.24 + 14.56) = 291.2 GJ.

Table 8.9 Electrical power absorbed at various flow rates for a system plus terminal

Flow rate		Fan total pressure (Pa)	Fan efficiency (%)	Fan power (kW)	Power absorbed (kW)
%	m^3s^{-1}				
100	27.0	1000	76	35.5	39.4
90	24.3	857	80	26.0	28.9
80	21.6	732	82	19.3	21.4
70	18.9	622	80	14.7	16.3
60	16.2	528	77	11.1	12.3
50	13.5	452	72	8.5	9.4
40	10:8	391	70	6.0	6.7
30	8.1	347	62.5●	4.5	5.0
25	6.75	331	55●	4.1	4.6

●These efficiencies are inferred from the fan powers quoted by the fan manufacturer

Table 8.10 Electrical energy consumed for each hour of the day in each month of the year

Month	Sun time (h)									Daily totals (MJ)	Average number of working days	Monthly totals (GJ)
	08.00	09.00	10.00	11.00	12.00	13.00	14.00	15.00	16.00			
	Energy consumed in each hour (MJ)											
January	16.6	16.6	16.6	16.6	16.6	16.6	16.6	16.6	16.6	149.4	20.3	3.03
February	16.6	16.6	16.6	16.6	16.6	16.6	16.6	16.6	16.6	149.4	20.0	2.99
March	16.6	16.6	16.6	16.6	16.6	16.6	16.6	17.3	17.6	151.1	21.9	3.31
April	21.9	21.9	20.6	18.4	17.5	19.5	22.0	25.2	26.6	193.6	20.0	3.87
May	31.3	31.4	29.0	24.9	23.0	26.4	30.9	36.1	38.2	271.2	21.0	5.70
June	41.1	41.1	38.4	33.8	31.2	35.2	40.2	46.4	49.5	356.9	22.0	7.85
July	43.5	43.3	40.8	36.4	33.8	37.8	42.3	48.7	51.3	377.9	21.0	7.94
August	42.5	42.5	40.1	35.8	33.3	37.2	41.8	48.2	50.9	372.3	21.3	7.93
September	30.5	30.7	29.2	26.4	24.7	28.1	31.5	35.4	36.9	273.4	21.6	5.91
October	17.4	17.5	17.4	17.0	16.9	17.8	18.9	20.4	20.8	164.1	21.3	3.50
November	16.6	16.6	16.6	16.6	16.6	16.6	16.6	16.6	16.6	149.4	21.9	3.27
December	16.6	16.6	16.6	16.6	16.6	16.6	16.6	16.6	16.6	149.4	19.7	2.94
Annual totals											252.0	58.24

Meteorological data for Heathrow airport[15] over the 10-year period from 1st January 1959 to 31st December 1968, on the frequency of occurrence of dry- and wet-bulb temperatures during each hour of the day and month of the year, may be analysed to show that between the hours of 08.00 and 16.00 sun time the dry-bulb exceeds 10°C for 1712.5 hours and the wet-bulb is greater than 5°C for 2225.5 hours, for 7 days a week. It may be inferred from this that the refrigeration plant will run for longer in the case of an induction system than for a variable air volume system, because the former can only provide free cooling when the outside wet-bulb is less than about 5°C whereas the latter can give it when the dry-bulb is below about 10°C. It might be reasonable, therefore, to multiply the utilisation factor for the induction system refrigeration plant in Example 8.3 by the ratio of $1712.5/2225.5 = 0.77$. However, in practice, there is a tendency for a refrigeration plant to be shut off in the winter months to economise on the electrical maximum demand charges, and this would bring the operational hours of the refrigeration plants in the two systems closer together. It is suggested that the ratio be increased to 0.82, which, when applied to the utilisation factor of 0.11 in the induction system gives a factor of 0.09 for the refrigeration plant of the VAV system. The average electrical energy demand for a VAV system, can now be calculated (Table 8.11).

Table 8.11 The average electrical energy demand for a VAV system

Item	Maximum power (kW)	Utilisation factor	Annual average power (kW)
Primary chilled water pump	22.5	0.09	2.025
Refrigeration compressor	370.0	0.09	33.30
Cooling water pump	31.0	0.09	2.79
Cooling tower fan	15.0	0.09	1.35
LTHW primary pump	3.0	0.28	0.84
LTHW secondary pump	3.0	0.28	0.84
Forced draught fans	6.0	0.20	1.20
Total			42.345

The electrical energy consumed by the plant, summarised in Table 8.11, is $42.345 \times 8760 \times 3600 \times 10^{-6} = 1335.4$ GJ which, with 291.2 GJ used by the fans, makes a total of 1626.6 GJ, or an annual specific consumption of 0.12 GJm^{-2}, which can be compared with 0.22 GJm^{-2} obtained for an induction system (Example 8.3). It should be noted that when comparing Tables 8.6 and 8.11 the chilled water pumps run through the entire occupied period for an induction system to give free cooling when the refrigeration plant is off and, therefore, have a higher utilisation factor.

A variable air volume system with perimeter heating will use more thermal energy than a non-changeover, induction system. Table 8.7 shows this. The minimum turn-down of the VAV system is 0.25, yet for much of the winter the airflow factor is less than this and in some cases no cooling air is wanted at all because there is a net heat loss, on average. The VAV system is thus overcooling at times and this must be cancelled by heating. Taking the difference between 0.25 and the factors in Table 8.7 that are less, the mean airflow can be calculated over a 9 hour day in each month that must be warmed from 13.5°C to 20°C, as follows: January–106.9(9 × 0.25 − 0.015 − 0.024 − 0.034 − 0.034)/9 = 25.5 m^{3}s^{-1}, over a working month of 20.3 days, and so on for the months of February, March, November and December, giving 19.3 m^{3}s^{-1} over 20 days, 4.3 m^{3}s^{-1} over 21.9 days, 14.7 m^{3}s^{-1} over 21.9 days and 24.2 m^{3}s^{-1} over 19.7 days, respectively. The average airflow to be heated is then calculated as 17.3 m^{3}s^{-1} and the average heating input is 17.3 × (20 − 13.5) × 358/(273 + 13.5) = 140.5 kW. The thermal energy that must be provided for this is, therefore,

$$\frac{3.6 \times 140.5 \times (20.3 \times 9 + 20 \times 9 + 21.9 \times 7 + 21.9 \times 9 + 19.7 \times 9)}{1000}$$

= 450.4 GJ annually.

The total heating requirement for the VAV system considered is therefore 15586 GJ (Example 8.1) + 450.4 GJ = 16036.4 GJ or 1.15 GJm^{-2}, to be compared with 1.11 GJm^{-2} for a two-pipe, non-changeover, perimeter induction system and 0.83 GJm^{-2} for a four-pipe system.

This is summarised in Table 8.12 and the energy used in the building is converted into primary energy as contained in fossil fuels like coal, oil and gas, by adopting fuel factors[6] based on work done by the Building Research Establishment[16]. These factors reflect the losses in producing energy as a usable medium from its fossil form and in distributing it to the building. Factors of 1.07 and 3.82 are taken for natural gas and electricity, respectively.

Table 8.12 Annual energy used in various systems

| | Annual energy used (GJm^{-2} floor area) | | | | |
| | Energy used in the building | | Primary energy used | | |
System	Heat	Electricity	Heat	Electricity	Total
Two-pipe non-changeover perimeter induction	1.11	0.22	1.19	0.84	2.03
Four-pipe perimeter induction	0.83	0.22	0.89	0.84	1.73
VAV with perimeter heating	1.15	0.12	1.23	0.46	1.69

8.4 Economic appraisal

To obtain a realistic view of the engineering economics of a system all the financial outgoings and receipts must be accounted over its estimated life. The technique currently most favoured for this is the present value method. This consists of establishing the discounted cash flow (DCF) throughout the life of the plant by converting all future expenditure and income into an equivalent sum of money at present day values, allowing for inflation and for the interest that must be paid on borrowed capital. Money lent cannot be used otherwise by the lender and the interest he receives after a period of time is a reward for his postponement of its expenditure. To convert a sum of money received one year from now, for example, into an equivalent sum today it must be divided by a discount factor determined from the interest rate paid. Thus an interest rate, or discount rate, of 10% per annum corresponds to a discount factor of 1.1 and so £1100 received in one year's time is equivalent to £1000 received today. Inflation is a different process that erodes the value of money and an inflation factor, corresponding to an assumed annual percentage for a future inflation rate, must be further applied to obtain a true picture of present value[17]. The product of the discount and inflation factors is termed the discount money factor. A sum of money received or spent in twelve month's time, when divided by the money discount factor, gives the equivalent present value of the sum. When estimating the discounted cash flow over the life of a system it is possible to apply different inflation factors to different elements in the analysis. For example wages, or energy prices, could be assumed to inflate more rapidly than the general inflation rate for the national economy.

Example 8.5 A plate heat exchanger, a static recuperator, is to be considered for transferring heat between the incoming fresh air and the outgoing vitiated air in an air-conditioning system. The total capital expenditure initially required is £7721 and it is estimated that the annual saving by energy conservation will be £799, at present day prices. Do a discounted cash flow analysis to establish the present value and so show if the project is worthwhile. Take a discount rate of 10% to reflect the passage of time and a general inflation rate also of 10% but assume that the cost of energy will double, in real terms, over the next 20 years. The life of the plant is considered to be 20 years and there are no maintenance costs.

Answer The calculations involved are all based on the formula for compound interest:

$$S = P(1+r)^n \tag{8.6}$$

where S is the sum of money received after n years if an annual interest rate of r, as a fraction, is charged on the principal sum, P.

Table 8.13 Cash flow calculations

| Year | At present day prices | | Specific energy inflation factor | Money cash flow● (£) | Money discount factor■ | Present value■ (£) | Progressive sum of the present values (£) |
	Cost of plant (£)	Energy saving (£)					
0	−7721.0			−7721.0	1.0	−7721.0	−7721.0
1		+799	1.139	+910.1	1.21	+752.1	−6968.9
2		+799	1.139^2	+1036.6	1.21^2	+708.0	−6260.9
3		+799	1.139^3	+1180.6	1.21^3	+666.4	−5594.5
● ● ●							
15		+799	1.139^{15}	+5628.6	1.21^{15}	+322.6	−77.3
16		+799	1.139^{16}	+6411.0	1.21^{16}	+303.6	+226.3
● ● ●							
20		+799	1.139^{20}	+10790.0	1.21^{20}	+238.4	+1272.9

●Energy saving at present prices × Specific energy inflation factor
■Money cash flow/Money discount factor

Equation (8.6) can be used to determine the annual rate of increase in energy costs if they are to double in twenty years because $S/P = 2$ and so $r = (2^{1/20} - 1) = 0.0353$, or 3.53% per annuma. The specific inflation factor to apply to energy costs is the general inflation factor, 1.1, times the real energy inflation factor, 1.0353, which is, therefore, 1.139. The money discount factor, to be used to convert future money receipts into present day values, is the general inflation factor, 1.1, times the discount rate, 1.1, which is, therefore, 1.21. The calculations of cash flow are summarised in Table 8.13.

The net present value at the end of the life of the plant is £1272.90, from Table 8.13, and the project is clearly cost-effective. It is worth noting that where a company is entitled to capital allowances these should be accounted since the tax saved constitutes an income throughout the life of the plant and the cost-effectiveness is improved[7].

A much cruder technique, that frequently provides a misleading answer and tends to underestimate the benefits of a proposed investment under inflation[17], is the calculation of the pay-back period. This simply divides the initial capital expenditure for a project by the estimated annual saving, at present day prices, to give the period in years needed for the return of the outlay. Thus, in Example 8.5 the pay-back period is £7721/£799 per annum = 9.66 years. Discount rates and general inflation are ignored and no attempt is made to assess the worth of the energy saved after the pay-back period has expired, up to the end of the life of the plant. The crude technique of the pay-back period should only be used for the most obvious, preliminary indications and should always be backed up by a discounted cash flow analysis, including the most realistic assumptions possible for future inflation. An essential feature of this method is an allowance for the life of the plant. Table 8.14 lists some suggested lives for items of plant.

Not all the parts of a piece of plant age at the same rate. For example, in the case of cooler coil, particularly sprayed cooler coils, the framework, which is usually of galvanised steel, invariably corrodes away before the fins and tubes because of the extreme, relative positions of copper and zinc in the electro-chemical scale.

The annual cost of a system is the annual sum of money that is equivalent to all expenditure and income and it is determined using similar principles to those in the calculation of present value, covering owning (capital) and operating costs over the estimated life of the system. The present value (PV), of £1 received annually over a period of n years and discounted at a rate of $100r$% is given by

$$PV = [1 - (1 + r)^{-n}]/r \tag{8.7}$$

and values for the solution of this are tabulated elsewhere.[7]

Example 8.6 Calculate the annual sum needed to repay a loan of £7721 over 20 years when the discount rate is 10% per annum.

Table 8.14   Some suggested life-times for plant[18,19,20]

Item	Life-time (years)
HPHW (high pressure hot water) and steam boilers:	
Shell	15–25
Water tube	25–30
M and LPHW (medium and low pressure hot water) boilers:	
Shell	15–20
Cast iron sectional	20–25
Steel sectional	5–15
Boiler plant ancillaries:	
Oil tanks	40
Combustion controls	15–20
Gas and oil burners	15–25
Fans	15–25
Heating equipment:	
Radiators	15–20
Convectors	15–20
Closed piping systems	25–60
Pumps in closed piping systems	20–25
Air-conditioning equipment:	
Vapour compression refrigeration plant	15–30
Cooling towers	10–25
Fans	20–30
Filters, excluding filter medium	15–25
Cooling coils—copper fins, tinned	20–30
Cooling coils—aluminium fins	15–20
Heater batteries	20–30
Sprayed cooler coils	10–20
Packaged air-handling units	8–15
Galvanised steel ductwork	30–60
Induction units	20–30
Fan coil units	10–25
VAV units	15–30
Double duct units	15–30

Answer From Equation (8.7)

$$PV = [1-(1+0.1)^{-20}]/0.1 = £8.514 \text{ per } £.$$

Since the present value of the sum borrowed is £7721 the annual repayment must be £7721/£8.514 per £ = £906.86.

Conversely, using Equation (8.6) and the method adopted in Example 8.5,

Table 8.15 shows the PV of £906.86 paid annually over 20 years with a discount rate of 10%.

Table 8.15   Cash flow calculation

Year	Cash flow (£)	Discount factor	Present value (PV) (£)
1	906.86	1.1	824.42
2	906.86	1.1^2	749.47
•			
•			
•			
•			
•			
19	906.86	1.1^{19}	148.28
20	906.86	1.1^{20}	134.80
Total present value			7721.00

In the past, the sum that must be paid annually to cover interest and the repayment of capital (sinking fund) was calculated by the reciprocal of Equation (8.7).

Maintenance costs, to include repairs, routine lubrication and cleaning, replacements, labour, tools, power, water and overheads, have often been disregarded or underestimated. It has been suggested[7, 12] that average costs of maintenance, including overheads, were £1.60 m^{-2} in 1968. Figure 8.2 shows that the index for 1968 was about 0.3, in relation to unity in 1977, implying a cost of £5.33 m^{-2} for 1977. This is in approximate agreement with £4.80 m^{-2}, obtained from another source[4] and it might, therefore, be concluded that a representative figure in 1977 was about £5 m^{-2} for air conditioned buildings. In subsequent years the application of an appropriate inflation factor should give an approximately correct estimate of annual maintenance costs. The owning and operating costs of air-conditioning systems are often compared by determining their annual costs.

Example 8.7 Estimate the owning and operating costs, i.e. annual costs, of two-pipe, non-changeover, perimeter induction and VAV systems for air conditioning the hypothetical office block (Section 1.2) in the year 1977. Take a discount rate of 10% per annum and assume energy prices to be 750 p GJ^{-1} (2.7 p kWh^{-1}) for electricity and 154 p GJ^{-1} (16.2 p $therm^{-1}$) for natural gas, consumed on the site.

Answer Using Table 8.14 a typical life-time of 20 years may be inferred for each system. From Table 8.3 and the conclusions drawn from it, and from Figure 8.2, approximate capital costs in 1977 can be taken to be (£53 + £99)/2 = £76 m^{-2} for the induction system and (£53 + £114)/2 = £83.50 m^{-2} for the VAV system. Maintenance costs can be assumed as £5 m^{-2} and Table 8.12 gives the energy used on site, after allowing for a mean seasonal boiler efficiency. From Equation (8.7) and Example 8.6, the annual repayment to cover interest and the money borrowed for a lifetime of 20 years and a discount rate of 10% is £8.514 per pound. The annual costs for 1977 were, therefore,

System	Induction		VAV	
Capitalised annual cost				
($£\,m^{-2}$)	76.00 / 8.514 =	8.93	83.50 / 8.514 =	9.81
Manintenance ($£\,m^{-2}$)		5.00		5.00
Fuel (Table 8.12)($£\,m^{-2}$)	1.11×1.54 =	1.71	1.15×1.54 =	1.77
Electricity (Table 8.12)				
($£\,m^{-2}$)	0.22×7.50 =	1.65	0.12×7.50 =	0.90
Total annual costs ($£\,m^{-2}$)		17.29		17.40

It has been shown[21] that these figures represent less than 3% of the average staff salaries in an office and, allowing for overheads, less than about 1.5% of the total costs of such employment. It is to be observed that if energy costs inflate sufficiently rapidly the annual costs of a VAV system may become less than those of an induction system (see Exercise 4). A major element in the economic appraisal of Example 8.7 is capital cost and this can vary greatly since it depends on many factors (Section 8.1). Furthermore, because of the way in which charges are usually made for electrical energy, involving the demand for maximum power as well as the cost of the energy actually used, the load factor exercises a significant influence. For example, in 1978 it was estimated that in the London area the approximate overall average unit charge fell from about 3.1 p k Wh^{-1} to about 2.5 p k Wh^{-1} as the load factor rose from 0.2 to 0.4, for an office building of 7000 m^2 treated area. Generalisations on comparative annual costs should, therefore, only be made with caution.

Exercises

1 Repeat Example 8.1 assuming that the U-values are 0.5 and 0.3 $Wm^{-2}\,°C^{-1}$ for the walls and roof, respectively and that only 30% of the two long, outer facades are glazed.

(*Answer* 13459 GJ, 0.96 GJ m^{-2})

2 Repeat Example 8.2 but assuming the same U-values and glazing as above. Assume useful solar gains are 17 Wm^{-2}.

(*Answer* 9472 GJ, 0.68 GJ m^{-2})

3 Repeat Example 8.5 but assume that energy costs will increase, in real terms, by a factor of five over the next twenty years.

(*Answer* Net present value = £5983)

4 Repeat Example 8.7 for the year 1984, assuming an annual inflation rate of 10% generally but that the cost of energy will increase in real terms at a rate that would correspond to a factor of five over twenty years.
(*Answer* Induction system annual cost £38.6 m^{-2}: VAV system annual cost £37.5 m^{-2})

Symbols

A	Element of area in the building envelope	m^2
$D_{15.5}$	Number of degree days in the year to the base of 15.5°C	°C days
F	Average annual usage factor	—
G	Heating benefit from casual gains	GJ
H	Total average annual consumption of fuel energy	GJ
P	Principal sum of money	£
Q'_h	Design fabric heat loss plus fresh air load	kW
$\bar{Q}_h$	Mean annual boiler power	kW
S	Sum of money	£
U	Thermal transmittance coefficient of an element in the building envelope	Wm^{-2}°C^{-1}
U'	$\Sigma AU + nV/3$	Wm^{-2}°C^{-1}
V	Volume of the treated space	m^3
f	Correction factor to cover: period of building occupancy, mode of system operation, class of building structure.	—
n	Number of fresh air changes per hour (natural and/or mechanical) or a period of time	h^{-1} or years
p_t	Fan total pressure	Pa or kPa
r	Annual rate of interest, as a fraction	—
t_o	Outside design temperature	°C
t_r	Inside design temperature	°C
$\dot{v}$	Volumetric airflow rate	m^{3}s^{-1}
W_f	Fan power	W or kW
η	Boiler or fan efficiency, as a fraction	—

References

(1) Swain, C. P., Thornley, D. L., and Wensley, R., The choice of air-conditioning systems, *JIHVE*, **32**, 7; 307, 1964

(2) Watson, R. B., *Capital and Running Costs of Air-Conditioning Systems*, CIBS/RICS/Inst of Refrigeration Conference on Air Conditioning and Energy Conservation, Nottingham University, 20–21 April 1978

(3) Symposium of High Velocity Air Conditioning, *JIHVE*, **28**, 225; 333, 1960

(4) Courtesy of Haden Young Ltd
(5) Indices of Cost of New Construction, *BSRIA Statistics Bulletin*, **3**, No. 3, 1978
(6) Building Energy Code, Part 2, CIBS, London, 1980
(7) *CIBS Guide*, Volume B, 1970
(8) Dufton, A. F., *Degree days, JIHVE*, **2**, 83, 1934
(9) Faber, O., and Kell, J. R., *Heating and Air Conditioning of Buildings*, The Architectural Press, 1945
(10) Fuel Note No. 7, Department of Energy, HMSO, London, 1978
(11) *Building Energy Code*, Part 1, CIBS, London, 1977
(12) Millbank, N. O., Dowdall, J. P. and Slater, A., Investigation of maintenance and energy costs for services in office buildings, *JIHVE*, **39**, 145, October 1971
(13) Statutory Instruments, 1978, No. 723, *Building and Buildings*, The Building (First Amendment) Regulations, HMSO, 1978
(14) Meteorological Office, *Average of Bright Sunshine for Great Britain and Northern Ireland*, 1921–50, HMSO, 1953
(15) Courtesy of the Electricity Council
(16) Energy Consumption and Conservation in Buildings, *Building Research Establishment Digest*, 191, July 1976
(17) Carsberg, B. and Hope, A., *Building Investment Decisions under Inflation, Theory and Practice*, The Institution of Chartered Accountants in England and Wales, London, 1976
(18) Hassan, A., *Reliability of HVAC Equipment—Introduction and Literature Survey*, HVRA Laboratory Report No. 56
(19) Eyers, J., Engineering insurance, inspection and breakdown of heating and ventilation plant, *JIHVE*, **35**, 163, September 1967
(20) Day, P. H., Capital investment appraisal for mechanical and electrical services in commercial buildings, *The Heating and Ventilating Engineer*, pp. 4–7, February 1976
(21) Pullinger, F. A., *Low Energy Air Conditioning—A Challenge for the Industry*, CIBS/RICS/Inst of Refrigeration Conference on Air Conditioning and Energy Conservation, Nottingham University 20–21 April 1978

9
Energy conservation

9.1 Building design

Before looking at energy conservation in systems it is worth examining the influence of the building itself on the cooling load and energy consumption. A study[1] in the design of buildings to minimise energy use, based on the hypothetical office block (Section 1.2), concluded that the following principles appear to apply:

(1) In the UK there is, at present, no economic justification for double glazing in office blocks but, for continuously occupied buildings, such as hospitals, there may be. This conclusion would be different for a country with a colder winter and/or higher energy costs.

(2) The influence of the mass of the walls on the cooling load is not significant. Floor slabs have a marginal effect, heavier floors slightly reducing the cooling load contribution from solar radiation through glass. Carpeting and furniture tend to insulate the floor slab from the solar heat gain and so reduce its effective mass.

(3) The mass of the roof slab is only significant for low-rise structures but should be heavy, rather than light, acoustic considerations and over-flying aircraft being relevant.

(4) U-values for walls and roofs should be 0.4 and 0.2 $Wm^{-2}\,{}^\circ C^{-1}$, respectively, or better[2], due consideration being paid to problems of condensation.

(5) The major building axis should point east-west, particularly when there is a lot of glazing.

(6) The amount of glass and its U-value dominates the energy flux through the building envelope and also affects the need for artificial lighting. Regarding human preference, it is likely that from 25% to 30% of the outer facade ought to be glazed. Some benefit accrues from the penetration of natural daylight and solar warmth[3].

(7) Large buildings are more economical than small ones, in terms of cooling load per unit area of usable floor[2].

(8) In the UK climate, the heating and air-conditioning systems in buildings should be operated intermittently, rather than continuously, when the structure is lightweight[4, 5] (Figure 9.1).

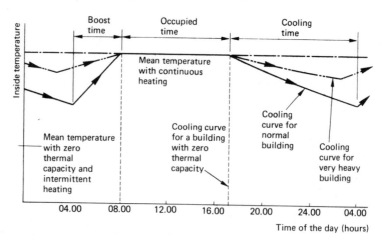

Figure 9.1   Intermittent heating

9.2 Energy conservation techniques in systems

Recirculating air

The well-established method of recirculating air minimises refrigeration load and running costs. It is one of the simplest and most effective techniques. The proportions of fresh and recirculated air are automatically mixed to reduce the fresh air component of the cooling load in summer and to switch off the refrigeration plant in winter when the outside air is cool enough to permit so-called free cooling, i.e., at about 5°C wet-bulb and 10°C dry-bulb for air-water and all-air systems, respectively, in the UK. Assuming normal office hours and a five-day week, the outside dry-bulb is less than 10°C in the London area for roughly 38% and the wet-bulb is below 5°C for about 21% of the occupied period. These figures suggest that significant benefit can result from free cooling with an air-water system and, in fact, the heat gains to be dealt with in marginal weather are less than the design summer loads and the outside wet-bulb that permits the refrigeration plant to be switched off can be a degree or so higher than 5°C. In any case, mixing control effects an energy saving in running cost during mid-seasons by using 100% fresh air when the outside wet-bulb is less than the room wet-bulb, the enthalpy of the fresh air being then lower than the enthalpy of mixed air. An analysis of the meteorological data for London (Heathrow) Airport shows that, during the occupied hours assumed, the outside wet-bulb exceeds the room wet-bulb, assumed as 16°C screen, for about 170 hours a year, i.e. for about 7.5% of a total working period of 2268 hours. This means that mixing is effective in saving energy for $100 - (7.5 + 38) = 54.5\%$ and $100 - (7.5 + 21) = 71.5\%$ of the time the refrigeration plant runs for all-air and air-water systems, respectively.

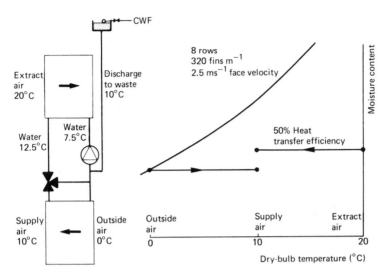

Figure 9.2   Run-around coils

Run-around coils

Run-around coils have also been used to a limited extent, for many years and they too provide an effective way of conserving energy, heat being transferred between the outgoing, vitiated air and the incoming fresh air. Figure 9.2 shows the principle for a winter case with a plant handling 100% fresh air, e.g. an operating theatre. Assuming 8-row coils with 320 fins m^{-1} and face velocities of 2.5 ms^{-1}, an approach efficiency of heat transfer of about 50% is possible[6]. The advantage of this method over some of the others is that the two coils need not be close together since the link between them is pipework. There is also no possibility of cross-contamination between the two airstreams.

Thermal wheels

Two types of thermal wheels are available, one having a fill of corrugated, inorganic, fibrous material with a hygroscopic property, air flowing along the channels formed by the corrugations, and the other being filled with a metallic material, e.g. aluminium, stainless steel or monel metal, in corrugated form. The first type transfers sensible and latent heat with efficiencies in the range 65% to 90%, as the face velocity declines from 5.0 to 1.0 ms^{-1}. The second type is primarily useful for exchanging sensible heat, but latent transfer can also occur if the colder airstream cools the metal to below the dew-point of the warmer airstream. Total heat transfer efficiencies of 65% and sensible transfer efficiencies of 80% can be obtained. Problems have occurred with failures of the seal wiping the face of the wheel (Figure 9.3) and, in the case of the metallic fill, with corrosion when the metal was wrong for the application. It is essential to

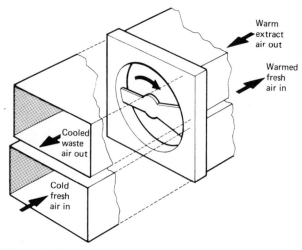

Figure 9.3   Thermal wheel

provide condensate drains to waste. With the hygroscopic fill, waterlogging can cause difficulties when very humid air is handled.

Static recuperators

Static recuperators are virtually air-to-air plate heat exchangers (Figure 9.4) with sensible heat transfer efficiencies of the order of 60% to 70%. Under certain conditions condensate will form within the passages which must, therefore, be drained to waste. It is also advisable to make arrangements for washing the plates during maintenance.

Heat pipes

Two versions of heat pipes are possible: one with horizontal tubes and the

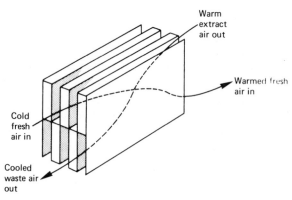

Figure 9.4   Static recuperator

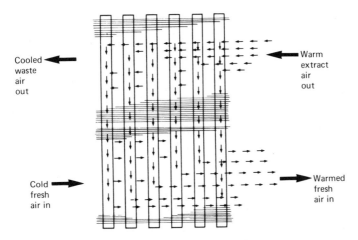

Figure 9.5   Heat pipe with capillary wick

other with vertical tubes. In the former (Figure 9.5) a wick transfers liquid by capillary action across the tubes, and in the latter rising vapour from the lower coil is condensed in the upper and returns to the lower by gravity. The wick in the horizontal type is often merely a concentric groove of small section and the fill is often water. The vertical type is usually filled with refrigerant 22. When transferring heat between moving airstreams efficiencies of 50% appear to be attainable but 70% and above does not always seem practical. The large heat transfer rate within the tubes, from one end to the other, cannot be matched by the heat transfer rate to the airstream which, for finned tube, is of the order of 80 $Wm^{-2} {}^\circ C^{-1}$. This may restrict their application in building services.

Heat pumping
Heat can only be rejected from a condenser if there is a cooling load at the evaporator. Also, heat pumping is only worth while if the rejected heat can be usefully deployed, i.e. if there is a fabric heat loss or a ventilation heating load. With all-air systems there is generally a cooling load when the outside temperature exceeds 10°C dry-bulb and a need for heating when it is below 20°C dry-bulb. In the London area, for the office occupancy assumed earlier, the outside temperature lies between these values for about 55% of the working time. For air-water systems the outside limits are 5°C wet-bulb and 20°C dry-bulb and the temperature lies in this region for about 70% of the working time. With smaller size installations, having cooling loads up to about 100 kW of refrigeration, fixed proportions of minimum fresh and maximum recirculated air are used throughout the year because this gives the lowest capital cost and, although the running cost is high, probably the lowest owning and operating cost over the life of the system. The conditions for useful heat pumping are then met for about 90% of the working time. In the above terms, the heat pumping

looks good for office blocks. The economic situation is not so favourable in many cases, however, because of the high extra capital expenditure involved in reclaiming the condenser heat and the relatively long pay-back period compared with the life of the plant. Nevertheless, if electricity is the only source of energy available on a site, heat pumping is the most economical way of heating, its coefficient of performance of about 5:1 making it a very cheap way of using electricity for heating (cheaper than using fossil fuels directly), if the low-grade heat produced at the condenser can be used.

There are several limitations on the use of heat pumps that it is well to consider:

(1) A positive displacement compressor, i.e. screw or reciprocating, should be chosen in preference to a centrifugal. This is because there is no risk of surge with such machines. A centrifugal machine tends to surge under the very conditions when heat pumping is most needed, i.e. when the outside air temperature is low and the cooling load is correspondingly low but high condensing temperatures are needed to give as much heat as possible.

(2) Screw compressors can operate at high condensing temperatures but these are restricted by lubrication and motor cooling problems. The open screw is much preferred because the hermetic model has its stator windings cooled by discharge gas and cannot therefore work at such high condensing temperatures.

(3) The compression ratio should be kept as low as possible if the desirably high coefficients of performance are to be obtained.

(4) The lowest possible cooling water leaving temperature ought to be adopted for the condenser. Although higher values have been used, a recommended upper limit is 40°C.

(5) Similarly, the lowest possible entering water temperature is desirable on the condenser and a suggested maximum is 35°C.

(6) Even if these suggestions are followed it is prudent to select the heater batteries to work with lower temperatures, say 38°C flow and 33°C return.

(7) The minimum design temperature difference between the chilled water and the water leaving the condenser is 14°C.

(8) Of the five methods, i.e. double bundle condenser, auxiliary condenser, open cooling tower with a plate heat exchanger, open cooling tower with cleanable tubes at the heater batteries, closed cooling tower, the most economical and practical is generally the open cooling tower with dirty water pumped from it to one side of a plate heat exchanger and clean water pumped from the condenser through its clean side, via the heater batteries.

(9) Hot gas air heater batteries can be used, in conjunction with conventional air cooled condensers and liquid receivers. Condensing and evaporating pressures must be controlled and a good deal of care must be exercised in the design, installation and commissioning of the system. In particular, control valves must be carefully sized.

Table 9.1 Comparison of methods of energy conservation in air-conditioning systems

Method	Face velocity $(m\,s^{-1})$	Heat transfer efficiency (%)	Pay back period (years)
Run-around coils	2.5–3.75	50–47	9–12
Non-metallic thermal wheels	3.3	70	13
Metallic thermal wheels	3.15–3.66	82–79	8
Static recuperators	3.33	66	13

To compare some of these methods it was assumed that the hypothetical office block (Section 1.2) was maintained at 20°C with the same moisture content inside as outside. A ventilation allowance of $1.3\,l\,s^{-1}\,m^{-2}$ was adopted and different methods of heat exchange between the incoming fresh air and the outgoing vitiated air were evaluated[7]. Although a discounted cash flow analysis would have been better it was felt that within the limitations of the simplifying assumptions made the cruder test of the pay back period (Section 8.4) was enough to show the trend. Meteorological data from London (Heathrow) Airport was used and analysed to yield the values of outside temperatures and their durations throughout the occupied working year. The total number of working hours for which the outside temperature was less than 20°C was estimated to be about 2085, or 90% of the working time. It was then possible to determine the heat energy requirement of the ventilation air. Because there is an air pressure drop across air-to-air heat exchangers, and a water pressure drop too for the run-around coils, a significant waste of electrical energy is involved. Such losses were debited to the energy saved. The results obtained varied a little because of the options possible when selecting a heat exchanger from a commercial range of sizes, and getting a selection at the best end of the commercial range is vital to making a good case for heat reclaim. Table 9.1 summarises the results.

The significance of the pay back periods in Table 9.1 can only be seen in relation to the estimated lives of the plant items in question (see Table 8.14). A life of 20 years can be assumed for the run-around coils and more than this for the associated pump and pipework, so a pay back in 9 to 12 years should give a positive present value over the life of the plant and make the method economically viable. Thermal wheels are more difficult to assess but it is possible that their life is a little shorter than that of run-around coils, because of the moving parts. Assuming a life-time of 15 years, a successful economic case is still obtained with a pay back of 8 to 13 years. Static recuperators could be regarded as similar to ductwork, with a life of more than 30 years but for these and the metallic wheels the economic case is less easy to establish because of the risk of corrosion giving a reduced life, particularly if condensate drainage is inadequate and maintenance poor.

It is to be noted that better cases can often be made with industrial applications, where the air temperatures are likely to be higher and the energy saved consequently greater. Heat pumps may also be used in industry with a more powerful economic justification than in commercial applications. It is possible to lift condenser cooling water to a leaving temperature of from 60°C to 110°C by pumping heat from a relatively low-grade source of fluid at between 27°C and 77°C. Notwithstanding what has been said earlier, the centrifugal compressor has been successfully used for this because its selection is possible in an area of performance remote from the surge condition, with the particular combinations of temperature and pressure involved.

9.3 System operation

The most potent way of conserving energy is by operating the system in a rational manner and in this respect there are two notable steps that should be considered.

(1) Intermittent heating—as has been indisputably demonstrated theoretically[4, 5] and verified in practice, switching off the heating system at night saves energy unless the building is of very heavy construction when the cooling down and heating up curves are so shallow that the system might just as well run continuously (Figure 9.1).

(2) Intermittent distribution—it is also possible to save large amounts of energy by operating the prime movers, i.e., fans and pumps, intermittently during the occupied period, if some variation in noise and air movement is acceptable to the occupants and if a temporary reduction in the rate of the fresh air supply is tolerable. It has already been seen that systems with automatic mixing of the fresh and recirculated air quantities only operate with minimum fresh air for about 7.5% of the working time and so, on average, will get much more than the minimum fresh air allowance, even if intermittent fan operation is adopted. The argument is that except at conditions of summer and winter design loads, when the plant must run continuously if conditions are to be maintained, it is possible to switch off a fan, say, for perhaps 10 minutes in each hour, allowing the heat energy or cooling capacity stored in the building structure to make good the temporary deficit, room temperatures falling or rising during the off period but remaining at acceptable values, although some individual thermostatic control is likely to be lost. For a large building, with mutliple air-handling units, the fans can be switched off in a planned sequence, certain areas of the building being given priority if necessary. The principle of fan switching, allowing the thermal inertia of the room to keep the temperature within reasonable limits, is not new. For many years fan coil units and room air conditioners have been controlled in this way (see Example 2.5). It is claimed that 15% to 20% savings in energy

consumption are possible if automatic, programmed switching is adopted for a commercial building.

References

(1) Jones, W. P., *Designing Air Conditioned Buildings to Minimise Energy Use*, Conference on Integrated Environment in Building Design, University of Nottingham, March 1974, Applied Science Publishers, 1974

(2) Jones, W. P., *Built Form and Energy Needs*, Joint Conference, Dept of Energy, Inst of Fuel, IES, CIBS, London, November 1975

(3) *Building Energy Code*, Part 2, CIBS, London, 1980

(4) Billington, N. S., *et al.*, *Intermittent Heating*, HVRA Laboratory Report, No. 26, November 1964

(5) Harrison, E., The intermittent heating of buildings, *JIHVE*, **24**, 145–196, 1956

(6) Holmes, M. and Hamilton, G., *Heat Recovery with Run-around Coils*, BSRIA, Technical Note TN2/78

(7) Jones, W. P., *Energy Recovery in Ventilation Systems*, Conference on Airflow and Building Design, University of Sheffield, 5–6 January, 1976

Appendix

Table A.1 Solar gains through internally shaded glass (reproduced by kind permission of Haden Young Ltd)
(a) For room surface density of 500 kg m^{-2}

		Solar air-conditioning loads (W m^{-2})												
		Sun time (hours)												
Month	Exposure	06.00	07.00	08.00	09.00	10.00	11.00	12.00	13.00	14.00	15.00	16.00	17.00	18.00
June 21	N	3	9	22	22	22	25	25	25	25	28	28	28	28
	NE	117	145	139	113	73	60	47	47	41	38	38	32	25
	E	106	183	205	199	164	110	76	69	63	57	50	44	38
	SE	6	73	123	158	173	170	148	113	76	63	54	47	38
	S	6	6	41	69	95	113	126	129	123	107	82	47	41
	SW	16	19	19	19	25	57	98	132	161	170	154	120	63
	W	22	25	26	26	28	28	28	57	113	170	208	214	189
	NW	16	19	22	22	25	25	25	25	38	82	126	161	157
July 23	N	3	9	10	19	19	22	22	22	22	22	25	25	25
and	NE	107	136	130	104	69	54	44	44	38	35	35	28	25
May 21	E	127	183	205	199	164	111	76	69	63	57	50	44	38
	SE	9	79	130	171	186	180	158	123	82	66	60	50	41
	S	9	9	44	79	107	130	142	145	142	120	91	54	44
	SW	19	22	22	22	28	66	111	155	183	196	177	139	85
	W	22	25	25	28	28	28	28	57	114	171	208	215	189
	NW	16	19	19	19	22	22	22	22	35	76	117	148	145
August 24	N	0	6	16	16	16	16	16	19	19	19	19	19	19
and	NE	88	111	104	85	54	44	38	35	32	28	28	25	19
April 20	E	123	177	199	193	158	107	73	66	60	54	47	44	38
	SE	9	85	142	186	205	199	174	133	88	73	63	54	44
	S	9	9	60	101	139	167	186	189	183	158	120	69	60
	SW	22	25	25	25	32	73	120	167	202	212	196	152	79
	W	19	25	25	28	28	28	28	54	111	164	202	208	183
	NW	13	16	16	16	19	19	19	19	28	63	95	117	117
September 22	N	0	6	9	13	13	13	13	13	13	13	13	13	13
and	NE	54	66	63	50	35	28	22	22	19	19	16	16	13
March 22	E	107	155	174	167	139	95	63	60	54	47	44	38	32
	SE	9	88	148	193	212	205	180	139	91	76	66	57	47
	S	13	13	66	117	158	193	215	218	212	180	139	79	66
	SW	22	25	25	25	32	76	127	174	208	221	202	158	82
	W	19	22	22	25	25	25	25	47	98	145	177	183	161
	NW	6	9	9	9	13	13	13	13	19	38	57	73	73
October 23	N	0	3	6	6	6	6	6	9	9	9	9	9	9
and	NE	28	35	32	25	16	13	13	9	9	9	9	9	9
February 20	E	82	117	133	127	107	73	47	44	41	38	32	28	25
	SE	9	85	142	186	205	199	174	133	88	73	63	54	44
	S	13	13	73	123	167	205	228	231	224	189	145	85	73
	SW	22	25	25	25	32	73	123	167	202	212	196	152	79
	W	16	16	16	19	19	19	19	38	73	111	136	139	123
	NW	3	3	6	6	6	6	6	6	9	19	28	38	35

ɔ) For room surface density of 150 kg m⁻²

Solar air-conditioning loads (W m⁻²)

Month	Exposure	Sun time (hours) 06.00	07.00	08.00	09.00	10.00	11.00	12.00	13.00	14.00	15.00	16.00	17.00	18.00
ʃne 21	N	0	6	22	25	28	28	28	28	28	32	32	32	32
	NE	136	186	177	142	88	60	47	41	38	32	28	28	16
	E	145	221	253	249	202	133	79	60	50	44	35	28	22
	SE	0	79	148	196	221	212	180	130	79	54	44	35	22
	S	19	38	79	114	139	155	158	143	101	88	44	28	19
	SW	6	9	16	19	22	60	123	177	212	224	205	158	69
	W	9	12	19	22	25	25	25	60	133	205	256	263	234
	NW	6	13	16	19	22	22	25	25	41	95	158	196	193
ʃly 23	N	0	6	19	22	25	25	25	25	25	25	25	28	28
nd	NE	127	174	164	133	82	54	44	38	35	28	28	25	16
ʃay 21	E	145	221	253	249	202	133	79	60	50	44	35	28	22
	SE	0	82	158	208	234	224	193	139	82	57	47	35	25
	S	22	44	88	130	158	177	180	167	114	101	50	32	22
	SW	9	13	16	19	25	63	130	186	224	237	218	167	73
	W	9	13	19	22	25	25	25	60	133	205	256	268	234
	NW	6	13	16	19	19	19	22	22	38	88	142	183	180
ʃugust 24	N	0	6	16	19	19	19	19	19	19	22	22	22	22
nd	NE	101	139	132	104	68	44	35	32	28	22	22	19	13
ʃpril 20	E	147	215	246	243	196	130	76	57	50	44	35	28	22
	SE	0	91	174	228	256	246	208	152	91	60	50	41	28
	S	25	57	114	167	205	231	234	218	146	133	63	44	28
	SW	9	13	19	22	28	69	142	205	246	262	240	183	79
	W	9	13	19	22	25	25	25	57	130	199	249	259	228
	NW	6	9	13	16	16	16	19	19	32	73	114	145	145
ʃeptember 22	N	0	3	13	13	13	13	16	16	16	16	16	16	16
nd	NE	63	85	82	66	41	28	22	19	16	16	13	13	6
ʃarch 22	E	123	186	215	212	171	114	66	50	44	38	28	25	19
	SE	0	95	180	237	265	256	218	158	95	68	54	41	28
	S	32	63	133	193	237	262	268	249	171	152	78	50	35
	SW	9	13	19	22	28	73	148	212	256	271	249	189	32
	W	9	9	16	19	22	22	22	50	114	174	218	228	199
	NW	3	6	6	9	9	9	13	13	19	44	69	88	88
ʃctober 23	N	0	3	6	6	9	9	9	9	9	9	9	9	9
nd	NE	32	44	41	32	19	13	9	9	9	6	6	6	3
ʃebruary 20	E	95	142	164	161	130	85	50	38	32	28	22	19	16
	SE	0	91	174	228	256	246	212	152	91	60	50	41	27
	S	32	69	139	205	249	278	284	265	180	161	79	50	35
	SW	9	13	19	22	28	69	142	199	246	262	240	183	79
	W	6	9	13	16	16	16	16	38	85	133	164	174	152
	NW	3	3	3	3	6	6	6	6	9	22	35	44	44

ʃable A.1 shows solar air-conditioning loads through windows in the UK only, for room surface ʃnsities of 500 kg m⁻² and 150 kg m⁻², expressed in Wm⁻². Values are for single plate or float ʃass and, where correction is necessary for other types of glazing, should be multiplied by the ʃctors given in Table A.2. The area to be used is the opening in the wall for metal-framed ʃindows and the area of the glass for wooden-framed windows. A haze factor of 0.9 has been ʃlowed. It is assumed that shades are not provided on the windows facing north and that all other ʃxposures have blinds that will be raised when the windows are not in direct sunlight. Scattered ʃdiation is included and the storage effect of the building taken into account. Air-to air ʃansmission is excluded.

Table A.2 Factors for use with Table A.1 (reproduced by kind permission of Haden Young Ltd)

		Blind position		
Outer pane	Inner pane	Internal	Between the panes	No blind
Clear sheet (4 mm)		1.00		
Clear plate or float		1.00		
Heat-absorbing bronze 49/66		0.96		1.43
Heat-absorbing green 75/60		0.92		1.30
Heat-absorbing grey 41/60		0.92		1.30
Heat-reflecting bronze 11/28				0.61
Heat-reflecting gold 15/22				0.50
Heat-reflecting gold 39/34				0.72
Clear plate or float	Clear plate or float	1.00	0.49	
Heat-absorbing bronze 49/66	Clear plate or float	0.80	0.47	1.17
Heat-absorbing green 75/60	Clear plate or float	0.73	0.45	1.03
Heat-absorbing grey 41/60	Clear plate or float	0.73	0.45	1.03

The factors given in Table A.2 are approximate and in each case are the ratio of the shading coefficient of the particular glass to that of clear glass with internal venetian blinds, taken as 0.53. Thus heat-absorbing bronze 49/66, which has a shading coefficient of 0.76, will have a factor to apply to Table A.1 of 0.76/0.53 or 1.43. Shading coefficients cannot be applied as factors directly to the solar loads given in Table A.3 for bare or externally shaded glass. This is because the shading coefficient is compounded of an instantaneous convective gain that is not susceptible to the building storage effect and a direct radiation gain that is susceptible to the building storage gain, whereas the values in Table A.3 refer to heat gains that occur largely by direct radiation through bare glass and, therefore, are heavily influenced by building storage effect. The procedure of relating the shading coefficient to that of clear glass with venetian blinds, for which the heat gain does have a significant instantaneous convective component, and referring it to Table A.1 is, therefore, proposed as an acceptable compromise. All the factors except the first refer to 6 mm plate or float glass. The figures quoted after the entries for the heat-absorbing and heat-reflecting glasses give the light and total heat transmitances, respectively. For types of glass having heat transmittances other than those listed, interpolation may be used to yield a good approximate factor to refer to Table A.1. For a more exact approach see Example 1.3.

Table A.3 Solar gains through bare glass (reproduced by kind permission of Haden Young Ltd)

(a) For room surface density of 500 kg m^{-2}

Solar air-conditioning loads (W m^{-2})

Month	Exposure	Sun time (hours)												
		06.00	07.00	08.00	09.00	10.00	11.00	12.00	13.00	14.00	15.00	16.00	17.00	18.00
June 21	N	6	19	25	28	32	35	38	38	41	41	44	44	32
	NE	82	136	164	171	158	148	117	104	95	91	82	73	69
	E	91	164	220	259	259	237	205	177	158	142	130	114	101
	SE	22	57	107	164	205	225	237	218	189	167	145	127	111
	S	22	19	38	63	95	123	152	171	183	180	167	142	117
	SW	41	41	38	41	41	66	101	145	196	234	246	237	205
	W	50	50	50	50	50	50	57	69	107	171	228	271	287
	NW	35	41	41	41	41	41	41	41	47	82	123	174	199
	Horizontal	28	63	104	155	206	259	310	354	391	420	436	443	434
July 23 and May 21	N	6	16	22	25	28	32	32	35	38	38	8	38	28
	NE	76	127	155	158	145	136	111	98	88	85	76	69	63
	E	88	164	224	259	259	259	237	174	158	142	130	114	101
	SE	25	60	114	174	218	243	253	234	202	180	155	133	120
	S	25	22	44	73	111	142	177	199	212	208	196	164	136
	SW	44	44	41	44	44	69	111	155	208	253	262	253	218
	W	50	50	50	50	50	50	57	66	107	167	224	268	287
	NW	32	38	38	38	38	38	38	38	44	76	117	161	186
	Horizontal	9	32	70	114	164	219	269	314	350	380	391	391	376
August 24 and April 20	N	3	13	16	19	22	22	25	25	28	28	32	32	22
	NE	63	101	123	127	117	111	88	79	73	69	63	54	50
	E	83	158	218	249	249	231	196	171	152	136	127	111	98
	SE	28	104	171	224	262	262	234	205	183	161	142	127	114
	S	35	28	57	95	142	186	228	256	278	271	253	215	177
	SW	47	47	44	47	47	76	120	167	228	271	287	278	240
	W	50	50	50	50	50	50	54	66	104	164	218	262	278
	NW	25	28	28	28	28	28	28	28	35	63	95	130	148
	Horizontal	0	9	32	70	114	161	209	253	285	306	316	310	285
September 22 and March 22	N	3	9	11	13	16	16	19	19	19	22	22	22	16
	NE	38	63	76	79	73	69	54	47	44	41	38	35	32
	E	76	139	189	218	218	199	171	148	133	120	111	95	85
	SE	28	66	130	196	248	275	287	267	231	202	174	152	136
	S	38	32	66	111	164	212	262	294	316	310	290	246	202
	SW	50	50	47	50	50	79	123	174	237	281	297	287	246
	W	44	44	44	44	44	44	47	57	91	112	139	223	243
	NW	16	19	19	19	19	19	19	19	22	38	57	79	91
	Horizontal	0	0	9	32	63	104	145	180	209	225	225	209	190

(b) For room surface density of 150 kg m^{-2}

		Solar air-conditioning loads (W m^{-2})												
		Sun time (hours)												
Month	Exposure	06.00	07.00	08.00	09.00	10.00	11.00	12.00	13.00	14.00	15.00	16.00	17.00	18.0
June 21	N	0	25	35	41	44	47	38	41	54	54	54	54	28
	NE	136	243	281	265	199	142	114	91	79	69	60	50	38
	E	152	281	378	413	384	300	215	152	123	101	85	66	50
	SE	0	82	186	275	335	357	335	278	205	148	107	82	66
	S	0	0	36	91	155	205	240	262	259	240	196	136	88
	SW	9	13	22	28	38	57	158	246	316	363	363	316	215
	W	13	15	28	35	41	41	44	72	164	278	378	428	422
	NW	9	16	22	32	35	38	44	44	57	117	208	281	316
	Horizontal	63	130	209	291	375	455	521	572	608	620	606	585	535
July 23	N	0	22	32	38	38	41	35	35	44	47	47	47	25
and	NE	127	224	262	246	186	133	104	85	73	63	57	47	35
May 21	E	152	281	374	409	381	297	215	152	123	101	85	66	50
	SE	0	88	196	290	354	378	354	294	215	158	114	88	69
	S	0	0	41	104	174	234	275	300	297	275	221	155	101
	SW	9	16	25	28	38	60	167	259	335	381	381	335	228
	W	13	16	28	35	38	38	44	79	164	275	374	425	419
	NW	9	16	19	28	32	38	41	41	54	107	193	262	294
	Horizontal	19	70	139	225	310	395	468	525	560	571	560	521	459
August 24	N	0	19	25	28	32	32	28	28	35	38	38	38	19
and	NE	101	189	212	199	148	107	85	69	57	50	44	38	28
April 20	E	145	271	363	397	368	287	205	145	120	98	82	66	50
	SE	0	91	215	319	387	416	387	325	237	174	123	98	76
	S	0	0	57	139	228	303	357	387	384	357	290	199	133
	SW	9	16	28	32	44	65	183	287	366	419	419	366	249
	W	9	16	28	32	38	38	44	76	158	265	363	413	406
	NW	6	13	16	22	25	28	32	32	41	88	155	212	237
	Horizontal	0	19	70	142	221	304	375	433	468	477	455	408	335
September 22	N	0	13	19	22	22	25	19	19	25	25	28	28	16
and	NE	63	111	130	120	91	66	50	41	35	32	28	25	19
March 22	E	130	237	319	347	322	253	180	130	104	85	73	57	44
	SE	0	101	224	332	403	432	403	335	246	180	130	101	79
	S	0	0	66	161	265	354	413	450	447	413	338	231	155
	SW	13	16	28	35	44	66	189	297	381	425	435	381	259
	W	9	16	25	28	35	35	38	66	139	234	319	360	357
	NW	3	9	9	13	16	19	19	19	25	54	95	130	145
	Horizontal	0	0	19	66	133	202	268	323	350	350	326	269	211

Table A.3 shows solar air-conditioning loads through unshaded windows in the UK only, fo room surface densities of 500 kg m^{-2} and 150 kg m^{-2}, expressed in W m^{-2}. Values are for sing plate or float glass and should be multiplied by the factors given in Table A.4 where correction necessary for external shaded or other treatment. The area to be used is the opening in the wall fo metal-framed windows and the area of the glass for wooden-framed windows. A haze factor of 0 has been allowed and scattered radiation is included, together with the storage effect of t building. Air-to-air transmission is excluded.

Table A.4 Factors for use with Table A.3 (reproduced by kind permission of Haden Young Ltd)

| | | Type of outside shading | | | |
| | | No shade | Light venetian blind | Light awning | Dark awning |
Outer pane	Inner pane				
4 mm clear sheet		1.0	0.15	0.20	0.25
6 mm clear plate or float		0.97	0.14	0.19	0.24
4 mm clear sheet	4 mm clear sheet		0.14	0.18	0.22
6 mm clear plate or float	6 mm clear plate or float	0.85	0.12	0.16	0.20
4 mm clear sheet, painted light colour		0.28			
4 mm clear sheet, painted medium colour		0.39			

Table A.5 Time lags for building structures

| | Approximate time lags (hours) | | | | | | |
| Density $(kg\,m^{-3})$ | Thickness (mm) | | | | | | |
	100	150	200	250	300	350	400
≤1200	2.7	4.9	6.8	9.0	11.2	13.3	15.2
1200–1800	2.7	4.9	6.4	8.0	9.6	11.2	12.7
1800–2400	2.7	4.6	5.8	7.3	8.6	9.9	11.2

Table A.6 Decrement factors for building structures

| | Approximate decrement factors | | | | | | |
| Insulation | Thickness (mm) | | | | | | |
	100	150	200	250	300	350	400
None	0.87	0.67	0.48	0.33	0.22	0.15	0.11
On the inside surface	0.67	0.47	0.33	0.22	0.16	0.11	0.08
On the outside surface	0.51	0.34	0.22	0.15	0.10	0.07	0.04

Table A.7 Equivalent temperature differences (reproduced by kind permission of Haden Young Ltd)

Exposure	Surface density (kg m⁻²)	Equivalent temperature difference (°C) Sun time (hours)												
		06.00	07.00	08.00	09.00	10.00	11.00	12.00	13.00	14.00	15.00	16.00	17.00	18.00
N	100	−3.9	−3.9	−4.5	−3.9	−3.4	−1.7	0	2.2	3.3	4.5	5.6	5.0	4.5
	300	−3.9	−3.9	−4.5	−3.9	−3.4	−2.8	−2.2	−0.6	1.1	2.2	3.4	3.9	4.5
	500	−1.7	−1.7	−2.2	−2.2	−2.2	−2.2	−2.2	−1.7	−1.1	−0.6	0	0.6	0.6
NE	100	0.6	5.6	8.9	9.5	10.0	7.8	5.0	5.0	4.5	5.0	5.6	5.6	5.6
	300	−2.8	−3.4	−3.4	0	10.0	8.9	7.8	5.6	3.4	3.9	4.5	5.0	5.6
	500	0	−0.6	0	0	0	2.8	6.1	5.6	5.0	4.5	3.4	3.9	4.5
E	100	−1.7	7.2	14.5	16.1	17.8	17.2	15.6	8.9	4.5	5.0	5.6	5.6	5.6
	300	−2.8	−2.8	−2.2	9.5	14.4	15.0	15.0	8.4	5.6	5.0	4.5	5.0	5.6
	500	0.6	0.6	1.1	2.2	5.6	8.9	11.1	11.7	11.1	8.9	7.8	6.7	5.6
SE	100	4.5	1.7	6.7	10.0	14.4	15.0	15.6	13.9	12.2	8.9	6.7	6.1	5.6
	300	−1.7	−1.7	−2.2	6.1	10.6	13.3	15.6	13.9	13.3	10.6	8.4	6.7	5.6
	500	2.2	2.2	1.7	1.7	1.7	5.0	7.8	8.4	8.9	9.5	8.9	7.8	6.1
S	100	−2.2	−2.8	−4.5	−0.6	1.7	9.5	15.6	18.3	20.0	18.3	16.1	11.1	7.8
	300	−2.2	−3.9	−4.5	−3.9	−3.4	3.9	8.4	13.9	16.7	16.7	17.2	14.4	11.1
	500	1.1	1.1	−0.6	−0.6	−0.6	0.6	1.1	4.5	7.2	10.0	10.6	11.7	11.7
SW	100	−3.4	−4.5	−4.5	−3.4	−2.2	0	1.1	9.4	13.3	18.3	22.2	22.8	23.4
	300	−0.6	−1.1	−1.7	−2.2	−2.2	−1.7	−1.1	2.2	5.0	12.2	17.2	19.4	20.0
	500	2.2	1.1	1.7	1.1	0.6	1.1	1.1	1.7	2.8	5.0	6.1	9.5	11.7
W	100	−3.4	−3.9	−4.5	−3.4	−2.2	−0.6	1.1	5.6	8.9	15.6	20.0	22.8	24.4
	300	−1.1	−1.7	−2.2	−2.2	−2.2	−1.1	0	1.7	3.4	8.4	12.2	16.7	20.0
	500	1.7	1.7	1.1	1.1	1.1	1.1	1.1	1.7	2.2	3.4	4.5	7.2	8.9
NW	100	−3.9	−4.5	−4.5	−3.4	−2.2	−0.6	1.1	3.4	4.5	8.4	10.6	15.0	18.3
	300	−3.4	−3.9	−4.5	−3.9	−3.4	−2.2	−1.1	1.1	2.2	3.4	4.5	8.9	13.3
	500	−0.6	0	0	0	0	0	0	0	0	0.6	1.1	2.8	4.5
Horizontal in sunshine	50	−4.5	−5.6	−6.1	−5.0	−2.8	1.1	5.6	10.6	14.4	17.8	20.0	21.6	21.1
	100	−2.2	−2.8	−3.3	−2.8	−1.1	2.2	6.1	10.0	13.3	16.7	18.3	20.0	20.0
	200	−0.6	−1.1	−1.1	−1.1	0.6	2.8	6.1	9.4	12.2	15.0	17.2	18.3	18.9
	300	2.2	1.7	0.6	1.1	0.6	3.3	5.6	8.9	11.7	13.9	15.5	17.2	18.3
	400	4.5	3.9	3.3	3.3	3.9	4.5	5.6	8.9	11.1	12.2	13.9	15.5	17.2

Table A.7 gives equivalent temperature differences for some typical walls and roofs at a latitude of 51.5° N in the UK, based on a 6°C difference between outside air temperature and room air temperature at 15.00 h sun time. For other temperature differences at 15.00 h sun time, add or subtract the appropriate correction in each case.

Table A.8 Sol-air temperatures at Kew

Sun time (h)	Air temperature (°C)	Sol-air temperature (°C)				
		Horizontal roof	North wall	East wall	South wall	West wall
01.00	19.1	19.9	19.9	19.9	19.9	19.9
02.00	18.6	18.6	18.6	18.6	18.6	18.6
03.00	18.5	18.5	18.5	18.5	18.5	18.5
04.00	18.6	18.6	18.6	18.6	18.6	18.6
05.00	19.1	24.1	25.2	34.7	19.9	19.9
06.00	19.7	30.3	28.2	44.6	21.0	21.0
07.00	20.6	37.4	25.5	49.5	22.4	22.4
08.00	21.6	45.3	24.0	50.8	28.1	24.0
09.00	22.7	51.7	25.8	48.8	34.7	25.7
10.00	23.8	57.9	27.0	44.3	40.9	27.2
11.00	24.8	62.0	28.3	32.8	45.0	28.4
12.00	25.7	63.2	29.3	29.3	47.2	27.3
13.00	26.3	63.5	29.8	29.8	46.6	39.9
14.00	26.8	60.9	30.1	30.1	43.9	47.3
15.00	26.9	55.9	29.9	29.9	38.9	53.0
16.00	26.8	50.4	29.1	29.1	33.3	56.0
17.00	26.3	43.1	31.2	28.1	28.1	55.2
18.00	25.7	36.3	34.1	26.9	26.9	50.5
19.00	24.8	29.8	32.0	25.5	25.6	42.0
20.00	23.8	23.8	23.8	23.8	23.8	23.8
21.00	22.7	22.7	22.7	22.7	22.7	22.7
22.00	21.6	21.6	21.6	21.6	21.6	21.6
23.00	20.6	20.6	20.6	20.6	20.6	20.6
24.00	19.7	19.7	19.7	19.7	19.7	19.7
24 h mean	22.7	37.3	25.6	29.9	28.6	30.2

Table A.8 shows the sol-air temperatures at Kew for a typical hot day in July, using a maximum outside air temperature of 26.9°C, assumed to occur at 15.00 h sun time. Also, a sinusoidal variation of outside air temperature with respect to time with a diurnal range of 8.4°C is assumed. The outside surface of the wall or roof is taken as absorbing 90% of the incident solar radiation and the value adopted for the outside surface film coefficient is 22.7 $Wm^{-2}°C^{-1}$. The values are based on maximum solar intensities, as originally published in the 1965 CIBS guide.

Table A.9 Approximate climatic refrigeration loads for office blocks in the UK, assuming a lightweight building (150 kg m⁻²) with a heavyweight roof (300 kg m⁻²)

Amount of glass (%)	Number of storeys in building														
	1			2			4			8			30		
	Sun time (hours)	Month	Load (W m⁻²)	Sun time (hours)	Month	Load (W m⁻²)	Sun time (hours)	Month	Load (W m⁻²)	Sun time (hours)	Month	Load (W m⁻²)	Sun time (hours)	Month	Load (W m⁻²)
Major building axis E-W:															
0	17.00	July	43	16.00	August	33	16.00	August	29	16.00	August	26	16.00	August	25
25	15.00	August	52	15.00	August	44	13.00	August	41	13.00	August	39	13.00	August	39
50	13.00	August	66	13.00	August	62	13.00	August	59	13.00	August	58	13.00	August	57
75	13.00	August	85	13.00	August	80	13.00	August	78	13.00	August	77	12.00	August	76
Major building axis N-S:															
0	18.00	July	46	18.00	August	35	18.00	August	30	18.00	August	27	18.00	August	26
25	17.00	July	67	17.00	July	56	17.00	July	51	17.00	July	49	17.00	July	47
50	17.00	July	89	17.00	July	79	17.00	July	74	17.00	July	71	17.00	July	69
75	17.00	July	112	17.00	July	101	17.00	July	96	17.00	July	93	16.00	July	92
Major building axis NE-SW:															
0	18.00	July	44	18.00	August	33	18.00	August	28	18.00	August	25	18.00	August	23
25	17.00	July	59	17.00	July	49	17.00	July	44	17.00	July	41	17.00	July	39
50	17.00	July	77	17.00	July	66	17.00	July	61	17.00	July	59	17.00	July	57
75	17.00	July	94	17.00	July	84	17.00	July	79	17.00	August	76	16.00	August	75
Major building axis NW-SE:															
0	18.00	July	47	18.00	August	36	18.00	August	30	17.00	August	28	17.00	August	26
25	16.00	August	62	16.00	August	53	16.00	August	49	16.00	August	47	16.00	August	45
50	15.00	August	82	15.00	August	74	15.00	August	70	15.00	August	69	15.00	August	67
75	15.00	August	104	15.00	August	97	15.00	August	93	15.00	August	91	15.00	August	89

The specific refrigeration loads listed in Table A.9 are based on the following assumptions: U-values $(Wm^{-2}{}^{\circ}C^{-1})$: glass, 5.6; wall, 1.7; roof, 1.1: Surface densities $(kg\,m^{-2})$: walls, 300; roof, 300; floor slabs, 150. The results are from a computer study (see Chapter 1, reference (9)) for a hypothetical building (very similar to that in Figure 1.1) with various amounts of single glazing on its two long faces but none on its short faces, fitted with internal Venetian blinds on all faces except north. The plan of the building is 86.4 m × 13.5 m with a floor-to-floor height of 3.3 m and a floor-to-ceiling height of 2.6 m. No natural infiltration is assumed. The loads are the maximum values for the whole building divided by the plan area × the number of storeys, and they include gains through the windows, walls and roof, plus the fresh air loads arising from the supply of $1.3\,1s^{-1}m^{-2}$ of floor area. They can, therefore, be converted into actual total refrigeration loads by adding the appropriate allowances for lighting, people, business machines, fan power, duct gains, etc. A sinusoidal variation in outside air temperature (Equation 1.1) based on meteorological data from Kew (see Chapter 1, reference (4)) is used and the inside state is taken as 22°C dry-bulb and 50% saturation in all cases. The solar loads through glass are calculated using the data in Tables A.1 to A.4, inclusive, based on the Carrier method, and equivalent temperature differences are adopted for the gains through walls and roofs.

The tabulated results can be regarded as typical of a modern, office block with carpeted floors. A heavyweight building (slab surface density $500\,kg\,m^{-2}$) gives results about 5% less for the higher rise structures with 75% and 50% glazing, but the times and months of the peak load are not greatly different. The same is true of buildings with lightweight roofs $(50\,kg\,m^{-2})$, except for single-storey constructions where, although the time and month of the maximum is virtually unchanged, the maximum load tends to be about 10% greater when there is no glazing.

Table A.10 Meteorological data for Kew: 5°28′ N, 0°19′ W, 5 m above sea level, for period 1931–1960

Item	Temperature (°C)											
	Jan	Feb	Mar	April	May	June	July	Aug	Sept	Oct	Nov	Dec
Mean daily maximum	6.3	6.9	10.1	13.3	16.7	20.3	21.8	21.4	18.5	14.2	10.1	7.3
Mean daily minimum	2.2	2.2	3.3	5.5	8.2	11.6	13.5	13.2	11.3	7.9	5.3	3.5
Diurnal range	4.1	4.7	6.8	7.8	8.5	8.7	8.3	8.2	7.2	6.3	4.8	3.8
Mean monthly maximum	11.7	12.1	15.5	18.7	23.3	25.9	26.9	26.2	23.4	18.7	14.4	12.2
Mean monthly minimum	−4.3	−3.6	−2.3	0.1	2.7	6.9	9.3	8.5	5.4	0.4	−1.4	−3.2
Absolute maximum	14.3	16.1	21.4	23.5	30.2	32.7	33.8	33.1	29.8	25.6	19.0	15.1
Absolute minimum	−9.5	−9.4	−7.7	−2.1	−1.0	4.8	7.0	6.2	3.0	−3.6	−5.0	−7.0

Based on information from Met O. 856c. Meteorological Office. Tables of temperature, relative humidity, precipitation and sunshine, Part III, Europe and the Azores, HMSO, London, 1972 (Reproduced by permission of HMSO, London).

Derivation of Equation (2.3)

Sensible heat gain = mass flow rate of supply air × specific heat capacity
× temperature rise
$$= \dot{m} \times c(t_r - t_s)$$

where t_r and t_s are the room and supply air temperatures, respectively.

Volumetric flow rate of air at temperature $t = \dot{v}_t = \dot{m}/\rho_t$

where ρ_t is the density of air at temperature t, and also

$$\rho_t = \rho_o(273 + t_o)/(273 + t)$$

where ρ_o and t_o are a standard density and temperature, respectively. Therefore,

$$\text{Sensible heat gain} = [\dot{v}_t \times \rho_o \times (273 + t_o)/(273 + t)] \times c(t_r - t_s)$$

If $\rho_o = 1.191 \ \text{kgm}^{-3}$ at 20°C dry-bulb and 50% saturation and $c = 1.026 \ \text{kJkg}^{-1}\text{°C}^{-1}$ then

$$\dot{v}_t = \frac{(\text{sensible heat gain})}{(t_r - t_s)} \times \frac{(273 + t)}{358}$$

If the sensible heat gain is in W, $\dot{v}_t$ is in ls^{-1}. I the sensible heat gain is in kW, $\dot{v}_t$ is in m^3s^{-1}.

Derivation of Equation (2.4)

Latent heat gain = mass flow rate of supply air × moisture pick-up in kgkg^{-1} air
× latent heat of evaporation in kgkg^{-1} water
$$= \dot{m} \times h_{fg}(g_r - g_s)$$

where g_r and g_s are the room and supply air moisture contents, respectively. As with Equation (2.3), $\dot{m} = \dot{v}_t \times \rho_o(273 + t_o)/(273 + t)$, therefore

$$\text{Latent heat gain} = [\dot{v}_t \times \rho_o \times (273 + t_o)/(273 + t)] \times h_{fg} \times (g_r - g_s)$$

If $\rho_o = 1.191 \ \text{kgm}^{-3}$ at 20°C dry-bulb and 50% saturation and $h_{fg} = 2454 \ \text{kJkg}^{-1}$ at 20°C then

$$\dot{v}_t = \frac{(\text{latent heat gain})}{(g_r - g_s)} \times \frac{(273 + t)}{856}$$

where $\dot{v}_t$ is in m^3s^{-1}, the latent heat gain is in kW and $(g_r - g_s)$ is in gkg^{-1} dry air.

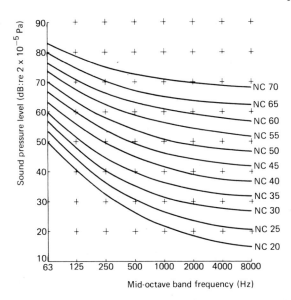

Figure A.1 Noise criteria curves (after Beranek; Reference (1), Chapter 7)

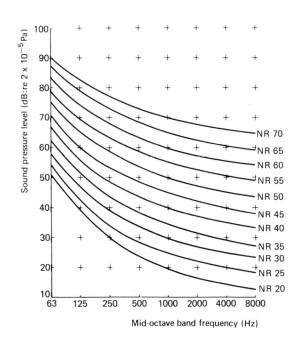

Figure A.2 Noise rating curves (after Kosten & Van Os: reference (3), Chapter 7)

Index